Multicultural Course Transformation in Higher Education

Related Titles of Interest

College Teaching Abroad: A Handbook of Strategies for Successful Cross-Cultural Exchanges
Pamela Gale George
ISBN: 0-205-15767-X

The Art of Writing for Publication
Kenneth T. Henson
ISBN: 0-205-15769-6

Sexual Harassment on Campus: A Guide for Administrators, Faculty, and Students
Bernice R. Sandler and Robert J. Shoop
ISBN: 0-205-16712-8

Shaping the College Curriculum: Academic Plans in Action
Joan S. Stark and Lisa R. Lattuca
ISBN: 0-205-16706-3

Multicultural Course Transformation in Higher Education

A Broader Truth

ANN INTILI MOREY

MARGIE K. KITANO

Editors
San Diego State University

ALLYN AND BACON

Boston   London   Toronto   Sydney   Tokyo   Singapore

Executive Editor: Stephen D. Dragin
Editorial Assistant: Susan Hutchinson

Library of Congress Cataloging-in-Publication Data

Multicultural course transformation in higher education : a broader
   truth / Ann Intili Morey, Margie K. Kitano, editors.
     p. c m .
   Includes bibliographical references and index.
   ISBN 0-205-16068-9
   1. Education, Higher--United States--Curricula.   2. Multicultural
   education--United States.   3. Curriculum change--United States.
   I. Morey, Ann I.   II. Kitano, Margie.
LB2361.5.M85 1996
378.1'99--dc20   95-44078
                                                                                  CIP

Printed in the United States of America
10   9   8   7   6   5   4   3   2   1   00   99   98   97   96

Contents

Chapter 12
Multicultural Infusion in Teacher Education: Foundations and Applications   192

Geneva Gay

Chapter 13
Integrating Transcultural Knowledge into Nursing Curricula: An American Indian Example   211

Karine Crow

Chapter 14
The Community College Curriculum   229

Desna L. Wallin

Chapter 15
Evaluating the Results of Multicultural Education: Taking the Long Way Home   242

Jeffrey S. Beaudry and James Earl Davis

Preface

This book is intended to assist faculty members, administrators, and faculty development professionals in colleges and universities to better prepare all students for effective functioning in a diverse society. It focuses on the inclusion of multicultural education in disciplinary courses and presents a framework and model for course change. In addition to content development, course transformation can entail rethinking instructional strategies, assessment procedures, and classroom dynamics. The book addresses these topics generally and then gives specific applications to the disciplines in community colleges and universities. Readers in any discipline will find stimulating and useful examples and suggestions in all of the chapters and are encouraged to explore the book in its entirety. Administrators and faculty development professionals will find useful information and insights that will guide their efforts to respond to our increasingly diverse student bodies and society.

Course transformation is a long-term, continuous, complex process requiring supportive organizational change and faculty development. Thus, the concluding emphasis is on evaluating impact and encouraging organizational change to support multicultural course and program transformation. The content also reflects our philosophy that *all* students, faculty, and administrators—not just those from diverse groups—benefit from multicultural education. One of the several goals of multicultural education is for higher education to share a broader truth through incorporation of the new scholarship and ways of knowing. Successful incorporation of multicultural education supports more comprehensive knowledge acquisition and critical thinking important to all citizens in a global society.

BACKGROUND

The impetus for the book stems from ten years of experience in planning and implementing systemic change to improve services to diverse learners in higher education. Our work initially focused on the need to prepare educators at San Diego State University with the knowledge and skills to create effective learning environments for a multicultural and multilingual K–12 student population. It became obvious to us that in order to transform the curriculum in Education, systemic/structural change of the College of Education itself was necessary as well as the transformation of courses in the academic disciplines.

More specifically, in 1985–86, the Dean and the faculty of the College of Education chose "serving the needs of the diverse learner" as one of their strategic choices. They began to design activities that would heighten the awareness of faculty regarding multicultural issues, expand faculty expertise in multicultural education, and promote course revision to reflect the importance of multicultural education. In 1990, the plans evolved into the Multicultural

Infusion Initiative. The major goal as articulated by the Initiative was to infuse the curriculum with multicultural content and strategies by changing both the individual and the organization. Plans and activities were collaboratively developed and implemented and institutional support structures put in place. The College of Education progressed in several areas as a result. Faculty reported not only changes to their curriculum but also dramatically increased focus on multicultural and multilingual issues in their research and reading. Recruitment efforts increased ethnic student and faculty representation fivefold to one third of their respective cohorts. Efforts to infuse multicultural content and strategies throughout the university curriculum had a strong influence on the development of this book.

The work at San Diego State University eventually evolved into the Multicultural Education Infusion Center, a national center funded by the U.S. Department of Education's Office of Bilingual Education and Minority Languages Affairs. The purpose of the Center is to increase the capability of Colleges and Schools of Education to prepare educators for a multicultural and linguistically diverse student population. Drawing upon the experience of the San Diego effort, the Center focuses on the development of faculty knowledge and understanding of multicultural education and systemic/structural change of the institutions themselves in order to support course and program transformation.

The Center provides professional development opportunities for faculty and administrators to increase their knowledge and understanding in foundational studies of multicultural and multilingual education, research-based instructional strategies appropriate for diverse students, and organizational development. It also provides on-site consultations to its member institutions, information dissemination, and other support services to assist member institutions in developing and implementing action plans, increasing the access of faculty to related research opportunities and supporting collaboration among its members. The Center currently supports a national consortium of 23 member universities and has 72 other collegiate institutions that have been involved in some of its activities. The learnings from our work in the Center are reflected in this book.

AN OVERVIEW OF THE BOOK

In Chapter 1, Margie Kitano provides a rationale and philosophical framework for multicultural course change in higher education. Based on the framework, she presents (Chapter 2) a general model for planning course change that encourages instructors to begin by making explicit their multicultural goals for the particular course. The model suggests that faculty members consider levels of multicultural infusion as well as four course components: content (Deborah Rosenfelt, Chapter 3), instruction (Eleanor Lynch, Chapter 4), strategies for assessing student knowledge (Rena Lewis, Chapter 5), and classroom interactions (Terry Jones and Gale Auletta Young, Chapter 6). In Chapter 7, Kate Kinsella specifically addresses accommodations for students whose first language is not English.

The next six chapters illustrate applications of various aspects of the framework to specific content fields: mathematics (Efraim Armendariz and Louise Hasty, Chapter 8), sciences (Judith Rosenthal, Chapter 9), humanities (Jackie Donath, Chapter 10), economics (Robin Bartlett and Susan Feiner, Chapter 11), teacher education (Geneva Gay, Chapter 12), and nursing (Karine Crow, Chapter 13). In Chapter 14, Desna Wallin discusses applications to the community college curriculum.

To ensure accountability, we encourage instructors to evaluate the impact of their multicultural course change efforts. Jeffrey Beaudry and James Davis (Chapter 15) examine evaluation issues and offer guidelines for assessing the impact of change. Ann Morey's concluding chapter (Chapter 16) focuses on the systemic organizational change that must occur in order to initiate, implement, and institutionalize curriculum transformation.

Our separation of the four components of course change—content, instruction, assessment, and classroom dynamics—is an artificial one useful for purposes of organization and communication. Clearly, all four components overlap and interact in implementing any course. However, we offer the components as a way for instructors to think about how to get started on multicultural course change. Moreover, analyzing courses by the four components provides instructors with optional approaches to course change that recognize individual differences by instructor and course. Readers who have a particular interest in multicultural change through transformation of course content will find useful examples in Chapter 3, which suggests content issues and readings through broad themes. Chapters 9 (sciences), 10 (humanities), 11 (economics), and 13 (nursing) provide specific examples reflecting varying levels of content change applied to the disciplines. Instructional change is the focus of Chapters 4 (general strategies), 7 (strategies for linguistically diverse), and 8 (mathematics). Readers who are considering program-level change will find helpful Chapters 12 (teacher education), 13 (nursing), and 16 (organizational change).

Planning for multicultural course change begins with the instructor's multicultural goals for the course. Chapters 7 (language diversity), 8 (mathematics), 12 (education), and 13 (nursing) are especially useful for faculty members concerned with the goal of improving the achievement of diverse students. Chapter 13 serves as an excellent resource on supporting American Indian students in any discipline. Where the multicultural goal focuses on providing a more comprehensive knowledge, Chapters 9 (sciences), 11 (economics), and 13 (nursing) offer excellent support.

Our purpose is not to prescribe but rather to provide a tool for instructors and administrators interested in transforming courses to address educational needs in a diverse society. We hope that this book stimulates individual and organizational efforts to improve access to knowledge and development of competent citizens for a highly diverse world. Multicultural course change is a long-term process, not a product. Similarly, the book represents a beginning, not an end.

As a supplement to this book, Carol Spirkoff Prime prepared an annotated bibliography. This bibliography offers additional sources for information on multicultural education, higher education in a diverse society, and what it means to be a person of color in the United States. It is divided into two sections: general and content-specific. The general section of the bibliography provides models and guidelines for multicultural infusion and essays about transforming college programs and courses to meet the needs of a diverse population. The content-based section of the bibliography serves as a resource for infusing multicultural content and strategies into course syllabi and for selecting readings within the disciplines. A copy of Prime's annotated bibliography may be obtained by writing to the Office of the Dean, College of Education, San Diego State University, San Diego, CA 92182.

We have tried to be sensitive to authors' preferences for terms that refer to ethnic and cultural groups. Regional, professional, and personal preferences lead to use of different terms (e.g., Hispanic, Latino, Chicano) and hence some inconsistencies across chapters. We have chosen to follow the guidelines of the American Psychological Association's *Publication*

Authors and Affiliations

Efraim P. Armendariz
Professor of Mathematics
University1 of Texas at Austin

Robin L. Bartlett
Professor of Economics
Denison University
Granville, Ohio

Jeffrey S. Beaudry
Assistant Professor
Department of Professional Education
University of Southern Maine
Portland, Maine

Karine Crow
Assistant Professor
Intercollegiate Center for Nursing
Education
Spokane, Washington

James Earl Davis
Assistant Professor
Department of Educational Studies
University of Delaware

Jackie R. Donath
Assistant Professor
California State University, Sacramento

Susan F. Feiner
Visiting Associate Professor of Economics
and Women's Studies
University of Southern Maine
Portland, Maine

Geneva Gay
Professor of Education and Faculty
Associate
Center for Multicultural Education
University of Washington, Seattle

Louise Hasty
Mathematics Department Head,
Riverside Campus, Austin Community
College, Austin, Texas

Terry Jones
Co-director, Center for the Study of
Intercultural Relations
California State University, Hayward

Kate Kinsella
Education Specialist, ESL and Bilingual
Education
"Step to College Program," San Francisco
State University

Margie K. Kitano
Associate Dean, College of Education
San Diego State University

Rena B. Lewis
Professor of Special Education, San Diego
State University
Faculty member, San Diego State
University-Claremont
Graduate School Doctoral Program

Eleanor W. Lynch
Professor, Department of Special Education
San Diego State University

Ann Intili Morey
Dean, College of Education
San Diego State University

Deborah S. Rosenfelt
Professor, Women's Studies
Director, the Curriculum
Transformation Project
University of Maryland at College Park

Judith W. Rosenthal
Professor, Biological Sciences
Kean College of New Jersey
Union, New Jersey

Desna L. Wallin
President, Forsyth Technical Community
College
Winston-Salem, North Carolina

Gale S. Auletta Young
Co-director, Center for the Study of Inter-
cultural Relations
California State University, Hayward

Multicultural Course Transformation in Higher Education

CHAPTER 1

A Rationale and Framework for Course Change

Margie K. Kitano, Associate Dean, College of Education
San Diego State University

Editor's Notes:
This chapter begins by offering a rationale for multicultural course change. Margie Kitano argues that incorporation of multicultural content and pedagogy has equal relevance for highly diverse and homogeneous campuses because a transformed course provides a broader, more intellectually honest view of the discipline and better prepares all students for world citizenship. Moreover, faculty members who engage in course transformation often experience their efforts as stimulating, challenging, and revitalizing. In examining additional reasons for multicultural course change, the author reviews current demographics specific to higher education as well as available empirical support for the efficacy of such change.

The second part of the chapter presents a general framework for thinking about multicultural education in colleges and universities. The literature documents numerous definitions of multicultural education. Kitano presents a highly inclusive, social reconstructionist definition of multicultural education and correlative goals, assumptions, and principles that serve as the basis for subsequent chapters. Among the key assumptions is the major role played by higher education faculty members in developing a more equitable society. ∎

Always interested in new ideas for enhancing his teaching skills, Professor Amatti has been attending a series of campus-based workshops on diversity. Observational research suggesting that teachers give more positive attention to male and mainstream students particularly concerned him. He determined to monitor his own classroom interactions to guard against biased treatment of students. In addition, he felt that the presentations on cultural differences in learning styles, women's ways of knowing, and the impact of low expectations on grading raised his consciousness and sensitivity. Indeed, the composition of his classes has changed over the past several years. This semester, he has several African American students, a few older students who are pursuing second careers, and a deaf student. In addition, several students from Belize are attending his classes. Professor Amatti wants to enhance the learning of all of his students while maintaining the university's high standards for achievement. Moreover, he knows that his professional organization's accreditation guidelines require that the coursework in his field "incorporate diverse ethnic, gender, cul-

tural, and disability perspectives." Yet in preparing for the new semester, he feels uncertain about precisely what modifications in content and instruction would be helpful to his students.

*   *   *

At 26, Toya Williams is taking her first upper division course, having transferred from a 2-year community college to a comprehensive state university. She forces herself to concentrate on the professor's orientation lecture, trying not to worry at this moment about how her two preschoolers are doing in the university day care center. She will try her best in Professor Amatti's class because she must maintain a 3.2 GPA in order to retain her scholarship. The demanding syllabus will require careful time management in order to juggle responsibilities related to her job, children, and elderly parents. She is hopeful that she will find a peer study group to support her learning of the course material. Looking at her fellow classmates, she notes that there are few students of color. She wonders if the swastika graffiti in the elevator has deterred them. The university advisor's suggestion that she enroll in non-credit basic study skill courses has shaken her self-confidence, particularly given her academic success at the junior college.

*   *   *

As Professor Amatti observed, the demographics of college classrooms in the United States are changing as they begin to reflect the increasing diversity of the country's population. And, like Toya, today's students enter colleges and universities with a range of backgrounds, experiences, and concerns that challenge the faculty to rethink long-standing assumptions about teaching and learning in higher education. Yet despite the critical role of teaching and learning in colleges and universities, few faculty members receive formal preparation in instructional strategies relevant for today's institutions. This book seeks to support faculty members'

efforts to apply content and instructional strategies that will enhance all students' success as they study, work, and interact in a multicultural society. Chapter 1 presents a rationale for multicultural course change and describes a philosophical basis for transforming courses to meet evolving needs.

THE RATIONALE FOR MULTICULTURAL COURSE CHANGE

Multicultural course change refers to the modification of a given course to appropriately incorporate multicultural content, perspectives, and strategies. Such change has as its objectives the following: provide a more comprehensive, accurate, intellectually honest view of reality; prepare all students to function in a multicultural society; and better meet the learning needs of all students, including those who are diverse. Course and pedagogy development as part of institutional change for responding to cultural diversity and combating racism is an ethical imperative for campuses with diverse student bodies (Chesler & Crowfoot, 1990). But it has *equal* relevance for more homogeneous campuses, whether a predominantly mainstream institution, a historically Black college or university, a single gender college, or a campus designed for students with disabilities. A transformed course's objectives of presenting new knowledge, helping students value diversity, and accommodating a range of learning strategies will better prepare *all* students for world citizenship.

Multicultural course change in higher education has potential for benefiting faculty, students from diverse backgrounds, and mainstream students. Surveys of higher education institutions demonstrate that concerted efforts to support the faculty's transformation of courses positively affects faculty vitality. Gaff (1992, pp. 34–35) found that "over seven of ten [institutions] surveyed noted a positive impact on faculty renewal. So strong was this effect that I was tempted to declare, during an early state of data analysis, that professors were the major beneficiaries of curriculum reform." Multicultural curriculum transformation challenges us to examine our own perspectives, engages us in intellectual struggles, and propels us across disciplinary boundaries as we search for resources to enrich our own knowledge. Across the country, collaborative projects among Women's Studies, Ethnic Studies, International Programs, and academic departments are enhancing awareness, provoking stimulating discussions, and resulting in innovative teaming arrangements for course development and implementation.

As instructors, we have a professional responsibility to enable our students to have access to comprehensive knowledge about our disciplines. Multicultural course change increases and transforms disciplinary knowledge. As Hilliard (1991/92, p. 13) cogently states, "The primary goal of a pluralistic curriculum process is to present a truthful and meaningful rendition of the whole human experience. This is not a matter of ethnic quotas in the curriculum for 'balance'; it is purely and simply a question of validity. Ultimately, if the curriculum is centered in truth, it will be pluralistic." History and literature textbooks often have been guilty of lying by omission in failing to acknowledge the contributions and perspectives of people of color and of women. In a later chapter of this book, Bartlett and Feiner report that introductory economics textbooks on the average devote less that 2 percent of their content to the economic status of women and minorities and omit new developments in the discipline that incorporate gender and race.

Textbooks often ignore the discrepancy between the ideal of equality and the reality of oppression caused by racism or sexism.

For example, American history texts in the past frequently omitted or provided only federal government perspectives on the confiscation of property and imprisonment of Americans of Japanese ancestry during World War II. Only recently have courses outside gender and ethnic studies programs begun to include and value scholarship related to the psychology, leadership, ways of knowing, and discourse of women and people of color. Clearly, the incorporation of multicultural content and strategies challenges instructors to recognize the limits of their training and to acquire broader knowledge to help students develop a more comprehensive truth.

In addition to our professional responsibility for comprehensive knowledge of the discipline, faculty members have a moral imperative to engage students intellectually and emotionally to encourage both learning and degree completion. The increasing diversity of students on our campuses coupled with disproportionately low rates of college completion by students of color demands transformation of our courses and programs. Courses that ignore the experiences of diverse students contribute to these students' feelings of alienation and their attrition from the university. The following statement from one student of color gives voice to many and reinforces the urgency for change.

> Part of studying history as an undergraduate turned me off, even though I loved history. When I took ethnic studies and women's studies, I realized that social history was missing from the way history was taught; basically it was what men did. It was elite history. I did not see myself or my community in the curriculum.

Finally, growing cultural heterogeneity requires of people from all backgrounds additional knowledge and social skills for effective participation as national and world citizens. All students, including those from traditional White, middle class backgrounds, have a right to expect that their courses present comprehensive knowledge and prepare them to succeed in a multicultural community. Understanding the perspectives of many groups enriches the lives of all students, supports cross-cultural competence, and promotes a more equitable society for all. Opportunities to critically analyze traditional canon (e.g., theories of moral development derived from data collected on male subjects) in light of new scholarship (e.g., Gilligan's critique based on women's experiences) expand students' knowledge and support higher level thinking. Further, multicultural education seeks to "close the gap between the Western democratic ideals of equality and justice and societal practices that contradict those ideals, such as discrimination based on race, gender, and social class" (Banks, 1991/92, p. 32). To achieve this end, all students—mainstream and nontraditional—need multicultural education.

Data from census studies document the range of demographic changes on college campuses. In addition, data indicating continuing disparities among groups in college completion rates support the need for curricular change. Finally, the literature indicates that institutional factors contribute to student attrition and retention and that faculty can positively influence student persistence and reduce prejudicial attitudes.

Increasing Population Diversity

The 1990 Census documented major demographic changes in this country over the last decade that are having and will continue to have significant impact on higher education. Between 1980 and 1990, the U.S. population grew by nearly 10 percent. According to Census figures (U.S. Department of Commerce, 1992):

- By ethnic group, the 1990 U.S. population figures were

Whites	199.7 million	(80.3%)
African Americans	30.0 million	(12.1%)
Hispanics (may be of any race)	22.4 million	(9.0%)
Asians or Pacific Islanders	7.3 million	(2.9%)
American Indians, Eskimos, or Aleuts	2.0 million	(0.8%)
Other and unknown	9.7 million	(3.9%)

- While the White population increased by 6 percent (11 million) since 1980, this group declined in proportion to the total U.S. population.

- The nonwhite population grew by 11 million, with African Americans experiencing a 13 percent increase; Hispanics a 53 percent increase; American Indians, Eskimos, or Aleuts a 38 percent increase; and Asian or Pacific Islanders a 107.8 percent increase.

It is projected that by 2010, although the nation will have grown in total population, the youth population will decline. At the same time, nonwhite youth will increase from 30 percent in 1990 to 38 percent in 2010 (Hodgkinson, 1991, p. 12).

Diversity characterizes people *within* the major ethnic groups as well. For example, the United States government recognizes over 400 Native communities, including Eskimo and Aleut. Asian and Pacific Islander Americans include people of Chinese, Filipino, Japanese, Asian Indian, Korean, Vietnamese, Cambodian, Hmong, Lao, Thai, Hawaiian, Samoan, and Guamanian ancestry. Hispanic Americans may have roots in Mexico, Puerto Rico, Cuba, or the many countries of South and Central America and may be of any race. Within each of the major groups and subgroups, individuals may differ in terms of language spoken, cultural values, level of acculturation, religion, socioeconomic status, education level, and generation in the United States. Moreover, immigrants within each group bring a variety of experiences from their countries of origin (e.g., urban or rural living; war or peace; oppression or freedom).

As the population increases in cultural and ethnic mix, the variety of spoken languages also is growing. The National Association for Bilingual Education (Waggoner, 1994) reports that 9.9 million school-age children and youth in the United States (over one in five) live in households in which languages other than English are spoken. Of these, approximately 60 percent (6 million) live in Spanish-speaking households. Children and youth who bring languages other than English live in every state. Interestingly, despite the predominance of school-age children who speak Spanish, children and youth from other non-English language backgrounds (e.g., Asian, Pacific Island, American Indian, African, European languages) in the aggregate outnumber their Spanish-language peers in the majority of states (Waggoner, 1994).

The Changing Classroom

Consistent with changes in the overall fabric of U.S. society, college classrooms reflect greater ethnic, cultural, and linguistic diversity. In addition, today's student body has a majority of women and a significant number of international students, older students, gay and lesbian students, and students with disabilities.

Ethnic Diversity

Differential high school attrition rates of students from some ethnic and cultural groups significantly affect their enrollment in institutions of higher education. Nevertheless, with the exception of African American students, the proportion of college enrollment comprised of diverse groups has increased steadily as the proportion of White, non-Hispanic students has declined. The absolute numbers of all diverse groups has increased (see Table 1).

Between 1980–81 and 1990–91, public and private 2- and 4-year institutions of higher education experienced a total increase in enrollment of 13.3 percent. Over the same period, the proportion of White, non-Hispanic students attending such institutions declined from 83.5 to 80.2 percent. Be-

TABLE 1–1   Enrollment in Higher Education by Ethnic Group

	School Year			
	1980–81		1990–91	
	(in thousands)			
Total enrollment in higher education	12,097	(100%)	13,710	(100%)
White, non-Hispanic	10,101	(83.5%)	10,995	(80.2%)
Black, non-Hispanic	1,137	(09.4%)	1,261	(09.2%)
Hispanic	484	(04.0%)	781	(05.7%)
Asian/Pacific Islander	290	(02.4%)	576	(04.2%)
American Indian/Alaskan Native	85	(0.7%)	110	(0.8%)

Adapted from U.S. Department of Education (1993a).

tween 1992 and 1993, enrollments of students of color rose by 2.6 percent, with all four major groups of color recording enrollment increases at four-year institutions. However, enrollments of African Americans and American Indians declined slightly at the two-year level (Carter & Wilson, 1995).

Gender

By 1980, women (51.5%) outnumbered men (48.5%) on college campuses. By the 1991–92 academic year, the proportion of women had increased to 54.7% (*Chronicle of Higher Education*, 1993), and the female majority is projected to continue (Editors of the *Chronicle of Higher Education*, 1992). Between 1970–71 and 1990–91, the percentage of bachelor's degrees awarded to women increased from 43.4 to 54.1. Over the same 20-year period, the proportion of doctorates conferred on women increased from 14.3 to 37.5 percent.

International Students

Although international students comprise only 2.9 percent of student enrollment nationwide (*Chronicle of Higher Education*, 1993), their numbers increased between 1978 and 1991 by 64 percent from 253,000 to 416,000. Commensurately, international students received 2.7 percent of bachelor's degrees awarded in 1990–91. However, during the same year, they earned 24.7 percent of doctoral degrees. One in four institutions of higher education reported an increase in the number of international students on their campuses in 1990–91 (National Education Association, 1992).

Age

Between Fall 1989 and Fall 1991, the percent of the freshman class over 18 years of age increased from 25.9 to 31.5. Age figures for Fall 1991 indicate that students over 24 con-stituted 40.8 percent of the total enrollment of full- and part-time students nationwide (*Chronicle of Higher Education*, 1993).

Gay and Lesbian Students

Gays and lesbians share experiences similar to those of members of other marginalized groups: lack of civil rights, societal censure, oppression, lowered self-esteem, physical violence, and hate campaigns (Elliot, 1993). Reliable estimates of the proportions of gay and lesbian students on college campuses are difficult to generate. Definitional and privacy issues may affect census-taking efforts. Nevertheless, Gonsiorek and Weinrich (1991) indicate that despite the considerable problems in definition and measurement, "the available research suggests that the incidence of homosexuality in the United States is currently in a range from 4% to 17%" (p. 11) and that gays and lesbians constitute one of the three most numerous minority groups in the United States. In her chapter on gay and lesbian issues in education, Fassinger (1993) notes that the literature well documents discrimination and harassment targeting gay and lesbian students in higher education. For example, she cites a 1984 survey conducted at the University of California at Berkeley indicating that 82 percent of the gay and lesbian students responding had been subjected to pejorative comments about gays by instructors and felt more uncomfortable in the classroom than did other minority groups.

Students with Disabilities

According to the *Chronicle of Higher Education* (Wilson, 1992), an estimated 10.5 percent of all college students have some form of disability. Of these students, nearly 40 percent have a visual impairment and 26 percent are deaf or hard of hearing. Institutions of higher education also serve students who have learning, physical, communication, or emotional disabilities that may require accommodation in the classroom. In response to section 504 of the Rehabilitation Act of 1973, most institutions of higher education routinely provide special services to ensure educational access to students with disabilities. More recent federal legislation (the Americans with Disabilities Act of 1990) extends provisions of the earlier act to the private sector, forbidding employment discrimination and requiring reasonable accommodation. Enrollments of individuals with disabilities are projected to increase in the future as the new regulations expand opportunities in the job market.

Degrees Awarded

National reports clearly document the disproportionately low numbers of individuals from some ethnic and cultural groups earning college degrees. Continuation of this trend in an era of increasing population diversity will result in undereducation of a significant portion of the population and diminish our individual and collective capacity. For example, a survey of the educational attainment of 1980 high school seniors by 1986 revealed that only 10.8 percent of American Indians, 9.9 percent of Black, and 6.8 percent of Hispanic students had attained bachelor's degrees as compared to 27.3 percent of Asian and 20.2% of White, non-Hispanic students (Editors of the *Chronicle of Higher Education*, 1992). The U.S. Department of Education (1993b) reports that Black, Hispanic, and American Indian students who graduate from college take longer as a group to complete their baccalaureate degrees than do Asian American and White students. According to the Department, taking longer may occur for a variety of reasons, including changing schools or majors, stopping out, or taking reduced course loads. The delay can result

in higher total costs for the degree and decreased lifetime earning potential.

As a natural result of demographic changes in the general population, students of color are enrolling on college campuses in larger numbers. However, their completion rates are disproportionately lower than for White students. At four-year colleges, 45 percent of all students in public institutions graduate in six years as compared with only 26 percent of African American and Hispanic students. Dropout rates of 60 percent for Hispanic and 71 percent for African American students are significantly higher than the 55 percent for Anglos (Fisk-Skinner & Gaither, 1992).

Similarly, students with disabilities evidence lower college completion rates than do students without disabilities. Students with disabilities enter college at a lower rate (15%) than do nondisabled students (56%), and of those entering, disproportionately fewer graduate. For example, 71% of students with hearing impairments leave college prior to completion as compared to 41 percent of students with normal hearing (English, 1993).

Institutional Contributions

Early investigators focused on background characteristics as the source of such underachievement of students from diverse groups. More recently, researchers have expanded the study of achievement differences to include structural factors, such as racial discrimination, that affect both students and educational systems. For example, discrimination on college campuses, an unsupportive social and emotional environment, and low expectations for student performance may contribute to student attrition. In addition, historical patterns of discrimination may indirectly affect student factors related to attrition, such as preparation, motivation, and nontraditional modes of participation, including delayed college entrance and enrollment interruptions (Fisk-Skinner & Gaither, 1992).

Aspects of campus climate that may affect students' level of comfort and their retention include overt acts of discrimination, the diversity of the faculty, and outcomes of academic debates related to multiculturalism. Each of these aspects sends explicit or implicit messages regarding the institution's valuing of diverse students.

Incidences of Overt Discrimination

Nationally, the incidence of oppressive acts on college campuses continues at an unacceptable rate. A 1991 survey of 444 two-year, four-year, and doctoral-granting institutions of higher education (National Education Association, 1992) revealed that 36 percent of reporting institutions had incidents of intolerance related to race, gender, or sexual orientation in the previous year. Of doctoral universities, 75 percent reported such incidents. In addition to overt acts of intolerance, campuses successful in recruiting diverse students and faculty are experiencing subtle racial tensions whose prevention or quick resolution are needed to maintain supportive climates. These situations include classroom interactions, comments, and instructional or grading practices that students and instructors with differing backgrounds attribute to cultural biases.

Faculty Diversity

Efforts to increase faculty diversity in higher education continue but are limited by low numbers of doctoral graduates of color in disciplines of high demand. For example, in 1993, of 6,496 individuals earning doctorates in the physical sciences, there were only 11 American Indians, 41 Blacks, and 89 Hispanics who were U.S. citizens. Moreover, on the average, only 20 percent

of doctoral graduates in the physical sciences plan postdoctoral employment in educational institutions! In 1991–92, of 520,551 full-time faculty nationwide, only 1,655 (0.32%) were American Indian; 26,545 (5.1%) Asian; 24,611 (4.7%) African American; and 11,424 (2.2%) Hispanic. Thus, a total diverse faculty of 12.3 percent serves a college enrollment that is approximately 23 percent diverse.

But in some areas of the country, the discrepancy between student and faculty diversity is worse than these nationwide statistics suggest. For example, a recent California report (Intersegmental Coordinating Council, 1991) compared the percentages of nonwhite undergraduate students and faculty for the University of California system (41% and under 15%), California State University (40% and under 15%) and the California Community College system (37% and 14.2%). A rough comparison (Table 2) of the proportion of diverse groups in the general population with their proportions among college students, graduates, and faculty supports the need for change in higher education to attract and retain more individuals of color.

Campus Debates on Multiculturalism and Diversity

Based on events of the early 1990s on college campuses across the country, the editors of the *Chronicle of Higher Education* (1992) predicted that debates will continue on issues related to diversity. Many campuses have made efforts to recruit and retain more diverse students and faculty. At the same time, critics have targeted admission criteria and scholarships that give preference to members of certain underrepresented groups. With the conservative Bush administration and voters' demands for change during the Clinton administration, colleges have experienced a backlash against affirmative action

TABLE 1–2   Comparison of Selected Characteristics by Ethnic Group

Characteristic	American Indian	Asian	Black	Hispanic	White	Total
U.S. Population (90)	0.8	2.9	12.1	9.0*	80.3	248,709,873
Enrollments 4-yr colleges (88)†	0.5	3.8	8.3	3.8	83.6	7,873,000
Conferred Bachelor's degree (88)†	0.4	3.9	5.9	3.0	86.8	988,267
Faculty, 4-yr colleges (87–88)‡	1.0	5.0	3.0	2.0	89.0	378,732

*May be any race

†Adapted from the Editors of the *Chronicle of Higher Education* (1992); does not include international students.

‡National Education Association (1992)

and "political correctness." Yet many institutions are broadening their curricula to include new perspectives related to race, gender, and class even while critics urge maintenance of traditional literary and historical views. And while some urge moderation in attempts to diversify students, faculty, and curriculum, others argue that colleges are moving too slowly.

The debate concerning curriculum transformation centers on what content best serves the vision of a society where diverse groups can retain their cultural heritages while simultaneously engaging in true cooperation to achieve universal ideals of equity and access for all. Efforts to change the curriculum have invoked arguments based on philosophical and value differences as well as pragmatic concerns related to the reality of a multicultural and interdependent world. Additionally, the question arises regarding the impact of curriculum change on students.

The Efficacy of Curriculum Change

While we might agree that a moral imperative exists to transform curricula in higher education, as responsible academics we search for evidence that such changes will make a positive difference for students. Are multicultural curriculum change efforts working? Attempts to empirically demonstrate the efficacy of multicultural training are relatively new and constitute a uniquely challenging and complex task. Beaudry and Davis's evaluation chapter in this book suggests that evaluation designs require research teams that reflect cultural and linguistic diversity and pay close attention to variables of race, gender, ethnicity, and social class in defining validity. Few studies have met these criteria.

Given the recent curriculum change efforts in higher education, Gaff (1992) argues that it is too early to determine outcomes. "Indeed, the major task confronting most institutions today is going beyond the rhetoric in implementing educationally useful programs and courses. After all, most educational innovations fail not because they are ineffective, but because they are never implemented" (p. 35). Nevertheless, data are emerging that support the efficacy of transformed courses in changing student attitudes.

Research on prejudice reduction in children and adults provides support for focused multicultural curricula. Banks' (1988, 1995) reviews of literature identify several variables that impact the effectiveness of multicultural education:

- Curriculum content (democratic versus ethnocentric curricula and materials supported the development of positive racial attitudes in children)

- Understanding of the discrepancies between reality and ideals related to race in this country (workshops demonstrated positive changes in adults)
- Specific objectives and strategies for multicultural education
- Strategies that increase cognitive sophistication (cognitive sophistication and critical thinking ability appear to correlate negatively with racial bias)
- Attitudes and predispositions of teachers as manifested in verbal and nonverbal interactions, reponses to students' languages and dialects, and accommodation of diverse learning styles
- Duration of training
- The hidden curriculum and institutional factors supportive of multicultural goals

These factors clearly apply to higher education as well as K-12. For example, MacPhee, Kreutzer, and Fritz (1994) recently described an evaluation study of a project to infuse multicultural content into a sequence of four human development courses taught by three faculty members at Colorado State University. The authors reported significant changes in the attitudes of students, who were primarily White (90%), relative to comparison groups. Specifically, students in the infused courses demonstrated decreased ethnocentrism, increased critical thinking skills, and a reduction in prejudicial and blaming attitudes toward minority groups. Results also emphasized the importance of multicultural infusion across a sequence of courses as opposed to a single course or session in enhancing multicultural sensitivity.

Data on incidents of discrimination on college campuses, faculty diversity, campus debates related to multicultural issues, and the demonstrated impact of multicultural curricula support the need for institutional change. Fisk-Skinner and Gaither (1992) argue that "rather than expecting the student to conform to the educational system, the system itself must share the burden of change" (p. 1664). In higher education, recruitment and retention have been the focus of change. Student recruitment is a logical beginning; transformation in higher education may follow a developmental progression commencing with an emphasis on student recruitment, proceeding to more comprehensive student services intervention, and finally to a recognition of the need for faculty involvement and change in academic practices and curriculum (Carter & Wilson, 1994).

Recommendations on outreach, student support, and faculty diversity components of recruitment and retention have been offered elsewhere (see Green, 1989; Sawchuk, 1992) and will not be repeated here. Rather, this book adopts the view that "what happens in the classroom—the interactions between teachers and students, the curriculum, pedagogy, human relationships—is the core of the academic experience" (Green, 1989, p. 131) and therefore has the highest potential among institutional factors for influencing students' success or failure. Specifically, the book focuses on curriculum and instructional strategies within faculty control as key elements in recruiting, retaining, and graduating students in a diverse society. The next section provides a multicultural education framework as the basis for curriculum and instructional change.

A FRAMEWORK FOR CURRICULAR CHANGE

Increasing population diversity, sensitivity to achievement differences, and recognition of institutional contributions to inequity have affected how institutions of higher education perceive their missions. Universities and colleges across the country are responding to these issues through increased emphasis on multiculturalism in the curriculum. A recent survey of 196 colleges and universities (Levine & Cureton, 1992) found that over one third of all such institutions have a multicultural general education requirement; that over half have introduced multiculturalism into their departmental course offerings, most frequently through the addition of new materials to existing courses; and that the overwhelming majority (72%) of vice presidents and deans at four-year institutions "talk about multiculturalism frequently or continually" (p. 29). The authors project that these data reflect "only a beginning of what is likely to be a very long process."

These findings give evidence that curricular change for diversity is occurring on significant numbers of college campuses. Yet the literature provides little evidence that institutions are monitoring the appropriateness of these changes. For example, the addition of required readings by ethnic or women authors might be viewed by some as a valid method for multicultural curriculum infusion. However, unless the new readings provide new perspectives on events, ways of knowing, values, or aesthetics, no substantive change has occurred. Clearly, as the multicultural curriculum movement expands, participating higher education institutions must focus on *quality* of change. One approach to addressing quality issues is to establish a framework for multicultural infusion of higher education courses and assess course development and revision in relation to the framework.

This book was developed within a coherent framework that addresses the foundational issues of diversity, achieve-ment, and access, and institutional contributions to equity as described in the previous section. The book was designed to assist faculty members who desire to incorporate multicultural content and strategies into their courses as a means of better meeting the needs of all students in a diverse society. This section describes the framework, including a definition of multicultural education, philosophical assumptions, guiding principles, and recommended practices.

Multicultural Education

Sleeter and Grant's (1987) comprehensive review of literature on multicultural education in K–12 education revealed that writers use the term in a variety of ways, often without explicit definition. To facilitate communication and progress in the field, they encourage authors to clarify their definition of multicultural education, including target groups, theoretical framework, assumptions and goals, and recommended practices. Sleeter and Grant suggest that five distinct approaches emerge from the literature: teaching the culturally different (equipping people of color to compete with Whites); human relations (helping students of different backgrounds get along); single group studies (teaching about a specific group); multicultural education (valuing diversity, equal opportunity, and equity in distribution of power); and education that is multicultural and social reconstructionist (preparing people to take social action against structural inequality). Although based on K–12 schooling, this taxonomy has relevance to higher education.

Specifically, as we make the decision to incorporate multicultural content and strategies in our courses, a critical first step is to make explicit the intended outcome—the **multicultural goal**. Is it to

- support diverse students' acquisition of traditional subject matter knowledge and skills?

- help students acquire a more accurate or comprehensive knowledge of the subject matter?

- encourage students to accept themselves and others?

- understand the history, traditions, and perspectives of specific groups?

- help students value diversity and equity?

- equip all students to work actively toward a more democratic society?

How we answer this question or prioritize intended outcomes has implications for how we approach curriculum change.

The authors of the book propose the following definition of multicultural education for higher education:

> **Multicultural education has as its purpose the development of citizens for a more democratic society through provision of more accurate and comprehensive disciplinary knowledge and through enhancement of students' academic achievement and critical thinking applied to social problems. It seeks to promote the valuing of diversity and equal opportunity for all people through understanding of the contributions and perspectives of people of differing race, ethnicity, culture, language, religion, gender, sexual orientation, and physical abilities and disabilities.**

This definition rests on a number of assumptions, each of which has implications for teaching and learning in higher education.

Assumption 1: Multicultural education is for all. A common perception is that multicultural education targets the im-

proved status of members of marginalized groups. Indeed, one major goal of multicultural education is the academic, social, and career attainment of diverse students. However, the broader concern of multicultural education is the promotion of a more equitable society whose realization will enrich the lives of all groups and individuals. No one group has the market on ethnocentricity; successful multicultural education invites all people to examine critically their own biases and to adopt the values and behaviors needed for social change. An act of discrimination against any individual or group dehumanizes us all.

Second, multicultural education is quality education. A multicultural curriculum broadens students' world views and enables them to appreciate different cultures, languages, values, and ways of thinking. A multicultural curriculum enriches the lives of all students and benefits the wider community with which they interact.

Finally, from a pragmatic viewpoint, successful multicultural education will enable all students to interact more effectively with individuals different from themselves. These skills increasingly are demanded by public institutions and businesses as the nation becomes domestically more diverse and as the world shrinks through international peace initiatives, cross-national hiring practices, binational cooperative ventures, and global telecommunications. In her presidential address at Association for the Study of Higher Education, Hackman (1992) concluded that higher educators in the 1990s and opening years of the twenty-first century must

- consider new ways of working with each other and in organizations, to learn from alternative ways of inclusion and communication what some have called African American, Native American, and women's ways.

- change how we prepare for and live on our increasingly interdependent globe.

- make a major shift in how we learn from and work with people of multiple backgrounds and cultures.

- participate fully in the age of knowledge and prepare ourselves, our students, and our institutions to play roles in this new age. (p. 15)

Assumption 2: Higher education seeks to disseminate truth, and teaching transformative scholarship offers students a more comprehensive truth. The traditional knowledge base transmitted through higher education was developed or compiled primarily by persons representing the views of the dominant (White male) power structure. For example, Banks (1993) describes Western-centric or mainstream academic knowledge in the social and behavioral sciences as having been established within mainstream professional associations and as providing the perspectives taught in U.S. colleges and universities. Transformative theory and research methods, developed in women's studies and ethnic studies, provide data and explanations that challenge, expand, and revise those established by mainstream scholarship (Banks, 1993). Transformative scholarship does not necessarily diminish the contributions or value of mainstream discourse and provides a more inclusive, comprehensive view of reality. "The truth about the development and attainments of multicultural education needs to be told for the sake of balance, scholarly integrity, and accuracy" (Banks, p. 22).

Assumption 3: All groups (e.g., cultural, gender) have the same underlying abilities; they may differ in preferred modes of acquiring and expressing competence (Cole & Bruner, 1971). Research from the fields of anthropology and cross-cultural psychology demonstrates that cultural experiences mediate how individuals and groups best acquire new information and express their acquired knowledge and skills. Instructors therefore can assume that all students have the ability to learn. And competent instructors use a wide repertoire of teaching methods to promote students' learning.

A number of authors argue that ethnic and cultural differences exist in cognitive and learning styles, or the ways in which individuals approach and perceive problem solving tasks. The topic has sparked much controversy primarily because of the potential produced for stereotyping different groups as having different types of styles (Anderson & Adams, 1992; Green, 1989) as compared to the mainstream standard. Research on learning styles has addressed differences between groups based on ethnicity, culture, gender, disability, and age. Based on their review of the literature, Irvine and York (1995) conclude that

> research on learning styles using culturally diverse students fails to support the premise that members of a given cultural group exhibit a distinctive style. Hence, the issue is not the identification of a style for a particular ethnic or gender group, but rather how instruction should be arranged to meet the instructional needs of diverse students. (p. 494)

Given our diversity, it is logical to expect that any given classroom would have students exhibiting a range of preferences in the ways they learn, communicate, interact, perceive, and compete. The implication is the same: competent instructors use a wide repertoire of teaching methods to promote students' learning and their expression of knowledge.

Assumption 4: Academic achievement is a critical factor in promoting equal opportunity. Diverse students' academic achievement is a necessary part of their empowerment; failure to demand academic competence perpetuates both social marginality and structural inequality (Sleeter, 1991). Given that all groups have the same underlying abilities, instructors can communicate high expectations to all students. No need exists to reduce demands for excellence. While some students across culture, gender, and other groups enter higher education underprepared, underpreparation should not be confused with lower potential. Instead, academic rigor can be combined with social support:

> When academically rigorous instruction is conducted within a community of scholarship accompanied by a system of social supports, then all students seem to benefit. But if culturally sensitive features are added to the curriculum without adding academically demanding curriculum, then minority students may not benefit and achieve. (Mehan, Lintz, Okamoto, & Wills, 1995, p. 141)

Equal opportunity does not result in declining standards when preparedness is supported, instructors maintain high expectations for student performance, and learning opportunities are structured to take advantage of student strengths.

Assumption 5: Academic achievement alone does not eliminate structural barriers to career attainment and social integration. Recent reports continue to demonstrate that, while correlated, academic achievement does not lead to equal opportunity for all in higher education or the workplace. In their review on lack of preparation as a factor in college attrition among diverse students, Fisk-Skinner and Gaither (1992) reported that "preparedness does not tell the whole story...even when past academic achievement is held constant, minority dropout rates are higher and GPAs are lower" (p. 1660). The authors suggest that historical patterns of discrimination and limited access have affected expectations, motivation, and real opportunities such that racial and ethnic background may exert a continuing influence independent of socioeconomic class.

Relatedly, the National Center for Education Statistics (1989) indicated that when economic status is controlled, a significantly smaller percent of African Americans and Hispanics attain bachelor's and graduate degrees than White non-Hispanic counterparts. Moreover, an OERI report on the class of 1972 (Adelman, 1991) found that of those with bachelor's degrees, White males' mean annual earnings were higher than those for White women, African American women and men, and Hispanic women and men. A U.S. Commission on Civil Rights (1992) report on Asian Americans in the 1990s noted that this group's professional advancement is not commensurate with higher educational achievement in studies that control for education level, work experience, English ability, and industry of work.

A 1994 report commissioned by the U.S. Office of Personnel Management on federal workers fired in 1992 found that African Americans are fired at nearly twice the rate of Whites even when allowing for differences in age, education, experience, job performance, and prior disciplinary history (Greve, 1994). The Federal Glass Ceiling Commission (1995) concluded that "at the highest levels of business, there is indeed a barrier only rarely penetrated by women or persons of color...The research also indicates that where there are women and minorities in high places, their compensation is lower" (pp. iii–iv). These findings suggest that racial bias and other structural factors continue to operate in societal institutions.

Assumption 6: Higher education faculty can play a significant role in develop-

ing a more equitable society. Faculty members contribute to social equity by fostering the academic competence of all students. But given assumption 5, a question arises regarding the responsibility of higher education faculty to go further than the dissemination of content knowledge and skills by working to promote equity beyond the classroom. For example, a chemistry professor with strong convictions regarding equity believes that she can best serve diverse students by motivating their learning through use of inquiry methods, discrepant events, cooperative learning, and linking of new information to previous experiences and concepts. Has she fulfilled her commitment to equal opportunity if she is successful in promoting diverse students' achievement in chemistry?

Like the chemistry professor, faculty members must determine their own goals regarding the extent of personal participation in social change. Faculty members in higher education reside in the center of a number of concentric spheres of influence. They can choose to become involved in social change within any or all of these spheres (see Figure 1–1):

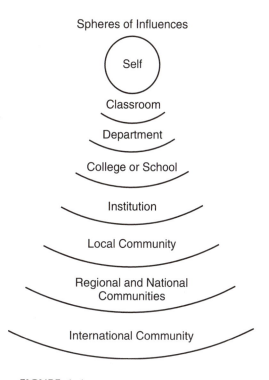

FIGURE 1–1

- *Self*: We can analyze our own attitudes, beliefs, values, knowledge, and behavior in terms of our own socialization experiences, those of other groups, and our interactions with students in the classroom. As individuals, we can behave in ways that acknowledge the value of diversity and speak out when we encounter an act of oppression; we can support scholarships or mentor students from underrepresented groups.

- *Classroom*: We can improve student achievement in our discipline, engage students in critical analysis of disciplinary perspectives, provide a rigorous and welcoming environment, and support students' development of tools important for active citizenship, such as critical thinking and social action skills.

- *Department, college or school, and institution*: Through advising, committee work, and governance activities, we can influence recruitment and retention of students and faculty, campus climate, and other structural features of the institution.

- *Community*: Our efforts can be extended to professional and personal service roles in the greater community as we interact with schools, government and social service agencies, business and industry, and charitable, arts, and religious organizations.

- *Professional activities*: As faculty members, we have local, regional, national, and international influence through our scholarship and work with professional organizations. We can focus research efforts on studies that will improve the quality of life for members of diverse groups, initiate special interest groups in professional organizations, or encourage the appointment of individuals from underrepresented groups to leadership positions.

This book focuses on the classroom sphere of influence. However, it encourages each of us to consider our responsibility and comfort level with extending social-change activities to additional spheres. Freire (1985) reminds us that every action (or inaction) by an educator is a political decision.

Principles and Practices

The principles and recommended practices that guide the development of this book stem from the foregoing issues, definition, and assumptions and are consistent with the current knowledge base in multicultural education (AAUW, 1993; Banks, 1988; NCSS, 1992; Suzuki, 1984).

1. Diversity should permeate the total campus environment. A comprehensive approach requires organizational management and change directed at diversity, focused hiring and faculty development, and specific attention to the informal, hidden curriculum.

2. Content and materials should reflect the cultural characteristics and experiences of the students, critically examine social realities and conflict in U.S. and world societies, include the study of various cultural

groups and their historical experiences, and present and analyze diverse perspectives.

3. Instructional strategies should communicate high expectations for achievement, capitalize on students' experiences and learning strengths, and include opportunities for personal participation and growth.

4. Objectives should include fostering of skills important to informed citizenship, such as critical thinking, decision making, social participation, and intergroup interaction.

5. Assessment procedures should include methods that accommodate students' strongest strategies for expression of accumulated knowledge and skills.

6. Evaluation should be ongoing and systematic with relationship to multicultural education goals and objectives.

Marchesani and Adams (1992) identified a four-dimensional faculty development model for promoting diversity in college classrooms. The four dimensions of teaching and learning focus on understanding how *students* from diverse backgrounds experience the classroom; encouraging the *instructor* to know herself or himself as an individual who brings a unique history of socialization, experiences, and assumptions; incorporating diverse perspectives into *course content*, and possessing a broad repertoire of *teaching methods* to accommodate different learning styles and preferences. Based on the principles articulated above, we suggest additional dimensions: *assessment procedures* that take advantage of student experiences; systematic *evaluation* of courses in relation to multicultural education goals; *informal processes* (hidden curriculum) supportive of diversity; effective *organizational management* and change.

This book assumes that readers recognize and appreciate the diversity of their students and understand the impact of their own socialization on classroom interactions. For this reason, the remaining chapters focus on curricular and instructional dimensions. The book's mission is to encourage faculty in higher education to modify their courses to better prepare all students for effective functioning in a diverse society. Course transformation is a long-term, continuous, complex process requiring supportive organizational change. Chapter 2 presents a model for course transformation that considers levels of multicultural change and entails rethinking four components: content, instructional strategies, assessment procedures, and classroom dynamics. Chapters 3 through 6 explore in detail multicultural change in each of these four components. Chapter 7 is devoted to improving instruction for students who have a primary language other than English. Chapters 8 through 14 represent examples of how some subject matter specialists approach the task of multicultural course change. The last two chapters offer recommendations for organizational strategies supportive of multicultural curricula and for evaluating the impact of multicultural change.

CHAPTER 2

What a Course Will Look Like After Multicultural Change

Margie K. Kitano, *Associate Dean, College of Education*
San Diego State University

Editor's Notes:

In this chapter, Kitano describes an integrated model for course change and syllabus revision. The author seeks to answer the frequently asked questions: What does a multiculturally infused course look like? How will I know when my course is transformed? Assumptions include the long-term, continuing nature of the course-change process and the conceptualization of multicultural change in terms of levels rather than a dichotomy.

Kitano analyzes various conceptions of multicultural curriculum change from the literature. Based on this literature, she derives a two-dimensional model or paradigm consisting of three levels of change (exclusive, inclusive, transformed) and four components: content, instructional strategies, assessment of student knowledge, and classroom dynamics. The paradigm suggests that instructors can approach course change by focusing on one or more of the components and identifying a target level, depending on the instructor's multicultural goals and the nature of discipline. The author suggests ways in which the syllabus can be revised to accurately reflect and communicate the course's multicultural intent. Examples from a variety of disciplines illustrate the interplay of components and levels applied to specific courses. Subsequent chapters detail the content, instruction, assessment, and classroom dynamics components of the paradigm; the subject matter chapters then apply aspects of the paradigm to specific disciplinary courses. ∎

Professor Navarro has volunteered to participate in her university's faculty development program on multicultural education because she has a strong interest in recruiting and retaining women and students of color in the College of Engineering. She wishes to discover ways in which her course on nonmetallic materials, dealing with the fundamentals of plastics and ceramics and the selection of materials for use in design, can be modified to better accommodate student diversity. As she uses an example from military technology, a bright, popular African American student comments appropriately on the example and then quips, "But it won't work if President Clinton lifts the ban on gays in the military." Professor Navarro would like to ignore this statement because opening a discussion of this issue would take time away from the course's content objectives. On the other hand, she wonders what message she will be conveying to students by letting the statement go by unchallenged.

* * *

What should Professor Navarro's course look like after multicultural change? In addressing this question, several assumptions must be made explicit. First, every course has several dimensions that can be considered in planning for change: content, instructional strategies and activities, assessment strategies, and classroom dynamics, including how instructors respond to student comments. Second, in terms of content, courses in some disciplines (e.g., sociology) are more easily modified than courses in other disciplines (e.g., nonmetallic materials; calculus). Third, course revision for multicultural change is a continuing and interactive process between the individual instructor and course as the former grows in multicultural sophistication. For this reason, describing an ideal end product for a specific course can be like sighting a moving target. Nevertheless, revision efforts tend to follow a logical continuum of degree and quality of multicultural change that can be described. Fourth, the course syllabus should accurately reflect multicultural intent. A comparison of syllabi with actual course instruction will demonstrate that the multiculturalism of some transformed courses is not reflected in their syllabi, while some courses with obviously multicultural syllabi do not demonstrate multiculturalism in practice. This chapter argues for consistency between syllabus and course implementation with the idea that the syllabus represents a tentative course guide. Moreover, all course goals, including multicultural goals, should be made explicit to students, actualized in content and instruction, and their attainment monitored. Finally, syllabi constitute a major source for external evaluation of program quality, including meeting of professional standards regarding multicultural content and strategies.

A MODEL FOR COURSE AND SYLLABUS CHANGE

As stated in the first chapter, the logical place to begin in incorporating content and strategies for a multicultural society within a given course is with intended outcomes— our multicultural goals. What do we hope to achieve for a particular course? Is it to

- support diverse students' acquisition of traditional subject matter knowledge and skills?
- help students acquire a more accurate or comprehensive knowledge of subject matter?
- encourage students to accept themselves and others?
- understand the history, traditions, and perspectives of specific groups?
- help students value diversity and equity?
- equip all students to work actively toward a more democratic society?

The framework for multicultural education presented earlier views these outcomes as noncompeting and supports their inclusion in all courses. But individual differences exist in faculty members' adoption of these values and in their readiness to implement them in a given course. This chapter suggests general strategies for working toward these goals within the higher education classroom with the assumption that the reader will select those consistent with his or her values. We begin first with a discussion of broad learning principles that serve as a basis for appropriate instruction at all levels of education. We then present a model for multicultural course change tied closely to syllabus development. Subsequent chapters detail suggestions for each component of the model.

Principles of Learning

Social and political values often stimulate recognition of the need for educational reform, as in the case of multicultural education. However, specific recommendations for change in teaching and learning must have foundations in current theoretical and empirical knowledge about the learning process. It is beyond the scope of this book to describe the various applicable theories of learning. For our purposes, general principles derived from the current knowledge base on teaching and learning, together with principles and assumptions of multicultural education presented in Chapter 1, create a workable underpinning for course change. The American Psychological Association's Task Force on Psychology in Education (1992) identified twelve psychological principles applicable to learners of all ages as guidelines for school redesign and reform. Recommendations for infusing multicultural content and strategies demonstrate consistency with these principles. The principles emphasize the need for instructors to recognize the critical contributions of individual experience, self-awareness, values, interests, and feelings to the learning process; to connect new information to previous knowledge and experience in order to promote the learner's construction of meaning; to create a comfortable, nonthreatening learning environment; to support learning opportunities through peer interaction; to provide meaningful and optimally challenging experiences; to value and accept students as individuals; and to accommodate individual differences in learning modes and strategies.

A Model

The model we present for multicultural change in postsecondary courses (Figure 2–1) suggests that course development and revision should be based on the instructor's goals for the course and students with regard to multiculturalism. These goals derive from explicit multicultural education and learning principles such as those just discussed. The goals are mediated by the nature of the course, particularly its amenability to multicultural transformation. The instructor's goals determine the level of course change and the course elements (content, instruction, assessment, and dynamics) that will be modified. The level and elements will be reflected in specific aspects of the course syllabus. A simple schematic of the model appears below and is followed by a detailed explanation of levels of change, course elements, and syllabus components.

The Nature of Change

In Chapter 1, we provided a broad definition of multicultural course change as the modification of a given course to appropriately incorporate multicultural content, perspectives, and strategies. This section embellishes the definition through an analysis of literature and terminology on multicultural change. The literature provides discussions of multicultural change applicable to different units—single courses, the larger university curriculum, the entire organization—and for different contexts—K–12 schools, higher education, business and industry. For example, Green (1989) describes five phases of campus-wide curriculum change in incorporating ethnic and women's studies. Ogibene (1989) applies a two-dimensional typology consisting of three ways to include ethnic and women's studies content and three categories describing how well subject matter lends itself to integration of such content. Jackson and Holvino (1988) present six sequential stages in the process of developing multicultural organizations. Table 2–1 provides a

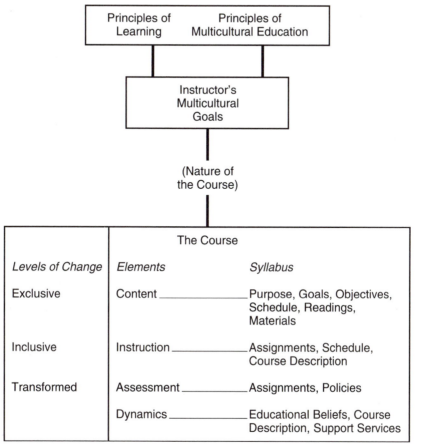

A MODEL FOR MULTICULTURAL COURSE AND SYLLABUS CHANGE

FIGURE 2–1

summary of selected conceptions of multi-cultural change.

Whatever the focus and context of these conceptions of multicultural change, consensus exists that change is a dynamic process describable in terms of levels rather than as a static outcome. While authors use different labels, they tend to agree that the lowest level represents traditional, main-stream perspectives while the highest focuses on structural transformation. In between the two extremes is a middle level that incorporates both normative and non-traditional perspectives and may encourage critical analysis of the dominant norm in light of the newer perspectives. Authors vary on what precisely constitutes the highest form of transformation. Banks (1993) suggests that the highest level goes beyond structural modification to provide students with the social action and decision-making skills necessary for participation as agents

TABLE 2-1 Conceptions of Multicultural Change

Source	Context	Level 1	Level 2	Level 3	Level 4	Levels 5, 6
Banks (1993)	K-12 Courses	*Contributions* Brings in discrete elements such as foods or holidays.	*Additive* Adds content but retains original structure.	*Transformation* Changes structure of curriculum to incorporate diverse perspectives.	*Social Action* Encourages decision making and social action	
Green (1989)	Higher Education Curriculum	*Exclusive Curriculum* Excludes works and perspectives of non-Western cultures and women.	*Exceptional Outsider* Adds superstar minorities/women but no structural change.	*Understanding the Outsider* Includes content to analyze and understand excluded groups.	*Getting Inside the Outsider* Provides many perspectives of "reality," switching from dominant to outsider.	*Transformed Curriculum* Incorporates new scholarship, methodologies, ways of thinking, ways of teaching/learning.
Schoem, et al. (1993)	Higher Education Courses	*First Stage* Restricts discussion of diversity to one part of the course.	*Second Stage* Includes additional information throughout to compare to dominant norm.	*Third Stage* Integrates additional information and critical analysis of norms and implications of inclusion/ exclusion.	*Fourth Stage* Diversity of content, process, faculty, and students leads to deeper levels of understanding.	
Ognibene, (1989)	Higher Education Courses	*Strengthening the Canon* Includes women and minorities to confirm stereotypes.	*Adding to the Canon* Adds significant people who meet traditional standards.	*Challenging the Canon* Provides alternative definitions from diverse perspectives.		
Jackson & Holvino (1988)	Organizations	*Exclusionary* Uses exclusionary practices.	*The Club* Allows entrance to limited numbers who have the "right" perspective.	*Compliance* Commits to access without disturbing the structure.	*Affirmative Action* Actively recruits, supports, and promotes.	*Redefining* Critcally examines policies, and changes to distribute power. Level 6 *Multicultural* Actively works to eradicate social oppression.

22

of social change. Schoem, Frankel, Zúñiga, & Lewis (1993) define transformation in terms of the coming together of multicultural curriculum content, process and discourse, and faculty and student diversity that permits learning to "rise to a new level of understanding, one that transcends particularistic knowing" (p. 4).

Like the forgoing, the paradigm for course change we present in this chapter recognizes levels of change. We propose three: exclusive, inclusive, and transformed. Our paradigm (Table 2–2) diverges from others in applying the levels to four components of teaching a course: content, instructional strategies, assessment, and the dynamics of classroom interaction. In this way, the paradigm addresses four elements that instructors can choose to modify, depending on their personal philosophies, readiness, expertise, and the demands of disciplinary content. Changing each component requires considerable planning, experimentation, and revision and should be considered an ongoing process over several semesters of implementation.

IMPLEMENTING THE PARADIGM

This section describes in greater detail the potential levels of course change and then applies these levels to the four course elements over which instructors have control.

Levels of Course Change

The extent and quality of incorporation of diversity content, instruction, assessment, and dynamics into a course depends on the instructor's view of the discipline with respect to multiculturalism. Three broad categories of course integration can be derived from these discussions: exclusive, inclusive, and transformed.

An **exclusive** course presents and maintains traditional, mainstream experiences and perspectives on the discipline. If alternative perspectives are included, they are selected to confirm stereotypes. The instructor conveys information in a didactic manner, and students demonstrate their acquisition of knowledge through objective or subjective written examinations. Classroom interactions are limited to question/answer discussions controlled by the instructor without attempts to support participation by all students. In the exclusive classroom, class time is not given to discussion of social issues not directly related to the discipline.

An **inclusive** course presents traditional views but adds alternative perspectives. Content integration in an inclusive course can range from simple addition of new viewpoints without elaboration to efforts at analyzing and understanding reasons for historical exclusion. The instructor uses a wide array of teaching methods to support students' active learning of course content. Evaluation of students occurs through several different types of assessments to ensure consideration of individual differences in expressing knowledge. The instructor monitors student participation and employs learning activities that support participation by all students.

A **transformed** course challenges traditional views and assumptions; encourages new ways of thinking; and reconceptualizes the field in light of new knowledge, scholarship, and ways of knowing. The instructor restructures the classroom so that the instructor and students share power (within the limits of responsibility and reality). Methods capitalize on the experience and knowledge that students bring and encourage personal as well as academic growth. Alternatives to traditional assessment procedures are used, including self-evaluation and projects that contribute to real-life change.

TABLE 2-2 A Paradigm for Multicultural Course Change: Examining Course Components and Levels of Change

Component	Level 1		
	Exclusive	Inclusive	Transformed
Content	Gives traditional mainstream experiences and perspectives; adds authors from different backgrounds who confirm traditional perspectives or support stereotypes.	Adds alternative perspectives through materials, readings, speakers; analyzes historical exclusion of alternative perspectives.	Reconceptualizes the content through a shift in paradigm or standard; presents content through nondominant perspective.
Instructional Strategies and Activities	Mainly lecture and other didactic methods; question-and-answer discussions; instructor as purveyor of knowledge.	Instructor as purveyor of knowledge but uses a variety of methods to • relate new knowledge to previous experience • engage students in constructing knowledge • build critical thinking skills • encourage peer learning.	Change in power structure so that students and instructor learn from each other; methods center on student experience/knowledge such as • analyzing concepts against personal experience • issues-oriented approaches • critical pedagogy.
Assessment of Student Knowlege	Primarily examinations and papers.	Multiple methods and alternatives to standard exams and papers; student choice.	Alternatives that focus on student growth: action-oriented projects; self-assessment, reflection on the course.
Classroom Dynamics	Focus exclusively on content; avoidance of social issues in classroom; no attempt to monitor student participation.	Acknowledgment and processing of social issues in classroom; monitoring and ensuring equity in student participation.	Challenging of biased views and sharing of diverse perspectives while respecting rules established for group process; equity in participation.

The levels and components provide an organized way of conceptualizing degrees of multicultural change. Applicability depends to a great extent on the specific discipline and course. Instructors may choose to modify each component at different levels. Through this book, we hope to demonstrate that the greatest majority of courses offered in a university, including those taught in a large lecture format, can become inclusive in all four components. It is important to note that the various levels are not discrete and will overlap. Moreover, in reality, it is impossible to separate out the four components of content, instruction, assessment, and dynamics. Finally, there exists no single correct way to transform a course or any of its components. The paradigm is intended to stimulate thinking about course change, and the possibilities for a creative instructor are vast.

Content

To move toward an inclusive course, instructors can select content, materials, and resources that reflect the cultural characteristics and experiences of the students; critically examine social realities and conflict in U.S. and world societies; include the study of various cultural groups and their historical experiences; and present and analyze diverse perspectives. To the extent that knowledge is socially constructed, the presentation of multiple perspectives provides a closer approximation of "truth."

Consider, for example, a course on leadership theories. An exclusive course might focus on traditional leadership theories based on studies of White male leaders. An inclusive course would provide at least equal focus to women's leadership and to non-Western theories of leadership. Such a course might further engage students in analyzing why theories on women's leadership have traditionally been omitted from the curriculum and the impact of including and omitting such literature. A transformed course might present a new paradigm of leadership that replaces the traditional norm with a new, inclusive norm. Similarly, the way an instructor conceptualizes the definition and identification of giftedness in a psychology course may shift dramatically as the instructor moves from an exclusive to transformed mindset. Exclusive identification strategies would focus on traditional standardized intelligence tests despite their bias against members of some diverse groups. An inclusive presentation might discuss multiple assessment strategies, alternative identification models, and a critique of the concept of giftedness as a means of furthering social inequities. A transformed discussion might provide a new conceptualization of giftedness that considers the complex interactions of cultural, sociohistorical, institutional (e.g., discrimination), individual (ethnicity, gender, class, personality, type of talent), and socialization factors that contribute to both an individual's identification as gifted and her or his fulfillment of potential.

The transformed level of course change, particularly with respect to content, applies most readily in disciplines whose knowledge is socially constructed—where experts select the content to be presented, generally based on tradition, politics, and power: history, literature, sociology, education, psychology, the arts. However, even the "objective" disciplines—mathematics, the sciences, engineering, medicine—can broaden students' views. A colleague in mathematics argues that mathematics has been constructed linearly by mathematicians, and new views could enhance the field. Calculus students can discuss when modeling is valid and not valid and what it means to be valid. Additionally, instructors in technical fields can incorporate readings and speakers by diverse professionals, acknowledge the contributions of mathematicians and scientists who are women and members of underrepresented groups, and discuss the diversity of cultural perspectives (e.g., non-Western or indigenous healing methods; algorithms used by different cultural groups; cultural considerations in applying mathematics, science, technology, and engineering to real life).

Burlbaw (1994) points to the developing fields of critical mathematics and ethnomathematics as encouraging the examination of mathematics within cultural contexts. For example, Burlbaw suggests that the contextualization of a mathematics problem within real-world social issues can enrich the discussion of mathematics. Specifically, students can be asked to analyze the percent of disposable income spent by people from various ethnic groups to provide for their basic needs such as housing, food, medical benefits, and recreation. The analysis lends itself to questions about equity and differences of quality and access.

Tetreault (1993) offers an example from the sciences of an activity that aims at curriculum transformation. Students read Evelyn Fox Keller's biography of Barbara McClintock, *A Feeling for the Organism*. McClintock won a Nobel Prize in 1983 for her work in genetics. Some authorities suggest that McClintock's insights into corn genetics were "feminine" in that her "empathy" for the organism led her to recognize that genetic elements move within the chromosomes. According to Keller, the approach challenged the predominant "command-and-control" model (considered a male approach) in mainstream cell biology, and her isolation as a scientist appears gender-related. McClintock's story prompts such questions as:

- What role do interests—individual and collective—play in the evolution of scientific knowledge?

- Do all scientists seek the same kinds of explanations?
- Are the kinds of questions they ask the same?
- Do differences in methodology between different subdisciplines ever permit the same kinds of answers?
- Do female and male scientists approach their research differently? (adapted from Tetreault, 1993, p. 144).

The major limit to content transformation is the instructor's multicultural knowledge and creativity.

Instructional Strategies and Activities

Instructors can work toward inclusion in the instructional component by incorporating teaching strategies and learning activities that capitalize on students' experiences and learning strengths; include opportunities for personal participation and growth; and foster skills important to informed citizenship, such as critical thinking, decision making, social participation, and intergroup interaction. Kafka (1991) offers an excellent example of applying instructional strategies that integrate critical thinking about social issues within a lesson on Shakespeare's *Othello*: She notes that in addition to the works an instructor chooses to teach (i.e., the content), what matters is the kinds of questions asked about them. Kafka (p. 183) asks the following, explaining that Afrocentric scholars have traced the beginnings of institutionalized racism to the sixteenth century:

1. What is Othello's status at birth? What is his rank when the tragedy opens? What is his race?

2. What is the basic reason for Iago's vendetta against Othello? Are race and class factors?

3. Why does Emilia obey Iago? How does Emilia's language and attitude toward sex, love, and marriage differ from Desdemona's? What does this show about the two women? Describe their relationship. Do they have similar or different relationships to their husbands?

4. What do the courtship and marriage customs seem to be in the various classes of society found in the play?

5. Are there any stereotypes which bother you in this play?

Mathematics instructor Aliaga (1993) similarly focuses on changing the instruction rather than the content itself. Her goal is to create a community of learners by encouraging students to participate, talk, debate, disagree, argue, take risks, and make mistakes. Strategies include helping students to visualize problems and relate them to their own experiences and organizing study groups that include peer support. According to Aliaga, study groups help students practice speaking the language of mathematics; members debate with and question each other to derive correct solutions. She requires each group to share, discuss, and agree on an answer. The answer is presented as the group's proposed solution to the problem, and the group receives a communal grade.

Critical pedagogy provides an example of transformed instruction. Proponents of critical pedagogy argue that altering curriculum content without transforming the traditional process of classroom interaction works to increase self esteem and content knowledge while simultaneously socializing students into a system that stifles development of critical skills and ignores goals for student empowerment. Darder (1991, p. 74), says that "content may be theoretically emancipatory but in practice is pedagogically oppressive." Because of critical pedagogy's critical nature and emancipatory goals, the approach offers no prescriptive rules for implementation.

Nevertheless, critical theorists appear to agree on two important elements. The first is an instructor thoroughly grounded in critical education theory and committed to empowering students and correcting social inequities. Critical theory has as its roots an understanding of links among culture, power, and economics and the goal of cultural democracy. The second is a teaching process that incorporates critical discourse, dialectical thought, and dialogical methods. Critical theory views knowledge as socially constructed; what is presented in classrooms as truth depends on power relationships in society. For example, traditional presentation of Columbus's impact on the New World occurs because of the dominance of Western cultural views over other views. Critical discourse encourages students to challenge the dominant ideology and frees students to act in their classrooms and greater world. Dialectical thought acknowledges, seeks out, and analyzes social contradictions, such as the U.S ideal of democracy in the face of institutionalized oppression (e.g., laws requiring racial segregation). Dialogical methods include problem-posing or issues-oriented educational approaches that take advantage of student experiences and encourage students and instructors to learn from each other (Darder, 1991). Ellsworth (1989) expresses important caveats to implementation of critical pedagogy. Among these are her findings that critical pedagogy fails to examine some of its own assumptions and that implementation requires high levels of trust that may be unattainable solely through in-class activities.

Assessment

Inclusive courses will provide students with multiple avenues for demonstrating their mastery of course content. Alternatively, instructors may want to permit students to choose from among several options that accommodate their strongest strategies for expression of accumulated knowledge and skills.

Assessment in transformed courses is based on a different conceptualization of mastery. Maher and Tetreault (1992) describe the traditional concept of mastery as rational comprehension of material from the expert's perspective: the right answer. In classrooms where knowledge is perceived as socially constructed, mastery refers to students' development of the ability to make meaning, or increasingly more sophisticated connections with topics, often through interaction with peers. This type of mastery is better assessed through students' evaluation of their own progress and through projects that empower students to apply their new learning in ways that produce change.

For example, an organizational management instructor can incorporate Banks's (1993) social action level of course transformation in assessment through a culminating assignment that asks students to synthesize their knowledge of change theories and apply them to specific situations that demand social change. Tatum (1992) requires students to work in small groups to develop an action plan for decreasing racism. "While I do not consider it appropriate to require students to engage in antiracist activity (since I believe this should be a personal choice the student makes for him/herself), students are required to think about the possibility" (p. 21). Tatum reports that students often go on to implement their plans.

Classroom Dynamics

The model for course change defines classroom dynamics as the human interactions that occur in the classroom: instructor with students and students with students. How the instructor initiates and responds to student questions and comments and initiates and responds to students' behaviors with their peers can send powerful messages about the instructor's valuing or devaluing of diversity. Classroom dynamics in inclusive courses encourage equity among students in their participation and unbiased behavior on the part of the instructor. Reviewing research on institutional factors affecting minority student retention, Carter and Wilson (1994) conclude that "quality interaction with faculty seems to be more important than any other single factor in determining minority students' persistence" (p. 33). However, studies indicate that classroom interactions, particularly at predominantly White campuses, favor mainstream students, to whom faculty provide more complete answers and direct more complex questions (Carter & Wilson, 1994). These authors argue the critical need for faculty members to hold high expectations for diverse students' success, to provide an engaging learning environment, and to divest ourselves of "sink or swim" attitudes.

Findings from observational studies in postsecondary classrooms attest to our need to be vigilant about our own behavior as instructors interacting with students in classroom discussions. Sadker and Sadker (1992) concluded from a review of research in higher education classrooms that

- compared to White males, female students of all backgrounds and males from underrepresented groups are more likely to be quiet in class and less likely to assume a powerful role in discussions.

- most instructors, regardless of gender, race, or ethnicity, have no awareness of their biased interaction patterns.

- informal segregation by race, ethnicity, and/or gender intensifies patterns of unequal participation because instructors are drawn to the part of the room where White males cluster.
- wait time after questioning is related to achievement, level of discourse, and participation; and instructors give White males more wait time than they give to women students and to students of color.

Fortunately, the Sadkers's work also demonstrates that simple charting by an observer will reveal interactional biases. Moreover, following their initial surprise at such results, most instructors are eager to find ways to create equitable classroom dynamics.

Consistent with the socially constructed view of knowledge, transformed classroom dynamics empower students to become equal participants and to perceive learning as a shared experience among instructor and students. The instructor assumes the roles of facilitator and resource. Activities such as personal journals and raising/answering one's own questions are selected to encourage students to find their own "voices" and perspectives and to make connections between their own lives and new learning (Maher & Tetreault, 1992).

Gawelek (1993) has observed that despite higher education's interest in content transformation, academicians rarely address the issue of how teaching is influenced by social-cultural differences. For example, in addition to general patterns of interactions with students, instructors' responses to specific comments related to diversity and equity constitute another critical component of classroom dynamics. An instructor may ignore a biased comment in the classroom because of a sincere desire to focus precious class time on imparting course content (e.g., nonmetallic materials in Professor Navarro's case). Yet a decision to do nothing in response to a biased comment in the classroom sends as powerful a message to students as a decision to agree with or confront the comment. Would Professor Navarro be remiss in taking time during the engineering class to discuss the issue of gays and lesbians in the military? Part of the answer depends on her goals for the course given our diverse society (e.g., to support students' acquisition of traditional and/or new knowledge; encourage acceptance of self and others; understand the perspectives of specific groups; help students value diversity and equity; equip all students to work toward social change). On the other hand, given the contribution of motivation and affect to the learning process as described above, one might argue that helping students value diversity and equity may influence students' acquisition of content knowledge. Said another way, how well will a gay student achieve in a class where the instructor either implicitly or explicitly communicates a bias against gays and lesbians?

Biased comments commonly occur during both formal and informal class discussions:

> *"Men are just better at math than women."*
> *"I never notice a person's skin color; to me, everyone's the same."*
> *"Asians always stick together."*

Weinstein and Obear (1992) found that faculty members express similar fears about confronting issues of racism and other biases in their classrooms. These include feeling guilty about the behaviors of members of one's own group; being confronted with one's own biases; worrying about making a mistake; feeling inadequate about handling intense emotions; needing students' approval.

Based on her experiences in teaching about racism and sexism, Tatum (1992, p. 2) reports that the introduction of issues about oppression "often generates powerful emotional responses in students that range from guilt and shame to anger and despair. If not addressed, these emotional responses can result in student resistance to oppression-related content areas." Tatum found four strategies useful for reducing student resistance and promoting their development: (1) creating a safe classroom atmosphere by establishing clear discussion guidelines; (2) providing opportunities for self-generated knowledge; (3) offering a framework that students can use for understanding their own process (e.g., a model for racial identity development); and (4) exploring strategies to empower students as change agents.

CHANGING THE COURSE SYLLABUS

Once the instructor has determined the multicultural goals for the course, the appropriate course elements to be modified, and the level of change, the instructor is ready to revise the course syllabus to reflect these decisions. A review of information that might be included in a syllabus (Altman & Cashin, 1992) indicates that there is general consensus on what constitutes the major components. The following sections suggest how a syllabus might reflect multicultural change based, with some additions, on sections identified by Altman and Cashin and the writers they reviewed.

Course and Instructor Information

Syllabi typically begin by detailing the course title, number, credit hours, location, meeting dates and times, and the instructor's name, office, office hours, phone number, and electronic mail address. Times and duration of office hours as well as flexibility to arrange appointments outside of office hours reflect consideration of work and family schedules, especially important for nontraditional students. Room choice, furniture

arrangement, and selection of furniture and equipment, while often not within the instructor's control, can determine accessibility to classroom facilities and instructor's office for students with disabilities.

Selection of venue for offering instruction also has implications regarding accessibility. Institutions of higher education increasingly support faculty to provide courses at community sites, for example, at K–12 schools, community centers, and business facilities. Moreover, courses are being offered through distance-learning technologies at remote sites and through virtual classrooms. Such alternatives have potential for increasing educational access to students. However, additional research on efficacy for traditional and nontraditional students is needed.

Educational Beliefs

Some writers encourage inclusion of a specific section in the syllabus that makes explicit the instructor's beliefs or assumptions about the learner, the purpose of education, and the teaching/learning process (Altman & Cashin, 1992). A statement of educational beliefs provides an excellent opportunity to communicate the instructor's multicultural goals for students and expected classroom dynamics based on principles of learning and of multicultural education. Whether or not the instructor includes such a statement as part of the syllabus, determining one's educational beliefs is critical to the planning process and implicit in the selection and implementation of actual content and instructional methods.

Course Description and Objectives

Instructors often copy the catalogue description of the course and its prerequisites. However, given the tendencies of catalogue copy to contain incomprehensively abbreviated descriptors, blatant or subtle inaccuracies, and overly general and ambiguous language, more helpful is a description of the course's general content, why the course is important, and the instructional methods to be used. The following two course descriptions demonstrate different levels of content change.

> This course offers principles and methods of effective composition, rhetorical techniques for achieving clarity, interest, and effective organization and development of ideas, based on the reading and analysis of selected texts. Readings have also been selected to reflect cultural diversity.
>
> This course explores the basic nature of literature and seeks to answer seminal questions: What prompts humankind to the creation of imaginative literature? What purposes does literature serve in the cultural life of humanity? What are its social, philosophical, spiritual, and aesthetic values? Specific works studied will be representative of several genres, cultures, and periods of literature. Students will be asked to engage in inquiry, comparing major theories and techniques of literary criticism to their own strategies and ideas as critical readers.

The second description suggests classroom dynamics and activities that convey a respect for the learner as knower. It gives a sense of validity to students' evaluative methods even while they acquire new strategies through comparisons with those of experts. Finally, the comparison incorporates the learning principle of encouraging students to construct meaning by connecting new information to their own experiences.

Course objectives for multiculturalism address cognitive, affective, and behavioral domains (NCSS, 1992; Sawchuk, 1993). Examples follow:

Cognitive

After completing this course, students are expected to

- demonstrate knowledge and understanding regarding the impact of culture on behavior.
- understand the history and contributions of various cultural groups.
- identify and understand conflicts in a multicultural society.
- understand relationships among economics, power, and oppression.
- understand that different groups may have different perspectives on the same historical or contemporary event.

Affective

Through this course, students are expected to

- appreciate and value diversity.
- demonstrate sensitivity to cultural differences.
- recognize their own and others' biases and understand their impact.
- develop a stronger self-identity, self-concept, and sense of efficacy.
- adopt attitudes supportive of a democratic society.

Behavioral (skill-oriented)

After completing this course, students are expected to be able to

- engage in critical thinking, analysis, and problem-solving about social issues.
- effectively participate in cross-ethnic interaction.
- evaluate social problems and make appropriate decisions regarding personal behavior.

- engage in social and political action directed at social change.

Some of these objectives can be incorporated readily into courses across disciplines. They can be adapted to specific content areas, as the following examples from psychology (Sawchuk, 1993) suggest:

- Students will understand the influence of ethnicity, social class, bilingualism, and gender on human development. (cognitive)
- Students will identify how these variables have affected their own development as individuals. (affective)
- Students will analyze the impact of current social policies on children and propose policy revisions. (behavioral)
- Students will explore the reasons underlying the absence of multicultural perspectives in the historical development of psychological theory. (cognitive)

Texts, Readings, and Materials

Syllabi generally list required and supplementary texts, readings, and other instructional materials and resources. The syllabus can demonstrate multicultural change through materials that include women authors and authors from culturally and linguistically diverse backgrounds, authors who present alternative perspectives, and authors who address critical issues related to diversity. These readings can be additive to traditional content or present a totally nontraditional perspective as modal, depending on the level of critical analysis encouraged by the instructor. Resources should present multiple viewpoints, including those representing people of various classes, not just the viewpoints of elites and heroes. Tying a course to diversity in the community can occur through use of community resources, such as guest presenters, field-trip sites, and exemplars. Texts, readings, and materials should support course objectives.

Tentative Course Calendar/Schedule

The course schedule indicates the topics to be covered for each meeting time, specific activities (e.g., simulations or role playing, field trips, speakers, videos), dates of assessments (e.g., tests, oral reports), and due dates for assignments. Thus, the schedule can indicate multiculturalism through the instructor's selection of content topics, instructional methods, learning activities, and assessment strategies.

Course Policies

The syllabus provides information concerning the instructor's expectations and policies regarding attendance, class participation, late or missed assignments, safety (e.g., laboratory procedures), academic dishonesty, writing style, and grading. The section on grading details how students will be evaluated, the criteria to be applied, and how evaluative marks are translated to a final grade. Level of multiculturalism will be apparent in this section through the instructor's selection of assessment strategies, including alternatives to traditional exams and papers and opportunities for students to choose among options. Additionally, opportunities for extra credit and for rewriting papers and projects after receiving feedback should be communicated. Such opportunities provide students with additional ways to improve their performance and demonstrate growth.

Available Support Services

Altman and Cashin (1992) suggest that listing in the syllabus services supportive of students' learning may encourage their use by students. Depending on the course, these services might include special library collections, learning centers, computer labs, research and data analysis consulting, tutoring, and services for students with disabilities (e.g., assistive technology, readers, interpreters). Instructors may want to encourage, help organize, or otherwise support informal study groups by building such opportunities into the course and syllabus.

Learning Activities and Assignments

The course calendar or schedule lists dates for learning activities, projects, and assignments to be completed in or out of class. Details can be described in the syllabus but more frequently are provided in a separate handout distributed to students at a later date. Multicultural change will be apparent in the variety of activities, goals, and procedures for accomplishment. Inclusive activities permit students to apply their preferred approach to problem solving while encouraging mastery of other approaches. Additionally, activities and assignments can present opportunities to take action on social problems. Consider the following examples:

- One assignment in a philosophy course on Existentialism asks students to compare the way three women deal with their life crises: Jessie (from *Night Mother*); Alice (from *Alice*) and either Moira or Offred (from *The Handmaid's Tale*). The goal is to explore the nature of their life crises and the response of each woman to her situation. Students are required to integrate in their analyses at least two traditional existential thinkers: Nietzsche, Camus, Sartre, and Heidegger (from Teays in Sawchuck, 1993).

- One U.S. history course assignment asks students to prepare and deliver a short speech on the meaning of democracy from the perspective of a notable figure from early or recent times, such as Thomas Jefferson, Elizabeth Cady Stanton, W. E. B. DuBois, César Chávez. Goals include encouraging students to demonstrate their knowledge of major issues related to democracy over time; to recognize and appreciate diverse perspectives; and to understand the complexity of democracy as a concept and as a way of life.

- An assignment in an elementary mathematics methods course for preservice teachers requires students to find an alternative algorithm for one arithmetic operation. The algorithm must be used by people from another country or culture. Students are encouraged to locate these algorithms by working with diverse school children and their parents. The assignment helps students to appreciate that different cultures have found different and equally correct algorithms. It reinforces the view that the algorithms we have come to use in the United States are a matter of convention and represent only one of many correct approaches (Philipp, 1994).

Course Evaluation

Finally, the syllabus can describe the process and timeline for evaluation of the course, which may include student and peer review. We view course evaluation as a means of improving instruction rather than as a tool for reviewing faculty performance. Consistent with the principles of multicultural education listed in Chapter 1, multicultural education goals for the course must be evaluated. At least two levels of evaluation are possible: the quality of multicultural transformation of the course and whether the students have met the instructor's multicultural goals. According to the paradigm presented in this chapter, quality and level of course change depend on the instructor's multicultural goals for the course, the nature of the course, and the instructor's values and philosophy with respect to transformation. The paradigm itself provides a framework for self-assessment and collegial consulting on the quality of change based on the instructor's goals for change.

Evaluation of student progress on multicultural education goals for the course (e.g., students will increase their appreciation of diversity) can occur through a variety of means. For example, instructors may add relevant items on standard student evaluation forms. Instructors can identify multicultural criteria in the assessment of student assignments and projects and analyze the extent to which students meet these criteria. Students can be asked to respond to content-related vignettes or case studies that require application of values and knowledge on diversity. Sawchuk (1993) offers a student questionnaire and discusses the use of post-course student focus groups on whether and to what extent the course supported students' achievement of multicultural goals. Chapter 15 provides a detailed discussion of evaluation.

So what does a course look like after multicultural change? The answer depends on the instructor's multicultural goals for the course, the nature of course content, and the instructor's objectives regarding level of change. The instructor will determine the goals and level of change in planning the course, as well as those elements of the course most appropriate for multicultural integration: content, instructional strategies, assessment activities, and classroom dynamics. The revised course syllabus will reflect the instructor's multicultural goals and provisions for achieving them. The remaining chapters support instructors' efforts to achieve their diversity goals by providing specific ideas on content and materials, instructional strategies, assessment, and the hidden curriculum.

CHAPTER 3

Doing Multiculturalism: Conceptualizing Curricular Change [1]

Deborah S. Rosenfelt
Professor, Women's Studies
Director, the Curriculum Transformation Project,
University of Maryland at College Park

Editor's Notes:
Deborah Rosenfelt's chapter focuses on the content component of multicultural course change. She addresses primarily the multicultural goal of enabling students to acquire a more accurate or comprehensive knowledge of the subject matter through a transformed content. She begins by acknowledging the almost overwhelming diversity of students in terms of ethnicity, culture, language, religion, sexual orientation, ability, and raises the question, "How can I do it all?" Her answer is to define content by examining overarching concepts that inform the scholarship on diversity across disciplines. Based on her extensive work with faculty on multicultural curriculum transformation, Rosenfelt identifies four concepts from which instructors can develop units within their courses:

- Race, gender, sexuality, and ability as socially constructed concepts
- Postmodern challenges to scientific views of objectivity
- The politics of representation in language and the media
- Tension between community and diversity—do we emphasize differences among groups or among commonalities?

In addressing these concepts, the author identifies critical readings and films that can be incorporated in courses ranging from the sciences to music and literature. Her examples illustrate how an instructor might incorporate the new scholarship in ways that redefine the canon. ∎

On a hot summer morning in College Park, Bonnie Thornton Dill, a black feminist sociologist, is leading a group of faculty participants in a curriculum transformation institute in a discussion of Women, Work, and Families. Drawing on her widely read essay "Our Mothers' Grief" (1988, 1992), she asks us to consider families from different U.S. racial-ethnic cultures—Black, Hispanic, Asian American, Native American—at different moments in U.S. social and economic history. The discussion encompasses as well the current nostalgia for old-fashioned family values.

Dill demonstrates clearly that the shape of families and the different experiences of women, men, and children in them have been structured by the economic and social circumstances of particular cultural groups—not that some sudden collapse of family values has produced the ostensible social disintegration we hear of every day. But the discussion does more than produce a cross-cultural family history. By the time we are through, we have called into question familiar meanings of a range of central terms: among them family, mother, work, power, public, private, and American. Such reconceptualizations define the process known as curriculum transformation: integrating into the curriculum materials and ideas acknowledging human diversity, especially the knowledge and perspective afforded by two decades of work in women's studies and ethnic studies—the largest tributaries to what we broadly call "multiculturalism."

Attendees at conferences and professional meetings on multicultural education frequently express a particular anxiety: "But how can I possibly do it *all*?" For "diversity" and "multiculturalism" are terms that do indeed imply a vast undertaking: the curricular incorporation of material on differences in, let us say, race, ethnicity, nationality, language, gender, class, sexuality, ability (developmental and physical), religion, and age. Every teacher can, at least potentially, create an inclusive classroom climate hospitable to diverse constituencies—women and men, those with varying abilities and disabilities, students of differing races, ethnicities, and religious and national backgrounds, lesbian and gay and straight and bisexual and asexual students, younger and older students. But no teacher can, in any given course, include in-depth content on the experiences, issues, and perspectives of all of these social groups. Perhaps it is best to think of "multiculturalism" not so much as

an end point, a goal, than as a process in which we try to be always mindful of the multiplicity of "knowledges"—a multiplicity derived from differences among those who do the knowing, differences in where and when and for whom the knowing is done, differences in how the knowing is acquired and conveyed.

One fundamental understanding arising from a commitment to the scholarship of diversity is that our knowledge is inevitably situated within and circumscribed by the parameters of our own social and educational backgrounds. For this reason, I want to clarify the relation of my work here to that process. I am writing from the standpoint of a "women's studies activist"—a White, Jewish female who comes to multiculturalism via two decades of feminist teaching and scholarship, particularly women's studies in literature. I have entered the field of multiculturalism, then, through the door of gender rather than through the door of race.[2] My discussion here inevitably reveals its feminist origins. This is a problematic point of entry since some multiculturalists argue that multiculturalism (as opposed to diversity) is a term that privileges differences in *culture*, defined as the values, practices, and histories of particular racial, ethnic, or national peoples—among whom women, or lesbians and gays, or working class people, let us say, are included, though they do not constitute a primary category of analysis.[3] There is a certain intellectual coherence in this argument, as well as a history in both educational policy and practice that often establishes multicultural education and nonsexist education as two related but distinct endeavors (Rosenfelt, 1994).

Increasingly, those who work on race and ethnicity and those who work on gender, class, sexuality, or disability are identifying common issues and sorting out the differences and crucial points of intersection among these social and analytic categories. The inclusive definition of multicultural education presented in Chapter 1 reflects the commonality. For most of us, some categories will remain or become more central than others—in this chapter, gender, race, class, and sexuality. But most important, contemporary scholarship can no longer examine any social group or conceptualize any individual identity as unitary. If there is one central substantive insight deriving from the various projects, conferences, and writings on diversity and curricular change, it is this: The identity of individuals and social groups is inflected across a spectrum of differences—through the intersections of class location, national, racial, and ethnic heritage, gender, sexual orientation, and ability—not to mention historical moment and geographic region.

The preceding chapter presented a paradigm for multicultural course change that proposes levels of transformation and four elements—content, instruction, assessment, and classroom dynamics—that instructors can change. This chapter addresses the content component and discusses concepts, texts, and materials that instructors might incorporate into their disciplinary courses. Because others have elaborated on levels of content change (see Chapter 2), I have chosen to use a principle of organization growing out of my experience in directing for a number of years a summer faculty development institute on curricular change. Specifically, I identify some (by no means all) of the overarching concepts and conflicts informing and addressed by the scholarship on diversity. I have not tried so much to detail the content of multiculturalism—an impossible task—as I have to elucidate some ways of thinking that have emerged from the scholarship of difference. I have tried to frame these concepts to reveal the interrelatedness of the various categories of difference and to deliberately transgress the boundaries of the traditional disciplines—though my disciplinary background in literature undoubtedly shows through.

These issues overlap one another. At least one overarching theme echoes throughout: a dialectic between oppression and resistance, victimhood and agency, the objectification as "other" and the assertion of subjectivity, whether in the study of groups denied social power or in the cultural productions of individuals in those groups. I identify some crucial readings in the course of discussion; some might best be used in advanced classes or as background reading for faculty, but I have identified a number of readings useful for introductory students. My sections are not teaching units; they elaborate on concepts from which such units might be constructed.

THE DEFINITION AND CONSTRUCTION OF RACE, GENDER, AND SEXUALITY: SOCIAL CATEGORIES AND CULTURAL IDENTITIES

Definitions and Discourses

A starting point for the integration of diversity materials in many courses might well be a discussion of the extent to which race, ethnicity, gender, sexuality, and even ability are social and historical constructs rather than innate, fixed categories of identity. Students often view certain practices as "natural" and certain qualities as innate or immutable: heterosexual romance and marriage are ordained by "human nature"; African American men are innately athletic; women are innately nurturant; and so on. Such assumptions, unquestioned, can justify maintaining the existing social order. Correspondingly, if students can understand the complexity and force with which race, gender, and sexuality, let us say, are socially and historically constructed, they can also begin to imagine possibilities for social change.

Class derives from a shifting set of relations to property, power, and the production of wealth; in the United States it is hard to get students to acknowledge the existence of class differences at all. A discussion of social construction, then, involves both issues of definition—what are race, gender, class, sexuality?—and issues of politics and power—if it is not biological determinism that supports hierarchies of power and privilege, then what does, and who benefits?

It is useful to read together two theoretical pieces about, respectively, gender and race by Scott (1986) and by Omi and Winant (1993), all historians. Both pieces are engaged in larger arguments that will not be apparent to students without help (Scott about the relationship of class to gender as categories of analysis for historians, Omi and Winant about the post-structuralist dismissal of race as "only" an ideological category). Still, each piece offers a complex set of definitions of gender and race that identify both as historical formations, constantly changing in response to different historical circumstances. These more theoretical formulations might be accompanied by specific accounts of gender and race relations in different historical and cultural locations. One might, for example, compare the rigid racial categories under South African apartheid, where "colored" (racially mixed) formed a category seen as naturally distinct from "Black," with the efforts under Mandela to deconstruct race as a socially significant category. Or one might use a piece of utopian or science fiction literature in which gender and/or race relations are imagined as egalitarian, as in Piercy's *Woman on the Edge of Time* (1976). Such readings can help to "de-naturalize" social arrangements that otherwise seem inevitable.

It is important to look historically at how race, let us say, has been constituted in the United States as a social category, reminding students that it has no validity as a biological category.[4] Takaki has argued succinctly for the particular ways in which race, as distinct from ethnicity, has been singled out and indeed constituted in the United States by a long history of legal discrimination. He demonstrates how United States law has contributed to the construction of racial identity (1987). Omi and Winant's *Racial Formation in the United States from the 1960's to the 1980's* (1986) similarly is a crucial text. These authors explore how race relations between African Americans and Whites and a Black movement for social change have structured understandings of and struggles over the meanings of African American identity.

Literary and cultural critics have contributed much thought concerning the construction of gender, race, and sexuality, emphasizing the primacy of discursive formations in constituting these categories—that is, both inscribing them in public language and enforcing their dualisms—male-female, colored-white, gay-straight. Butler, in *Gender Trouble* (1989), argues that gender is in effect a performance, a series of conventional gestures that enact cultural codes for masculine and feminine. De Lauretis writes that gender, "as both representation and as self-representation, is the product of various social technologies, such as cinema, and of institutionalized discourses, epistemologies, and critical practices, as well as practices of daily life" (1987, p. 2). Correspondingly, Higginbotham (1992) sees race as a "metalanguage," a system of meanings with different significations in different historical contexts, contributing to and constructed by discourses on gender, class, and sexuality as well.

In these essays, race and gender are conceptualized as relationships, processes, formations—never as static *things*. They draw on and are related to important neo-Marxian reformulations of class (e.g., Aronowitz, 1992; Braverman, 1975; Ehrenreich & Ehrenreich, 1979), though discussions of class inevitably emphasize the material over the discursive. Sennet and Cobb document powerfully *The Hidden Injuries of Class* (1973); Amott and Matthei (1991) show how class, race, and gender in the United States have mutually constructed one another. The accessible but conceptually rich section on class in Rothenberg (1992) is useful for introductory classes.

Work on how the discourses of Western science have constructed race and gender and contributed to the legitimation of social inequities is also dramatic and effective in the classroom. An essential text in this regard—useful in many other contexts as well—is Harding's anthology, *The Racial Economy of Science* (1993). Gould's essay on "American Polygeny and Craniometry before Dawn: Blacks and Indians as Separate, Inferior Species" is particularly effective at demonstrating the circular relationship between assumptions about the racial nature of Blacks and Indians and experiments demonstrating their supposed inferiority.

Films like *The Pinks and the Blues*, on sex-role socialization; *Still Killing Us Softly*, on the power of advertising in enforcing social definitions of femininity; and *Ethnic Notions* and *Color Adjustment*, on the caricatures of African Americans in popular culture and their impact on cultural definitions of Blacks are effective in visually demonstrating how gender and racial differences are constructed and maintained.

Identity and "Difference"

If gender, race, and class are social formations derived from and shaping the interactions of groups, they are also experienced by individuals in gendered and racialized societies as components of individual identity.

Biologists and psychologists concerned about the trajectories of individual development and identity formation have contributed to the discussion, particularly about gender. Biologist Ann Fausto-Sterling's book *Myths of Gender* (1992a) contains a lucid argument for the insignificance of innate gender differences in cognitive development and achievement. Feminist psychologist Sandra Bem (1991) makes a similar argument against biological essentialism. Both acknowledge the extent to which our society, including our scientists, have been consciously or unconsciously invested in biological explanations for women's subordinate status, and both explore how biologistic assumptions have led to biased conclusions. Harris and Wideman (1988) apply psychoanalytic concepts to examine how gender and disability as social constructions interact in the process of identity formation in girls born with disabilities.

When considering sexuality, it seems especially important to encourage students to move beyond a simple tolerance for difference to an understanding of the relations of power that maintain and structure it. Rich's (1980) classic essay, "Compulsory Heterosexuality and Lesbian Existence" argues that heterosexuality is a compulsory institution, imposing substantial penalties on women who deviate from its strictures. Rich's essay has been critiqued for its ahistoricity and its implicit assumption, an essentialist one, that women would love other women if only society and culture did not dictate otherwise (e.g., Ferguson et al., 1981). But it challenges heterosexual readers to alter their own assumptions that heterosexuality is the only norm for sexual identity. Rich's positing of a lesbian continuum raises the definitional question, What is a lesbian? She argues that sexuality is really a continuum of desires and practices and that women can derive their greatest emotional satisfactions from other women without engaging in genital sexuality—by no means an uncontroversial stance.

In another important essay, Epstein (1987) uses the work of Omi and Winant on racial formation to ask if lesbian and gay experience in this country might constitute a social formation analogous to race or ethnicity. On the question of the origins of homosexuality, Epstein is something of an agnostic. He refutes simplistic notions of biological determinism but acknowledges that strict social constructionism does not seem to account for aspects of sexuality that are experienced as innate. Yet the social practices through which sexuality—heterosexuality or homosexuality—are expressed vary from culture to culture, from era to era, from class to class.

The burgeoning field of "queer studies" deconstructs dichotomies between gay or lesbian and straight, between bisexual and monosexual, and argues instead that human beings engage in a range of sexual practices expressing a complex field of desires not reducible to, and inevitably misrepresented by, categories of fixed identity. Duberman (1993) asserts that queer theory "has taught us to distrust categories as needless calcifications of what is purportedly our fluid, meandering erotic natures. We are told to move beyond Freud's notions of inherent bisexuality to posit a malleable sexuality that, if allowed to run free, would create all sorts of trisexual permutations" (p. 22). Such theory can be very affirming to students who sense that their own sexuality is in flux; it is also important for those whose sexuality feels immutable and who assume that all sexuality is experienced that way.

All these definitions deconstruct notions of race, gender, and sexuality as being permanent, fixed structures, either in the self or in society, constructed rather than innate. At the same time, there is no doubt about the extent to which the experiences of groups and of individuals are shaped by these constructions. There is, then, no substitute for the personal voice in conveying to students what it means to be female, or lesbian and gay, or a person of color, or a person with disabilities, or a working-class person. Indeed, all these "or's" are misleading, for many of us are more than one of these things. As Higginbotham (1992) writes, speaking of African American women, we must not "bifurcate the identity of black women (and indeed of all women) into discrete categories—as if culture, consciousness, and lived experience could at times constitute 'woman' isolated from the contexts of race, class, and sexuality that give form and content to the particular women we are" (p. 273).

For this reason, it is helpful to use in classes the essays and autobiographical writings of those who meditate on the complexities of their identity. Such writers might include Minnie Bruce Pratt (1991) and Irena Klepfisz (1990), who write of class, region, ethnicity, and sexuality as Christian and Jewish lesbians respectively; the feminist women of color who write in *This Bridge Called My Back* (Moraga & Anzaldua, 1981); Audre Lorde, Black lesbian socialist feminist poet (1982, 1984); Michelle Cliff, light-skinned, middle class Jamaican and lesbian novelist (1983); Nancy Mairs, who writes of living with disability (1986) and a wealth of others. See the anthologies of Andersen and Collins (1992); Anzaldua (1990); Brown and Ling (1993); and Rothenberg (1992) for many fine examples of male and female writers of many different races and ethnicities. See also Brown et al. (1985) and Saxton and Howe (1987) for work by and about women with disabilities.

Integrating the experiences and perspectives of women, people of color, working-class people, and lesbians and gays should be a central mandate of curricular change. But we must remember that it is not only women whose experience is gendered nor "people of color" whose experience is racialized, nor lesbians and gays for whom sexuality is an issue, nor working-class people who have a class location. A number of texts in men's studies, for example, examine the construction and strictures of masculinity (e.g. Gilmore, 1990; Hearn & Morgan, 1991). Recent books by Frankenberg (1993) and Roediger (1991) provide accounts, respectively, of how "whiteness" functions in the lives of some contemporary White women and of how class and color historically collaborated in the construction of the identity of White working-class men. McIntosh's (1988) reflection on "White privilege" works well for students at all levels in revealing the multiple daily ways in which Whites benefit from living in a racist world. Her essay draws its strengths of immediacy and concreteness (and its dangers of oversimplification) from her use of her own experience.

Equally important to explore is the question of how categories of difference, when describing identity, interact in their mutual construction and how such categories, when deployed analytically, sometimes fail to acknowledge the lived complexity of human experience. Roediger's (1991) book provides one such example, as he examines how working-class identity shaped and was shaped by the construction of racial "difference." Evelyn Torton Beck (1988) writes about how feminist scholarship, in its litany of "race, class, and gender" as central categories, has failed to take into account and therefore rendered invisible the complexities of Jewish experience. She describes this experience as one which cannot be defined as simply ethnic, simply religious, or simply cultural, and which is lived differently by Jewish men and Jewish women of different nationalities. Enloe (1990), White (1990), and R. Williams (in press) are among the writers who

have examined how an assertion of national identity is sometimes linked to a valorization of masculinity and sometimes to an accompanying homophobia.

Borderlands and Boundaries

Without immigration, there would be no American history and culture. If the image of the melting pot and the narrative of assimilation have been replaced by the image of the mosaic and the narrative of resistance, the terrain where individual and group identities are forged is one where cultures meet, clash, and transform one another. The tensions between Old World and New, between tradition and change, between generations linked to the past and those trying painfully to forge their futures permeate the literatures of immigration, from Cahan's *Yekl: A Tale of the Ghetto* (1896) to Rodriguez's *Days of Obligation* (1992). These tensions acquire a particular poignancy for the daughters of immigrant parents as they struggle over different cultural constructions of acceptable femininity. This struggle is inscribed in novels and memoirs from Yezierska's *The Bread Givers* (1925) to Hong Kingston's *The Woman Warrior: Memoirs of a Girlhood among Ghosts* (1975).

Cultural encounters are becoming more fluid and less unidirectional through the increasing movements of people and capital across borders and through contemporary communication technologies. Simultaneously, the notion of pure identities for cultural groups and individuals becomes increasingly problematic, increasingly mythic. An important body of multicultural work today draws on the imagery of the borderland, the liminal space between territories, acknowledged as both geographical and psychic. This is especially true for Chicano and Chicana writers, rooted in the distinctively hybrid culture of the border region between Mexico and the United States.

The concept of borderlands, of a hybridization of culture and identity simultaneously troubling and liberating, is related to queer theory about the fluidity of sexual identity and even to speculative fiction about the dissolution of boundaries between humans and machines (e.g. Piercy, 1991). Anzaldua's (1987) writing has been especially influential. For Anzaldua, borderlands occur "whenever two or more cultures edge each other, where people of different races occupy the same territory, where under, lower, middle and upper classes touch, where the space between two individuals shrinks with intimacy." Those who consciously inhabit the borderlands develop a new consciousness, "la conciencia de la mestiza," a tolerance for contradictions that leads to new ways of thinking and being (see especially Ch. 7, pp. 77–91), new alliances, and new strategies of resistance.

THE CHALLENGE TO OBJECTIVITY: STANDPOINT THEORIES AND SITUATED KNOWLEDGES

The Sciences, the Humanities, and the Pursuit of "Truth"

Feminist and ethnic studies scholarship shares with other bodies of postmodern thought a presumption that differences in gender, race, ethnicity, class, national origin, and sexuality figure not only as objects of inquiry but as determinants in the shaping and transmission of knowledge and in the production of culture. In accord with their Enlightenment heritage, the sciences, social sciences, and humanities have all valued, in different ways, notions of objectivity, truth, and universality. The physical sciences, and the social sciences modeled on them, relied on positivist, empirical, quantitative models to gather and analyze data, assuming that good science would eliminate the vagaries of human perception and produce results that would be universally "true" as descriptions of physical or social reality. The humanities have always been more interpretive, but the preeminence in the fifties of new critical and subsequently of structuralist methods in literature, art, and music—ostensibly giving "objective" accounts of how their various languages worked to create coherent wholes—can be understood now as corresponding in some ways to the empirical methods and functionalist assumptions of the sciences. The work of art constituted a self-contained world, and the business of the critic was to determine how its constituents worked to accomplish that wholeness. The quest for universal objective truths about the natural and physical universe in science paralleled the quest for universal criteria of aesthetic and moral value in the humanities.

Marxian and neo-Marxian thinkers have challenged such assumptions for decades, exploring the hegemony of both dominant cultural expressions and dominant scientific practices in maintaining class relations advantageous to the more privileged classes. Oppositional work on gender and on race also has a long history. Virginia Woolf's *A Room of One's Own* (1927) remains one of the most articulate feminist critiques of dominant methods for reading literature. She insists on, and her prose enacts, the paramount importance of understanding the contexts in which women write—their material circumstances, and their relation to their male and female forebears and audiences. Similarly, the writings of W. E. B. Du Bois (1903) challenge ideas about the homogeneity and ostensible rectitude of American society even as they insist on looking at the cultural productions of Blacks in slavery—such as their "sorrow songs," or spirituals—on their own terms. Until the 1970s, though, most scholarship assumed the legitimacy of something called "the scientific method" in establishing verifiable truths, and most assumed the viability of received standards of greatness in art. And even oppositional theories like Marxism theorized historical change by offering a singular "grand narrative" of class struggle in the context of the economic relations of capitalism.

The personal and theoretical writings of feminists and people of color in this country and the work of postmodernist theorists like Derrida, Lacan, Lyotard, and especially Foucault, jointly call into question the possibilities for objectivity in the quest for knowledge, for unified accounts of social life and social change, and for universal agreements about what constitutes beauty, goodness, and truth. Women writers of color have called attention to the specificity of their own experiences and to the inapplicability of many generalizations from both "White" women's studies and ethnic studies to the experiences of their group (e.g. Anzaldua, 1990; hooks, 1984; Lorde, 1984; Mohanty, 1991). Similarly, postmodernist thought argues against all "totalizing narratives," suggesting that both the construction of knowledge and the dynamic of struggle and resistance can be only partial, provisional, and local, circumscribed by the cultural and social contexts in which researchers, theorists, and activists undertake their work. In doing multicultural work, a genuine commitment to an inclusivity of vision and action is both necessary and destined to bring us up against the limitations of our own enculturation, even as we work to exceed them.

Difference, Methodology, and Epistemology

In the sciences and social sciences, an acknowledgment of the limits of objectivity and the provisional nature of knowledge has invited extensive discussion of difference, methodology, and epistemology: the analysis of bias in the work of existing scholarship, texts, and curricula; an exploration of the ethical and power relations between researcher and researched; and the search for new, more viable grounds on which to base knowledge claims, including "strong objectivity," "standpoint epistemologies" and the concept of "situated knowledges."

Masculinism and Bias

Keller (1983) has argued that science as practiced has an intuitive, subjective dimension not acknowledged in the rhetoric of objectivity; a rhetoric which nonetheless resulted in the marginalization of a figure like Barbara McClintock, whose empathic "feeling for the organism" led to major breakthroughs in the genetics of corn (see Chapter 2 for an example of content transformation based on Keller's biography of Barbara McClintock). In *Reflections on Gender and Science* (1985), Keller draws on the influential feminist-psychoanalytic work of Chodorow (1978) to argue that the insistence on a sharp subject-object dichotomy in the rhetoric of scientific methodology derives from the differing developmental trajectories of women and men, unnecessarily "masculinizing" the field. Rosser details the consequences of this masculinization in a very useful overview (1993):

> When scientific hypotheses are held up for critique to the scientific community, biases and flaws in the hypotheses are likely to go unseen to the extent that the scientific community holds a relatively homogeneous perspective. This homogeneity in gender, race, and class is what caused the scientific community to fail to include women and men of color in definitions of problems for study, as experimental subjects in drug tests, and in applications of research findings. (pp. 214–215)

If for Keller, science has never been as free from subjectivity as its rhetoric claims, then for Rosser (as for Fausto-Sterling in her critique of work in the biological sciences on gender differences, *Myths of Gender* [1992a]), the goal is "strengthening the rigor of the scientific method" (Rosser, 1993, 215) by incorporating more diverse perspectives in the sciences and thereby eliminating the biases that have weakened that method's applications. A short accessible piece representing this stance is Cannon et al. (1991), which demonstrates the problems and possibilities of setting up a social studies research model within the positivist tradition that consciously avoids bias. Fausto-Sterling, though, in a useful piece written some years after *Myths of Gender*, goes on to question "what it means that so much 'bad science' is done by so many 'good scientists,'" and admits that asking that question of her own work led her to abandon her framework of science as "an objective search for the truth" (1992, p. 8).

The Researcher and the Researched

Sandra Harding argues in *Feminism and Methodology* (1987) that three features have characterized feminist methodology: (1) the centralizing of women's experiences; (2) the designing of research for women, and (3) placing the researcher and the researched in the same critical plane, so that the researcher appears "not as an invisible, anonymous voice of authority, but as a real, historical individual with concrete, specific desires and interests" (1987, pp. 6–10; quotation, p. 9). Harding's more recent work has included a critique of both mainstream science and feminist methodology and science writing for their racism and ethnocentrism. She reminds feminists that women of color and third world women might have as much in common with the men of their group as with White Western women (1991). But her sec-

ond and third ideas—that scientific research should be acknowledged as being *for* particular groups rather than simply about them, and that the location of the researcher be acknowledged and explored—are important dimensions of the feminist and ethnic studies critiques of methodology.

A body of interesting work examines the relationship between researcher and researched, questioning the ethics and the relations of power involved. Students at any level can benefit from the essays in Gluck Patai (1991). These essays ask hard questions about the practices of oral history and ethnography: Is it possible for U.S. academics to do ethical research about third world women? Is the effort to put researcher and researched "on the same critical plane" really possible, or does it lead to hypocrisy and the abrogation of a fraudulent and temporary friendship? What if we find the politics of those we interview unexpectedly offensive, or if we feel that our subjects are misleading us as a defense against our cultural and political difference?

"Strong" Objectivity and Standpoint Epistemologies

A frequent critique of multiculturalist endeavors is that they render all judgments relative. Harding (1991) argues that there is a difference between "judgmental relativism," or the assessment of cognitive adequacy, and "historical relativism," which emphasizes the legitimate perspectivity of different historical constituencies at different moments of time. She rejects the former and accepts the latter. In place of either an ostensible value-free scientific objectivity on the one hand and "judgmental relativism" on the other, she argues for "strong objectivity"—an objectivity which is heightened by the very acknowledgment of the specificity and commitments of scientific projects. Harding argues that the sciences need to legitimate the examination of historical values and interests as part of scientific research itself, "in order to elucidate the cultural agendas that shape scientific undertakings." Such scrutiny, she argues, will maximize objectivity, not relativize judgment (pp. 138–163).

Strong objectivity in scientific methodology is related to the development of "standpoint" epistemologies. Standpoint epistemology derives from Marx's idea that the location within a working class and the engagement in class struggle enabled a particular kind of consciousness, a point of view from which to produce an analysis of the otherwise silenced inequities of class. Hartsock (1983) developed this idea further for feminist thought, positing the possibility of a feminist standpoint based on women's experience but achieved through resistance. Collins (1990) also makes an important contribution to standpoint theory, arguing that Black women in the United States have developed a particular epistemological vantage point based in their material experiences of race and gender in a racist, sexist world and in shared cultural traditions (1990). Their positions were anticipated by writers like Joyce Ladner (1972, 1973), who shares how she brought to her work as a social scientist studying young Black women the attitudes, values, and beliefs, the "Black perspective," of her own background. This perspective gave her a vested interest in her project and enabled her to see imaginative strategies for coping where others saw only social pathology.

The possibility for *a* singular feminist standpoint, or even a singular Black feminist standpoint, has been critiqued as essentialist (e.g. White, 1990). And the assumption that oppressed people have an unobstructed view of "reality" is countered by attention to the multiplicity of each human's identity; a middle-class Black heterosexual woman may be very aware of racism and sexism but less experientially attuned to issues of class and sexuality. Still, the concept that those who have experienced oppression might offer a version of reality different from and indeed more complex, complete, and liberatory than those in positions of power and privilege remains at the heart of a progressive multiculturalism. And since a standpoint is "achieved" rather than innate, it is also possible that through empathic learning, political coalition, and friendship, those in positions of relative power can understand the view of those to whom power has been denied. (See, e.g., Lugones, 1992.)

Situated Knowledges

Postmodernist thought offers a more radical critique of scientific "objectivism." The concept of "positionality" refers to the importance of the location of the subjects who do the knowing. This concept questions the viability of any position of epistemological privilege—even the vantage point of the oppressed, too easily rendered as innocent and exotically "other." At its most depoliticized, this tendency can lead to the kind of relativism feared by conservative critics of both multiculturalism and postmodernism. Feminist postmodernists have proffered in lieu of relativism the useful notion of "situated knowledges"—the insistence that knowledges, inevitably partial and inevitably shaped by the particular cultural habits of thought and agendas that produced them, can contribute in unevenly cumulative ways to an increasingly accurate account of the social and physical processes that constitute our world. According to Donna Haraway,

> The alternative to relativism is partial, locatable, critical knowledges sustaining the possibility of webs of connections called solidarity in politics and shared conversations in epistemology...it is precisely in the politics and

epistemology of partial perspectives that the possibility of sustained, rational, objective enquiry rests. So…I want to argue for a doctrine and practice of objectivity that privileges contestation, deconstruction, passionate construction, webbed connections, and hope for transformation of systems of knowledge and ways of seeing." (1991, pp. 191–192)

Teachers of undergraduates can easily find examples to demonstrate these issues. Harding's *The Racial Economy of Science* (1993) contains a number of articles that examine how Western science has been partly constructed in the service of racist and ethnocentric agendas, as well as how oppositional scientific practices have developed in particular social locations. More advanced students could grapple with Haraway's (1989) *Primate Visions: Gender, Race, and Nature in the World of Modern Science*. This essay shows how modern primatologies give accounts of nature that depend on and reproduce the social relations of their countries of origin. An effective approach is to contrast accounts of "received" knowledge with accounts from different perspectives, different "standpoints." For example, one might compare the enthusiastic accounts of the human genome project purveyed in the popular press with the critiques by some feminists, lesbians and gays, and people with disabilities (see *Women's Review of Books*, 1994). Or one might compare Moynihan's report on "black matriarchy" (1965) with the critiques and alternate versions of Black feminist scholars (e.g., Collins, 1990). Students might benefit from such work as Judith Rollins's *Between Women* (1985) or Romero's *Maid in the U.S.A.* (1992), which look at domestic work from the perspectives, respectively, of African American and Latina maids. The South African film *Maids and Madams* similarly offers the differing perspectives of the White "madams" who employ maids and that of the maids themselves. These are some of the specific materials and strategies which can drive home the power of our social location in shaping our vision and our ways of knowing.

THE POLITICS OF READING AND REPRESENTATION

"Representation," as I use it here, is the cultural production of linguistic artifacts; the inscription in language, broadly defined to include verbal, visual, aural, and social texts, of the values and ideologies of particular groups of people. A multiculturalist approach to the politics of representation requires some intellectual moves analogous to those in the sciences—not surprising, since the practices of reading and interpreting these representations are the "methodologies" of the humanities. The sciences have been asked to include new constituencies as subjects of study in order to correct generalizations based on the assumptions of middle-class masculine norms. Similarly, canons of art, literature, and music have been revised to correct the long omission of works by women, people of color, and working-class people—with necessary revisions as well in periodization, and discussions of affiliation, influence, tradition, and value. Interpretive strategies have questioned traditional notions of universality, instead unmasking the power of dominant ideologies as inscribed in cultural texts, asserting the importance of context in textual production, and locating in reading and writing from positions of marginality various strategies of resistance.

Race, Gender, and Language

Addressing the politics of representation starts with an attention to language itself.

There has been a great deal of work on sexism in the English language (e.g., Thorne et al., 1983). A good summary piece, one that looks at gender differences in both patterns of speech and in grammar and lexicon is Adams and Ware, "Sexism and the English Language" (1989). Students enjoy Tannen's *You Just Don't Understand* (1990). But her popular book is problematic in its failure to consider how class and racial diversity might complicate the generalizations she makes about gender differences in communication. Moreover, it disregards the ways in which differences in language use also inscribe differences in power.

The latter issue is given compelling attention by Carol Cohn (1990). She analyzes how sexual, domestic, and birthing images interact with a language of abstraction in the written and oral exchanges of defense strategists, almost all men, to sanitize the horrors of nuclear war. Moore's "Racist Stereotyping in the English Language" (1992) details how deeply embedded in language and imagery is a hierarchy of values that associates "white" and "light" with goodness, innocence, and purity; and "black" and "dark" with evil, guilt, and impurity. Occasionally the essay errs in its association of particular words with racial meanings (e.g., "niggardly"), but it works well in introductory classes to make students aware of how symbolic systems like the pervasive imagery of light and dark can take on racial significance and can harm those whose skin color is so devalued. Many publishers, professional associations and journals, and universities have guidelines for their own publications on nonsexist and inclusive language use. Reviewing these guidelines with students works well in both introductory and advanced courses to acquaint students with the issues and to show how they too can intervene in the conventions of language use as agents of change.

Decoding the Dominant Culture

Decoding the gender, racial, and sexual ideologies in literature, art, the media—in virtually every discursive arena—constitutes one of the preeminent critical tendencies of our time. The initial "images of" approach is relatively unsophisticated, sometimes involving a static typology (e.g., women as madonnas, whores, earth mothers), sometimes rejecting otherwise valuable cultural expressions because of their negative portrayals of particular social groups, sometimes looking for "positive role models" in literature, film, textbooks. Yet such an approach can help students understand some of the power of language and imagery. Kent (1988), for example, writes movingly of her tough search for role models in literature featuring women with disabilities. Rigg's film *Ethnic Notions* is a devastating exploration of the images of African Americans in popular culture. Beck (1988) explores the sources of the Jewish American Princess image in the interactions of sexism and anti-Semitism among contemporary Christians and Jews. Tajima analyzes and deplores the images of Asian women in film (1989).

But the problem is not simply negative images or the distance between image and reality. Language, deployed in the discourses characteristic of particular time and social milieu, not merely describes reality but constitutes it by naming and organizing our perceptions. For example, Stepan (1993) examines how analogies between race and gender cooperated to constitute a scientific order in which women and peoples of color constituted the lower ranks, along with children and apes.

Discussions of the politics of representation in cultural texts examine how dominant ideologies are inscribed in the processes of narrative, the deployment of tropes, the depiction of human bodies, and structure of visual space. Morrison's *Playing in the Dark: Whiteness and the Literary Imagination* (1992) can represent this approach. Morrison eloquently locates in the traditional canon of American literature traces of a pervasive "Africanism," analogous to the "orientalism" that Edward Said (1978) finds in the literary and political discourses of Western Europe and, by extension, the United States of the Colonial and post-Colonial periods. These terms denote the complex processes by which White-dominated cultures produce their understandings of themselves through the racialization, exoticizing, and control of "oriental," native, and darker-skinned "others." Racial and gender ideologies have even been analyzed in classical music. For example, McClary (1991) makes a case for the narrative enactment of contests over gender, sexuality, and power in some of the canonical works of the Western musical tradition. She draws also on work on colonial discourse to examine the intersections of sexuality and Eurocentrism in music.

Students can learn much about the power of representation through examining the textual dimensions of contemporary events. Gooding-William's anthology, *Reading Rodney King, Reading Urban Uprising* (1993), contains some excellent pieces on the cultural representations of race that fueled the events surrounding King's beating, the cultural meanings of the subsequent uprising, and media representations of the conflicts among Blacks and Koreans. Morrison's anthology, *Race-ing Justice, En-gendering Power: Essays on Anita Hill, Clarence Thomas, and the Construction of Social Reality* (1992) performs a similar service. For instance, Crenshaw's "Whose Story Is It, Anyway? Feminist and Antiracist Appropriations of Anita Hill," brilliantly demonstrates how Hill is in effect silenced because her story falls between two tropes: the lynching trope, which calls up visions of injustice to Black

men, and the rape trope, which is activated on behalf of white women (1992). Faludi's *Backlash* documents the conservative reaction against feminism in the Reagan-Bush years. One of the strongest sections of this book recounts the evolution of the immensely popular film, *Fatal Attraction*, from a short film sympathetic to the "other woman" character and critical of the married man who uses her, to a story of a single career woman turned homicidal by frustration and rejection (1991). The massive anthology *Cultural Studies* (Grossberg, Nelson, & Treichler, 1992) contains a number of such analyses, including two good essays on representations of people with AIDS.

Resisting Readings

The preceding works on the whole emphasize the hegemonic power of dominant cultural representations, though some also discuss oppositional textual practices. Other cultural critics refuse to accord such monolithic oppressive power to dominant discourses and offer the possibility for resisting readings. Two essays useful to students at all levels are Zimmerman (1991), "Seeing, Reading, Knowing: the Lesbian Appropriation of Literature" and hooks (1992), "The Oppositional Gaze: Black Female Spectators," respectively, on lesbian readings of novels and Black women's viewing of films. Sarris writes more for teachers in "Keeping Slug Woman Alive" (1993), a discussion of the challenges of reading in reservation classrooms and of reading strategies more empowering for students as individuals and more sustaining for their cultural communities.

Reconstructing Canons

A vast body of work examines the circumstances and contexts of cultural production, looking at the social and cultural milieu, class location, historical moment, gendered and sexual relations, available discourses, and biographical experiences that shape cultural artifacts. The effort to contextualize such artifacts—which range from literary, musical, and artistic texts to the Hollywood film—matters a great deal, because only through this kind of historical understanding can we demystify and democratize existing canons. We begin to understand the canonical elevation of White-male–authored literature, for example, as the product of a particular class of men in response to a particular set of social circumstances. And we begin to ask different questions: not so much, what makes this book "great" but what have been its uses and meanings to particular groups at particular moments—including ourselves. Lauter's *Canons and Contexts* (1991), which addresses gender, race, and class as formative of the received canons of American literature, is essential reading on this issue; he makes an argument for the study of American literature as comparative literatures.

Perhaps the best accounts of the circumstances of cultural production, though, are those of artists themselves. A few teachable books and essays: Baldwin's *Notes of a Native Son* (1955) and *Nobody Knows My Name* (1961); Lorde's "biomythography," *Zami, A New Spelling of My Name* (1982), on coming of age as a Black, lesbian poet; Momaday's *The Names: A Memoir* (1976), a lyric family memoir capturing the merging of Momaday's Kiowa and Cherokee origins; Olsen's *Silences* (1978), which tells how gender and class circumstances can impede creative expression; Bernice Johnson Reagon and Sweet Honey in the Rock's *We Who Believe in Freedom* (1993), on the roots of Reagon's and the singing group's background in the Black church and the Civil Rights movement; Rich's "Split at the Root: An Essay on Jewish Identity" (1986); Alice Walker's *In Search of Our Mother's Gardens*

(1983), especially the title essay, which can be usefully read with Marshall, "The Making of a Writer: From the Poets in the Kitchen" (1983), since both emphasize the daily creativity of their mothers as examples and sources of imaginative power; Walker's "Advancing Luna and Ida B. Wells" (1981), a powerful meditation on the difficulties of writing with integrity as a Black woman in a racist society about an incident involving a White woman's rape by a Black man (this piece can be effectively paired with Crenshaw, 1992). Among the many excellent films that feature the cultural production of women of color are *Hearts and Hands,* on women's quilts in U.S. history; *Identifiable Qualities: A Film on Toni Morrison; Mitsuye and Nellie: Asian American Poets; Visions of the Spirit: A Film about Alice Walker;* and *Wild Women Don't Have the Blues,* on Black women blues singers.

Difference, Oppression, and Resistance

Much of the cultural production of women, people of color, working-class people, and lesbians and gays can also be read to show how they encode or directly articulate strategies of resistance. Works of the dominant culture may also be read for their subversive and liberatory possibilities. While naming specific works could only be wildly arbitrary, some recent anthologies may prove useful. The *Heath Anthology of American Literature* (Lauter, 1994) reorders the very categories for the organization of American literature to accommodate a new inclusiveness. Brown and Ling have edited two excellent multicultural anthologies, *Imagining America: Stories from the Promised Land* (1991) and *Visions of America: Personal Narratives from the Promised Land* (1993). Fisher (1980) and Anzaldua (1990) provide good selections from the works of women writers of color; Zandy (1990) has edited a fine collection by working-class women.

Not that even resistance literature is free of the traces of dominant ideologies, about one's own social group or about other "others." Harriet Beecher Stowe's *Uncle Tom's Cabin* relied on ideologies of domesticity and accepts ideologies about Negro "nature" to make an argument against slavery. Male writers of the proletarian novel called for class struggle while often inscribing conservative ideologies of gender and sexuality. These examples can be endlessly multiplied. A progressive multiculturalism can unpack these ideological dimensions of writing—still with us, of course—in a way that historicizes and critiques without facile condemnation.

Needless to say, work by White ethnic women, by writers of color of both genders, by lesbians and gays, by working-class writers, is not limited in its texts or subtexts to accounts of oppression and resistance; it addresses every dimension of human experience and desire. Yet the presence in their consciousness and cultural production of a history not only of difference but of subordination cannot be ignored. Henry Louis Gates, Jr., one of today's most influential literary critics, writes ambivalently about the Bill Cosby show, applauding its success "at depicting (at long last) the everyday concerns of black people (love, sex, ambition, generational conflicts, work and leisure) far beyond reflex responses to white racism." But he acknowledges how small a percentage of Blacks in the United States live the deracinated upper-middle-class life of a Huxtable, and goes on to quote Mark Crispin Miller:

> "By insisting that blacks and whites are entirely alike, television denies the cultural barriers that slavery necessarily created: barriers that have hardened over years and years, and that still exist"—barriers that produced different cultures, distinct worlds. (1992, p. 316)

Michael Eric Dyson, in *Reflecting Black: African American Cultural Criticism* makes a similar argument about the same show. It's fine, he suggests, to identify issues that transcend race, "but that does not mean we should buy into a vacuous, bland universality that stigmatizes diversity, punishes difference, and destroys dissimilarities" (1993, p. 87). Slavery, the holocaust, the internment of Japanese Americans and the dropping of the atomic bomb on their homeland, the long history of Colonialist brutality toward Native Americans, the occupation of Hispanic territories—one cannot "do" multiculturalism and ignore this history, though to do only this history is insufficient. To analyze and intervene in the politics of representation is to assume that language has power both to marginalize and to liberate, to represent and to change.

EQUALITY AND DIFFERENCE[5]

Policy Implications

The issue Gates (1992) and Dyson (1993) have delineated—the mandate to acknowledge simultaneously the commonalities of human experience and the differences that different social and familial histories have constructed—represents a tension that pervades feminist and ethnic studies thought. This double consciousness is one of the hallmarks of multiculturalist thinking; it is often expressed as a tension between "community" and "diversity." By no means, however, do feminists and ethnic studies theorists and activists agree on the degree of emphasis to be placed on either side of the conjunction.

Gates and Dyson locate this tension in the realm of cultural criticism, but it acquires a special urgency in history and social theory, where policy decisions are at stake. Here, "commonality" can mean a common or equal claim to social goods and legal rights. Do we minimize difference in the service of our aspirations to equality, or do we acknowledge the social construction and history of difference (and subordination), risking the reification of difference in law and policy?

In women's studies, these issues came to a head in the Sears vs. EEOC sex-discrimination suit of 1986, filed because women were so underrepresented in the lucrative arena of commission sales. Feminist historians Rosalind Rosenberg and Alice Kessler-Harris testified for opposing sides. Rosenberg argued that sex differences between women and men led to different work priorities, exonerating Sears from charges of discrimination. Kessler-Harris, trying unsuccessfully to situate Sears' policies in the context of a history of discriminatory labor practices, argued that women and men in the absence of discrimination would have equal access to higher-paying positions (see Milkman, 1986). In this instance, an argument about women's "difference" from men had the effect of penalizing women. Yet affirmative action law and policy tries to remediate a history of social injustice by acknowledging that certain groups, having been socially constructed as "different" and simultaneously as subordinate, now require different measures to ensure their genuine equality.

The Emphasis on "Difference"

An emphasis on "difference"—respectively, gender differences and racial differences—was characteristic of an influential body of both feminist and ethnic studies work in the 1970s and 1980s. In ethnic studies thought, the emphasis on difference is sometimes aligned with nationalism—for example, the African American delineation of a pan-African experience, the Chicano emphasis on "La Raza." Asante's *The Afrocentric Idea* (1987), for example, argues that Black Amer-

icans can look to Africa for an epistemology and moral philosophy different from, and superior to, the Eurocentric tradition. Allen, in *The Sacred Hoop* (1986), makes a similar argument about Native American worldviews. Both emphasize the existence of a way of thinking based in a sense of community, a reverence for and participation in a natural and cyclical order, a sense of the sacred as part of rather than separate from daily life, a way of knowing that does not seek domination over nature. Collins (1990) argues for a Black feminist standpoint, growing from the position of Black women in a society both racist and sexist. In feminist thought, the valorization of difference has sometimes taken a form similar to the organicism of Asante and Allen. Indeed, Allen is a feminist who consciously seeks connections between American Indian thought and "women's ways of knowing."

The experience of maternality lies at the heart of many works about gender difference. Ruddick (1989) for example, poses the possibility that women's experiences as mothers—the embodied experience of pregnancy, the requirement of a particular kind of sustained attention to human needs for love and growth—generate a particular way of seeing the world, more concerned than men's vision with the preservation of human life. Chodorow's (1978) and Gilligan's (1982) work have been enormously influential in focusing attention on gender differences. Chodorow's psychoanalytically informed work emphasized the different developmental trajectories of women and men. Gilligan focused on their ostensibly different ethics—a masculine ethic of justice that assumes equality, a feminist ethic of care that assumes differential needs for nurturance and assistance. Stacey (1994) calls Tannen's *You Just Don't Understand* "the purest progeny" of Gilligan's *In a Different Voice*, since it assumes profound gender differences in communication analogous to those Gilligan finds in moral reasoning. And, like Gilligan's first book, it appeals to a mass audience apparently hungry to understand the sources of friction between contemporary men and women, at least those of the White middle classes.

The Critique of "Difference"

This tendency to valorize "difference," racial or gendered, has been critiqued by other feminist and ethnic studies writers on a number of bases. First, it essentializes the groups in question, implying if not asserting a quasi-biological core of being and leading to an acceptance of the status quo rather than to a struggle for social change. Second, it masks differences, fractures, and conflicts within particular gender and ethnic groups. Third, its proposals fail to describe accurately the experiences of significant constituencies within those groups. For example, White (1990) critiques Asante and Collins for ignoring gender and class differences among Africans in the diaspora and African Americans, arguing that nationalist thought often mystifies and distorts history in an effort to recuperate a mythical past. Krupat (1992) disagrees with Allen and others who posit a simple opposition between Native and Western cultures. He argues that such metaphors as the sacred hoop as a symbol of wholeness, though they do have a place in many Native cultures, are "essentially helpless before the complex facts of Native American and Western cultural diversity" (p. 42). hooks (1990) critiques essentialism among African American writers and activitists, but argues that there is a "radical difference between a repudiation of the idea that there is a black 'essence' and recognition of the way black identity has been specifically constituted in the experience of exile and struggle" (p. 29).

Spelman (1988) is only one of many critics who have taken Chodorow to task for assuming that gender is a primary and undifferentiated category in accounts of human development. Auerbach et al. (1985) critique Gilligan's work on similar grounds, and Stack finds that Gilligan's generalizations about a specifically female ethic of care do not apply to the rural African American community in her study (1990, 1994). Williams talks about how nationalism in the Black community is partly constructed by masculinist and heterosexist ideologies, used as a defense against the damages inflicted by racism. She brings issues of "difference" back to the classroom, by asking implicitly how, if, and when we as teachers mobilize our own identities in the interests of teaching "difference"—as she did in revealing to her Afro-American studies course her identity as a Black lesbian feminist (1994).

Beyond the Binaries

A number of theorists have made an effort to move beyond the dichotomies of equality/difference, or nationalism/assimilation, or community/diversity, by historicizing and deconstructing these binaries. Taylor's (1992) *Multiculturalism and "The Politics of Recognition"* traces the development in western social thought of a politics featuring the equalization of rights and entitlements and a subsequent and opposing politics of difference, based on the development of modern notions of identity. He suggests that a politics of equal recognition—the acknowledgment of the existence, value, and worth of cultural "others"—might render these divergent politics less oppositional. He proposes a liberal framework that struggles to advance certain "universal" principles—like the impermissibility of murder—while assuming that very different cultures "that have provided the horizon of meaning for large numbers of human beings, of diverse characters and temperaments, over a long period of time…are almost certain to have something that deserves our admiration and respect…"(quotation p. 72). Hooks (1992) looks at the "multiple experiences of black identity that are the lived conditions which make diverse cultural productions possible" and rejects the view that sees "black folks as falling into two categories: nationalist or assimilationist, black-identified or white-identified" (p. 29).

In feminist theory, at least two major anthologies and one major study are devoted to this historicizing and deconstructive project (Bacchi, 1990; Bock & James, 1992; Rhode, 1990; Stacey, 1994). Cott (1986) traces the tension in U.S. women's history since the nineteenth century, arguing that for much of the women's rights movement "the two strands of argument, 'sameness' and 'difference'…were not seen as mutually exclusive, but as juxtaposable" (p. 51). Even today, when

> the value accorded to "sexual difference" in feminist theory has increased at the same time that the universality of the claim for sisterhood has been debunked,…stress on women's socially constructed "difference" from men can go along with recognition of diversity among women themselves, if we acknowledge the multifaceted entity…that is the group called women. That acknowledgment allows coalition building, the only realistic political "unity" women have had or will have. (pp. 59–60)

In a clarifying essay, Joan Scott (1986) thinks through the uses of postmodernism for deconstructing "equality versus difference." In a related piece, she shows implicitly how debates about "equality" and "difference" elide into debates in the university today about "community" and "diversity." She argues that we must construct a sense of community that simulta-neously recognizes the existence of irreducible historical differences among us (1991). Minow (1990) tries to think past the same-difference issues that have inhered in legal and policy struggles among feminists, especially in the areas of parental leave and pornography. In a way, the entire field of critical legal theory arose in recognition of the necessity to think past the polarization between a discrimination-blind equal rights policy and a facile reification of difference.

Not all these issues and texts will be accessible for undergraduates, who can perhaps best approach them through the issues that touch their own lives most closely. Equal opportunity or affirmative action? Equal funding for women's athletics or an acknowledgment of physical "difference" (a physical difference that may also be partly or even largely socially constructed)? Are "mommy tracks" desirable because they acknowledge the reality that women mother and provide a less competitive place for women in the world of work, or undesirable because they reify parenting as a maternal rather than a parental responsibility and relegate women to dead-end jobs? Can political action be based on identities like "woman" or "African American," or do these categories dissolve on inspection into an endless proliferation of differences within difference—and if so, on what basis do we organize for social change? What does seem important is that teachers who wish to integrate multiculturalist perspectives recognize and be able to interpret this tension and its deconstructions, so that they do not misrepresent or oversimplify multiculturalist discourse.

CONCLUSION: SOME PARTING ANECDOTES

At a state university on the West Coast, a professor teaching a course on American architecture participates in a curricular change project. At the outset, he decides that instead of beginning his course with "colonial" architecture, he will spend a session or two on American Indian architecture. Over time, he comes to spend the first three weeks of the course on what he calls the Hopi mesa condos and the movable architecture, or tipis, of the Plains Indians. In the process of adding these new materials, he also redefines both "American" and "architecture"—the central organizing terms of his course. And now he inevitably touches on the displacement of tribes in the processes of White colonization.

Participating in a curriculum-transformation project on the East Coast, a professor of American Literature decides that for his individual reading project he will examine the literature of turn-of-the-century Black women writers—Nella Larsen, Jessie Redmon Faucet, and others. He wants to integrate them into his survey course, which is organized chronologically into three periods: realism, naturalism, modernism. He finds that their cultural productions do not fit his chronology; their work is "out of sync." Does he treat them as an exception and keep his chronology and his periodization? Rather, he struggles to change the structure of his course to acknowledge the inadequacy of his previous "data base."

A feminist biologist for some years has been confronting the exclusion of women as subjects in scientific experiments on health issues and the masculinization of the field of science. She decides to structure a new course to feature the proposed new national Women's Health initiative, investigating the impact on women's health of hormonal replacement therapy. She hears a talk by Ruth Zambrana, Latina sociologist, who carefully critiques the initiative for replicating in its design some of the same exclusions for racial-ethnic minority and poor women that White middle-class women

had complained of initially. She tries to redo her course on gender and science to avoid facile narratives of progress—either Western enlightenment narratives, or White feminist notions of progress as leading to one culminating health initiative for an undifferentiated "woman."

These are some of the more dramatic experiences of participants in curriculum transformation projects as they re-examine their courses through multiculturalist lenses. Ultimately, each teacher will need to discover for herself or himself what changes such an angle of vision will mandate. Whenever I speak of this process, I always think of the words of one of the characters in the film *Salt of the Earth*. A working-class Mexican-American woman, she comforts her friend when the friend's husband rages over her new-found independence in marching on a picket line: "These changes," she says softly, "come with pain." Yet they come with pleasure too. As Barbara Ehrenreich puts it:

> The "unenlightened"—the victims of monoculturalism—are oppressed too, or at least deprived. Our educations, whether at Yale or at State U, were narrow and parochial and left us ill-equipped to navigate a society that truly is multicultural and becoming more so every day. The culture that we studied was, in fact, one culture, and, from a world perspective, all too limited and ingrown. Diversity is challenging, but those of us who have seen the alternative know it is also richer, livelier and ultimately more fun. (1991, p. 84)

ENDNOTES

1. It is not possible to acknowledge in notes how deeply indebted this essay is to the work and ideas of Betty Schmitz, the founder of the Curriculum Transformation Project at the University of Maryland at Col-

lege Park and the director of its first summer institute. Also thanks to Rhonda Williams and Alaka Wali, who co-directed the institute in different summers (Rhonda Williams did it twice), and of Sandra Patton, first graduate assistant and subsequently assistant director for the institute. Rhonda Williams and Sandra Patton also provided valuable feedback on a draft. I am also grateful to Bonnie Thornton Dill, Sara Silverton, and Dabrina Taylor for their careful readings. The essay's limitations are my own.

2. Spelman (1988) uses this imagery of "doors" to caution against the perspective that privileges one door, one lens over another, since the experience of, let us say, Asian American women is not divisible into the "female" and the "Asian American." I am acknowledging here how difficult her mandate is, at least for me.

3. For example, the New York State Social Studies Review and Development Committee has argued for the primacy of race and culture over other categories; Taylor in his influential essay on multiculturalism and the politics of recognition assumes the primacy of ethnic and national identity and never mentions other forms of diversity.

4. "...Only one-quarter of 1 percent of our basic genetic information can be ascribed to what we call 'racial' differences." Hitchens (1994, 640).

5. As I was working on this section, I received from Judith Stacey the manuscript of a review essay (1994) and from Rhonda Williams the draft of a forthcoming teaching unit on equality and difference, expanding on work that we had done together for the summer institute at College Park. This section is indebted to both.

CHAPTER 4

Instructional Strategies

Eleanor W. Lynch, Ph.D.
Professor, Department of Special Education
San Diego State University

Editor's Notes:
Eleanor Lynch's chapter elaborates on the instructional strategies component of the course change model. She notes that despite the considerable research, theory, and practice confirming individual differences, colleges and universities continue to employ narrow modes of instruction that fail to consider these differences. Her chapter focuses on information about teaching, learning, and diversity that can be used to improve instructional practices for diverse learners.

Lynch believes that the first step is create a climate that honors, respects, and encourages diversity. Curricula, instruction, and pedagogy based on a model of empowerment provide the foundation for demonstrating that all students are valued and recognized for what they bring to the learning experience. In this regard, she discusses a number of contextual variables important to creating such an environment (e.g., cooperative vs. competitive environment, student and faculty behavioral styles, language and communication, and respect for authority and elders). The author then suggests some specific instructional strategies for teaching a diverse student body, including preassessment, role play, simulations and games, case methods, assignments/activities that promote critical thinking and problem-solving, cooperative learning and journaling. Subsequent chapters of this book contain examples of these strategies applied to specific disciplines. ∎

Throughout the United States, college and university students are becoming increasingly diverse. Faculty members and administrators are engaged in discussion, dialogue, and debate over the impact. The increased student diversity has outpaced faculty diversity. Although 20 percent of the total U.S. population is racially and ethnically diverse, only 11 percent of faculty members are diverse (Robbins, 1993). Not only does the faculty not mirror student diversity, but perhaps of even greater significance is the cultural milieu in which most of these faculty were trained. Most earned degrees from traditional doctoral programs prior to national consciousness-raising related to issues of gender, culture, race, and ethnicity. Few were ever taught how to teach at the college level. Although many have served as graduate teaching assistants, their models and mentors were from even earlier generations of faculty who came from even more traditional programs. As a result, many current faculty are struggling with the demands of students who differ from their expectations; and many are re-thinking their courses as well as their instruction. This chapter is designed to address issues related to instruction and diversity. It includes sections on diversity on campus, our understanding of diversity and instruction, creating a climate for effectively reaching and teaching diverse students, and employing strategies that build upon gender, cultural, linguistic, ethnic, racial, and disability diversity.

DIVERSITY ON CAMPUS

Issues of diversity have received renewed attention on university and college campuses in recent years. It is not uncommon to find these issues highlighted in articles in *The Chronicle of Higher Education*, to receive announcements of workshops to help campuses recruit and retain students of color or ensure compliance with the Americans with Disabilities Act, and to find literature in an increasing number of disciplines addressing student and faculty diversity. Within that literature, however, the greatest emphases have been on recruitment and retention of underrepresented students (Oliver & Brown, 1988; Terrell & Wright, 1988), re-aligning the curriculum (Buchen, 1992), and examining the campus climate that has led to intergroup tensions and intolerance (e.g., Harvey, 1991; Noley, 1991). Within these frameworks, the traditional approach has been to focus on forms of student assistance, lending credence to the belief that the problems or barriers to success lie within the student (Smith, 1989). But, as Smith (1989, p. v) states, "many institutions have broadened these efforts to include *institutional accommodations* which acknowledges that some of the barriers to success rest with the institution itself."

The increased concern over institutional barriers has given rise to a critical examination of the politics of teaching, often described as critical pedagogy (Castenell, 1993; Luke & Gore, 1992; Schmitz, 1992). However, despite the increased concern over institutional barriers and the politics of teaching, the literature on diversity and *instruction* in higher education is less robust. A great deal remains to be learned about what occurs in college and university classrooms and faculty offices that supports or inhibits the success of diverse students. Establishing an inclusive climate, supporting positive classroom interactions, and organizing instruction to accommodate a wide range of learning preferences has been a topic of great concern at the elementary and secondary levels; and that literature provides a foundation for developing strategies that can be applied in college classrooms.

TEACHING, LEARNING, AND DIVERSITY

Research, theory, and practice have all confirmed that each individual differs from every other; yet college and university classrooms have traditionally made few allowances for these differences. Exposed to a Eurocentric, male-biased curriculum using narrow models of instruction, students who differ in *any* way from the norm may feel isolated and alienated from the educational goal that they are pursuing. Some of these students—re-entry women, students of color, those who are differently abled—will adapt and succeed. Others will not. This section of the chapter focuses on information about teaching, learning, and diversity that is being used in higher education and other educational settings to improve instructional practices for diverse learners. However, one caveat obtains. Defining individuals unidimensionally does not lead to enlightenment. Knowing a student's age, race, cultural background, language, disability, family income, or place of origin provides information, not insight. Although much of the work cited in the paragraphs that follow has been done in relation to broad cultural or racial groups, within-group differences are as great as those across groups (Hanson & Lynch, 1995). Thus, the information that follows must be considered and applied individually to those students for whom it is appropriate rather than to all students from a given group.

Cooperation and Competition

One of the hallmarks of higher education is competition. The admissions procedures alone confirm or deny each applicant's ability to compete. Although higher education in the United States is egalitarian by many countries' standards, it is nonetheless based on a premise of exclusion rather than inclusion. For many students of color, international students, and many women, cooperation is more highly valued than competition (Lynch & Hanson, 1992). Individuals who are socialized in societies or groups that place a higher value on cooperation than competition may have difficulty in university classes in which only independent performance is encouraged or allowed. For example, feminist pedagogy suggests that cooperative rather than competitive models of learning may be more effective for women (Maher & Tetreault, 1992). Joe and Malach (1992) discuss the educational implications of the importance of relationships as opposed to individualism for American Indian students; and Chan (1992) describes the importance of relationships as opposed to egocentric and individualistic perspectives in the socialization of Asian children. For students accustomed to settings in which problems are solved by the group or those in which work is shared based upon one's ability to contribute, the typical university classroom that does not support cooperation may be uncomfortable and alienating.

A corollary to the competition/collaboration issue is related to the way in which achievement is acknowledged. Within the Anglo-European tradition of schooling, students' achievements are often publicly acknowledged. Compliments from the instructor on the excellence of a student's paper or response to a question are typical. In fact, they are viewed as very reinforcing, and many students who have been socialized within this system work hard for public praise and acknowledgment from faculty. However, being singled out for one's personal accomplishments is not universally appreciated. Perhaps the feelings that such praise can evoke are best explained by the following Japanese proverb, "the nail that raises its head is hammered down" (Chan, 1992, p. 181). Warner and Hastings (1991, p. 6) make a similar comment in relation to American Indians: "Individual success in education (or any enterprise) is generally not valued." Putting oneself above others is not viewed positively by many cultural groups. Thus, individual praise may be disquieting rather than reinforcing for many diverse students.

In summary, competition and acknowledgment of individual accomplishment are highly valued in traditional academic settings, but they may not have the same positive valence for students whose socialization has been outside the dominant U.S. culture. As a result, faculty members may need to reconsider these dimensions of their instruction and develop additional ways of structuring their classes and responding to student achievement. Group projects in which the emphasis is on overall contribution, and all group members receive the same grade is one strategy. Instead of responding to student comments by praising the individual's comments, a more neutral response based on the content can be used to prevent singling students out for public praise. For example, rather than saying, "That was an excellent comment, Rhonda," the instructor might say, "Rhonda is suggesting that this poem reflects the grief that is experienced with any loss. What do some of the rest of you think?"

Learning and Behavioral Styles

Literature in psychology and education is replete with discussions and studies of learning styles. For many years it has been appealing to imagine that each individual has a modality, or way of learning, that is uniquely suited to her or him. Some of the work in this area has attempted to describe learning styles by sensory systems, personality types, or approaches to problem-solving. Although each of us may have learning preferences and recognize that we are somewhat stronger in one approach than another, the majority of adults learn in a variety of ways and do not have a learning style that can be readily defined.

Although work in the area of learning modalities and learning styles has not been fruitful, there is information that suggests that individuals learn various behavioral styles that influence their learning preferences. Hilliard (1989) suggests that what is known about behavioral styles is too limited to lead to instructional strategies, but he does address behavioral style in relation to misperceptions of students, especially African American students. He suggests four ways in which behavioral style may result in misperceptions. Although his emphasis was focused on students in elementary and secondary schools, his observations are equally applicable in college and university classes. The first misperception that Hilliard (1989) describes is related to underestimating students' intellectual ability. The example cited is the learned

preference for many African American students to focus on the global aspects of a problem rather than the specifics. Although an understanding of the big picture is becoming increasingly valued in many settings, academic institutions typically place more emphasis on analytical rather than holistic approaches to problem-solving. Thus, a student tackling a problem holistically may be dismissed, discouraged, or graded lower than one who uses an analytical approach. Hilliard (1989) points out that the goal is to have all students learn to apply both approaches, but he suggests that we should not discount or make negative judgments about students who first operate holistically.

The second area that Hilliard (1989) describes is a behavioral style in storytelling—which can be extended to include expository writing and responding in class—that is spiraling rather than linear. Citing Orlando Taylor, a sociolinguist who has done considerable work on language and African American children, Hilliard (1989) suggests that the Anglo-European approach is extremely linear with a clearly defined beginning, middle, and end with few departures from the central points. Among African American children, however, there are often many seeming departures from the main point that spiral back to create an enriched whole. When these differences are assumed to be lack of skill or competence rather than a different approach that has been learned over the years, faculty may misjudge the students' abilities. In speaking and writing there are forms that all students need to learn; but students' overall level of competence should not be underestimated because they have had more practice with one than another.

Hilliard (1989) also discusses the role of faculty expectations in relation to behavioral styles. Faculty may have greater difficulty establishing communication and rapport with students who differ significantly from themselves in culture, ethnicity, language, race, gender, socioeconomic status, or other salient variables. Sensing this lack of communication and rapport, students may feel less adequate and perform less well. The research of Allen and Niss (1990) seems to support a portion of Hilliard's (1989) hypothesis. In their study of seven professors at a midwestern university, an analysis of videotaped classes showed that faculty tended to be more critical of the comments made by students of color (mostly African American) than White students; and they were more apt to respond positively to the remarks of White students and foreign students than students of color from the United States. Although not addressed by Hilliard (1989), Allen and Niss (1990) also found that both male and female faculty responded more positively to male students than to female students. In an extension of that theme, Hall and Sandler (1982) report that faculty are less likely to develop the points made by women in class, and that women students are more likely to be interrupted by the instructor or male students than are their male counterparts.

Finally, Hilliard (1989) describes language differences as another dimension in which faculty may misjudge students' capabilities. A more comprehensive discussion of the ramifications of language differences is included in the subsequent section.

Behavioral style is a complex issue that is similar to a double-edged sword. Not acknowledging style differences among individual students may result in misunderstanding and misperception; however, assuming that all students of one cultural, ethnic, or racial group share the same style may lead to unwarranted and inappropriate stereotyping. Perhaps Hilliard's (1989) own words related to this issue are most instructive.

Educators need not avoid addressing the question of style for fear they may be guilty of stereotyping students. Empirical observations are not the same as stereotyping. But the observations must be empirical, and must be interpreted properly for each student. We must become more sensitive to style out of a basic respect for our students, for their reality, and for their tremendous potential for learning. (p. 69)

Language and Communication

College and university classes rely more heavily than any other level of education on verbal interactions. The lecture method, though less prevalent than in decades past, is still ubiquitous. This dimension of the college experience is especially challenging to students whose primary language is other than English, whose dialect differs from that spoken in classes, and whose verbal metronomes are adjusted to a different speed than their instructors'.

An increasing number of individuals in the United States are not native English speakers. Census data from 1990 indicate that 1 in 7 individuals speaks a language other than English at home ("1 in 7 Don't," 1993). Even for nonnative speakers who appear fluent in English but speak another language in their everyday interactions, the cognitive academic language proficiency described by Cummins (1981) that is required in university classes produces additional demands. Students who consider their spoken English skills to be insufficient in an academic setting may withdraw from responding to questions or offering observations and comments in class. Although their thinking may be far superior to that of some of the students who are fluent and articulate, instructors have less opportunity to gauge this and may view the quiet students as less involved or less competent.

Students whose dialect differs from the English of the college classroom may experience some of the same difficulties as non-native speakers. In fact, students whose native language is English and who have been educated in English may feel and be even more excluded from the language of academics than many non-native speakers. Dialects such as Black English (Willis, 1992) or Hawaiian Pidgin (Gollnick & Chinn, 1990) may interfere with students' participation in class as well as their writing. Students with dialectical differences may require additional assistance in performing according to the academic formula, but their language differences should not be viewed as a reflection of their cognitive potential.

A third issue of language is related to the rhythm of language or the metronome of speech that is used by native speakers of any language (Oleska, 1993). In each language there is a cadence or rhythm that is as important as the vocabulary, grammar, and syntax. The metronome that one uses when speaking the language is influenced first by the language itself, then by the characteristics of the geographic region, and finally by the personal characteristics of the individual speaker. One of the salient characteristics in conversation, or in questions and answers in a class, is the amount of pause time that is allowed between speakers (Oleska, 1993; Tafoya, 1993). For example, in mainstream American English, if a speaker pauses for approximately one second, it is signal that it is the conversation partner's turn. Responding after a pause as short as one second is not viewed as interrupting, and waiting longer may even lead to a feeling that an awkward silence is occurring. However, speakers of other languages and some individuals with expressive language disorders or cerebral palsy may have a very different metronome; and they may use that rhythm when they are speaking. Tafoya (1993) describes the pause time of the Taos

Pueblo people as between four and five seconds; and Oleska (1993) suggests a similar pause time for many Alaskan Natives. As a result of these different rhythms, interchanges across cultures may be unsatisfying to both speakers. The mainstream speakers may feel that things are not happening quickly enough and may feel that they are having to jump in to keep the interchange going. Speakers with longer pause-times may feel that they are not being respectfully listened to and that their comments are being discounted. Perhaps the best way to imagine a conversation of this sort is to recall the discomfort that is felt in a long distance or conference call when there is a delay in the line. Pauses, people talking simultaneously, and the overall uncertainty of whose turn it is, are similar to conversations that occur when the speakers are using different metronomes.

These differences may show up in college classes that include diverse students. Imagine a professor from New York City with a very rapid delivery interacting with a student whose pause-time is three times as long as his. The typical result—besides frustration for both—is for the speaker with the faster metronome to dominate the dialogue. For example, an open-ended question that is not immediately answered is often made into a verbal multiple-choice. If the answer is not selected quickly enough from this menu of options, the faster speaker tends to reduce further the question to a true and false. If the slower speaker still does not respond, the faster speaker tends to move to someone else or provide the answer (Oleska, 1993). In this situation, the speakers with the longer pause-time have never had the opportunity to share their thinking.

Language is a part of almost every human transaction. Although its primary function is communication, culture, physical challenges, and different ways of speaking may interfere with successful interactions. Cheng (personal communication, January 15, 1993) suggests that the cultural, language, and ideological differences that occur in communication can lead to "difficult discourse," and difficult discourse can lead to misperceptions and misunderstandings between students and faculty.

Authority and Respect for Elders

In each of the areas considered in this section, individual differences may be more potent than differences in culture; however, there are powerful cultural norms related to authority and respect for one's elders. Respect for position, role, and authority are greater in many cultures than in the dominant U.S. culture. In other cultures, such as Latino, Asian, and Filipino, professors and teachers are accorded considerable respect by their students and the larger community (Lynch & Hanson, 1992). Combined with traditions that value ancestors, age, and the wisdom that comes with it, students of color may maintain a very reserved and respectful manner in the presence of faculty members. In some Asian cultures, asking a question would indicate that the professor had not adequately explained the information, and therefore would cause the professor to lose face. The student may prefer to remain puzzled rather than put the professor in a position that the student would regard as humiliating (Chan, 1992). When asked whether or not students understand the material, some may nod affirmatively to show their respect rather than ask questions.

Respect for elders and anyone who is older than oneself may compound the problem. The majority of faculty members are older than their students, making it even more difficult for students to ask questions. The U.S. mainstream norm of questioning authority and one's elders is anathema to most of the rest of the world. Faculty who value lively argument, debate, and discussion in their classes may misread the reticence of students from other cultural backgrounds and presume that they are not learning as quickly or as well as their more talkative classmates (Committee for Economic Development, 1987; Cheng, 1987; Lewis & Doorlag, 1991). Respect may be viewed as insecurity with the material and limited expressive skills when in fact it is a learned behavioral style that is valued within the student's family and culture (Lynch & Hanson, 1992).

The preceding discussion of cooperation versus competition, learning and behavioral styles, language and communication, authority and respect for elders provides general information that may help faculty members consider their instructional methods in relation to students' needs and preferences. As with all information, when applied to any individual it may or may not inform. Culture, language, race, ethnicity, gender, and disability are dimensions rather than definitions of each individual.

CREATING THE CLIMATE FOR DIVERSITY IN THE CLASSROOM

The first step in making a class more responsive to a diverse student body is to create a climate that honors, respects, and encourages diversity. Curricula, instruction, and pedagogy that are based on a model of empowerment provide the foundation for demonstrating that all students are valued and recognized for what they bring to the learning experience (Sleeter, 1991). Because the basic commodities in almost every college or university class are knowledge and ideas, diversity should be a given. However, the diversity of knowledge and ideas have had boundaries—boundaries that represented Eurocentric, male-dominated perspectives. Thus, the climate must be created anew every term in every class to ensure that the old boundaries are expanded. There are several strategies for creating a climate that is responsive to diversity, and the paragraphs that follow provide general suggestions related to climate.

The Climate in Words and Language

It is difficult to change the cadence of one's speech, but there are a number of changes in language that can be addressed by all faculty members. The old aphorism, "Sticks and stones may break my bones, but words will never hurt me," is not true. Words can and do hurt; but perhaps even more important, words can influence expectations. The Women's Movement has been quite successful in helping the nation change from sexist to nonsexist language. Grown women are no longer referred to as girls, and the male pronoun is no longer used to represent all people. However, despite these changes, there are still college classrooms in which the vocabulary has not changed. Using inclusive language is something that every faculty member can do and demonstrates an increased commitment to acknowledging diversity.

The words that are used to describe groups of people also make a statement about how much the speaker honors diversity. Because labels have typically been chosen and applied by the dominant group, choosing the way that a group is referred to is a particularly sensitive issue. For example, "African American" is the term that has been selected by the African American community as the term of preference. The terms "Negro," "Black," or "Afro-American" are no longer terms of choice. The same is true for other groups, although there are often more regional differences. For example, in many areas of the country, individuals with roots in Latin America, Central America, and Mexico prefer to be referred to as "Latino." In other areas of the country, or within certain groups who share these roots, "Hispanic" might be an acceptable term. In some areas of the Southwest, individuals with roots in Mexico prefer the appellation "Chicano," whereas in others that would be an insult.

The primary issue is that the words chosen to describe any group should reflect the group's preferences, and it is incumbent upon the speaker to determine the words that are appropriate for the time and the region. Faculty who use "Afro-American" when they are discussing issues related to "African Americans" are demonstrating that they do not consider it important to use the words that are preferred by the group. This, in turn, communicates an attitude that interferes with a climate that is supportive of diversity.

Words also make a difference in another area. Among consumer groups and professional fields such as special education and rehabilitation, "person first" language has emerged (Stahlman & Pusch, 1992). Just as the words suggest, the emphasis is placed upon the person, not his or her disability or challenge. For example, instead of mentioning the "handicapped student who is in a wheelchair," it would be more appropriate to mention the "student who uses a wheelchair." Descriptors such as "crippled," "physically handicapped," and "physically disabled" have given way to "individuals with physical disabilities or physical challenges." Although skeptics have suggested that these changes in language are euphemistic, consider the image that comes to mind in these two different phrases: "wheelchair bound" versus "uses a wheelchair." The latter suggests someone in control; the former does not.

If the classroom climate is to be one that fosters diversity, the words that are used are important. Words that convey respect, that honor group preferences, and words that empower rather than enfeeble must become the *lingua franca* (common language) of colleges and universities.

The Climate of Acceptance

Colleges and universities are built upon difference—different disciplines, different ways of thinking about the world, different methods of research, and different perspectives among colleagues. Little is as treasured as academic freedom. However, the freedom that is so cherished among faculty members may not always find its way into classes. Students bring their own values, beliefs, and ideologies that they have learned through family, culture, religion, and schooling. Although one of higher education's missions is to create and transmit knowledge, colleges and universities are not the keepers of all wisdom. Students bring with them their own ways of knowing; and the college experience should expand their ways of knowing without discounting the differences that they bring (Banks, 1993). For example, the life experiences of a re-entry woman in her mid-40s may provide valuable information to the entire class about issues of child care, role expectations, and even the trickle-down theory of economics. Just as the traditional healing practices of a Nigerian physician may broaden the knowledge of all participants in a public health class, so too may the political wisdom of the son or daughter of an American Indian rights activist. Using the knowledge that students bring can inform both the knowledge within the subject area and the process for conveying it.

The challenges posed by diverse students—a traditional Muslim woman, a Rastafarian man, a re-entry grandmother, a star football player, and a woman who is blind—are the challenges of the entire society. Accepting and capitalizing on these differences in the college classroom provides a model for their acceptance and inclusion in the larger community.

The Curricular Climate

Class and course content at most colleges and universities is determined through a series of departmental, college, and university curriculum committees. The basic content is dictated by the discipline, but individual faculty members have considerable freedom in interpreting that content: writing the syllabus, selecting textbooks, and utilizing other resources. It is this area in which faculty have an opportunity to create a curricular climate that supports diversity.

Several issues may arise as faculty review their courses from this perspective: Are women, people of color, and people with disabilities represented as authors of textbooks or other readings for the course? Are videotapes or other materials that are used in the course non-biased, non-sexist, and person-first in their language and presentation? Do guest lecturers, field supervisors, or lab instructors represent the diversity of students? These issues are easier to address in some courses than in others, but elements of each can be addressed in every course. For example, a course on Shakespeare might include readings on contemporaneous literature from other areas of the world, thus examining the differences in thinking, expression, and values of those times. A course in aerospace engineering may include journal articles by women and people of color in the syllabus, as well as teleconferences or videotaped conversations with professional colleagues around the country who are from underrepresented groups. A course in philosophy may examine cultural values related to disability, their origins, and their influence on ethics in contemporary society.

Because each faculty member is the expert in his or her own courses and discipline, it is not possible nor advisable to be prescriptive. However, it is essential to broaden the standard course of study in meaningful and inclusive ways. Honoring differences by providing access to others in the discipline who are from diverse cultural, language, gender, and racial groups invigorates the curriculum and creates a climate that supports diversity.

The Office and Advising Climate

Academic freedom is most sacrosanct in faculty offices! From brimming desks in the corners of rat labs, to the dusty paper piles and bookshelves in arts and letters, and from the posters and primary colors in child development to the chalky chaos in the sciences, faculty offices tend to mirror their occupants. Offices make nonverbal statements that reflect values, beliefs, and sometimes biases.

The way in which office hours are posted, if at all, provides students with clues about accessibility and openness to dialogue. Cartoons, books, photos, and decor define the occupant to everyone who enters. Is the furniture positioned to encourage interaction or to erect barriers? If there are posters, cartoons, objects, art, or humor, what are their messages? Are the cartoons sexist, racist, ageist? What does the art communicate? For example, posters celebrating Columbus's "discovery" of the New World and the conquistadors that followed are not messages of welcome to most Latino and American Indian students.

A considerable amount of advising, career planning, and academic support occurs in faculty offices. They are places in which students as well as faculty should feel comfortable. As in previous sections, the goal is not to reduce faculty offices to politically correct cubicles. The purpose is to engender reflection and discussion about the statements that are made without words—the messages that faculty offices communicate to a diverse student body.

STRATEGIES FOR TEACHING A DIVERSE STUDENT BODY

Despite the appearance of homogeneity among many students, their abilities, personal concerns, weaknesses, motivations, and needs may differ considerably. College and university classrooms, however, are typically organized as if these differences do not exist. There is a tacit assumption that university admission denotes a level playing field, and that the responsibility for winning or losing the game belongs to the student. There is often little opportunity to get to know students by name, let alone by need.

This section of the chapter describes a variety of strategies that can be used to improve opportunities for learning for all students with particular attention to strategies for women and underrepresented students. Many strategies can be used across the curriculum, while others are more appropriate in some disciplines than in others. Each strategy also contains a "comfort component" that is based upon the faculty member's style, preferences, and skills. Some strategies may be comfortable for some faculty and not for others. However, no strategy should be judged exclusively by how comfortable the faculty member is. Rather, each should be weighed in terms of its potential for increasing the success of diverse learners.

Pre-Assessment

It is often the unknown that is most fearsome. Many students entering higher education have doubts about their ability to measure up, to meet their goals. Even those who appear confident may be deeply concerned about their ability to perform. Pre-assessment at the beginning of a course, or each new area of content within a course, provides an opportunity to adjust course content, to allay students' fears, and target problems for which students can seek help. Pre-testing students' knowledge and skills for information rather than for a grade shows the student what is expected and enables the faculty member to determine areas of strength and weakness among class members and gear the instruction accordingly.

Learning that many students lack prerequisite skills does not mean that the instructor must water down the instruction. It means that the instructor may advise some students into other classes, assist in organizing study groups, refer some students to other resources on campus such as Study Skills Centers, or provide additional sessions for students who need to catch up. Pre-assessment may also provide information that allows the instructor to include more advanced material because students already have basic knowledge. Eliminating the need for review can save multiple class sessions and increase the depth or breadth of the content.

Pre-assessments can be done in a variety of ways, depending upon the course. A two-minute extemporaneous talk in a communications class, a multiple-choice, computer-scored test in mathematics, or a one-page writing sample in a composition class can help faculty members determine how to proceed and help students learn what is expected. When students do lack prerequisite skills, it is essential to talk with them about it. No one likes to give students bad news, and the faculty may be reticent to discuss skill problems with students. This reticence may be even more pronounced if there is a climate on campus in which charges of racism are frequently heard. Despite these concerns, students deserve thorough, sensitively delivered explanations about academic deficiencies and suggestions and referrals for remediating them. If students are already involved in campus programs that assist with basic skills or provide counseling, working with the program may be helpful for the faculty member and the student. Students who receive services to help them compensate for specific disabilities often need to have faculty members work with the campus service center to alter testing strategies, obtain special equipment, or have people resources such as sign-language interpreters or notetakers available.

Contextualized Learning

There is no argument that those things that are meaningful to us are learned more quickly and retained longer. Abstract facts and information unrelated to one's life experience, interests, or goals are more difficult to master. Gay (1977) has described this principle in relation to diverse students as cultural context teaching. Such contextualized instruction draws upon examples, analogies, and experiences that reflect students' lives in order to make material more meaningful to them. Contextualizing education is also recommended for reaching all adult learners (Knowles, 1970, 1973).

For faculty, the issue becomes *how* to contextualize information that must be taught but may be outside the realm of student experience and interest. In almost every situation, activities that are interactive and call upon the real-world knowledge, skills, and experiences of students are more apt to provide a meaningful context than those that don't (Franklin, 1992). Thus, teaching through role play, simulations and games, and critical-thinking and problem-solving provide excellent opportunities to maximize each student's learning.

Role Play

Role playing activities provide students with opportunities to practice new skills in context. Although they may be difficult for some students who are particularly shy or who are uncomfortable with ambiguous situations (Nagata, 1989), they can be extremely effective for others. Role plays vary in their degree of structure. In structured role plays, students are assigned to roles and given scripts that provide information about their role and character. For example, in a social-work course, students may role play an interview situation. To give the activity structure, the instructor may create descriptions to get the role play started: The student playing the social worker is working in a large child welfare office and is responsible for conducting the interview with a family who is petitioning to have their children returned to them after 18 months in foster care. The children were originally removed from the home because of the parents' drug use. During this 18-month period, the father and mother have participated regularly in a drug-rehabilitation program and have requested that they and their children be reunited. The students role playing the mother and father also would be given descriptions that provide a framework for their roles and characters. The goal of the role play would be for the social worker to gather information about the parents' current status in order to make a recommendation regarding the children's placement. Students playing the roles would stay in character throughout the interview and try to respond from the perspective of the character that they are playing.

Role plays also can be conducted without the structure of character descriptions. In this format, the instructor would describe a brief scenario and assign students in the class to take the roles. Each student participant would play the role in the way that she

or he chooses, without relying on a set description provided by the instructor. This type of role play might occur in a management class in which the scenario revolves around a senior manager conducting a performance review of a staff member. Without further instruction, the participating students would begin the role play. After a preset number of minutes has expired, or at the instructor's discretion, the role play would be stopped, and the entire class would share in the debriefing and discussion.

Role plays provide excellent vehicles for allowing students to practice applying the skills and knowledge that they are learning in the course. These practices allow for feedback and discussion that involves the entire class, and they enable the instructor to monitor student performance before students use their skills in practicum or internship settings. As such, they are valuable tools for including students from a wide range of backgrounds. There are, however, cautions that should be exercised. Role playing should be voluntary, especially if the content is highly charged, such as issues related to child abuse, disability, sexual preference, and so forth. Faculty must be prepared to carefully observe those taking roles, their extent of identification with the role, and their apparent comfort or discomfort. Faculty must also debrief role plays carefully and thoroughly to ensure that the intended points were made and that unexpected issues have been dealt with.

Simulations and Games

Simulations and games provide additional techniques for instructing students from diverse backgrounds. Greenblat (1988, p. 2) defines simulations as "...an operating model of central features or elements of a real or proposed system, process, or environment." Simulations can be mock-ups of scientific or technological systems such as spacecraft, wind tunnels, or ecosystems. They can also be mock-ups of social systems such as state government, a small business, or a hospital emergency room. Simulations in which the outcomes are based partly or entirely on players' decisions are referred to as games. Instructional simulations and games often have role playing as an element, but they differ in structure from the role playing previously described. Simulations and games are built upon interactive, dynamic models in which there are more structure and rules that determine the consequences of each action (Greenblat, 1988).

Commercially available simulations and games are available in many formats, including print materials, game boards, computer, and interactive video. *The Guide to Simulations/Games for Education and Training*, edited by Robert Horn and Anne Cleaves (1980) describes over 1,000 simulations and games that are available on a wide range of topics. For those who are interested in developing their own, *Designing Games and Simulations: An Illustrated Handbook* by Greenblat (1988), provides invaluable information.

Simulations and games provide a structured experience in which all students can participate. They vary in length from a class period to many weeks but can often be modified to suit the needs of the instructor. Because they are built on dynamic models with preset decision rules, extremely complex scientific and social issues can be addressed. Through the experience, students can increase their knowledge about the topic as well as their understanding of interactivity of the elements of problems and possible solutions. As a result, students must think critically and apply their knowledge to the activity.

Case Methods

In many university departments and content areas, case methods provide an oppor-

tunity to contextualize instruction. Presenting real-world cases or problems can enliven instruction, stimulate critical thinking, and ensure problem-solving. Real or fictitious scenarios can be presented as examples to illustrate the material being taught. In an accounting class students can be presented information about the bookkeeping system of a charity and asked to evaluate the system for its level of compliance with state and federal legislation or its compliance with the standards of the profession. Students in veterinary medicine can be given scenarios of symptoms and asked to determine the most likely diagnosis and the preferred course of treatment, or students in special education may be given information about a student's performance and asked to develop an Individualized Education Plan.

Case methods are familiar to faculty from a wide range of disciplines. They encourage student engagement and participation, provide a connection to real-world application of the content, and heighten interest in the material being taught. They can be extremely effective when used with diverse students because the instructor can construct cases in which there is a range of responses but no single correct answer. This allows students to bring their own knowledge, creativity, and perspective to the situation. Students can also be asked to work in groups to create their own case studies to be given to other students.

Critical Thinking and Problem-Solving

Two overriding goals of instruction in most disciplines are to help students develop their ability to think critically and to solve complex problems. Activities that promote these goals can also support diverse students. For example, a course in health science might include small-group problem-solving activities that require students to conduct needs assessments of their own communities related to knowledge about high-risk health behaviors. Their next responsibility may be to develop a strategy that could be implemented in their community to reduce those behaviors, pilot the strategy, and evaluate its success. A class in psychology might have students interview members of their own families to determine what strategies were used to motivate, reinforce, or encourage children in the family to reach their goals. Information from the interviews could be discussed in a report in relationship to theories of motivation. Students in an astronomy course may be given the task of determining what concepts are important for elementary school children to know and to devise ways to present the information to a third-grade class that they have adopted. Or a class in architecture may be required to design a house that is accessible to individuals who are physically challenged. As a part of their assignment, they would be required to work with students on campus who have physical disabilities to determine their needs as well as their preferences. Finally, a class in film, dance, or drama may be asked to select a pressing social problem and bring it to public attention through the medium of their art.

Including interactive activities is critical to contextualizing instruction. The more students can identify with the concepts and apply those concepts in settings with which they are familiar, the greater the likelihood that they will master the material. Contextualization is a hallmark of high-quality instruction for all people at all levels of learning.

In addition to its value for students, there is a reciprocal to contextualized learning. To use real-world instruction most effectively, faculty members themselves must be open and willing to, commit time to learning about life circumstances that differ from their own (Giroux, 1988). Participating in, rather than studying, the life of various groups and communities enables instructors to bring additional meaning to their content and to understand the meaning that diverse students bring to learning.

Cooperative Learning

Cooperative learning is typically described as an instructional strategy in which students work together in small groups (Slavin, 1987; Tiedt & Tiedt, 1990). The development of the Network for Cooperative Learning in higher education has contributed to increased interest in this strategy in colleges and universities (Cooper, 1993). Within the group the students contribute their own talents, are responsible for learning through their own contributions as well as those of others, and are rewarded for the performance of the group rather than the performance of individuals (Gollnick & Chinn, 1990). If competitiveness is introduced, it is between rather than within groups. Research on cooperative learning based on college and university students suggests that this approach has beneficial effects on student involvement in learning as well as on student-to-student interaction which supports leadership characteristics (Astin, 1993).

Cooperative learning is an instructional strategy that can be used in any content area. One of the best examples of cooperative learning is demonstrated in the sciences and engineering. Throughout the nation there are a number of competitions that accept teams from various universities. The teams work on solutions to specific problems, such as designing an electric or solar-powered car. This form of problem-solving teamwork need not be reserved for national competition but can be routinely utilized in university coursework. In other disciplines, cooperative learning groups are equally easy to implement. Class projects can be designed and implemented by teams, research studies can be conducted cooperatively, and study groups can be organized.

Cooperative learning can be used as a strategy that supports diverse learners in college and university classrooms. In addition to the advantages for many students from diverse backgrounds, there are advantages for all group members. Besides opportunities to learn together in a mode that reduces competition, students learn to negotiate, assert themselves, compromise, and resolve conflict—all marks of those who are truly educated. For a more thorough discussion of cooperative learning and suggestions for using it in the college classroom, see Chapter 7.

Journal Writing

Journal writing is suitable for many classes within the social sciences, arts, letters, and professional schools. In its most elemental form, students keep journals that discuss personal experiences, reactions to course content, or situations in practicum settings that they feel are significant to their personal or professional growth. The journals are shared with the instructor at specified times, and the instructor reacts to the content of the students' writing. The goal is to help students increase their understanding of themselves and their professional and/or academic interactions; the goal is not a perfect composition or mastery of course content. Through journals, students often share content that allows faculty members to know more about them and to understand their concerns. Journals also can be used to discover gaps in learning or application that the instructor can help students remediate.

Journals may be assigned for a more specific purpose. The author uses journals to encourage students' discussions of their concerns, experiences, and issues related to cross-cultural competence. In a course designed to acquaint students from a wide range of disciplines with early intervention for young children with disabilities and their families, students keep a journal of issues that arise related to the diversity that they find in practice. Because the journals pinpoint those areas that are most troublesome for students, as well as the insights that they are gaining, it is possible to tailor instruction to meet individual and collective needs.

Journals provide a communication link between students and professors that is safe (ungraded, nonjudgmental feedback). They provide a vehicle for personalizing instruction and getting to know students in ways that are seldom possible in class. By their nature, journals require thought, reflection, and writing—all goals that are a part of most university classes.

CONCLUSION

Instruction that supports diversity is instruction that is effective for *all* students. It is not instruction that is less rigorous or watered down. It is not instruction that can only be used in one academic area and not in another, nor is it instruction that requires more time than any faculty member has to give. It is simply an attitude that is inclusive, a repertoire that is broad, and a commitment to infusing pluralism into all aspects of teaching and learning. It is intellectually challenging, personally rewarding, and academically sound.

CHAPTER 5

Assessment of Student Learning

Rena B. Lewis, Ph.D.

Professor of Special Education, San Diego State University
Faculty member, San Diego State University–Claremont
Graduate School Doctoral Program

Editor's Notes:

Rena Lewis's chapter examines specifically the assessment component of the multicultural course change model presented in Chapter 2. She begins by engaging readers in one of the assessment strategies she recommends. The author maintains our engagement throughout the chapter with her highly accessible wisdom communicated through personal examples and activities. After taking us through an analysis of our current assessment practices, she offers two approaches to achieving more equitable evaluation of student progress in a course. The first approach is to modify traditional assessment tools. The second involves employing alternative strategies because "no course can be considered multiculturally infused if it utilizes only traditional assessment procedures." Lewis' suggestions focus on the multicultural goal of improving diverse students' learning through assessment strategies sensitive to a range of learning needs. However, as she also emphasizes, moving assessment from exclusive to inclusive to transformed supports the knowledge acquisition of *all* students. ■

In college courses, the process of assessing student learning does not begin on the day of the first exam. It begins far earlier: when the course is first conceptualized, when course goals are identified, and when the course syllabus is prepared. At these stages, the professor determines the content of the course, the instructional strategies that will be used to teach that content, and the types of activities in which students will participate to demonstrate what they have learned.

In this chapter, *assessment* is defined as the process of gathering information about student performance in order to evaluate progress toward mastery of course goals. This process involves a series of steps including specification of desired student outcomes, selection of an assessment strategy, design of the assessment task, data collection, and evaluation of student performance.

In recent years, leaders in the higher education community have begun to focus increased attention on the ways in which student achievement is assessed in an attempt to improve the evaluation process (Banta, 1992; Ewell, 1991). One major strategy has been the development of new types of assessment tools as supplements to or replacements for traditional measures. Before reading further in this chapter, please experiment with one of these tools, the concept map. Take a blank sheet of paper and write the words "classroom assessment" in the middle. Draw a circle around those words, then jot down other concepts that come to mind when you think about classroom assessment. Draw lines to join related concepts together as needed. For example, if I were drawing a concept map of "desserts," I might begin with subordinate concepts such as "sweets" and "fruit," then develop each of those (e.g., the concept "sweets" might be linked with "cakes," "pies," "cookies," and so on). Your map for "desserts" might look quite different, however. Concept maps are used for several purposes, including gathering pretest data on learners' knowledge of and attitudes toward a subject prior to instruction. For example, in a women's studies course, students were asked to prepare a concept map of "feminism" on the first day of class; the instructor then used the results as a basis for class discussions and to structure lectures and other classroom activities (Angelo & Cross, 1993).

In developing your concept map on "classroom assessment," you likely included one or more of the most typical tasks used to assess student learning: exams, written assignments, and projects. Some college courses, particularly those with large numbers of students, require only exams (for instance, a midterm and a final). Others combine exams with a project such as a term paper. In others, frequent quizzes replace exams and students complete several written assignments in lieu of a major term project.

However, traditional assessment tools are not always the best choice for nontraditional students. Included in this group are students from diverse cultural and linguistic backgrounds, women (particularly in majors where women are traditionally underrepresented), and students with disabilities. Traditional assessments present three barriers to the optimal performance of students such as these. First, there may be a mismatch between the content knowledge that students bring to the class and the knowledge required to successfully participate in assessment activities. For example, one woman student nearly failed a midterm exam in a statistics and probability class, not because of her lack of knowledge of the course content but because many of the test questions asked students to compute the probability of different types of poker hands, a game with which she was not familiar. Second, there may be a mismatch between students' skills and the skills required to demonstrate learning on traditional assessment tools. For example, a multiple-choice exam written in dense, cryptic English may not fairly assess how much a student from Cambodia knows about the United States Constitution. Likewise, an in-class writing exercise may unjustly penalize the student with a physical disability who writes well, but slowly.

Third, there may be a mismatch between the values held by students and those inherent in the assessment activity. For example, in one of my earliest teaching experiences, I tried to motivate Native American students from the Navajo Nation to excel on the first exam of the course by promising public recognition of all who earned A's. One of my students kindly took me aside and explained that in his value system the achievement of the group is prized over the achievement of an individual.

It is critical to note that *all* students, not only those from nontraditional backgrounds, may benefit from efforts to rethink our classroom assessment procedures. Students in every group, including White middle-class males, exhibit a range of individual differences in how they best demonstrate what they know.

There are two major approaches to overcoming barriers that assessment procedures may place on students' abilities to demonstrate what they have learned. In the first, traditional assessment tools are modified to make them more equitable for nontraditional students (and more accessible to all students). In the second, alternative strategies for assessment are used instead of, or in addition to, traditional methods. This chapter will discuss both approaches. The chapter begins by exploring the factors to consider when selecting or designing assessment tools. The next sections provide a strategy for analyzing and then modifying assessment practices. The final section presents alternative methods of assessment and principles for their incorporation into a course curriculum.

The suggestions offered in this chapter are based upon a set of assumptions regarding the assessment of student learning. These assumptions serve as the guiding principles for the design of appropriate assessment procedures for all students.

- *The tasks selected for assessment must be directly related to course goals.* This is a validity issue. If one course goal is that students will be able to deliver a 5-minute extemporaneous speech, a written exam on extemporaneous speaking is not a valid measure (McLoughlin & Lewis, 1994).

- *Assessment tasks should reflect the most important course outcomes.* What the task reflects is also a validity issue. It is usually not possible to assess all of the outcomes that a course is designed to bring about. When choices are made, priority should be given to major topics, not minutia. Also, the topics selected should be a representative sample of the entire domain under assessment, not just one or two aspects of it. If a course covers

the history of the United States from the colonial period to modern times, half of the final exam should not be devoted to questions on the Civil War.

- *Assessment techniques should be designed to bring out the best performance of students.* Implementing this principle requires that the professor consider student strengths when making decisions about assessment strategies. Although this consideration is important for all students, it becomes essential when attempting to promote the academic success of students from nontraditional groups.

- *Assessment strategies must not only be effective, they must be efficient.* Holding 30-minute conferences with each student at the end of the term may be an effective way to gauge learning. It is not efficient when there are 200 students—and only one instructor—in the class.

FACTORS TO CONSIDER IN ASSESSMENT

When professors sit at their desks, pen or keyboard in hand, and draft a course syllabus and course requirements, they are making several decisions about assessment. These decisions may be made on the basis of history and tradition, that is, the professor's own experiences as a student and member of an academic discipline ("in my field, we only use essay exams") and/or on the basis of past teaching experiences ("This is how I've always done it and it works"). Or professors may decide to try a new technique that they have read about in the literature or heard discussed by colleagues. In many cases, however, decisions are made without conscious consideration of the factors that make up the assessment process. Those factors become important when thinking about ways to improve assessment practices, and it is useful to have a model that describes them. These factors include (1) the characteristics of the assessment task, (2) how tasks are weighted, (3) the scheduling of assessments, and (4) procedures for grading and feedback to students.

The Assessment Task

Exams, term papers, oral reports, tests, abstracts, essays, reaction papers, debates, critiques, quizzes—these are but a sampling of the different types of assessment strategies that professors use to obtain information about student learning. Each strategy also represents a range of options; exams, for example, can be objective or essay, in-class or take-home, open or closed book, performance or paper-and-pencil, and so on. One way to sort through the options when selecting or designing a specific assessment task for a particular course is through analysis of the dimensions that characterize all assessment tasks.

Task Level

The level of an assessment task refers to the type(s) of cognitive demands it places upon students. Asking students to name the current head of state in country X clearly imposes different demands than asking them to discuss the forces that led to that leader's rise to power. One way to conceptualize task level is through the *Taxonomy of Educational Objectives* proposed by Bloom and his colleagues. In the cognitive domain (Bloom, 1956), this schema classifies course goals into six hierarchical levels:

- *Knowledge,* or the recall of information
- *Comprehension,* or the understanding and interpretation of information
- *Application,* or the use of information
- *Analysis,* or the breakdown of information into its component parts

- *Synthesis,* or the production of new information
- *Evaluation,* or judging the value of something in relation to a specific purpose

Although this schema does not apply equally well to all disciplines and all courses, it provides a basis for thinking about task level and the cognitive demands that different types of course goals impose.

Consider, for example, two assessment tasks that might be used in a beginning level foreign language class. One goal of the course is that students will learn basic vocabulary. This is a knowledge goal (as defined above) that could be assessed with a paper-and-pencil test. A second goal is that students will be able to use their new knowledge of the language in authentic communication situations. This is an application goal. To assess it, the instructor might require students to interview a native speaker, then present an oral report of that interview to the class.

Input Mode

This dimension is concerned with the types of inputs students receive prior to the assessment task. The most obvious type is the set of instructional activities that make up the course: lectures, text, and other required readings, demonstrations, discussions, and laboratory work. In some cases, course activities are supplemented with additional experiences that form part of the assessment task; the interview of the native speaker, discussed below, is an example.

The directions for the assessment task itself are another type of input. Directions may be as brief as one sentence written at the top of a test ("Read each question carefully; answer all questions"). If the assessment task is a writing assignment such as a term paper, the professor may supplement written instructions with a thorough discussion of the parameters of the assignment and grading criteria.

The knowledge, skills, and experiences that students bring with them to a course represent a third type of input. Often called "prior knowledge," this input is the foundation upon which students build their competence in specific course content. Professors base their expectations for student performance upon assumptions about prior knowledge ("Of course sophomores know how to use the library"); these assumptions form part of the hidden curriculum. For example, in most college classes, professors assume that students can read the textbook and other required readings with understanding, that they are able to take notes from lectures, and that they know how to study for and take exams.

Response Mode

Response mode is the medium students use to express their ideas when completing an assessment task. The most typical response modes in college courses are writing and speaking. Students write exams, reports, projects, and papers; they present oral reports and participate in class discussions and debates. Courses related to the arts may require other response modes: singing, playing an instrument, designing a stage set, drawing, painting, sculpting, and so on. Each response mode can be further described in terms of the type of product required. For example, in writing, the response may be as simple as writing one letter to answer a multiple-choice test question or as complex as writing an original poem, short story, or play.

Use of Aids

Aids are supplements that assist students as they respond to assessment tasks. For instance, students might be allowed to use a calculator on a math exam, a print, or electronic dictionary when writing an essay exam. In an "open book" exam, students have access to their textbook(s) and sometimes class notes and handouts. Likewise, some professors encourage (or require) students to take advantage of aids as they complete written assignments. For example, when writing a term paper, students might take part in a library tour, attend a term-paper clinic, use a word processor with a spelling and grammar checker, review a model paper from a previous semester, and confer with the course instructor or a teaching assistant.

Language Requirements

Assessment tasks differ in the types of language demands they impose on students. In college classes, however, tasks are typically language-intensive, requiring high levels of skill in reading and writing. When written language skills are de-emphasized, oral language skills often take their place. For some students, the difficulty level of the assessment task is directly related to the degree of language proficiency required. This rule holds true no matter what the subject matter of the course. Reading a chemistry textbook, giving an oral report in a marketing class, and writing an essay in a comparative literature course are all language-based activities.

Speed and Quantity Requirements

Speed and quantity requirements are concerned with how much work the assessment task entails and how quickly that work must be accomplished. These two variables can sometimes interact. A 25-item short-answer quiz does not appear lengthy if students have the entire 50-minute class period to complete it. However, the magnitude of the task seems to increase when the time period for the quiz is shortened to 5 minutes.

Participants

In many college-level assessment tasks, students work as individuals. Each student completes his or her exam; each student writes his or her own paper. In some situations, it is also possible for students to work in pairs or in small groups or teams. Group assignments can be structured in two ways: all of the members of the group can collaborate on all aspects of the task, or each student can take responsibility for a separate portion of the work. Another option is for students to first complete their work individually, then act as peer reviewers or editors for each other.

Location

Students can complete assessment tasks in class or at some other location. Although in-class exams are most common, some professors also use take-home exams. Other possible locations are university facilities (e.g., library or computer lab assignments) and community venues. For example, students might visit an art museum or see a play, observe a city council meeting, or complete a practicum in a business or public school setting.

Weighting

Another important factor to consider is the weighting of assessment tasks in relation to students' final course grades. Most professors use some type of system that assigns differential weights to various tests and assignments. Class quizzes might be worth 20 percent of the final grade, a library research paper 20 percent, the midterm exam 25 percent, the final 30 percent, and class participation 5 percent. In a class where the grade is based on three exams, each might make up 33 percent of the total grade; or, the first test might count for 20% and the other two for 40 percent each. The

advantage to the latter arrangement is that students can use the first test to become familiar with the professor's style. In some courses, there is only one assessment task: a senior paper, a thesis, or some other type of major project. In cases like these, students can be graded as they complete portions of the task; typically, however, the final product accounts for a major part of the grade.

Scheduling

Scheduling is concerned with the frequency of assessment tasks and their timing during the semester or quarter. If quizzes are one of the methods used to evaluate student performance, they could be given every class session, every week, every month, or at varying intervals throughout the term (as is often the case with "pop" quizzes). Many professors structure their courses so that they are able to monitor student progress several times, including at least one assessment task early in the semester. When university calendars permit, the first test or assignment can be scheduled so that it can be returned to students before the official course drop date. Early assessment provides useful feedback both to the students and to the professor; because the course has just begun, there still is time to make changes. Scheduling assessment tasks at spaced intervals throughout the semester also has advantages. Students receive periodic feedback, and the bulk of their grade does not rest on tasks to be completed in a flurry of activity in the last weeks of the term. Professors also avoid some of the stress associated with the end-of-the-term grading crunch.

Grading

There are several variables related to the process of assigning grades to student tests and assignments. First of all are the criteria used to judge student performance. Criteria can be objective, subjective, or somewhere in between. The answer key for a multiple-choice exam is an objective standard; a checklist or rating scale used to evaluate a written assignment is more subjective. In some courses, grading criteria are explicit; at the start of the course or as each new task is assigned, students are informed about the standards that will be used to evaluate their performance.

A second variable is who does the grading. In most instances, the grader is either the professor in charge of the course or a teaching assistant (although, with some assessment tasks, it is possible for students to participate by completing self-evaluations). When the professor delegates grading responsibilities to someone else, she or he must also communicate the grading criteria and, if necessary, train the assistant.

Third, once the grader has marked the errors on a test or made comments on a written assignment, a final grade must be assigned. Some professors use an absolute grading system. If there are 10 items on a quiz and the student misses 3, his or her grade is 7 or 70 percent. Others prefer to grade on a curve. In this system, students whose scores fall in the middle range of the class receive a C, those in the next highest range receive a B, those with the highest scores receive an A, and so on. The ranges associated with the various letter grades can be set statistically (e.g., those falling within one standard deviation of the class mean earn a C) or by "eyeballing" the data. The advantage to the use of curves is that some students will receive A's, even if the highest grade in the class is 65 percent. The disadvantages are that students compete against each other (rather than striving to meet course goals) and that minor variations in performance (e.g., 34 versus 37 points out of a possible 60) can result in different grades (C versus B).

A fourth consideration are the consequences for poor performance. Some professors offer students strategies for remedying poor grades; others do not. One strategy is a "forgiveness" policy; for example, the lowest quiz grade is dropped or the lowest test score is raised one letter grade. Or, students may be allowed to take a make-up test or complete an alternative assignment to offset a failing grade. The grades of the two attempts can be averaged, or the second grade can replace the first. Extra credit work is another option. In this system, students take on an extra project or assignment to raise their overall class average or as a hedge against a future low grade.

Feedback to Students

The assessment process is not complete until students have received feedback about their performance. Knowledge of results is one type of feedback, and it can be as simple as a grade on a test. Informing students about which test items they missed, their overall score, and their standing in relation to others in the class helps them evaluate their progress. Such information may or may not assist them to learn the material they missed or to do better the next time. Improvement is more likely to occur if corrective (or informative) feedback is given. This type of feedback includes information on the types of errors students have made and provides direction for rectifying those errors. For instance, if a student knows that his or her essay on the abortion debate received a grade of C– because its organization was difficult to follow and it failed to address both sides of the issue, he or she can use that feedback to begin to improve his or her writing skills.

When feedback occurs is another important concern, and a distinction from the field of evaluation (Worthen & Sanders, 1987) is useful here. In summative evaluation, the purpose is to judge the quality of an undertaking *after* it has been completed. In formative evaluation, data are gathered *during* the undertaking in order to improve it. In assessment, tests and exams are typically summative strategies. Providing students with feedback on a draft of a term paper would be a formative strategy.

A final issue is the timeliness of feedback. For feedback to have an impact on student learning, it must be received in time for students to act upon it. Returning the midterm three weeks before the final gives students little chance to revamp their study regimen.

THE FIRST STEP TOWARD INFUSION: ANALYZING CURRENT ASSESSMENT PRACTICES

The first step in improving assessment for students from diverse groups is analysis of current practices. The factors described in the previous paragraphs provide a schema for analyzing current practices. As Table 5–1 illustrates, assessment strategies can be described in terms of the course goals they address, the assessment tasks themselves, and other dimensions such as weighting, scheduling, grading, and feedback. Analyzed here are the two strategies mentioned earlier for measuring student progress in a beginning-level foreign language class.

As can be seen from this analysis, the two assessment strategies differ on several dimensions. Among the most salient differences are the types of goals they address (knowledge versus application), their language demands (written versus oral), their frequency of occurrence (weekly versus once per semester), and the grading criteria employed (objective versus more subjective). For professors interested in analyzing their own current assessment strategies, a blank analysis worksheet is provided in Appendix A of this chapter.

MODIFYING TRADITIONAL ASSESSMENT PRACTICES

There are a number of relatively minor changes that professors can make in their courses so that their assessment practices are more responsive to the needs of all students, but especially those from culturally diverse groups and other nontraditional students. Four types of changes are discussed in the sections that follow. The first and the last deal with issues of classroom climate and the hidden curriculum: instructor expectations and grading practices. In the middle are suggestions for modifying the two assessment tools most commonly used in college courses, exams, and papers.

Checking Assumptions

When planning a course, professors make assumptions about the skills, knowledge, and attitudes that students will bring with them into the classroom. These assumptions, warranted or not, then translate into expectations for student performance. Dissonance occurs when these expectations are not met. One way to prevent this disjuncture is to gather information early in the term about students' past experiences and current skill levels. There are several ways to go about the task of checking one's assumptions, as the following suggestions illustrate.

1. *Determine whether students have completed prerequisite coursework and other relevant university requirements.* There are many reasons why a student might enroll in a class for which he or she has not met the prerequisites. Some, not convinced of the necessity for prerequisites, treat university regulations quite casually. Others have received poor advising and are not aware of the requirements. Still others select classes that fit into their schedule of work hours, childcare, and/or family commitments.

TABLE 5–1 Analysis of Assessment Strategies

	Task 1	Task 2
Instructional Goal	acquire basic vocabulary in language X	use basic vocabulary in authentic communication situations
Assessment Task	paper-and-pencil quiz	interview native speaker, give oral report on interview
• level	knowledge	application
• input mode	vocabulary lists in each text-book chapter; English words on the quiz	all course activities; class hand-out with suggested interview topics; interview native speaker in language X
• response mode	write language X equivalent for each English word or phrase	give oral report in language X
• aids	none	class notes, text, handouts, dictionary to prepare interview; note cards for report
• language requirements	reading and writing; spelling counts	listening and speaking; in the oral report, students are graded on intelligibility, fluency, word choice, and overall communicative competence
• speed & quantity requirements	15-minute quiz with 20 to 30 items	10-minute interview; 5-minute oral report
• participants	students work alone	students work alone
• location	in class	interview takes place on campus or in the community, oral report in class
Weight	quizzes are 30% of course grade	10% of course grade
Scheduling	every Friday (class meets 3 days a week)	assignment given at midterm; oral reports take place in the last two weeks of the semester
Grading	percentage correct	professor completes rating sheet during report
Feedback	items marked if incorrect; quizzes returned the next class period	rating sheets given to students on the day of the final

Thus, at the start of each class, it is wise to review the required prerequisites with students and explain the rationale behind them and their importance. If deemed necessary, students can be asked to furnish verification of successful completion of prerequisites. As Chapter 4 mentioned, it is also possible to administer a pretest to directly assess mastery of prerequisite skills. Pretests can be structured like traditional course exams with objective and essay questions or, as discussed earlier in this chapter, the instructor may want to experiment with techniques such as concept maps.

2. *Check students' reading and writing skills.* Students' ability to read and understand the class textbook and other required readings can be assessed quite easily with a technique called the cloze procedure (Bormuth, 1968; Jongsma, 1971). This method evaluates silent reading skills. The professor chooses a 250-word passage, leaves the first and last sentences intact, and replaces every fifth word in the rest of the selection with a blank. Students read the passage and write in the missing words (or suitable substitutions). The material is at an appropriate reading level when students are able to predict 50 percent or more of the missing words.

The professor can gain general information about writing skills by asking students to spend 10 or 15 minutes writing a brief essay. An in-class writing sample is preferred because it controls the time variable and the use of aids such as computers with spelling checkers. Having students write a short autobiography or explain their reasons for taking the course also helps the instructor become better acquainted with the students and their experiential backgrounds.

3. *Find out about students' study skills.* Notetaking is one study skill that almost all professors take for granted. As the professor lectures, he or she assumes that students are listening (and comprehending), identifying the major points and important details, and taking careful notes. To assess the accuracy of this assumption, ask students to turn in their class notes at the end of a lecture. Results are always interesting (and often surprising). They also provide almost as much information on the instructor's lecturing style as they do on students' notetaking skills. Angelo and Cross (1993) suggest two other strategies that provide useful information about students' comprehension of lectures and other classroom activities. In the Minute Paper, students write brief answers to two questions at the end of a class session: "What was the most important thing you learned during this class?" and "What important questions remain unanswered?" (p. 148). In a similar activity, Muddiest Point, students describe the portion of the class activity that remains most unclear to them.

Other study skills of interest are strategies for reading and taking notes from the textbook, techniques for preparing for exams, test-taking strategies, amount of time devoted to course activities, and knowledge and use of campus resources such as the library. These skills are best assessed via a student questionnaire. To increase the likelihood of honest answers, questionnaires should be turned in anonymously. With their names on the paper, students might be tempted to exaggerate a bit when asked, "Not counting class time, how many hours do you spend per week on this course?"

4. *Maintain high expectations for all students.* The information gathered about students' skills and knowledge before the course begins is used to modify and improve instruction and to link students with appropriate campus-based resources and support services (Richardson, 1989). Although the professor may need to rethink some of his or her assumptions, this rethinking should not result in lowered expectations. If students lack prerequisite coursework, the solution is enrollment in another class, not lowering standards. If students need to improve their reading skills, they should be advised about options such as peer tutors and study groups, not excused from course reading assignments. As the literature on education and students from diverse groups clearly indicates (e.g., Banks, 1993; Rodriguez, 1991), high expectations play a powerful role in fostering academic success.

Exams

Tests, quizzes, and exams are an accepted part of college coursework. These traditional assessment tools are an efficient method of gathering information about student performance, although they may not be the most effective way, particularly for students for diverse groups. To reduce the barriers that tests present to some students, the measures themselves can be modified and changes can be made in the testing process.

1. *Prepare students for testing.* Test preparation involves informing students about the characteristics of the test they will take and reminding them of (or introducing them to) effective test-taking strategies. Professors can share information about:

- the content that the test will cover (e.g., what chapters or readings are included, a list of the most important terms and concepts, etc.)
- the types and numbers of questions on the test (e.g., 50 multiple-choice items, two essays)
- the weight of each part of the test
- grading procedures (e.g., if partial credit is possible)
- any necessary materials or equipment (e.g., calculator, dictionary, special answer sheet, number 2 pencil)
- strategies for taking the test (e.g., read each item carefully, budget your time, leave difficult items till last, spend the most time on the parts of the test that count the most, and so on)

2. *Create a classroom climate that reduces test anxiety* (Ramsden, 1992). Preparing students for testing is one way to reduce test anxiety; explaining what will occur on test day helps to demystify the assessment process. The general classroom climate is another important contributor. Test anxiety is much less of an issue in classrooms where students feel valued and supported.

3. *Monitor the linguistic complexity of test items.* Test items that are difficult to read pose real problems for some students, particularly those who speak English as a second language. Students are likely to have trouble with sentences that contain double negatives. Long sentences, particularly those with parenthetical remarks (whether those remarks are placed within the confines of parentheses or not), tend to be more difficult to read than shorter sentences. It is also important to point out that abstruse vocabulary and complex sentence structures can have an egregious impact on difficulty level as can sentences which are written in the passive voice. Tests should assess course content, not reading skills. So, avoid double negatives. Write short sentences. Monitor vocabulary level. Use the active voice.

4. *Use performance data to evaluate and revise test items.* After tests are administered and graded, the professor should review and evaluate how students performed on individual test items. When tests are scored by computer, two statistics are typically available for each item: item difficulty and discrimination index. Difficulty level is the percentage of students who pass the item. Brown (1981) recommends a difficulty level of 0.60 to 0.75 (i.e., 60% to 75% of the students respond correctly). When more than half of the students miss an item, it is useful to analyze their responses to determine if a pattern exists. Some professors have a policy of throwing out test items that a majority of the class misses.

The discrimination index compares how well high-scoring students do on an individual test item compared to low-scoring students. The class is divided into two groups, those with total test scores in the upper half and those whose scores fall in the lower half, and the percentage of students who answer each item correctly is computed separately for each group. The discrimination index is determined by subtracting the percentage of lower-half students from the percentage of upper-half students. The index can be positive or negative. For instance, if one-fourth of the higher-scoring students and two-thirds of the lower-scoring students are successful on a particular item, its discrimination index is negative ($0.25 - 0.67 = -0.42$). Gay (1985) suggests that items show adequate discrimination when the index is +0.30 or greater.

Similar analysis techniques can be used when tests are scored by hand. At minimum, professors should look for questions that posed significant challenges for large numbers of students. High error rates can be caused by unclear directions, ambiguous wording, or even an incorrect answer key.

5. *Consider using a variety of testing options.* This strategy requires the professor to re-think his or her current practices and consider alternative methods of testing. Possibilities include:

- *Give power tests instead of speed tests* (Boone, Kaiser, & Litowitz, 1988). Is speed an important component of the knowledge or skills the test is designed to measure? If not, reduce the number of test items, increase the time allowed for the test, and/or consider giving take-home rather than in-class tests.

- *De-emphasize rote memory.* Is rote memory the cognitive skill under assessment, or is it a higher level skill such as problem-solving? If memory is not the major concern, consider options such as open-book and take-home exams.

- *Vary the types of test questions.* There are a number of choices for objective-type questions: true-false, multiple-choice, matching, completion (fill-in-the-blank), short answer, and problems

(McLoughlin & Lewis, 1994). Essay questions are another option. Ramsden (1992) advocates less use of objective items and more emphasis on essays and other types of questions that require students to demonstrate their understanding of the course material.

- *Allow the use of aids.* If spelling skills are not the target of assessment, let students use dictionaries. Likewise, if computational skills are not being evaluated, students should be permitted to use calculators.

- *Replace two or three big tests with several smaller ones.* Students are under less pressure when assessment occurs frequently. They also have more opportunity to benefit from the feedback from one test to prepare for the next.

- *Provide ways for students to recover from one bad grade.* Among the possibilities are "forgiving" the lowest grade, giving make-up tests, and accepting additional work for extra credit.

6. *Be prepared to work with students with disabilities on accommodations for testing.* Students with learning disabilities often request extra time for exams (most typically time and a half). Students who are blind will need a braille copy of the test or a reader to read the test aloud to them. Other common testing adaptations are use of a dictionary, electronic spelling aid, or word processor; a scribe to record the student's oral responses on the test form or answer sheet; and test administration in a quiet environment free from distractions.

Papers

Like exams, term papers and other types of written assignments are a common feature of university coursework. Papers draw upon a different set of student skills from those required by exams, and so the strategies used to adapt them are somewhat different. However, the first consideration in either case is preparation of the student.

1. *Communicate expectations clearly.* The professor should explain the task and the procedures for accomplishing it. If the assignment is a research paper, for instance, it is helpful to review the various steps in the process (selecting a topic, searching the literature, reading and notetaking, etc.) and to suggest timelines for each step. Length, style, and formatting requirements should be discussed as well as the criteria for grading the final product. If a rating sheet, checklist, or feedback form will be used in grading, give students a copy when the paper is assigned. Students are more likely to spend their time wisely if they know that the summary and conclusions section of the paper is worth 25 points whereas the introduction and problem section is worth only 7. Also helpful are model papers from previous semesters.

2. *Encourage the use of aids and resources.* Students should be encouraged to use dictionaries, thesauruses, word processors with spelling and grammar checkers, and other pertinent aids as they write their paper. In addition, they should be made aware of campus resources where they can obtain these aids and other types of assistance. Students may not be familiar with campus services such as a word processing lab, computer literature searches, reference librarians, interlibrary loan, or term-paper clinics run by the academic skills center.

3. *Consider making peer editing part of the assignment* (Harrison, 1992). Peer editors read and critique each other's work. Typically, the professor structures the editing process by providing students with a list of areas to consider or questions to answer in their review. For instance, peer editors should provide feedback not only on the weaknesses of a paper but also its strengths.

Peer reviews are usually written rather than oral and, in some classes, they are graded as part of the assignment.

4. *Break large writing tasks into smaller chunks.* Big assignments such as term papers can be broken down into a series of smaller tasks. For example, students could turn in a one-paragraph description of their topic in week 3 of the semester, their note cards in week 6, an outline of the paper in week 9, and a rough draft in week 12. These intermediate tasks may be graded or simply critiqued. In either case, students benefit because they receive feedback on their work-in-progress.

5. *In grading, separate form and content issues.* Instructors are influenced by the appearance of a paper (Good & Brophy, 1987) and by any errors it contains in spelling, grammar, punctuation, and the like. One way to counteract this bias is to grade the content of a paper and its form separately. For instance, if content is the major concern, it can be weighted so that it accounts for 90 percent of the grade and form is the remaining 10 percent.

Grading Practices

Although grading has been mentioned in relation to modifications for exams and papers, there are some general considerations that apply to any type of assessment task. Each relates to classroom climate and the messages professors send to students as they evaluate their work.

1. *Be aware of the impact of your written and verbal comments.* Imagine spending over a month writing a paper, then getting it back bloodied with red ink and without a single positive comment. This experience is all too common in college classrooms. It takes only a few seconds more to add a few words of encouragement when grading a paper. And it is just as easy to grade a test with green or purple ink, colors less associated with failure. Similar caveats apply to verbal feedback. Words, whether spoken or written, have the power to wound or to spur students on to greater achievements.

2. *Do not encourage competition among students.* Competition is not equally valued by all cultures. As Chapter 4 pointed out, some cultures and many women prefer cooperative interactions to competitive ones (Lynch & Hanson, 1992). Professors can inject a competitive spirit into grading in big ways and in small ones. Grading on a curve is a major endorsement of competition. Contrasting the performance of different groups (the men in the class versus the women, the English majors versus the Education majors) when discussing results of a test or assignment is more subtle, yet equally distasteful to some groups.

3. *Be cautious about singling out students for individual recognition.* No one likes to be singled out for criticism. In some cultures, individuals are equally uncomfortable being singled out for praise.[1] Thus, it is best to confine laudatory remarks to written comments or private conversations, at least until students' preferences on this issue can be determined. One simple way of discovering students' wishes is to distribute a brief questionnaire at the start of the semester or quarter. That questionnaire might ask students to comment on their preferences for feedback and recognition and to share their views on other topics such as the types of instructional activities to be used in the class and the scheduling of office hours for the instructor and any teaching assistants.

ALTERNATIVE ASSESSMENT PRACTICES

No course can be considered multiculturally infused if it utilizes only traditional assessment procedures. As professors move their courses along the course-change continuum described in Chapter 2—from exclusive to inclusive to transformed—they must begin to develop new ways of thinking about the assessment process. This final section of the chapter provides an introduction to some of those new perspectives.

Support Student Learning with Peer, Campus, and Community Resources

One professor, by himself or herself, cannot hope to meet the needs of every member of every class. This caution does not mean, however, that those needs cannot be addressed. To successfully accommodate students' needs, two things must occur: an expansion of the concept of "classroom" to include places outside the classroom walls, and a broadening of the concept of "teacher" to include persons other than the professor.

There are many campus and community resources that can assist nontraditional students to succeed in higher education. Several have already been mentioned earlier in this chapter and in previous chapters. Richardson (1989), in a report of successful strategies for increasing the scholastic success of students of color, identifies a range of effective campus-based services related to the academic program:

- Tutoring is widely available to students who need it.
- Assistance with reading, writing and math skills is available on a walk-in basis.
- Instruction in study skills, note-taking and test preparation is provided to all students as needed.
- Students who follow nontraditional patterns of attendance have access to an educational service center that provides counseling, developmental coursework, tutoring, critical reading and library research skills, time management and study skills. (p. 12)

Another source of assistance—one that is often overlooked—is the student members of the class. Students can help each other in a variety of ways: as tutors, academic advisors, mentors, editors, consultants, and sources of encouragement and support. Rodriguez (1991) describes a program at Berkeley where African American students were brought together in study groups. The program was started because Uri Treisman, its founder, noticed that "Black students [who were failing] studied alone, even if for many long hours, while Asian students, who were passing, studied in groups. Through study groups Asian students tutored, criticized and supported each other" (p. 7). (Chapter 8 describes an adaptation of Treisman's model for Latino, Black, and other underrepresented students in freshman calculus.)

Cooperative learning is another strategy that involves peers as teachers. Students work collaboratively in groups on common tasks or to solve common problems (see Chapter 7 for a detailed discussion). Cooperative learning can extend into assessment. A colleague of mine teaches a doctoral level statistics course in which students work in cooperative groups throughout the semester. On the nights of the midterm and final, the students meet as groups to discuss the test questions before each writes his or her individual answers (Santa Cruz, 1993).

Contextualize Learning and Its Assessment

In many cultures, knowledge is considered worth learning only when it is perceived as relevant to real-world issues and the solution of real-world problems. In addition, in many cultures, children are reared to value interactions with people above interactions with things.[2] These value systems carry with them three important implications. First,

learning (and its assessment) should be contextualized so that students perceive it as both relevant and important. When studying learning in a basic psychology course, for example, students might be asked to provide examples of how they have applied course content in their own studying (Angelo & Cross, 1993). Second, whenever possible, learning and its assessment should include opportunities for social interaction. Cooperative learning strategies provide these opportunities as do course assignments in which students interact with others outside the classroom walls. For example, students in a political science course might participate in a local election; students in a history course might interview community members about their recollections of and participation in the civil rights movement. Third, learning and its assessment are tied to real-world issues, and students are encouraged to use critical thinking skills to apply course content to the solution of real-world problems. For instance, as a culminating activity for a course on child development, students might be asked to draft a set of recommendations to improve the well-being of children in their community, state, or the nation as a whole.

Use Multiple Evaluation Techniques

Contemporary theories of intelligence recognize that ability is not a unidimensional trait. Gardner (1987), for example, describes seven types of intelligence: linguistic, logical-mathematical, spatial, musical, bodily kinesthetic, interpersonal, and intrapersonal. In Sternberg's triarchic theory (Sternberg, 1984; Sternberg, Okagaki, & Jackson, 1990), intelligence is contextualized. It includes not only an individual's mental mechanisms for processing information but also the tasks and situations in which that processing occurs and the sociocultural context in which the individual lives.

Theories such as these call attention to the multidimensional nature of human ability. Strengthening this position is the information available on the ways in which some women, individuals with disabilities, and persons of color prefer to engage in cognitive tasks. For example, as earlier chapters have described, some groups prefer holistic approaches to problem solving rather than analytic approaches.[3]

Student achievement can be enhanced by providing multiple ways for students to demonstrate their mastery of course competencies. There are many ways to vary the assessment process, and the model described in the first part of this chapter outlines a number of dimensions to consider. For example, the most typical input modes for assessment tasks, reading the textbook and listening to lectures, are routinely altered for students with disabilities (Lewis, 1993). Those who cannot read because of a vision loss or a learning disability listen to Talking Books or books on tape. Those who cannot hear watch an interpreter as he or she translates the lecture into sign language. Similar types of alternatives can be made available to all students. Among the possibilities are reading related fiction as a supplement to the textbook, watching a movie or video (with captions, if the class includes students with hearing losses or those for whom English is a second language), conducting an interview or observation, and participating in a community service activity.

The response modes for assessment tasks can also be altered. For example, a traditional term paper assignment might be replaced with a reading log or a series of abstracts annotated with students' personal reactions. A traditional exam might be replaced with a concept map exercise where students must fit several key concepts into a map prepared by the instructor (Seymour, 1993). In addition, writing can be replaced

by other response modalities such as speaking, artistic expression, music, or performance art. Many years ago, when I was struggling to teach undergraduate students about learning disabilities, I asked them to develop a personal definition of this condition using any medium they wished. The "papers" I remember best are a poem, an original piano composition, and a macramé wall hanging.

Performance-based assessments allow students to demonstrate in some concrete way their mastery of course material. For example, in mathematics, a student might be asked to solve a complex problem and explain the process used to arrive at the solution. In education, a student might videotape a lesson he or she has taught to document competence in instructional techniques. Banta (1992) provides several other examples including an in-basket activity where students in dietetics must respond to mail received by a hospital dietitian and an activity for theater majors which requires them to view a videotape of a portion of a play and, depending on their specialization, critique the acting, directing, or set design.

Portfolio assessment is a technique that can incorporate a range of response modes (Abruscato, 1993; Feuer & Fulton, 1993; Grady, 1992; Wolf, 1991; Worthen, 1993). Portfolios contain samples of student work collected over time (e.g., over the duration of a course or the completion of an academic major) to document progress and record accomplishments. As Banta (1992) comments, portfolios can contain a variety of student products:

> …course assignments, research papers, materials from group projects, artistic productions, self-reflective essays, correspondence, and taped presentations. Student performances can be recorded using audio- or videotapes. Potential materials for the cassette-recorded

portfolio are speeches, musical performances, visual arts productions, foreign language pronunciation, group interaction skills, and demonstrations of laboratory techniques or psychomotor skills. (p. 1688)

Two characteristics make portfolio assessment a good choice for students from diverse groups: students themselves are responsible for selecting the work samples that go into the portfolio (with some initial guidance from the professor), and one of those samples is typically a self-evaluation. When logistically feasible, portfolios should be reviewed as part of a professor-student conference.

Empower Students to Make Choices

It is not enough to incorporate many types of assessment tasks into a course; students also must be able to choose among them. What we as professors see as benign assignments may be perceived as insulting, degrading, or extremely distasteful by some students. A colleague of mine tells a story from her high-school years about being assigned to compete against her best friend in a debate. As Japanese American young women, they were horrified with being forced into competition against one other.

Choice-making is a means of empowerment. Giving students options acknowledges their competence and the value of their preferences. It also helps them begin to assume responsibility for setting their own goals, directing their own learning, and participating in the evaluation of that learning. That beginning is an important part of the true commencement: the start of lifelong learning.

Take out a blank sheet of paper and draw a concept map of "classroom assessment." Compare this map with your original version to evaluate how your thinking has changed. If you would like further information about current trends and issues in classroom assessment, see the work of Banta (1992) and Ewell (1991). For specific suggestions and examples of classroom assessment techniques, consult the handbook prepared by Angelo and Cross (1993).

ENDNOTES

1. Authors such as Cheng (1987), Joe and Malach (1992), Kitano (1973), Pepper (1976), and Walker (1988) report that persons with Asian roots and persons with Native American roots tend to value cooperation rather than competition and achievement of the group rather than achievement of the individual. However, it is extemely important to recognize that descriptions of cultures are by their nature generalizations. Lynch (1992) warns: Culture is only one of the characteristics that determine individuals' and families' attitudes, values, beliefs, and ways of behaving…Assuming that culture-specific information…applies to all individuals from the cultural group is not only inaccurate but also dangerous—it can lead to stereotyping that diminishes rather than enhances cross-cultural competence. When applying culture-specific information to an individual or family, it is wise to proceed with caution. (p. 44)

2. For example, authors such as Franklin (1992), Willis (1992), and Zuniga (1992) suggest that persons with African American roots and persons with Latino roots place high value on the importance of the family, interpersonal interactions, and the solution of real-world problems, particularly those related to social issues such as inequality.

3. Chan (1992), for example, notes that persons identifying with the traditional Asian culture favor "contemplative, circular thinking" whereas those identifying with the dominant Anglo-European culture favor "analytic linear thinking" (p. 251).

TABLE CHAPTER 5, APPENDIX A   Worksheet for Analyzing Assessment Strategies

	Task 1	Task 2	Task 3
Instructional Goal			
Assessment Task			
• level			
• input mode			
• response mode			
• aids			
• language require-ments			
• speed & quantity requirements			
• participants			
• location			
Weight			
Scheduling			
Grading			
Feedback			

CHAPTER 6

Classroom Dynamics: Disclosing the Hidden Curriculum

Terry Jones and Gale S. Auletta Young
Co-directors, Center for the Study of Intercultural Relations
California State University, Hayward

Editor's Notes:
Terry Jones and Gale Young address the fourth component of course change—classroom dynamics—through a discussion of the hidden curriculum. The hidden curriculum refers to unstated but clearly reinforced rules about the knowledge and behaviors valued in the classroom. The authors, both professors, share their experiences with the hidden curriculum from their perspectives as an African American, first-generation college student (Jones) and as a European American woman (Young). These experiences give a personal voice to the negative impact of implicit rules on students of color and women. Their personal voice carries over and infuses the discussion of how we perpetuate the hidden curriculum and how we can promote change.

The authors describe the hidden curriculum as operating to divide culturally conforming from culturally diverse students, as supporting the valuing of traditional knowledge and of White male students, and as enforcing unequal power relationships between instructors and students. They argue that instructors' recognition and open acknowledgment of the implicit rules will enhance equity and support students' learning. Strategies for disclosing the hidden curriculum include monitoring our language, discussing oppressive comments, encouraging student participation, and employing student-centered instructional methods. Examples of the strategies illustrate their use in practical settings.

Jones and Young address electronic technologies as a new aspect of the hidden curriculum that has potential to further divide students or to enhance the learning of all students. They call for concerted efforts to develop the new instructional technologies with specific attention to the needs of culturally and linguistically diverse students. Current trends related to technology and diversity can be combined to produce culturally sensitive, effective instruction provided that considerations for diversity are integrated from the beginning rather than added on at the end. ∎

Normally we project a blended voice in our writing, but the topic of the hidden curriculum hit such a nerve with each of us that we will open this chapter with our individual stories. The first voice is that of Terry Jones, an African American professor of sociology and social services, recounting his first experiences with college and the hidden curriculum. Gale Auletta Young, a European American female communications professor, follows with her reflection on how the hidden curriculum slowed her academic development. When we fall back into the blended voice we will discuss ways in which faculty unknowingly perpetuate the hidden curriculum and its exclusionary practices as well as provide strategies for disclosing and thereby dissolving the hidden curriculum.

TWO EXPERIENCES

Terry Jones

Entering college for the first time in 1960 was for me a brave new world: full of hope and anticipation, yet overflowing with fear and anxiety. These feelings persisted throughout college and kept me focused, on edge, and directed toward the prize of a college degree. In retrospect I wonder if college shouldn't have been more fun. Why did I have to feel constant tension and anxiety?

What fueled such a mixed bag of emotions? For me, an African American male, straight out of what is now called a ghetto (we called where we lived a "neighborhood"), hope sprang from what I thought a college education would mean to my life. The anticipation was the result of the excitement and the challenge of wanting to "get it on." I had recurring dreams about what it would be like to be away from home, living in a dorm, meeting people from faraway places, and sitting in class and raising my hand to give the "right" answer. I was thrilled that a college actually wanted me, yet so fearful that I would not have what it took to make it. After all, I had known people from my neighborhood, many of them much smarter than I, who had gone off to college only to be unceremoniously sent

home because they had "flunked out." With such emotions churning away, do I need to say more about anxiety?

I entered college with a steel-trap memory. In elementary, junior high, and high school I was rewarded for my memory and socialized into believing that I was both smart and educated. College, however, became an entirely different story. Unknowingly, I ran into my first bout with one dimension of the hidden curriculum. Professors expected me to know already how to compare and contrast, to apply concepts and theories, and to deal in broad theoretical frameworks and modes of analysis. I was lost; the harder I studied the more confused I got. No connection existed between the effort I exhibited and the results returned. As good as my memory was, it could not uncover the hidden theories, concepts, and other abstractions. The students who were doing well in class had long ago acquired these skills. I saw the professors as unwilling to stop and teach me how to compare and contrast. I felt their judgment—I was unprepared, "not college material"—simply for not having been taught.

I was naive enough to assume that the professors would be completely honest with me and that their teaching practices and curriculum would offer me the skills to progress in their classes and the knowledge to negotiate and succeed in the world. So if I wasn't getting it I assumed it was my fault. Now I see clearly how so much of the meaning and function of a college education was locked away and hidden from me. There was no way I could "get it." While I recognize that a lot has changed during the thirty or more years since I entered college, much has remained the same. How often do we presuppose skills, never even listing them as prerequisites? How often do we unknowingly perpetuate the hidden barriers that prevent our students from success?

Gale Auletta Young

I come from a long line of highly educated European American women, and it was assumed I would succeed in college or be a family embarrassment. I felt less than a success by not making the grades to get into the Ivy Leagues as my mother, aunts, and female cousins had done. Unlike Terry, my memory for isolated facts is slow in both programming and recall. I now know that I am a "field sensitive" learner. I learn best by knowing how the facts relate and connect to real-life matters and relationships. Field-sensitive teaching and learning was an alien concept in the 50's and 60's. Unknowingly I learned the epistemological and ontological perspectives and actions of "Americans," what I now understand as the specific public doings of Northern European American upper-class male leaders, their history, social studies, and literature.

Memorizing isolated facts, computations, theorems, and formulas in mathematics and science was like trying to catch water in a sieve. I hungered to know what these facts had to do with my life, my body, my experiences. I loved the idea of flying and thought often about Amelia Earhart's life. A math or science instructor could have hooked me for life if he or she had found out about my infatuation with flying and connected that with what Earhart needed to know. Intently curious about relationships, about the lives of women and people who weren't in power, I wanted to know how decisions were made and what mattered to these people. My questions, when I dared to voice them were laughed at and silenced. Even in college, the predominant teaching style favored field-independent learners. Not until graduate school, when synthesis skills were valued did I begin to excel. While it required time to learn, I took to relationship building among ideas like a duck to water. Today I would be excluded from graduate school because my high school and undergraduate grades of B's and C's revealed far more about the incompatibility between my learning style and the schools' teaching style than my potential.

DEFINING THE HIDDEN CURRICULUM

For Terry the hidden curriculum included the prerequisites of conceptual thinking and analytic writing. For Gale, it meant the overarching assumptions that only facts by and about upper-class Northern European American males mattered and that field-independent styles would be rewarded. Our first encounters with the hidden curriculum provide just two brief examples of a far more pervasive problem. By hidden curriculum, we refer to those attitudes, policies, actions, non-actions, behaviors, practices, and objects that lurk beneath the surface of the day-to-day operation of higher education. We mean as well the implicit value choices of what is included and excluded in the curriculum, teaching practices and assessment methods. Glatthorn defines the hidden curriculum as:

> Those aspects of schooling, other than the intentional curriculum, that seem to produce changes in student values, perception, and behaviors. (Glatthorn, 1987, p. 20)

In describing the hidden curriculum in K–12 schooling, Jackson (1968) noted that students often learn more about "crowds, praise, and power" in classrooms than they do about academic knowledge. In college classrooms, the hidden curriculum similarly teaches students about their place within the crowds, what knowledge and behaviors are valued (praised) by the institution, and about power relationships.

Dividing the Crowd

As Terry's story demonstrates, the hidden curriculum can function to build a gap between traditional and nontraditional students through expectations that are not explicitly stated. These expectations—assumptions that students enter college practiced in the teachable skills of analysis and negotiating with faculty—may be consistent with traditional students' experience but foreign to the experience of others. Reflecting on studies related to the hidden curriculum and its impact on minority children, Florio-Ruane (1989) noted that "Analysts find that problems stemming from the school's hidden curriculum exacerbate the difficulties of pupils who enter school with a cultural background or first language different from that of the United States middle class" (p. 169). The mismatch between cultural expectations of the hidden curriculum and students' backgrounds can have serious consequences. However, instructors aware of the hidden curriculum can prevent potential failure by understanding their students and facilitating a better match:

> ...cultural differences which are unspoken and misunderstood can yield pupil withdrawal and the imputation of indifference and even incompetence to minority pupils. This work sensitizes both beginning and experienced teachers to the need not only to understand the norms regulating communication in their schools and classrooms, but to the fact that these norms, as social constructions, may not mirror the social norms or values of the cultural groups to which their pupils belong. It also demonstrates that miscommunication and cultural conflict can result in school failure and alienation. This realization alone can be a significant intervention into teaching if it encourages teachers to seek greater understanding of their students. (Florio-Ruane, 1989, p. 170)

In both K–12 and higher education, understanding or intuiting the unwritten rules of the hidden curriculum benefits those students who are most like the professors and severely burdens those students whom the professor sees as being the least like him or her. Hidden rules include about what and when to talk to professors; how to respond to a professor's questions in class; what questions to ask; what knowledge to value.

Some have said that teaching is the second most private activity. But given the media's open portrayal of sex, we suspect that in fact the curriculum, teaching methods and in particular grading and assessment are far more private and are far less talked about than sex. As we prepared for our college instructor roles, most of us were told in many ways: "Teaching to the exam is bad; teaching from the textbook is anti-intellectual; too many A's and B's means you are a soft and easy teacher; every good teacher of _____ must teach _____." These unwritten rules become the hidden values and invisible forces that drive the curriculum and snare our students. The presupposition is that the "successful student" will just know or intuit what will be on the exam and what the teacher values. This student will accurately interpret the subtle messages that point to the professor's value system and ways of reasoning. Moreover, if the professor is under pressure to give only a few A's, then this successful student will know what questions to ask the professor to entice him or her into talking more about what an "A" answer might look like. Because this successful student is so much like the professor and thus can be "perceptive" enough to ask the "right" questions, that is, the question the professor likes, not only will the professor be predisposed to like the student, but the student will be predisposed to give the "correct" answers.

What Is Valued

Gale's experience illustrates how the hidden curriculum communicates implicit values. Her professors' negative reactions to her questions about the perspectives of women and people of color reflected the instructors' valuing of the knowledge and behaviors associated with middle-class White males. Simultaneously, Gale learned that her interests were not valued. Unfortunately, Gale's experience was not unique. Synthesizing their own research and that of others, Sadker and Sadker (1994) concluded:

> At the highest educational level, where the instructors are the most credentialed and the students the most capable, teaching is the most biased...We discovered how hidden lessons, rooted in elementary school and exacerbated in high school, emerged full-blown in the college classroom. (p. 168)

The hidden curriculum discourages women's active involvement in the classroom to the point that "women's silence is the loudest at college" (Sadker & Sadker, 1994, p. 170). When they speak, they are more likely than men to be interrupted. Men talk more often in class and for longer amounts of time. Professors are more likely to remember the names of male students and give men more attention, more eye contact, and more time to answer.

Like women, students of color experience differential treatment in the classroom, similarly communicating values favoring White males. Reviewing the multicultural education research literature, Grant and Tate (1995) conclude that "this research suggests that teachers perpetuate and reinforce the stereotypic beliefs associated with girls (e.g., reserved and quiet) and people of color (low achievers)" (p. 154).

Power Relations

The hidden curriculum we unknowingly perpetuate represents an ideology, thought, and action that works to both perpetuate power relationships, cultural hegemony, and political relationships and to impede the progress of those without the ability to identify and understand its existence. Power and politics are at the heart of most institutions, yet we in the university make a fine art of denying their existence and importance. Most academics want to contend that knowledge is value free and academically neutral. To some extent this unexamined faith is like believing in Santa Claus or the Tooth Fairy, except far more harmful.

Bourdieu and Passeron (1990) remind us that the ruling class of any society uses its educational system to conceal its power relations and claims its legitimacy on other grounds:

> Not only are "the ruling ideas, in every age, the ideas of the ruling class," but that the ruling ideas themselves reinforce the role of that class, and that they succeed in doing so by establishing themselves as "legitimate," that is, by concealing their basis in the (economic and political) power of the ruling class. (p. vi.)

Colleges are the powerful social instrument for the dominant class to "reproduce the cultural beliefs and the economic relationships that support the larger social order, regardless of the particular nature of the larger social order" (Glatthorn, 1987, p. 21).

The classroom is the place where the issue of control is paramount, yet rarely mentioned. It is an essential part of the hidden curriculum. Many of our students come from environments where they are accustomed to being in one down situations, where they are being told what to do, how to do it, and when to do it. On the other hand, we have faculty who are accustomed to being in charge, of having power, especially in the classroom. The classroom is where students often learn conformity, complying with rules, and docility. At a Black Panther rally years ago Terry heard Eldridge Cleaver, then the Minister of Information for the Party, describe ghetto schools as places where they prepared students to stand in lines, to raise their hands, and to be compliant, all essential skills for surviving in prison. In a less dramatic fashion, Glatthorn (1987) notes:

> Control is achieved through the differential use of power; the teacher uses several kinds of power to control the selection of content, the methods of learning, movement in the classroom, and the flow of classroom discourse. Control also is achieved by the skillful use of accountability measures; teachers spend much time evaluating and giving evaluative feedback. In such a classroom, students unconsciously learn the skills and traits required by the larger society; they learn to be punctual, clean, docile, and conforming. (p. 21)

What is gained by not including these arbitrary power relations as topics and issues within the curriculum? Actually, the question should be, "What is lost and hidden away by not including these power relations as topics and issues within the curriculum?" No matter how fair and equitable an organization may appear on the surface, its real practices and intent can only be ascertained by looking beneath the surface and at its informal unwritten institutional culture and practices. Here is where the actions are taken or not taken that produce the inequities in resources and participation by race, gender, sexual orientation and class. In this institutional underground

everything is "understood" and European Americans maintain historic racial and cultural privileges while, at the same time, professing and giving the appearance of fairness (Bowser, Auletta, Jones, 1993, p. 2).

STRATEGIES FOR DISCLOSING THE HIDDEN CURRICULUM

Exposing the tilted playing field in the examples we discussed earlier begins with stating prerequisite skills in the syllabus, grading only what we teach, making the criteria for what constitutes an "A" explicit, stating our predominate teaching style, and explaining our biases for what knowledge we value and the learning styles we prefer. However, to actually level the field we must consider how we interact with students in both formal and informal ways. Additionally, we must examine our selection of instructional strategies, including electronic technologies. These are the secret mazes that as faculty, we can use our power to recognize and correct. On the other hand, we can ignore them and perpetuate the concealed traps in the educational process.

Teacher-Student Interactions in the Multicultural Setting

How we interact with students sends powerful, implicit messages about our values and expectations. Three aspects of interacting with students are embedded in the hidden curriculum: our selection of language, how we respond to statements reflecting ethnocentric and other biased views, and how we encourage student participation. In each case, we communicate our intent to include or exclude.

Language in Higher Education Classrooms

Moving onto a college campus for many of our students parallels moving to another country because the language, customs, rituals, practices, and traditions are so dramatically different than any of their previous experiences. For the first time in their lives students are exposed to such terms as matriculation, breadth requirement, cohort, prerequisite, major, the canon, liberal studies, interdisciplinary studies, provost, plagiarism, dean's list, baccalaureate, and concurrent enrollment, just to mention a few. Does anyone here speak English? With each new course comes a whole new set of jargon. While these terms are useful and appropriate, they often overwhelm, distance, intimidate, and shut down students.

These are the kinds of terms you find in upper- and upper-middle-class homes and schools. These are not the terms that everybody else grows up hearing as they sit around the dinner table, in their communities, or even in their schools. Students are unlikely to look up the meaning in the dictionary or ask the user to explain. Because of their fear and insecurity, students assume that they should know the meaning, that everyone else knows, and that it would appear ignorant to ask or not appear to know. In actuality, we are losing some of these students before they even have a chance to connect. Such language reinforces for students the feeling that they should not be in college, that they do not have what it takes to make it. After all, the student might think, if I cannot even understand the instructions I am getting to apply for financial aid or to register for classes, what is going to happen to me when I finally get into class?

As faculty, administrators, and staff we need to be much more aware that our students often come from environments that are significantly different than those we expect for college students. If we are aware that some of the terms and language we use serve to intimidate and slow students down in their pursuit of higher education, we might want to consciously look for alternative modes of communicating our ideas and intentions.

Accommodating our language to meet student needs is not a matter of asking faculty, staff, or administrators to water down their communication or to lower standards, or to censor their first amendment rights. It is more a matter of common decency and courtesy. With regard to academic jargon we suggest seeing it through the eyes of students. Assume they don't know what these terms mean. Explain the words with a focus on what these terms mean to them and why they are useful for the student to know.

Responding to Biased or Oppressive Comments

As faculty we become so accustomed to jargon that it flows from our tongues like water from a stream. Rarely do we see how often our students tighten up and become immobilized. If academic jargon can build walls, imagine the power of covert racially or sexually coded words to exclude. Such words can be a blow to the stomach. They intimidate, make you feel inferior, or even make you so angry that effective learning is nearly impossible.

Most faculty are far too civil to knowingly make offensive remarks or use sexist language, but some have mastered the art of sophisticated code words that are almost as hurtful to women and students of color. For example, most students of color (and faculty of color) bristle when they hear European Americans talk about "qualified minorities" or "affirmative action hires" or note that "this quarter I have a much more intellectually stimulating group of students." People of color often translate such discussions to mean that the speakers have found a person of color acceptable to them and there are no minority students in the class this quarter, respectively. How would mainstream students (and faculty) react to the term "qualified White"?

Reducing racist and sexist perceptions or beliefs is far more difficult to do. We suggest that faculty honestly address the problem by first inquiring into their own mental chatter, emotional waves, and actual knowledge base regarding these issues. We cannot begin to listen to the students' experiences or to reduce our complicity in their perceptions of racism until we understand our own struggles with these issues. The social rule of racial silence is so ingrained in the hidden curriculum that we may very well need professional help to sort through our feelings and myths. However, once the personal process is engaged we suggest cultivating empathic listening as a method for encouraging healthy and educational interracial dialogues. This method requires the instructor to listen without judgment and gently inquire in order to learn the student's perspective. The "without judgment" part is far easier said than done, especially with a student whose racial biases and intolerance boil over. Yet it is in this very situation that if we have compassion for our own struggles that we can gently but firmly invite students to examine their own beliefs.

If we encounter a student who makes a biased comment, we can model questions for the student or inquire into the beliefs behind the statement. And then, we can turn to the rest of the class and suggest that many times one student will voice what others are too embarrassed or strategic to voice yet believe. Then students can be invited to write their own "dangerous questions and concerns" and turn the papers in with or without names. If the instructor is especially skilled, brave, or comfortable with these issues he or she could engage the class in a discussion. A New Age saying admonishes, "Grow where you are planted." The teaching equivalent is "Teach where your students are stuck." Every time we deny, ignore, or belittle a student's experience we miss an opportunity to teach and to learn.

Student Participation

The Sadkers' work, cited earlier, attests to the power of faculty to systematically encourage or discourage participation by selected groups of students. What specific behaviors communicate our welcoming or rejecting of student comments? Jenkins (1992) interviewed 77 students at San Francisco State University as part of a study designed to glean student views through anecdotes to help faculty understand the experiences and perceptions of students of color. The sample included American Indian, Latino, Black, Asian, White, and international students. Among Jenkins' findings were the following:

Students felt encouraged to participate in their classes when instructors used methods such as calling on students by name; offering encouragement through facial expressions and nonverbal gestures; giving students time to respond; and treating everyone equally. In general, students appreciated faculty who were responsive to their contributions and gave them positive reinforcement for participating. (p. 2)

- Students identified behaviors that discouraged participation, such as not really listening; ignoring the speakers' content; shutting up the speakers or cutting them off; treating them patronizingly or contemptuously; and acting surprised when they did well. Students reported that faculty, even those who professed to want student participation, seemed to get so caught up in their own lectures that they had no time to call on students. (p. 2)

- Students believed that instructors encouraged some students to participate more than other students.

- Most of the students interviewed were pleased when instructors included materials pertinent to their cultural group and were more likely to partici-pate when materials were culture-spe-cific. Though some were embarrassed at feeling "singled out," others resented the absence in most classes of materials relevant to their cultures....Students who had taken ethnic studies classes wanted to introduce this material in other classes, but were often afraid to do so because of the risks involved. (p. 3)

- It appears appropriate to encourage students to share culture-specific knowledge and experience, but inap-propriate to ask students to act as a spokesperson for their group. Half of the students interviewed indicated that on at least one occasion they had been asked to be a spokesperson. Responses were largely negative. In an English class, when students were reading the novel *Sula*, a middle-class Black female student was asked what it was like to live in the ghetto. Another Black woman reported a similar incident in an English class in which she was asked to read an excerpt from a novel in Black dialect, even though she did not speak this dialect. (p. 3)

- Many students felt that race and/or gender affected faculty expectations or evaluations of their performance (p. 12). Moreover, students of color felt they had less opportunity for improve-ment because they were not receiving as much feedback as other students. (p. 13)

Faculty need to regularly drop out of the "I am the Instructor" pattern and listen as a learner. We need to be open to what the students have to teach us about their expe-riences, especially those experiences that have been silenced by the academy—their race- and gender-based experience. The heart of the issue is making students feel

comfortable enough to take risks. Milem (1992) reports that "peer and faculty norms can have an important impact on the racial attitudes of students. They can "set the tone" (p. 75). Students' experiences and percep-tions should matter dearly to us. If we do not make a conscious effort every day to include and listen to students from their perspective, we will perpetuate excluding them.

We teach a lot of culturally diverse stu-dents. We want them to change. We assume that our knowledge will transform their lives. Is it too much to ask that we as faculty, administrators, and staff might also have to do some changing in order to make these students comfortable enough to absorb more of what we have to offer? More impor-tantly, shouldn't we expect ourselves to be open to changing, to assume that our inter-actions with the students and their knowl-edge and experiences could transform our lives? Part of the hidden curriculum has been to assume that education is a one-way learning process.

Instructional Strategies

In the traditional institution of higher edu-cation the faculty member sits or stands at the front of the class and presents him or herself as the dispenser of knowledge. The image of faculty as all wise, all knowing and spewing down knowledge like water from a mighty stream may be only a slight exag-geration. In most colleges and universities the lecture or lecture-discussion format is the most common mode of instruction. This approach, referred to as the banking model by Freire (1970, p. 58) relies on the professor to "deposit" knowledge and information into the students. There is a subtle, to not-so-subtle assumption that students are to adapt to the knowledge of the professor, adapt to the world the way it is, and not to be concerned with change or transforma-tion (Ventimiglia, 1994, p. 5). This teacher-centered learning approach hides its culture-based accommodationist orientation and the fact that there are other ways of knowing and other ways of teaching. Thus, the teacher-centered approach to education both hides the fact that certain subjects and certain approaches are chosen over others and that students are turned into compliant, nonthinking dependents.

Although the teacher-centered approach dominates, we constantly hear about bad student attitudes. Rarely is the focus on the attitudes of the faculty that remain hidden but are integral to the content of higher education. Often European American faculty judge our students as if they were idealistic eighteen-year-old, European American, middle to upper class, residential, single, living in the dorm, and from the suburbs. In reality, our students are increasingly adults, working, with children, married, urban, female, and people of color. Such students resent being talked down to, want to be more involved in their education, and bring more in terms of life experiences to the classroom. These students want to be treated as the adults they are and increasingly want to be engaged as partners in the educational experience.

Faculty often come to the educational experience with an attitude about what constitutes a good student, what is appropriate student behavior, and what the proper student faculty relationship ought to be. Students who deviate from this image in the faculty mind are often labeled as deviant, inadequate, or deficient. These students are saddled with the burden of being perceived as lacking and less than, needing to catch up. Some faculty do a good job of working with students they see as underprepared; however, others demonstrate an attitude of superiority and spend an inordinate amount of time complaining about the students and wondering how they got into college in the first place. Such attitudes are frequently passed on to our students. Students internalize these attitudes, become defensive, and withdraw.

Many students—across cultural and ethnic groups—except at the very elite institutions, are underprepared in one or more areas *but not incapable.* A far healthier attitude might be to recognize the cards we have been dealt and get on with finding the best ways to play them. If we are teachers, what can we do to create an inclusive learning environment for a classroom of students with varied academic preparation? How can faculty learn about what the student brings to the educational setting and then provide ways for the students to connect their personal knowledge to the new knowledge? Asking this question at every step along the way in curriculum development opens the range of possibilities for formulating educational plans that are meaningful and useful to the student.

However, we also understand that faculty need to be supported by the institution. Just as asking the questions opens the door, the university must provide the time and resources for faculty to engage in on-the-job training. The following story illustrates for us the subtle nature of the hidden curriculum and the need for such training. Recently we were called in to consult with two European American theater instructors developing a multicultural student touring company. The plan called for students of color to enact short plays about such issues as drugs, violence, and living in low-income areas. We suggested that they first create and enact plays that grow out of the life experiences of the students being educated and then frame the scenes in such a way that focuses on the students' experiences with the wider causes of such problems as well as on students' overcoming challenges. We cautioned them about the dangers of creating and generating new stereotypes. One of the instructors very honestly responded, "I don't know how to teach that. What we have proposed is what I do know how to teach." This brief moment of honesty frames for us what is at the heart of higher education. We teach that which *we* know and value. What we know is valuable, but what we teach often gets interpreted as being *all* of knowledge, and not just the piece that we value. This practice subtly socializes our students into accepting and adapting to what we have to offer as "knowledge" (Minnich, 1990).

We know that faculty come to the classroom with a vast store of knowledge, with credentials, expertise, and prestige. What we do not know is the significance of the knowledge and experiences the student brings to the classroom. Our goal is to do a better job of connecting the two.

Learning is linking new information to prior knowledge and experience; connecting the two allows us to tap into what our students know and what is important to them by knowing about them, their communities and their life experiences. We go even further when we delve into how our students learn and begin to tailor our curriculum, our assignments, and assessments based on our findings about our students and their learning styles.

W. E. B. Du Bois (1973) contended that in order for education to be relevant for African Americans, it had to focus on their life experiences: "You are teaching American Negroes in 1933, and they are subjects of a caste system in the Republic of the United States of America and their life problem is primarily the problem of caste" (p. 92). In arguing for an education that recognized the conditions in which African Americans exist, Du Bois was not excluding other areas of education. Quite the opposite; he believed in the importance of "starting with present conditions and using the facts and the knowledge of the present situation of American Negroes and then expanding toward possession and the conquest of all knowledge" (p. 95).

There are multiple ways for teachers to learn about their students, their life experiences, and the communities from which they come. Asking students to keep diaries, to write autobiographies, to apply concepts from our various disciplines to conditions and experiences in their families or communities, are all successful ways to learn and share students' experiences within the context of the course material. In other instances it may be appropriate to have students do field assignments, visit agencies, or interview family members or other persons significant to the students. In addition faculty can learn by reading ethnic-specific literature, attending community events, theater, and art exhibits, to mention but a few of the opportunities for enlightenment. Learning about our students and their life experiences does not have to be a laborious and painful experience. Their completed assignments become not just a means for the faculty to assess student learning but also a means for faculty to increase their education as well.

One of the quickest ways we have found to dismantle the teacher-based classroom is to integrate throughout the course what we've come to call "prepared participation." We combine the spirit and practices of cooperative learning (see Chapter 7) and writing across the curriculum. From cooperative education we assume that teachers and students can learn from each other. From writing across the curriculum we assume that writing in and of itself is a vehicle for not only improvement but also reflection and preparation for participation. The essence of the process is to ask students to respond in writing to any question or idea you want them to explore. Then, in any number of structured ways, have students summarize and explore the implications of what they have written and share it with the whole class or with a small group.

Let's take a typical walk through how this structure might work in the course of a term. The instructor walks in and asks the students to write for 2 to 5 minutes on what they learned from the readings or the previous lecture/discussion, what distracted or annoyed them about the material, and what questions they have about the ideas. The instructor might ask students to provide examples from their own experience that illustrate certain major ideas, or what concepts the students "liked" the best, and which concept(s) bothered them, confused them, or that they just plain didn't like? The teacher then gives them a moment to write a sentence or two that they want to share with the class. In a small class of up to 30 students, each student can respond in one or two sentences, without any responses from the teacher or class. In a larger class, or when time is short, 2–3 students in each row or section of the class can respond. The instructor then summarizes the responses and replies to them as a whole or invites students to respond to the ideas presented.

Another structure involves putting students into small groups and assigning them communication roles, including that of the facilitator, the timekeeper, and recorder. Each person is given a structured time to report or read what he or she has written, and then a structured time period, for example, 2 minutes apiece, for other group members to question or discuss with the person reporting out. After students have presented their materials, and their ideas have been discussed by the whole group, the group members note the similarities and differences among all the experiences or ideas. At the end, the recorder will work with the group to make sure the major themes have been accurately recorded. Finally the recorder will read to the entire class a summary of the major themes discussed in the small group. This process prepares each student to participate and provides the structure for each student to participate. It focuses on sharing knowledge, ideas and experiences. The facilitator enforces the communication structure while the timekeeper enforces the time limits. Providing a communication structure is as important as the content guidelines. Without the communication structure the small group will become a microcosm of the competitive classroom where some students monopolize the talk time and others withdraw. Moreover, this structure encourages and affirms all voices. Many faculty initially fear this teaching method because the student's learning, rather than the instructor's expertise becomes the focus of the class. Using this structure, the faculty member shares some power with the students in constructing the knowledge base.

Students in a multicultural society need skills and models that prepare them for effective participation in an increasingly multicultural and multiracial society. We must begin to move away from the teacher-centered approach to education and move toward the learner-centered approaches where students are thrust to the center of the educational process. The Ventimiglia (1994) and Johnson, Johnson, and Smith (1991a, 1991b) studies confirm that such approaches to education improve student self-esteem, develop interpersonal relationships, and increase racial tolerance. These are important, though often ignored, learning objectives.

Placing students in the center of the learning process and making them active participants uncovers the hidden power faculty exert when they claim responsibility for guiding and teaching knowledge. While we seldom realize it, faculty dominance and control of the learning process create dependence, apathy, and indifference. The visible reaction to such an approach to teaching is tardiness, absenteeism, low attention levels, disruptive behavior, and poor academic performance.

Cooperative and collaborative education does not mean that the teacher is no longer important or that she or he is forever forbidden to lecture. Quite the contrary. The role of the instructor is paramount to preparing effective learning assignments which must be well thought out. As for the lecture, there are times when it is the very best method of delivering information to students. We do suggest, however, that faculty ask themselves why they are lecturing. Is it to give a good performance, to show competence, to exercise control, because it is the only way they know how to teach? Or does it meet student needs? Often faculty are more interested in showing students how smart, knowledgeable, and well prepared they are, instead of helping the student discover for themselves.

Applying Electronic Technologies

Higher education's embracing of electronic technologies just as student populations are becoming increasingly diverse prompts a specific discussion on applications of technology in instruction as a new aspect of the hidden curriculum. Ironically, just as learner-centered teaching methods are making inroads, the move toward distance education and other mediated forms of instruction present opportunities to perpetuate existing barriers to access or to ensure that these new tools expand equity and excellence in education.

It seems as if distance learning and other electronic technologies will become as integral a part of the educational landscape as computers. Both economic necessity and the demand for more effective ways of educating an increasingly nontraditional student population has precipitated such a move. But many institutions lack clear, coherent strategies for connecting their diversity-supporting goals and their goals for expanding technology applications. Just as the numbers of women and people of color on our campuses have begun to increase, we discover distance learning. Just as we begin to seriously discuss campus climate issues, we invest millions of dollars in electronic educational capabilities that could serve to separate students even further. On the one hand, such approaches have the capacity to reach even more diverse students. On the other hand, we have this nagging fear: If we cannot adequately teach diverse students now, and if we have yet to ensure an inclusive learning environment when we have students physically in front of us, can we expect appropriate, inclusive instruction using electronic media?

The introduction of distance learning and other electronic technologies is a potential opportunity for those interested in infusing the multicultural perspective in higher education. It is an opportunity for us to learn from our past mistakes and to consider the needs of our diverse student populations from the beginning of the development process. Discussing K–12 education for culturally and linguistically diverse students, Soska (1995) suggests that multimedia technologies have numerous advantages. Used properly, they can provide multisensory delivery of instruction; promote active learning; yield opportunities for collaborative learning; enhance communication skills; promote cross-cultural understanding by linking students around the world; increase student interest and motivation; and support speaking, listening, reading, and writing skills. A positive example from higher education is exemplified by Coombs' work at the Rochester Institute of Technology. Coombs has been successful in using vax notes and e-mail computer conferencing as an interactive mode to discuss African American history, racism, welfare, and other social issues.

However, computer applications are not culturally neutral. In her review of the literature, Taylor (1994) reports a number of findings relevant to the interface between technology and diversity. First, existing software tends to exclude or present biased representations of African Americans, Latinos, Asians, and women. Second, gender differences may exist in the conditions that promote effective use of technologies as learning tools. For example, women students may achieve better with computer learning in the context of cooperative settings. Third, technologies that rely on reading do not consider potential effects of the strong oral traditions of some cultures. Additionally, universities that do not provide a personal computer for every student must resolve the problem of access. Moreover, disparities may exist between income groups in prerequisite skills related to computer literacy.

The potential for reaching greater numbers of students and in stimulating ways through interactive technologies is tremendous. Our caution stems from our observation that diversity and multicultural issues are being tacked on to the policies and practices of technologically transmitted education. They are not considered elemental to the process. We suggest that all plans for the development of distance learning consider diverse learners and multicultural issues as core elements. We need serious research and design plans to inquire into how educational technologies, including distance learning, can and cannot meet the needs of our diverse student populations. While the delivery of information is important, the very nature of the media can perpetuate the teacher-centered paradigm and communicate implicit messages about exclusion. We need to be vigilant in guaranteeing that the two-way nature of learning is incorporated in all educational electronics. While some will argue that the very nature of technological advances ensures the protection of the two-way process, we are unsure. Adapting the cooperative and collaborative methods we've described above to the at-distance and electronic educational media will require even more faculty preparation. Given the academy's past slowness in allocating funds for faculty development, we might anticipate that untutored use of distance/electronic technologies may perpetuate an even more deadly form of teacher-centered education. We must protect students' access to experiential learning and one-on-one contact with the instructor. With these caveats, current interests in technology and diversity create a unique opportunity to develop effective and engaging instructional modalities based on the strengths of our multicultural population.

CONCLUSION

Nothing in the curriculum should be hidden. Everything should be explicit. Exposing the unwritten rules of the curriculum requires faculty to be honest and open about the choices we make in teaching materials and strategies, our actual criteria for grading, and our justifications for our choice of assessment methods. Everything should be laid on the table for students, including our attitudes and biases.

Disclosing the hidden curriculum is a simple but difficult task, for several reasons. First, aspects of the hidden curriculum have been in place for so long that they have become synonymous with "a good education." One first step, as indicated in Chapter 2, is to make our expectations explicit in the syllabus. Second, in acknowledging and disclosing the hidden curriculum, we may face challenges to dearly cherished beliefs about what constitutes knowledge. Third, changing the hidden curriculum requires a willingness to share power with students. We are talking about relating to students in open, honest ways. All students will benefit from our sharing of the hitherto implicit rules for success in higher-education classrooms.

CHAPTER 7

Creating an Enabling Learning Environment for Non-Native Speakers of English

Kate Kinsella
Education Specialist, ESL and Bilingual Education
"Step to College Program," San Francisco State University

Editor's Notes:

Kate Kinsella's chapter primarily addresses two components of course change: instructional strategies and classroom dynamics. While her focus is on students who are not native speakers of English, many of the ideas she presents are useful for any instructional situation where the professor wishes to be more inclusive of students and promote learning among all. The strategies are at least at the inclusive level on our model; they represent a wide range of teaching methods to promote students' active learning of course content. The methods also further the development of communication skills in English. Some of Kinsella's suggestions would transform a course as they empower students and draw upon students' experience and knowledge.

Kinsella's chapter is a rich source of information on creating a learning environment for non-native speakers of English. Her review of research furthers our understanding of language acquisition and the academic performance of students who are learning English as a second language. Kinsella provides insights into the different groups of non-native speakers, particularly focusing on how culture and prior educational experiences shape their understanding of the American college classroom and their academic performance.

Kinsella outlines several general instructional strategies which promote language and concept development for non-native speakers of English. These strategies increase students' motivation and assist them in becoming more confident and competent learners. Emphasis is placed on those strategies which promote active listening and notetaking. She also details strategies for enabling lectures, more equitable class discussions, and effective group-work design and implementation. Thus, Kinsella's chapter is valuable reading for anyone who wants to know how to employ more effective instructional strategies and learning activities. ∎

RECOGNIZING THE GREAT DIVERSITY AMONG NON-NATIVE SPEAKERS OF ENGLISH

The initial step in creating an enabling learning environment for linguistically and culturally diverse students is to better understand who they are and what their varied needs might be in a college classroom. In this chapter, the term "English as a second-language" (ESL) student is used to refer to any student who is not a native speaker of English. This label encompasses a wide range of students in American higher education. Among the ESL students who may enrich a student body include the following: international students, United States–born English-dominant bilinguals, immigrants who arrived during childhood or adolescence, recent immigrants, political and religious refugees, and individuals from a migrant background. These students differ in such outwardly recognizable features as age, gender, ethnicity, language background, and degree of comfort interacting in English. They also differ significantly in less evident characteristics such as their communities, cultures, socioeconomic status, personalities, learning styles, attitudes toward English and North Americans, reasons for studying English, prior English language instruction and primary language schooling, and opportunities to regularly use English for a range of communicative purposes.

A pedagogy of inclusion with regard to ESL students in higher education is grounded in an understanding of their distinct personal characteristics:

- ESL students may be recent high school graduates or graduate students who have already attained a degree in the United States or abroad.

- An ESL student may be the first family member with a high school diploma and access to a college degree, or a child from a family with a long tradition of higher education.

- ESL students may receive considerable financial support from their families or government scholarships; in contrast, they may work thirty hours per week to make ends meet while managing a full academic course load.

- They can be middle-aged adults who achieved high academic and professional status abroad but experienced occupational and social downgrading during the process of migration, and who are now struggling to improve their English language skills to re-enter their professional domain in a new society.

- They may have immigrated as adolescents and be recent graduates of U.S. high schools.

- ESL students may be visiting scholars from the People's Republic of China or Southeast Asian refugees who relocated in the United States as youngsters after completing limited schooling in their first language and spending formative years in a refugee camp, waiting for resettlement.

- An English-dominant bilingual student may be a Native American or a Chinese American who speaks English and has been schooled in English, yet has been exposed to the family's other language through parents, relatives, and family friends. This student may comprehend a great deal of the parents' native language and may be able to interact within the community, using a social variety of the language, but have more academic language proficiency in English.

- ESL students may come to a North American college having achieved a high level of formal education and academic literacy in their primary language, complemented by extensive English-language preparation. They may also enter college after having immigrated during early adolescence following a disrupted educational history, which required them to acquire a new language along with grade-level competency in subject matter taught exclusively in English.

While individual students from these varied groups may respond positively to similar instructional approaches (discussed in this chapter), they come to our classes with unique histories, contexts, and perspectives which warrant special consideration. Often the only commonalty among ESL students in a heterogeneous college class is that English is not their first language. It is challenging for college educators who are committed to educational access and equity to get to know their diverse students and to be sensitive to the wide variations in cultural and educational background, socioeconomic status, and personality. We can begin by striving to better recognize the range of learners we regularly encounter in our classes within our respective disciplines, and to better understand the more critical variables which can dramatically impact their academic and social success.

Identifying the Various Non-Native Speakers Within Classes

There are a number of ways to obtain practical background information about the various learners in our classes without being intrusive or offensive. Through information sheets, brief questionnaires, biographical sketches, or journal entries an instructor can better ascertain the percentage of the class who are non-native speakers of English and the various communities to which they belong. One simple way is to distribute an information sheet at the beginning of the term, being careful to explain the purpose: to have a more accurate class profile. A student information sheet may include: preferred name, country of origin, home

language, length of time in the United States, school system in which a high school diploma was obtained, English coursework completed to date, current class schedule, and job responsibilities.

In creating positive rapport and interacting successfully with non-native speakers in class, it is important to first learn what name they prefer to be called. Students from many cultures are uncomfortable with the informality in American higher education and with addressing an instructor by his or her first name. They also are shocked being called by a first name when even close family members do not do so. Within the same class, some ESL students may prefer an adopted American name, while others will feel strongly about maintaining their ethnic identity. If an instructor conveys a genuine interest in accurately pronouncing foreign names, students will generally respond enthusiastically, and in some cases with surprise, after having been routinely assigned a variety of American approximations of their names in previous classes.

It is helpful to learn whether non-native speakers who are new to the campus are familiar with student organizations and support services which may ease some of the potential confusion and isolation of the first year in college. An international student may be extremely lonely and homesick or have a healthy support system of friends and acquaintances on campus from the home country. A resident student may be quite acculturated and have an active social life which includes friends from a diversity of backgrounds or have very little interaction with individuals outside his or her community.

It is additionally worthwhile to identify students who may have overwhelmingly busy work and school schedules which may provide some explanation for underachievement in coursework and failure to avail themselves of support services such as departmental tutoring, study groups, or instructor office hours. While an international student may be enrolled in a full load of courses but have no legal work possibilities in the United States, an immigrant student may be juggling an equally demanding number of courses along with a full-time job and additional family responsibilities.

Such information can help us ascertain the nature of ESL students in a class. We can better gauge whether they have had extensive schooling in English or relatively little to meet the language and literacy demands of higher education. After analyzing initial exam or assignment results and reviewing these profiles, we can better discern which ESL students might benefit from some learning assistance, either during office hours, in a study group, or with a tutor. In order to encourage our non-native English speakers to avail themselves of campus resources, we need to familiarize ourselves with the various learning assistance services offered. For many ESL students, the university is quite alien in its institutions and in norms. Taking a few minutes in class to talk about conventions for office hours and the various forms of study groups or tutoring one can take advantage of on campus helps to demystify the university. In summary, simply identifying a few key pieces of information can alert faculty to potential academic and interactional challenges for different students and help us to be more sensitive, informed educators and student advocates.

International Students Versus United States Resident Students

Perhaps the most significant distinction to make among students who speak English as a second language is between international students and permanent United States residents or immigrant students. International students and resident students can have quite differential preparation for success in North American institutions of higher education. This differential preparation may include formal English language instruction and substantive curricular and critical literacy development in the native language. As an example, international students are customarily required to attain a relatively high score on the Test of English as a Foreign Language (TOEFL) as part of their admission to any college or university in the United States. In order to receive an acceptably high TOEFL score (475–550), a student must display a relatively sophisticated understanding of English grammar and syntax and comprehend complex vocabulary and reading selections. Many institutions additionally require a passing composition score on the Test of Written English (TWE) as a further gauge of academic English preparation for the complex literacy demands of higher education.

To prepare for these rigorous English-language exams, some international students benefit from a strong English-language component integrated throughout their secondary school curriculum abroad, while others have the financial means to avail themselves of a costly though effective pre-university intensive English program on an American campus. Further, international students are customarily accepted to colleges and universities in the United States based on a relatively successful prior academic track record in their home country. It is even frequently assumed that international students represent the scholastic elite of their countries. Although many are indeed highly accomplished scholars and researchers, others may be quite average or have lacked high enough secondary school baccalaureate exam scores to admit them to competitive or prestigious universities back home. Nevertheless, whether their scholastic records are exceptional or merely adequate, all international students at least come to higher education in the United States with a strong academic foundation in another language. In their home country, they have already mastered cognitively and linguistically demanding secondary subject matter across the content areas and have completed complex reading, writing, and examination tasks in their native language. They are not only highly literate in their first language, but in many cases considerably more proficient in writing and reading English than their conversational interaction and listening comprehension might suggest.

In contrast, many permanent-resident students converse with ease and confidence, particularly those who have attended secondary school in the United States. As an illustration, college freshmen of immigrant origin who have recently graduated from American high schools are generally quite familiar with the slang, trends, and icons of American teen culture and appear to be comfortable, confident users of social interactional English. They may, however, be less skilled than many international students in writing and reading in English for academic purposes as well as the analytical and synthetical competencies critical for success in higher education. Furthermore, depending on their age at immigration, degree of schooling in their native country, and access to quality bilingual education upon arrival in the United States school system, they may or may not be literate in their native language and primarily speak a social rather than an academic variety of that home language.

A resident bilingual student's academic English and study skill foundation for higher education is contingent upon multiple variables. For example, there are great discrepancies around the country in secondary school responses to the needs of ESL students. Effective bilingual education at the secondary level is often difficult to provide, either because there are too few students from the same language background to warrant hiring a bilingual teacher, or because there are no adequately trained and certified bilingual teachers and appropriate instructional materials available. Inconsistencies in program goals and offerings can impact very heavily on the chances for secondary school success for U.S. immigrant students, in particular for those who aspire to a college degree. It is not surprising that ESL students from diverse backgrounds who have recently graduated from inner-city schools would feel that even their Advanced Placement courses had failed to adequately prepare them for the demands of the university (Brinton & Mano, 1994).

Few studies have addressed the length of time that it takes to become proficient in a second language for educational purposes and to reach native-speaker norms in academic achievement. However, Collier (1987; Collier & Thomas, 1988) and Cummins (1981a) provide compelling evidence that second language proficiency and academic achievement do not occur quickly for immigrant students who are schooled exclusively in English upon arrival in the United States, which has been the case for most of our immigrant students.

Collier (1989) additionally reviewed studies of public school achievement test scores in order to determine how long it takes second-language learners to attain native-speaker norms in content areas. Perhaps the most significant finding is that bilingual education is by far and away the most effective way to initially prepare ESL students for success in content area classes, although bilingual education is currently not available for many students throughout the nation. Collier also found that the students who take the longest time to reach national norms in content areas, if indeed they ever do, are those who arrive as youngsters with little or no formal schooling in their first language and who receive no early bilingual literacy and content area instruction. These are students who often slip through the cracks in the public school system and never receive early literacy development in their native language or special ESL support in reading and writing because of their apparent oral fluency in English.

In summary, the ESL students likely to find college coursework most challenging are those whose general education has been interrupted due to the immigration process or to mainstream secondary school classes with inadequate English language or curricular foundation. This is vital information for today's higher-education faculty to recognize, as it describes the educational history of thousands of immigrant and refugee students pursuing a college degree across the United States.

SCHEMA THEORETICAL RESEARCH AND THE ROLE OF BACKGROUND KNOWLEDGE IN SECOND-LANGUAGE COMPREHENSION AND RETENTION

Collier's (1989) findings point to the primacy of a strong conceptual and organizational framework along with study skill development for mastery of complex subject matter in English as a second language. These conclusions are consistent with schema theory and research in the area of second language comprehension and retention. The relatively recent emphasis on the role of prior knowledge in understanding instruction in a second language and culture is an outgrowth of the impact of *schema theory* (Rumelhart, 1980). Schema theory claims that understanding discourse involves far more than extracting information from a text or lecture; in fact, learners cannot extract anything for which they do not

have some kind of existing knowledge structure. That which is previously experienced and learned is stored in the brain in categories called *schemata* (singular is *schema*). These units of organized information are incomplete and are constantly being revised or further developed. The schema for supermarkets in the United States, for example, would contain information about checkout stands, cashiers, baggers, packaging, bar codes, and discount coupons. As a newcomer student sees pictures of, reads about, watches television images of, or visits a suburban supermarket, each experience expands and reforms the student's existing schema for supermarket.

Efficient English-language comprehension for non-native speakers therefore involves activation of appropriate schemata, assimilation of new knowledge into existing schemata, accommodation of existing schemata to fit new knowledge, and creation of entirely new schemata. Prior knowledge can facilitate interpretation of a written text, film, or oral presentation by providing an overall context for the textual information being encoded, comprehended, and recalled. When ESL students are not familiar with the various schemata of a particular lesson, the more they will struggle to construct an accurate meaning, particularly from culturally based and culturally biased content.

An analysis of the main forms of background knowledge which may exist within a given text (spoken or written) can shed light as to why ESL students who have recently entered U.S. colleges rank understanding lectures and reading and studying textbooks highest on survey lists of academic difficulties (Christison & Krahnke, 1986; Ostler, 1980; Smoke, 1988). Carrell (1983) makes a useful distinction among three forms of schemata: *linguistic, content,* and *formal. Linguistic schemata* includes knowledge of letters and their corresponding sounds, phonics, grammar, social and academic vocabulary, idioms, word-attack skills, and distinctions between spoken and written forms. *Content schemata* refers to an individual's knowledge about the topic being addressed, involving world knowledge, life experiences, culture, and concepts within and across particular disciplines. As an example, participation in the U.S. public school system presumes knowledge about teacher and student role relationships, appropriate classroom behaviors, and criteria for specific homework assignments. *Formal schemata* is background knowledge and expectations about differences among the rhetorical organizational structures in which information is presented.

To illustrate, effective readers of English text within higher education must be able to recognize common types of expository paragraphs and essays, such as cause and effect, problem and solution, and comparison and contrast. Within pieces of expository writing, they must know how to identify controlling ideas stated in a thesis or topic sentence and correctly interpret transitional expressions like "consequently" and "moreover" which establish logical relationships between items. Students must additionally be familiar with the differences in structure and format of the diverse genres they are exposed to across the school curriculum, such as expository essays, textbook chapters in various content areas (e.g., mathematics versus social sciences), short stories, myths, poetry, lab reports, and professional articles. The rhetoric and conventions of formal oral discourse in English can pose unique comprehension challenges for listeners from diverse linguistic and cultural heritages. For example, in order to competently follow a lecture or distinguish significant information for notetaking, ESL students must be able to recognize the verbal and non-verbal cues which signal the speaker's agenda,

overriding organization, presentation highlights, and sheerly anecdotal remarks, much of which may be culturally influenced but not characteristic of oral presentation patterns in other educational systems.

Many ESL students appear proficient in English due to their conversational fluency but may lack the knowledge to perceive complex core curricula in a culturally authentic way. Bloome and Greene (1984) maintain that reading selections reflect socially acquired schemata in the form of frames of reference, value systems, and processes as well as idiosyncratic facts and beliefs held between the writer and the reader. To successfully interact with a text, a student must gain access to information possessed by members of the social group for which the text was intended. Similarly, to successfully follow sustained, complex oral texts such as films, seminar presentations, lectures, or class discussions requires a sophisticated array of formal, conceptual, and linguistic schemata—forms of background knowledge that instructors in higher education often take for granted and rarely consciously factor into lesson design.

Language Proficiency and Academic Achievement

Cummins (1981b) offers a complementary theoretical framework for conceptualizing the linguistic and conceptual demands of secondary and postsecondary education for a non-native speaker of English. In mastering English, non-native English speakers must obviously have considerable exposure to the target language. This input may come from a variety of formal and informal sources in either oral or written form. Depending on the nature of the learner's English language input, the student will have decidedly different strengths in comprehension and communicative competence. Cummins (1981b) distinguishes between two types of language proficiency, language used for social and academic purposes: *basic interpersonal communication skills (BICS)* and *cognitive-academic language proficiency (CALP)*.

BICS is the social language which enables students to speak and understand the English of everyday face-to-face conversational exchanges. Students largely acquire BICS naturally in daily interactions at school, work, or government offices, running errands, and socializing with peers. This surface English proficiency includes ability to manage relatively complex communicative tasks and activities with the aid of contextual clues such as paralinguistic feedback from the other speaker (e.g, facial expressions, nods, gestures, intonation) and other situational clues to meaning.

The more opportunities students have to communicate in a variety of contexts in English both in and away from school, the faster they will master the conventions and discourse of daily social interactional English. As stated earlier, immigrant students who have completed a fair amount of formal schooling in the United States and who often have jobs which require English language skills may have a fairly solid foundation in BICS and converse very fluently in face-to-face interactions. Many other non-native English speakers have had far fewer regular opportunities to interact with proficient English-language users in a wide range of contexts. For example, many resident students must dash from a demanding school schedule to an equally demanding work schedule, often to a job within their own linguistic community, which leaves them little or no time for socializing on or off campus and acquiring more interpersonal communicative competence in English.

International and immigrant students who arrive with weak listening comprehension in English and less fluent communicative patterns similarly struggle to find opportunities to interact with native speakers of English or fluent bilinguals. They may excel at reading textbook assignments or objective tests but feel overwhelmed by the flow of uncontrolled rapid language they encounter in oral presentations and discussions during class and even when engaging in relatively simple exchanges after class or during office hours. Although they have mastered an impressive English vocabulary and grammar foundation through formal study and extensive reading, international and immigrant students who have spent relatively little time in the United States rarely are familiar with the discourse conventions of American classroom discussions or small-group process which would enable them to participate more dynamically, appropriately interrupt the flow of a lesson to request clarification, or raise a contrary point of view.

Most activities in college classes across the disciplines require a strong foundation in BICS and an even greater proficiency in CALP, the academic language which enables students to deal in more cognitively demanding and context-reduced learning tasks and communicative situations such as formal lectures, lengthy class discussions, standardized tests, textbooks and journal articles. Collier's (1989) review of ESL student achievement in public schools supports Cummins's (1981a) finding that it takes students who are beginners in English approximately two years to acquire surface fluency in BICS after their arrival in the United States, but at least five years of rich and varied exposure to the English language to acquire native-like competence in CALP. Academic language proficiency includes background knowledge and specialized terminology of various academic disciplines along with the linguistic features of academic English prose versus conversational English. Understanding the distinct expectations for performance on assignments which stipulate directions such as *compare, justify, analyze,* or *evaluate* and recognizing the critical shifts in focus when writers employ transitional signals such as *moreover* or *nevertheless* or *consequently* are examples of the multiple forms of academic language proficiency necessary for success in higher education. This academic language proficiency is primarily developed through extensive reading in a variety of academic contexts and through years of repeated exposure to academic terminology during class discussions, lectures, films, and assignments.

Students who have completed less than five years of schooling in English and who do not have the opportunity or inclination to read widely in English are thus at a disadvantage with regard to development of CALP. Yet many ESL students enrolled in mainstream secondary and college classes have limited familiarity with sophisticated English vocabulary and academic tasks, compounded by below grade-level literacy in English and no extracurricular reading habit in either English or the native language. This situation helps to account for the fact that students who speak social English with fluency and confidence may have surprisingly weak reading and listening skills in English and vast gaps in their academic English proficiency.

To further clarify the distinction between BICS and CALP, Cummins has proposed that language uses be located on a quadrant with two continua. One axis distinguishes between **context embedded** communicative situations which offer a variety of contextual clues to assist in the comprehension of language (e.g., facial expressions, gestures, real objects, and feedback from the speaker/listener) and **context reduced** communicative situations which offer few clues (e.g., a formal lecture, a textbook page, a calculus equation). The other extends from *cognitively undemanding* to *cognitively*

demanding communicative situations. The distinction between these two terms may be explained as the difference between a subconscious control of the routines of everyday life (undemanding) and a conscious focus on comprehending new language, concepts, and material (demanding).

Provision of Comprehensible English Input

Many academic activities within college classes are *both* cognitively demanding and context-reduced, making comprehension and retention of material extremely challenging for students who have not yet acquired full English language proficiency. Krashen (1985) claims that an ESL student acquires new vocabulary, grammar, and concepts in English only by understanding messages or "comprehensible input" at a level of difficulty just slightly beyond the learner's current level of English ability. If the English input is not roughly tuned to the student's ability to understand, then the spoken or written communication becomes meaningless. Krashen's "input hypothesis" has been influential in providing a rationale for content instructors to become more comprehensible by adjusting their spoken delivery and building in greater contextual support for lessons. Instructors across all academic disciplines can greatly enhance learning and participation for non-native speakers of English by making a concerted effort to add linguistic and contextual support to their lessons and ensuring maximum "comprehensible input." In so doing, an instructor is not "watering down" lessons, but rather increases curricular access for non-native English readers and listeners.

Christison and Krahnke's (1986) interviews with eighty non-native English speakers studying in U.S. colleges indicated that the quality most valued in an instructor was *comprehensibility*, the ability to provide students with a rich but understood experience with academic language and content. However, Chiang and Dunkel's (1992) examination of the effect of speech modification and listening proficiency on how well adult ESL listeners understood lectures revealed that what comprises comprehensible oral input can be different for different English learners. Their results indicated that for students with higher listening proficiency, providing redundant information through repetition, paraphrasing, and synonyms greatly augmented their comprehension of extended lecture material, whereas it did not appear sufficient to improve comprehension for students at lower levels. Students with weaker comprehension and retention of material presented through lecture/discussion need additional modifications of input. These specific modifications are echoed in the research-based recommendations of Hatch (1983) and Chaudron and Richards (1986) and include the following: (a) clearer articulation; (b) slower speech rate; (c) emphatic stress; (d) rhetorical signaling or framing; and (e) clearly signaled macromarkers (e.g., *What I plan to discuss today*) rather than non-facilitative micromarkers (e.g., *OK, all right*). These results suggest that an instructor with ESL students ranging from more proficient to more challenged listeners will need to rigorously monitor their speech delivery to equitably involve non-native listeners in the discourse of the classroom community.

GENERAL INSTRUCTIONAL STRATEGIES THAT PROMOTE LANGUAGE AND CONCEPT DEVELOPMENT FOR NON-NATIVE SPEAKERS OF ENGLISH

Although considerable variation exists among ESL students, there are a number of instructional strategies which should be appreciated by all non-native English speakers and no doubt many native-English speakers. The findings of schema and second-language acquisition research have many practical implications for educators across the disciplines who aspire toward creation of a more democratic learning environment for linguistically and culturally diverse students. In essence, theory and classroom practice in content-based second language instruction point to the primacy of: (a) subject matter; (b) background knowledge; (c) comprehensible English input; (d) contextualized language development; and (e) effective study skills.

The remainder of this chapter describes both general and specific instructional strategies that enable ESL students to achieve second language acquisition during the process of learning academic subject matter and study skills. Instructors in any discipline can use the following general strategies: (a) enhance lessons with greater contextual and linguistic support for English learners; (b) model effective learning and study approaches for specific subject matter; and (c) provide greater opportunities for classroom interaction, making new concepts, language, and tasks more comprehensible and memorable.

Consciously Modify and Monitor Your Speech Delivery

- Use a slightly slower but natural speech rate.
- Enunciate more clearly.
- Exaggerate intonation to emphasize key words and phrases.
- Add considerable redundancy, using examples, anecdotes, expansions, and paraphrases.
- Pause adequately between phrases or statements to allow time for thought-processing, question formation, and notetaking in English.

- Limit use of idiomatic expressions, understanding that many non-native English speakers may be unfamiliar with culturally based references and metaphors.
- Provide definitions, examples, synonyms, antonyms, or other clues for challenging concepts and words with multiple meanings.

Support Verbal Explanations with Context Clues

- Provide visuals to clarify key concepts: pictures, photos, films, chalkboard illustrations, diagrams, outlines, charts, maps, globes, models.
- Use gestures and facial expressions to dramatize meaning.
- Give clear step-by-step instructions and model procedures for new tasks.
- Distribute models of completed assignments that students can emulate: essay exam responses, lab reports, speech outlines, problem analyses, lecture notes, journal entries.

Encourage Student Interaction and Active Participation

- Incorporate regular opportunities for students to work with a partner or a small group.
- Expect all students to participate and call on them in an equitable manner.
- Precede class discussions and question-answer sessions with some form of prepared participation (e.g., a quick write, review of lecture notes or assigned reading and question formulation) to encourage voluntary participation from less confident English users.
- Do not constantly pose questions to the group at large, allowing a minority of

more confident or impulsive students to dominate the discussion.
- Increase wait time (3–5 seconds) after inviting a non-native English speaker to respond in order to allow adequate time for question processing and thought formulation.
- Focus on the content or the meaning of student responses rather than on the pronunciation or grammatical accuracy.
- Elicit responses to student questions first from fellow classmates to allow peers greater opportunities to share and construct knowledge.

Design Appropriate Lessons

- Design topically focused units with lessons that integrate language, concepts, reading, writing, and study-skill development.
- Identify and explain lesson objectives, major concepts, and critical academic vocabulary for students to aid them in following the lesson.
- Activate and build on prior knowledge and experiences at the beginning of challenging lessons with brainstorming, visuals, and small-group activities.
- Precede reading and writing activities with listening and speaking activities.
- Scrutinize your assignments to see if there are any direction words or format conventions with which students may not be familiar.
- Provide adequate modeling and demonstrations for all new assignments.
- Coach your students in effective learning strategies within your academic discipline; share successful yet manageable approaches to lecture notetaking, reading and annotating chapters

and articles, synthesizing reading material for study, mastering new terminology, brainstorming ideas for reports or essays, problem-solving, test-preparation and test-taking.

- Structure opportunities for active, hands-on learning.

Carefully Monitor Comprehension

- Review at regular intervals while covering a topic.
- Make frequent comprehension checks using different questioning types.
- Throughout the lesson assign brief tasks to ascertain comprehension problems: oral summaries of main points, quickwrites, or prepared written questions.
- Provide opportunities for students to rehearse information and demonstrate comprehension in a variety of ways: oral, written, graphic organizers.
- Make yourself accessible after class and during office hours for students who may feel too apprehensive to seek clarification or modeling in front of native-speaker peers during the class session.

Instructors who utilize these general instructional practices throughout the academic year can make great strides toward motivating ESL students and assisting them in becoming more confident and competent learners. However, the critical integration of *academic language, subject area background knowledge,* and *study skills* known to enhance learning for bilingual/bicultural students requires conscientious planning and cannot be left to chance. The approaches for structuring learning through lecture, discussion, and small-group formats described in greater detail in the following sections demonstrate how through relatively easy modifications instructors can enhance their

lessons to enable more involved and productive learning for students pursuing an education in a foreign language and culture.

Strategies Which Promote Active Listening and Notetaking

While lectures, discussions, and more spontaneous explanations and demonstrations are at times the most efficient method of introducing subject matter, they present particular difficulties for students who are still in the process of acquiring English language proficiency. Listening to sustained oral presentation of academic material is a highly intellectual activity involving successful processing and interpretation of incoming information. Following and accurately recording content delivered through lecture or discussion is a complex comprehension process in which a student must grasp ideas, assess their relative importance, and connect these ideas to other ideas. Lectures are an unusually concentrated form of oral communication that require all students to put higher-level attention, thinking, and responding skills into play and place non-native listeners at a distinct linguistic disadvantage. In a review of information-processing in bilinguals, Dornic (1979) emphasized that processing oral input in a second language takes more time at every stage: decoding, rehearsal in short-term memory, organization of information for storage, and retrieval of information from long-term memory. Many international and immigrant students have limited opportunities outside the classroom to use English for social purposes and thereby improve their interactional fluency and comprehension, let alone to engage in prolonged discussions of cognitively and linguistically demanding subject matter. Listening for several hours of academic English in a series of content area classes can therefore easily overwhelm a non-native English listener and result in cognitive linguistic overload.

Adamson's (1993) naturalistic investigation of how adolescent and adult ESL students accomplished academic tasks in content courses confirmed that even the most academically and linguistically prepared students had considerable difficulty taking good notes from lectures. A frequent observation in the case studies was that instructors across disciplines thought that their ESL students were following the course material much better than they actually were. However, throughout the semester, these instructors rarely interacted in or out of class with their ESL students and therefore didn't realize that most were struggling with homework assignments and classroom activities.

In addition to weak sustained listening comprehension in English, ESL students often lack the specialized terminology of academic disciplines and a sophisticated repertoire of idiomatic English usage. Comparatively weak vocabulary recognition and unfamiliarity with higher education classroom practices in the United States make it all the more difficult to pick up on the variety of verbal and nonverbal cues that instructors provide to signal that information is indeed worth noting. Examples of such signals are intonation, pausing, posture, movements, and gestures as well as emphasis words (e.g., "the principal problem was ..."), transitions (e.g., "now let's examine ..."), and enumerations (e.g., there are three potential effects ..."). As a result, ESL students can experience difficulty distinguishing main ideas in lectures and discussions from less important supporting information. Some students only copy information written on the board and miss illustrative examples and elaborations of points, leaving class with a very sketchy record of the lesson. Frustrated by their relatively unproductive efforts to follow the

stream of discourse and simultaneously take coherent notes, many non-native speakers opt to simply sit back and listen in hopes of grasping more of the main points.

Another common reason that many immigrant students do not take effective class notes is that this basic skill is rarely integrated systematically across the secondary curriculum in the United States. In few core content area classes are students introduced to discipline-specific learning and study strategies, then given sufficient opportunities to practice with constructive feedback in order to master the skills. International students can enter higher education equally underprepared for the active listening and notetaking challenges of lecture/discussion formats. Benson (1989) investigated an international graduate student's actual listening activities at a U.S. university, following completion of a pre-university intensive English program. The researcher found that the various activities in the student's graduate courses bore little resemblance to anything he had done in his intensive English program. Furthermore, recent immigrants and international students frequently arrive in college classes with different schema knowledge of teacher expectations and strategies for successfully meeting these expectations, what Saville-Troike and Kliefgen (1986) refer to as "scripts for school." Without adequate clarification of course expectations as well as integrated study skill development, students educated abroad are apt to use inappropriate strategies for reading textbooks, writing papers, taking lecture notes, and participating in discussions based on the scripts for school they learned in their native countries.

Active listening and notetaking are among the most neglected of the skills taught in school, despite research that shows they are crucial to secondary and postsecondary academic achievement. Conaway (1982) found listening comprehension to be a primary factor in college students' achievement and retention. "Among students who fail, deficient listening skills was a stronger factor than reading skills or academic aptitude." Palmatier and Bennett (1974) found that 75 percent of college students who failed courses had never before taken notes. In contrast, 99 percent of high-achieving students took lecture notes although only 17 percent had ever received any formal instruction in notetaking.

Given the complexities of following classroom discourse and taking effective notes for ESL students, it seems reasonable to expect concerned instructors to modify their delivery, activate and build high-level schemata, and model "learning to learn" in our respective disciplines. Instructors in all subject areas may utilize the following strategies while presenting critical information orally during lessons to facilitate accurate listening comprehension, active engagement, and notetaking for non-native speakers of English and other students who do not have a strong auditory learning modality.

Enabling Lecturing Strategies

1. Early in the term, teach your students a notetaking system. One system which has been proven successful for students within many disciplines is the Cornell Method, also called the Recall Clue Note-taking System. Spend adequate time explaining and modeling a manageable system such as this one and also sharing examples of well-taken notes on a particular lecture.

2. Encourage native English-speaking students or fluent bilinguals who take effective notes to share them with peers who are less proficient note takers. A teaching assistant can also compare and review lecture notes in a follow-up study session.

3. Help structure the notetaking process and lighten the listening load for stu-

dents by providing a partially completed "skeletal" outline of your lecture that organizes main ideas into headings and subheadings. This advance organizer is particularly helpful when presented in the format of the notetaking system that you have already introduced and modeled in class. Fill in key terms, phrases, and definitions on this outline as you progress through the lecture. Provide a handout for lengthy presentations of information and utilize the board or overhead projector for simpler outlines which students may easily copy. Do not, however, display a completed outline of your lecture; this will reinforce passive learning and busy students with copying rather than focus their engaged listening and participation.

4. Assist students in writing more quickly and selectively in English by providing them with simple shorthand guidelines along with a key or glossary of abbreviations and symbols for common words and recurring terms in your discipline.

5. Emphasize the importance of completing assigned readings, taking reading summary notes, and formulating questions for the instructor before attending a lecture on a particular topic. Prereading the material encourages coming to class with some familiarity with the topic.

6. At the beginning of the lecture, establish connections with recent lessons. Begin with a brief review of the main ideas covered in the previous class session. You can also ask students to summarize the main points of the previous lesson first in pairs, then as a unified class.

7. Clarify the topic and key objectives of your lecture at the very beginning. Help students identify the major purpose of the lecture (e.g., to clarify assigned reading, to present supplemental material, to demonstrate a pattern or trend).

8. Write as legibly as possible on the board or on overhead transparencies, keeping in mind that students educated abroad are often unfamiliar with cursive writing and only recognize printing in English.

9. Allow and even encourage usage of a tape recorder during lectures and discussions so that students with weaker listening abilities can review the material as many times as necessary to better comprehend and retain information.

10. Before and during the lecture, identify key terms, and write all important vocabulary and points on the board or an overhead transparency.

11. Modify your normal conversational style to make your formal delivery as articulate and comprehensible as possible for non-native listeners: use a slightly slower speech rate, increase volume, enunciate clearly, exaggerate intonation to emphasize important points and transitions, limit idiomatic expressions, and pause adequately at the end of a statement to allow time for thought-processing, question formation, and notetaking.

12. Follow an orderly progression of ideas and stick closely to your outline, avoiding constant digressions, thereby enabling students with less academic English proficiency to more readily identify essential lesson information and reduce potential "linguistic clutter."

13. Complement challenging information relayed orally with visual aids: e.g., illustrations, charts, advance organizers, concept maps, demonstrations.

14. Include many concrete examples and analogies so that students can conceptualize concepts within a more familiar context, and also invite relevant examples from students. Stop the lecture after introducing a key concept to encourage students to write down a relevant example in their notes. Asking everyone to first reflect in this manner will generally elicit more voluntary contributions from ESL class members.

15. Build in considerable redundancy with repetitions, examples, anecdotes, expansions, and paraphrases.

16. Relate information to assigned readings whenever possible and give the precise place within the text or selection, thereby enabling students who need more written reinforcement to indicate these page numbers in their notes and find the information later for study or review.

17. Highlight major points and transitions with broad gestures, facial expressions, purposeful movement, erect posture, and exaggerated intonation. You can additionally focus your students' listening and notetaking by using clear, consistent verbal signals or cues (e.g., *furthermore*, *in summary*) that indicate the structure and progression of your ideas.

18. Make regular eye contact with all your students to help keep them engaged and to better note potential confusion.

19. Check for comprehension regularly rather than at the end of the lecture. Predetermine critical transitions and stop the lecture at these junctures to ask students to summarize key points first in pairs and then as a unified class. Ask students to review their notes up to that point, either individually or in pairs, and write down any questions they would like answered. Prepared question formation in pairs or small groups affords self-conscious English users and less academically prepared students a chance to first rehearse material with peers, promoting greater comprehension and retention of subject matter while instilling confidence to pose thoughtful higher-order questions before the entire class.

20. Save adequate time at the end to summarize the main points, again making sure to have a visual reinforcement, even if it be a sketchy outline on the chalkboard.

21. Allow students a few minutes at the end of class to compare and edit their notes in small groups or pairs, and then formulate

any final questions for the unified class and/or instructor which they could not answer within their small group. This will build in crucial rehearsal of information and ensure that students have articulated any confusion before leaving to complete follow-up individual assignments.

Strategies for Facilitating More Equitable Class Discussions

Topically focused class discussions potentially offer ESL students rich exposure to new vocabulary and opportunities to interact in a variety of academic situations—reporting information, summarizing, synthesizing, responding, and debating. However, discussions require far more active involvement and participation than do traditional lectures and may be quite challenging for non-native speakers of English to follow, get involved, and identify more significant information for study notes. Few instructors who have had a variety of ESL students in their classes will be surprised to learn that ESL college students investigated in both Benson (1989) and Adamson's (1993) case studies were extremely reluctant to speak up in class, even when they had vital contributions to make or crucial questions to ask. Linguistically diverse students will remain relatively passive participants in whole-class discussions for varied reasons, including insecurity about their listening comprehension, pronunciation, word choice, and appropriate interactional conventions. In heterogeneous classes, many feel reluctant to compete with confident, outspoken native speakers who often dominate the discussion, or report having encountered impatience and intolerance in previous efforts to respond or ask questions. Further, many of the participants in Adamson's (1993) case study came from countries such as Vietnam and Japan where student involvement in class is nonexistent.

Fear of being ridiculed because of imperfect English and unfamiliar scripts for classroom interaction can leave many bilingual/bicultural students tongue-tied in their various college classes and reticent to share their unique perspectives.

Instructors may draw from the following strategies to lead more equitable, carefully orchestrated class discussions which provide language-promoting assistance and facilitate more engaged, voluntary participation for non-native speakers of English:

1. Create a supportive classroom environment for less confident English users by encouraging all students to talk in turn, to listen actively while others talk, and to offer assistance rather than impatience and intolerance for classmates who need some assistance in understanding or responding.

2. Show your students that you expect them all to participate in oral activities by regularly inviting every member of the class to contribute, calling on students by name when possible, and attempting to call on both native- and non-native English speakers in an equitable manner.

3. Build in regular opportunities for prepared participation to assist non-native speakers in responding more regularly and voluntarily. Allow students to do a focused quickwrite in response to a key question at the beginning or during a class session. Assign questions for students to complete before coming to class. Allow students to share observations and questions and generate examples with a partner to increase learning and ESL student confidence and motivation to contribute to a unified class discussion.

4. Be sensitive to the linguistic and conceptual demands of discussion questions and activities. Don't inhibit future participation by pushing students to communicate too far beyond their current level of English proficiency.

5. The easiest content for less proficient English users to handle is often related to their everyday lives and activities. Make a concerted effort to build in opportunities for ESL students to share relevant information about their cultures, communities, and histories.

6. Attempt to activate students' existing relevant background knowledge on topics, and provide through schema-building activities (e.g., brainstorming, mapping, advance organizers) requisite linguistic, conceptual, and cultural information which would otherwise prevent them from active learning and participation.

7. Move purposefully around the room to enable as many students as possible to enjoy having close proximity to the instructor, which should also encourage students to remain more alert and willing to volunteer responses and questions.

8. Do not constantly pose questions to the group at large, allowing a minority of more confident or impulsive students to dominate the discussion.

9. Ask a question before naming the respondent to encourage active learning by allowing all students to "attend" and decide how they would answer.

10. Draw in less confident students by asking them to respond to an open-ended question after they have heard a variety of responses from their classmates.

11. Call on English learners to answer not only safer, less demanding knowledge questions based on the course material, but also more challenging, open-ended questions which provide opportunities for thoughtful and extended use of their second language.

12. Increase wait time (3–5 seconds) after asking a non-native speaker to respond to allow adequate time for the student to successfully process the question and formulate a thoughtful response.

13. When trying to draw a specific ESL student into a discussion, it often helps to first pose the question and make direct eye contact with the student while stating her name; then pause a few seconds for the student to recover and focus before restating the question verbatim.

14. Discourage classmates from routinely blurting out responses and either interrupting or intimidating shy or less confident English users.

15. If a student asks a question or responds in a very soft, unintelligible voice, politely ask the student to repeat the contribution so that the entire class can benefit. Frequently, non-native speakers will muffle well-stated responses out of insecurity about a self-perceived accent or inappropriate usage.

16. Do not interrupt a student's thought processes after asking a question by immediately posing follow-up questions. These tandem questions greatly confuse rather than assist English learners who may not realize that the instructor is attempting to rephrase the initial question. It greatly facilitates ESL student listening comprehension and responding if the instructor pauses and formulates a single, clearly worded question, then pauses again for a student response.

17. Encourage students to talk through nonverbal means such as establishing eye contact, waiting adequately and patiently, smiling, and nodding in approval.

18. Make any corrections indirectly by mirroring in correct form what the student has said. For example, suppose a student says *"Majority immigrants San Francisco from Pacific Rim."* You can repeat, *"This is true. A majority of the recent immigrants in San Francisco come from the Pacific Rim."*

19. Use English interactional discourse conventions (see following list) regularly during class, and in so doing model for all of your students how to use them appropriately within class discussions and small-group work to more successfully convey their thoughts and concerns:

confirmation checks	*So you believe that…*
	You are suggesting that…
	If I understand you correctly…
	So what you are saying is…
clarification requests	*What do you mean by that?*
	Could you give me an example of that?
	Would you mind repeating that comment?
	Sorry, I didn't quite follow your last comment.
comprehen-sion checks	*Do you understand what I'm saying?*
	Have I made myself clear?
	Do you see my point?
	Are you with me?
interrupting	*Excuse me, but…*
	Sorry for interrupting, but…
	May I interrupt for a moment?
	Can I ask a question?
correcting oneself	*What I mean is…*
	What I meant was…
	Let me restate/rephrase that…
	Let me put that another way…

Strategies for Effective Group Work Design and Implementation

Over the past decade English-as-a-second-language specialists have documented the multiple benefits of small-group classroom learning in terms of second language acquisition, content mastery, and prosocial development. Small-group activities have been shown to provide English learners with more opportunities to initiate and practice real-world communication with a wider range of language functions (Long & Porter, 1985). Interactions such as restating and il-

lustrating allow second language users opportunities to clarify their contributions, elaborate explanations, and resolve disagreements. These interactions help develop understanding of the English usage and discourse strategies as well as lesson material. McGroarty (1989) describes how cooperative learning arrangements encourage ESL students to take a mutual and active role in the acquisition of knowledge and language skills. Cooperative activities additionally promote a more positive affective climate in which non-native English speakers feel more comfortable and willing to take risks in their second language. Working with peers, ESL students are allowed to serve as experts on certain topics and to learn from one another and native-speaker peers rather than receiving information from the teacher or the text alone. McGroarty further notes that in classes marked by linguistic heterogeneity, competitive individualistic learning approaches run the risk of primarily rewarding native speakers and those who have close to native-like language abilities. Regular inclusion of cooperative activities promotes more positive cross-ethnic relationships than do solely competitive or individualistic college learning experiences (Johnson & Johnson, 1989). Moreover, cooperative structures enable college students from different backgrounds to learn the thinking, communication, and social skills vital to success in an increasingly interdependent workplace and world.

Despite these benefits of task-based cooperative activities, faculty who have tried to introduce small-group learning in classroom settings with students from diverse cultural backgrounds can speak to a variety of implementation obstacles. Many teachers of ESL students encounter difficulty in adapting the collaborative instructional practices introduced in workshops or resource guides designed for native-English speakers. Efforts to create a more demo-cratic learning environment may be met with considerable reluctance by diverse English learners. This result is in part due to the fact that most instructional resources and professional training on cooperative, small-group learning do not adequately address the needs of large, heterogeneous adult classes—diverse in personality, socio-economic status, home languages, cultures, English-language proficiency, prior school-ing, educational attitudes and biases, first and second language literacy, learning styles, and academic achievement. Students clearly enter our classes with differential preparation and predispositions to operate effectively in heterogeneous work groups.

Students with years of formative edu-cation abroad generally require special con-sideration before they can confidently and competently work with peers within a class-room setting. International and immigrant students educated in a traditional, hierar-chical system customarily regard the instructor as an unquestioned authority on subject matter. These students are likely to expect this revered scholar to deliver formal unchallenged lectures while they assume a receptive role taking verbatim notes. Stu-dents coming from an authority-centered educational system may additionally be socialized to accept anything from a profes-sor as truth and to never entertain opinions different from those of the expert. They may consequently expect considerable direction from the instructor and perceive little aca-demic value in class discussions or activities in which classmates share and construct knowledge. For students who are non-native speakers of English, reticence to par-ticipate in small-group activities can also be attributable to insecurity about perceived English language proficiency and a general lack of familiarity with small-group pro-cess, pragmatics, and language functions.

Immigrant students who have com-pleted some schooling in the United States before entering college may voice similar reservations about participating in small-group activities with native-English-speak-ing peers. Despite the relatively recent infu-sion of cooperative learning into the K–12 curriculum, a great number of students graduate from high schools in the United States with little training in the skills neces-sary for small-group work. They come to college classrooms underprepared for the social, linguistic, and academic challenges of complex cooperative tasks. In addition, some ESL students have had frustrating or unproductive prior experiences working with classmates, stemming from intolerant or alienating behavior from fellow group members or from inappropriate tasks or inadequate guidelines and modeling on the part of the instructor.

To encourage students with diverse educational backgrounds and diverse class-room work-style preferences to perceive learning from peers as a viable instructional approach, faculty can begin the semester by asking students to articulate their prior experiences working with classmates and the variables that contribute to making peer collaboration a positive or negative learning experience. Using a questionnaire or jour-nal assignment, for example, you may dis-cover that the majority never had a positive prior experience working with peers in class. Initial activities will understandably require considerable justification, structure, modeling, facilitation, and validation of both academic and social achievement. In another class, you may discover that the students are unanimously enthusiastic about working collaboratively but want the instructor to establish the small groups throughout the semester, rather than place individuals in the often uncomfortable situ-ation of selecting a work group.

Drawing from research in learning styles and second-language acquisition as well as practical teaching experiences in multicultural college contexts, Kinsella and Sherak (1993) offer the following suggestions for implementing successful small-group learning in heterogeneous college classes. These instructional practices feature careful design structure, modeling, guidance, and evaluation, enabling students with a wide range of personalities, learning styles, English language proficiency, and educational preparation to find cooperative activities more academically and personally rewarding.

1. At the beginning of your course, provide a compelling rationale for inclusion of group activities in your curriculum (e.g., opportunities for interaction, information-sharing, problem-solving, practicing the democratic process, collaborative skills valued in the workplace, a more student-centered classroom).

2. Incorporate shorter group activities regularly into lessons rather than assigning one major group project; collaborative learning skills develop over time, with exposure to varied task types and experiences with different roles and group dynamics.

3. Make sure the tasks assigned to groups provide a clear incentive for students to work as a team rather than as individuals within the group. Ideally, the activity:

a) lends itself to collaboration, creative problem-solving, knowledge construction

b) is clearly tied to ongoing course content and integrated into a thematic unit with a variety of other individual and group assignments

c) is intrinsically motivating

d) promotes a positive affective climate

e) is centered around a specific task to be completed

f) has clearly articulated outcomes and manageable steps for achieving those outcomes

g) builds confidence with subject matter and academic skills so that students can successfully complete a subsequent independent assignment (e.g., a brainstorming prereading activity before completing a textbook chapter)

4. In general, form teacher-selected heterogeneous groups including students of diverse gender, ethnicity, and academic preparation. Heterogeneous teams produce greater opportunities for achievement, tutoring, and peer support, and improve cross-race relations and integration. Self-selection runs the risk of promoting status hierarchies in the classroom. When integrating spontaneous, less time-consuming, and perhaps less complex small-group tasks, students could be allowed to form self-selected groups or partners.

5. Assign students to heterogeneous groups and keep them in these same groups for one month, thereby allowing them to work in three or four base groups over the course of the term. This practice will allow students adequate time to develop more familiarity and confidence with their group members and to experience a variety of roles within that same working group. Sustained teamwork also helps students acquire the skills necessary to work effectively on a variety of task types with people from different backgrounds under varied conditions and ensures a more productive and collegial group process.

6. A recommended team size is four because it is large enough to allow for greater heterogeneity and richness of contribution while small enough to enable more manageable group processes and more responsible, equitable participation.

7. Establish consistent routines and procedures for group work so that class time devoted to small group activities can proceed efficiently and yield more time on task.

8. When introducing an activity, relate it to previously covered material or similar completed tasks so that students see its function within the ongoing curriculum.

9. Make the academic purpose and expected outcome of the activity explicit so that students will perceive learning with and from peers as a justifiable activity in higher education.

10. Give clear oral instructions for the activity accompanied by a visual aid; write the steps on a handout, the chalkboard, or an overhead transparency.

11. When assigning a more complicated or unfamiliar task, provide illustrative examples and sufficient modeling.

12. Build in time for students to request clarification of the task demands before they move into their small groups so that you don't have to go from group to group responding to questions.

13. Establish the time frame for the activity, making sure that you have provided sufficient time for successful completion of all components of the task and follow-up reports, processing, and evaluation.

14. Explain the various group member roles with expected behaviors necessary for completion of the task.

15. Take an active, facilitative role when the groups are working; check progress, provide guidance and validation, and get students back on task.

16. Allow sufficient time after completion of the activity to process it as a unified class, clarifying what was learned and validating what was accomplished.

17. Make sure that students see the relationship between what was generated or accomplished during this group activity and any follow-up individual assignments.

18. Incorporate listening and responding tasks for students to complete during group reports to facilitate task processing and ensure active learning and accountability (e.g., note-taking, summarizing, question formation).

19. Provide opportunities for students to evaluate their individual and group performance and to inform you of any difficulties they may be experiencing by way of quickwrites, journal entries, or feedback forms.

20. Provide clear, constructive feedback to working groups on both their prosocial skills and academic accomplishments, using a simple, consistent evaluation process and form.

CONCLUDING REMARKS

ESL students must not only learn English for diverse communicative purposes; they must also master demanding academic content and skills taught in an unfamiliar educational system. Whether they are immigrant, refugee, or international students, entering U.S. higher education means competing in the arena of language and culture against native students. Due to prior inadequate educational opportunities, some bilingual students must work even more diligently than others to surmount the dual hurdles of academic English language and literacy. Colleges across the nation are generally underprepared to assist these students in attaining academic and social success by providing vital support systems. Even when campuses offer tutoring and academic advising, these services often amount to little more than a stop-gap measure. A higher-education environment that fosters pluralism is one in which members of all groups have equal educational opportunities. Unless individual instructors assume responsibility for reassessing their instructional delivery and curriculum to see that students who bring special educational histories and needs to the classroom are affirmed and enabled, then we cannot say that we are truly responding to diversity. All bilingual/bicultural students bring novel perspectives, processes, and questions that can energize the classroom and challenge both our curriculum and methodology. If educators across disciplines strive to create democratic learning environments that are inclusive of the histories and accomplishments of different communities and which support English language, conceptual, and study skill development, we can help all non-native English speakers make their unique contributions and benefit more fully from what U.S. higher education has to offer.

CHAPTER 8

Making Mathematics Instruction Inclusive

Efraim P. Armendariz
Professor of Mathematics
University of Texas at Austin

Louise Hasty, *Mathematics Department Head*
Riverside Campus, Austin Community College,
Austin, Texas

Editor's Notes:

Efraim Armendariz and Louise Hasty approach multicultural change in freshman calculus by describing the Emerging Scholars Program at the University of Texas, Austin. The program, based on Uri Treisman's work at Berkeley, employs structured cooperative learning groups as a vehicle for increasing the mathematics achievement of African American, Hispanic, rural, and urban students who have high mathematics potential and who are at risk for academic underachievement.

Some mathematics educators, such as ethnomathematician Marcia Ascher (*Ethnomathematics: A Multicultural View of Mathematical Ideas*, Pacific Grove, CA: Brooks/Cole, 1991) seek to modify mathematics *content* by infusing culture-specific material. In contrast, the authors of this chapter focus on changes in *instruction* to increase the probability of success for underrepresented students. Their explicit multicultural goal is to raise the mathematics competence of ethnic students through challenging rather than remedial instruction. Their changes in instruction are inclusive in their use of cooperative groups and intellectually demanding problems. The instruc-

tional model moves toward transformation as the groups mature into communities of learners, equalize power relations among leaders (doctoral-level teaching assistants) and freshman participants, and enhance students' mathematics self-concepts and independence.

The Emerging Scholars Program also involves changes in classroom dynamics, as staff clearly attend to students' social and emotional needs outside the classroom. The selection of instruction as the focus of the mathematics chapter is not intended to suggest a valuing of instructional over content modification in the field. Rather, its purpose is to provide one example of instructional change targeting one clear multicultural goal: raising underrepresented students' achievement. ∎

Mathematics constitutes an important foundation for many modern university subjects: physics, economics, technology, engineering, agriculture, management, and business among others. These disciplines use mathematics in increasingly sophisticated ways. The quantification of public policy issues such as the population explosion, nuclear

126

policy, information technology, Third World debt, AIDS, and other global health concerns signals the need for greater mathematics literacy among college students.

Despite the role of mathematics as an underlying structure in so many arenas of human activity, the need for mathematics competence has not materialized in increased student interest or in improved mathematics instruction. Researcher Sheila Tobias points out that the perception in the United States is that mathematics instruction must occur within "a certain mode of thinking and way of transferring information" (cited in Hoots, 1992, p. 301). A perceived elitism creates mathematics anxiety among many students, an attitude which "disables women and minorities more than others" (Tobias, 1991, p. 91). Tobias, an advocate of "mathematical mental health," says that "this mental health translates into better career choices, decisions made from strength and certainty instead of from weakness and avoidance, more risk-taking in college, and more persistence on the job" (Tobias, 1990, p. 49). Mathematics professor Lynn Steen, in his foreword to Sheila Tobias's work, *Succeed With Math* (1987), warned that rapidly changing demographics in this country are contributing to a crisis in "the equality of opportunity to learn" (p. xvii). In particular, African American and Hispanic students are dramatically underrepresented in mathematics classes and majors.

Uri Treisman's work at the University of California, Berkeley, stands out as the most successful and innovative program targeting diverse students in mathematics in recent years. Originally his doctoral dissertation, Treisman's study evolved out of a simple observation that two groups, African Americans and Chinese Americans, evidenced disparate success rates in first-year calculus at Berkeley. Informal analysis of this discrepancy led to the finding that the Chinese students combined social and study time, while African American students almost uniformly studied alone. Treisman's original goal was simply to recreate the sharing and community that the Chinese students had evolved for themselves and make it available in group workshops to African American and Hispanic students, with some modifications (Fullilove & Treisman, 1990). Treisman began with the premise that traditional remedial and counseling approaches have proven ineffective in achieving significant results for first-year underrepresented students in mathematics and engineering classes. Treisman chose instead to presume the possibility of academic excellence in all students, which provided an alternative foundation for new strategies aimed toward high achievement (Landis, 1985). Evaluations of the program stress three main findings: 1) the workshops foster an environment for members that values success and academic achievement; 2) workshops structure study time efficiently; and 3) skills learned tend to be transferred over to other academic activities, creating a greater sense of commitment in students and leading to higher success levels throughout the college years (Fullilove & Treisman, 1990).

Others have been applying Treisman's workshop model in various ways. Olson and Olson (1991), examining the deficit model of student assessment, recommend instead a competency model which builds on existing strengths of the student. They cite Treisman's work as an example of successful alternative teaching strategies. Fischbach and Johnson (1992) have taken Treisman's collaborative workshop model and applied it to vocational and technical mathematics courses in community college settings. By 1990, over 25 institutions of higher education had adopted Treisman's model (Conciatore, 1990, p. 5).

Treisman's model represents a systematic effort to change the instructional component of a mathematics course with the specific multicultural goal of supporting the mathematics achievement of diverse students. The program requires adaptation and integration into the specific university or college system. One very successful adaptation to the Treisman model that will be discussed here is the Emerging Scholars Program at the University of Texas at Austin. This chapter seeks to enable interested faculty to design a similar program for their institutions. The chapter begins with a rationale for the program followed by a description of program components including student selection, content and processes, and instructor role. Outcomes and recommendations are discussed.

RATIONALE, CONTEXT, AND PURPOSE

In Fall 1988, Dr. Efraim Armendariz, Professor of Mathematics, and Ms. Jacqueline McCaffrey, Program Development Specialist in the College of Natural Sciences, established the Emerging Scholars Program at the University of Texas at Austin. The program was designed using as a basis the Professional Development Program workshops in mathematics which had been started and developed at the University of California, Berkeley, by Dr. Uri Treisman (Watkins, 1989).

Dr. Armendariz became interested in the Berkeley mathematics program upon learning that the workshops accentuated and extended the strengths of diverse students rather than following a path of remediation. A second and perhaps more important factor was the observation that the program was based on academic achievement, structured around an academic course in the mainstream of the curriculum rather than a social support structure. The Emerging Scholars Program (ESP), a joint program of the Department of

Mathematics and the College of Natural Sciences, thus became the only program designed primarily for diverse students at the University of Texas to incorporate all of these features.

The Berkeley workshops intrigued Ms. McCaffrey because she counseled many students of color, rural, and women students— the groups now targeted by ESP. A high proportion of these students historically failed to complete the calculus sequence at the University of Texas (UT). Before the establishment of the Emerging Scholars Program, Ms. McCaffrey observed that time after time students from these population groups entered the university with high motivations and expectations to be successful, yet were unable to translate these strengths into achievement in college courses. The intensive nature of the Berkeley workshops and their ability to greatly increase the success of these students impressed her.

As a result of their common concerns, Ms. McCaffrey and Dr. Armendariz studied the program at Berkeley, worked with Dr. Treisman, and organized a trial workshop at UT. The success achieved in the first year of operation resulted in the formal establishment of the Emerging Scholars Program at UT. Although modeled directly on the Berkeley workshops, the adaptation designed for use at Austin has proven highly successful. The UT program possesses many features which demonstrate the transformation of instructional strategies to support achievement in a mainstream mathematics sequence for a diverse student population (McCaffrey, 1991).

The philosophy incorporated in the establishment of ESP is consistent with that of the Berkeley Professional Development Program. When Treisman initiated the intensive mathematics workshops at Berkeley, he set them up as an honors program. His research findings substantiated the view that remedial assistance failed to retain students of color in mathematics and science disciplines (Treisman, 1992). The conventional explanations offered for poor minority performance did not hold for most of the students he observed. Rather, he found that these students lacked effective skills for coping with life as science and mathematics students at Berkeley. As a result, the workshops were designed to create a community of mutual support for students in an atmosphere of academic excellence.

PROGRAM OVERVIEW

The Emerging Scholars Program targets freshmen at the University of Texas at Austin who, despite their placement in a calculus course, are at risk for underachievement or attrition. These students typically have high SAT scores in mathematics and good standing in their high school graduating classes. These students also belong to population groups which have a history of failing calculus at UT. The ESP is a year-long program which encompasses both semesters of the calculus sequence. It is structured as an honors-type program for students who have potential to excel in mathematics.

The formal structure of ESP consists of the following:

- A student development specialist in the office of the Dean of Natural Sciences. The specialist screens students and acts as a resource for them after they are admitted to the program. This person acts as an advisor, informal counselor, and source of financial aid information for students in the program.
- Instructors of calculus classes who have agreed to have ESP workshops associated with their lecture sections.
- A workshop with 18 to 26 students for each ESP calculus section. Each workshop is led by a TA and has two student

assistants who were previous ESP participants. The workshops meet three days a week for two hours each meeting. Students sign up for the workshops on a credit/no credit basis. Each workshop entails group work focusing on a worksheet of calculus problems designed for a specific calculus topic. The worksheets are coordinated with the material presented in the lecture. The workshops constitute the heart of the program, and central to the workshops are the worksheets.

Students begin with an orientation meeting in the fall prior to the beginning of semester classes. A picnic is also held in October for all ESP participants. While the first ESP group consisted of one section with 17 students, the program has experienced substantial growth. During the fall semester of 1993 there were five Emerging Scholars Workshops with enrollments of approximately 25 students per section.

Selection of Students

Students are chosen to participate in the Emerging Scholars Program on the basis of membership in an underrepresented group, scholastic achievement, and personal interviews. During the spring and summer of each year, a student development specialist in the office of the Dean of the College of Natural Sciences screens entering freshman applications. The specialist identifies those who are African American, Hispanic, female, rural, or inner-city high school students.

Following this initial screening, a second screening is conducted to identify students with SAT mathematics scores of 600 or over (for indicated ability) or high class standing (evidence of motivation). Students who meet these criteria comprise the target group. Males with SAT mathematics scores between 550 and 600, or those with particularly high class standing, also are included. Program evaluation data indicate that females with SATs below 600 generally have difficulty with the program. An effort is made to ensure that equal numbers of men and women participate in the program. Additionally, inclusion of rural students as another target group provides workshops with a diverse mix by ethnicity (primarily African American, Hispanic, and White) as well as gender.

Following their selection, students receive a letter describing the Emerging Scholars Program and inviting them to inquire further. Students who express interest are interviewed by phone and at summer orientation sessions either individually or in small groups. During these interviews, students become acquainted with the expectations for participation in the workshops, which include:

- Work is very hard and at a higher level than the work required in their calculus classes.
- Students must be prepared to work in groups since the difficulty level of most problems presented precludes independent solutions in the allotted time.

Students need two courses to complete the calculus sequence. However, ESP does not require a full-year commitment because not all academic majors mandate a full year of calculus. The program specialist looks for a commitment to the work for one semester. Throughout the interview, the specialist emphasizes that the students are considered to be more than just competent. Students' prior record and performance are stressed as primary reasons for their being invited to participate in this honors-type program.

Frequently, students who do not meet the group membership and achievement criteria learn of the program and request inclusion. Such students are permitted to participate if they present a convincing case of their determination and commitment and if they would otherwise be able to enroll in the calculus course. Often students are encouraged to strengthen their preparation as a condition for participation, especially when the advising occurs early in the orientation period. For example, one such student, an African American woman, lacked the necessary mathematics background. The specialist advised her to take a precalculus course at the community college in her home town as a prerequisite for permission to enroll in ESP in the coming fall. The student complied and subsequently participated in ESP, earning a solid B in each semester of calculus. In contrast, an African American man who did not fit the required profile was referred to the program by another department. He had a very high SAT score but was ranked in the middle of his high school class. His high school mathematics achievement was not impressive, but he indicated a willingness to work. He attended the workshops but did not do his homework, failed the first two calculus tests, and dropped the course.

Components and Procedures

This section of the chapter answers questions typically asked about the content and instruction of the workshops.

What constitutes an ESP workshop? An ESP workshop's participants consist of

- a concerned teaching assistant (TA)
- two student assistants who are ESP alumni
- 18 to 26 students who have agreed to meet for six hours a week to work on challenging calculus problems

The focus of each meeting is group work on a worksheet of challenging problems.

What comprises a worksheet? Each TA prepares a worksheet for each workshop that extends the concepts the instructor is discussing in the lecture. Each worksheet should meet the following criteria:

- It should be challenging, not remedial.
- It should have five to eight problems coordinated with the topic being discussed in the lecture.
- Each problem on the worksheet should have several related parts.
- The worksheet should bring out the subtleties of the ideas in calculus.
- It should require use of the mathematical "tricks" and techniques that mathematicians typically employ to approach challenging calculus problems.
- The worksheet should be too challenging for students to complete during one workshop session.

The TAs do not provide students with solutions to the worksheets even when the students do not finish them in class. The intent is to illustrate, within a highly supportive environment, that students may not have all the answers to a set of mathematics problems, yet still can be successful in mathematics. Constructing worksheets is not a simple task. However, a large bank of problems is available from the workshops at Berkeley and at UT. TAs also use other texts and occasionally the more difficult problems at the end of the sections in the course textbook. In addition, they share problems and worksheets when appropriate. Two sample worksheets appear at the end of the chapter.

What happens the first day in an ESP workshop? On the first day the TA starts the workshop by introducing him or herself and the two student assistants. The TA then discusses his/her expectations of students. These expectations include:

- Group work: the students are expected to work on the worksheets in groups at each class meeting.
- Consistent attendance: roll is taken at every meeting, and students are instructed to notify the TA if they must miss a workshop.
- Mathematics presentation: each student presents to the class at some time during the semester the solution to a challenging problem from the worksheets.

The TA asks the students to introduce themselves to the group. Finally, the students choose their own groups of three to five and work together on a worksheet. From the first day, ESP emphasizes hard work on difficult calculus problems.

What activities take place in the workshop? At almost every meeting, students spend an hour and fifteen minutes to an hour and a half in group work on a worksheet. In addition, one or more of the following may occur:

- 10 to 15 minutes answering homework questions
- 30 to 45 minutes of students presenting problems from a previous worksheet
- a presentation by a guest speaker

The TAs arrange for three or four speakers each semester, which provides a unique opportunity for freshmen to hear a presentation about mathematics at their level. By the third or fourth week, the students know each other. When they enter the classroom they joke, talk, and settle in. They feel comfortable questioning the TA about the more difficult problems on their homework. When a student presents a worksheet problem to the entire workshop, the listeners actively request clarification to ensure their understanding and correct any errors committed by the presenter. This openness engages men and women of all ethnic backgrounds as a community of mathematics learners.

How do the groups work? When students divide into their small groups, they visit at first, settle in, and then start on the worksheet problems. They concentrate at times to the point of being oblivious to activities going on in the room. Pauses in their work occur, and they start again.

Sometimes the TAs assign students to groups. At other times students might select a group by counting off, identifying common birth months, or by finding another creative strategy. After several weeks they seem to be comfortable working with most of the other students. Occasionally, students encounter a particularly difficult peer, and the TA diplomatically counsels the peer and other group members. Occasionally, a student will fall behind on the homework or perform poorly on a test. The TA may assign this student to a specific, supportive group, or may ask a student assistant to spend additional time with him or her.

As the students begin working on the worksheet the TA and student assistants circulate around the room, exchanging a word, answering a question, checking a problem when asked. Occasionally students, the TA or student assistants approach the chalk board to explain a particularly complex idea or remind each other of some "trick" that they need for a problem. Students are expected to read ahead in their text and to work without the text in the workshop.

In the course of visiting different workshops we have been impressed with students' increasing ability to work in groups. From the first day, we observed some students willingly break into groups and share ideas. Within the groups, some at first tend to work alone or to merely tell each other how to solve a particular problem. After six weeks the students increasingly talk together about the approach to a problem, and they raise and answer each other's questions. As they continue working together, many students learn to help each other using the "Socratic" method of asking questions to guide their peers toward solutions. A student assistant commented that about six weeks into the semester his job became easier. When asked why, he responded that the students had fewer questions for him. The students were learning how to learn from each other.

What are some pitfalls to avoid in the workshops? From two workshops observed during a past semester, it became evident that the class of eighteen was slightly outperforming the class of twenty-six. The workshop of eighteen met in a large classroom with space for the TA and student assistants to circulate freely. The larger workshop occurred in a small room which limited the ability of the TA and student assistants to circulate among groups. Students in the larger workshop still scored higher than the lecture class average, but they were not performing as successfully as the class with eighteen. Class size and space should be considered in establishing workshops.

A second consideration is that teaching assistants must agree with the program's guiding principles. Two years ago, a TA in charge of one workshop was unable to attend any of the orientations for TAs and additionally never managed to treat the workshop as a chance for enhancing students' calculus skills. This TA developed all the worksheets from a remedial perspective. Students in the workshop finished the course with the same average as the rest of their lecture class. The lesson gleaned from this error supports the honors orientation intended by the Emerging Scholars Program. Remediation can raise students to a class average, but the Emerging Scholars Program implemented as it is intended will raise participants' average above the class average.

Finally, at Texas, as at other schools who have attempted similar programs, we are discovering a need for TAs and student assistants who are women and/or persons of color. Absence of such diversity inhibits workshop performance. This finding may stem from the fact that target students more readily identify with minority and women TAs and welcome their involvement in the students' learning.

Instructional Staff

What about the TAs? The TAs are chosen for their teaching ability and their in-depth knowledge of calculus. Generally they are advanced doctoral students in mathematics. We have observed that ESP students benefit from interacting with TAs who themselves are facing challenges in mathematics. Where possible, novice TAs apprentice as assistants in a veteran TA's workshop. In conjunction with the College of Natural Sciences, the UT Austin Mathematics Department holds an orientation for new TAs. This orientation has proven to be so successful that attendance now includes a significant number of participants from other colleges and universities who are interested in learning about the Emerging Scholars Program.

The orientation for TAs takes place in the middle of August and spans two days. Faculty and staff, TAs and former ESP students talk with the participants about the significance of the various aspects of the Emerging Scholars Program. A major portion of the orientation involves participants in submitting problems for worksheets on a calculus topic. Participants then arrange themselves into groups to construct a worksheet. Attendees report that this exercise serves as a helpful process for understanding the requirements of a successful program.

What do the TAs do? The TAs do far more than lead the workshops.

- They maintain contact with the lecturer so that the worksheets are directly relevant.
- They spend one to three hours constructing each worksheet and an additional half hour before each workshop discussing the worksheet with their student assistants. They ensure that the assistants understand the problems, generate appropriate hints, and know what the students should discover on their own.
- Normally the TAs do not grade papers. However, if they observe that the students are not sufficiently involved, they will collect and grade samples of the students' work on the worksheet problems.
- TAs frequently will hold a study session before a test outside of workshop time and then go out with the class for pizza afterward.
- Occasionally the TA or the students themselves will organize an intramural athletics team to participate in the University progam.

TAs frequently are the first people to recognize that a student is having a problem. They contact students who miss workshops and monitor those who are experiencing difficulty with exams. If they think a student is having a personal problem, they will try to ensure that the student receives appropriate assistance. The TAs' responsiveness to their charges' academic, social, and emotional needs exemplifies a modification in the interactional dynamics component of the course change model described in Chapter 2.

What are the TAs' reactions to the Emerging Scholars Program? When TAs are asked what they enjoy most about the

ESP workshops, they tend to identify the workshops themselves. Some have pointed to the excitement of working with calculus students in groups on difficult problems and seeing these students' skills develop. They get to know the students well and are not required to assign grades or formally evaluate them. TAs recognize that the workshops represent a uniquely positive teaching situation, one where the majority of students in a mathematics "class" are successful. The TAs also find it exciting to observe changes in students' self-concept with respect to mathematics. Students initially view themselves as being successful in mathematics and as the workshops progress, begin to view themselves as mathematicians. One TA related the experience of working with a Mexican American student who planned to be an aeronautical engineer. As a result of the workshops, the student discovered that he enjoyed thinking about mathematics in depth. At the end of his sophomore year, he attended a summer institute in mathematics at Berkeley to pursue this additional interest.

From the perspective of teaching assistants, the most difficult aspect of working in the Emerging Scholars Program appears to be their worrying about individual students. TAs develop strong personal concern for their students' success as a result of the interpersonal relationships that emerge. TAs often assume personal responsibility for ensuring that every student achieves.

Who are the student assistants? The student assistants are sophomores who participated in the Emerging Scholars Program during their freshman year. They are chosen for their strong mathematics ability and interpersonal skills. The TAs identify prospective candidates and make recommendations to the Mathematics Department for student assistant positions. The student assistants review each worksheet with the TAs, taking notes so that they know how to help participants as they circulate among the small groups. Under the direction of the TAs, they spend extra time with students who are struggling.

Most of the student assistants are mathematics majors or are considering majoring in the field. They are enthusiastic about their own experience in ESP and often have concerns about current participants who lack such enthusiasm. It is not uncommon to hear a student assistant express strong opinions to an ESP participant for not doing homework. One student assistant emerged from a workshop session with a big grin, "on a high" because he had "made a participant's day" by assuring her that she had worked a problem correctly. This student assistant does not major in mathematics but enjoys tutoring calculus and plans to continue tutoring after his student assistant role ends.

Many student assistants in the Emerging Scholars Program have numerous, competing commitments that make the program critical for their success. For example, one current student assistant works six hours a week as a student assistant in addition to the time she takes to review the worksheets before the workshops. She also continues her job at a fast-food establishment where she worked through her freshman year. Without the support of the Emerging Scholars Program, students such as this one might not find the needed academic, social, and personal encouragement to succeed in university calculus.

Who are the Emerging Scholars instructors? Instructors for the calculus courses with an attached ESP workshop are selected for their fair treatment of students and well-organized class presentations. They give reasonable exams that are not routine and incorporate the subtleties of important concepts in calculus. In addition, ESP instructors are accessible, both in and outside the classroom. Students feel that they can communicate with these instructors. Instructors are sought who encourage in-class questions about the topic at hand, discuss the theoretical aspects of calculus, and work several examples in class.

How do the instructors approach their ESP classes? Once the instructors have been selected, they conduct their classes in their own varying styles as they would if there were no ESP workshop attached. The one change requested of instructors is that, if they grade on a curve, the curve omits the grades of ESP students so that they do not adversely affect the grades of non-ESP class members. The instructors teach classes of 120 to 130 students for 3 hours each week. Students not associated with ESP meet with TAs in groups of 30 for 2 hours per week for the standard discussion sections. Students participating in ESP do not attend these regular discussion sections.

The ESP instructors demonstrate diverse approaches to teaching their classes. Some instructors answer homework questions in class and others do not. Some provide an overview of the daily or weekly topic and then explain each in detail. Some present an outline on an overhead projector, use reading assignments in the text, and employ a study guide. Tests occur on different schedules. The number of exams given by instructors over one semester has ranged from four to seven.

Does ESP change the calculus classes? Though instructors are not asked to change the way they conduct their classes, ESP students influence the class process. We find that

- ESP students not only ask more questions but also more in-depth questions.
- ESP students' questions seem to inspire more in-depth consideration on the part of other students in the class.
- ESP students rarely use the instructors'

office hours. Several instructors have speculated that these students receive sufficient assistance within the workshops. Certainly, the students have adequate opportunity to have their questions answered during the workshops.

- The most notable change is the success of a group of students whose background might otherwise have predicted risk for failure in mathematics.

Generally, instructors do not advertise their course's affiliation with ESP workshops. One instructor's announcement that an ESP section was attached to his class generated some resentment from students not participating in the ESP workshop. However, when such resentment has surfaced, it has quickly dissipated when students are informed of the extra time requirements demanded of ESP participants. Further, any student may join an ESP workshop if space is available and the student is willing to abide by the program's principles. Most instructors are more comfortable allowing students to discover the workshop for themselves. When TAs and students who are not participating in the ESP workshops learn about ESP students' performance, a friendly competition sometimes develops to improve the performance of students from the regular discussion sections.

What have been instructors' reactions to the Emerging Scholars Program? Instructors express enthusiasm about ESP. They identify a variety of advantages:

- ESP takes a group that historically has experienced a higher-than-average failure rate in calculus and gives them a higher-than-average success rate. The program enhances students' confidence and provides coping skills that facilitate success in other science and mathematics courses.

- ESP exposes students to the excitement of working on challenging mathematics problems within a learning community and may influence more under-represented students to major in mathematics.

- A significant benefit of ESP on a large campus is to build a sense of community and to structure opportunities for students to learn to work effectively in groups with a wide variety of people.

One instructor described as follows the difference the ESP workshop made for several students. She had an African American student who earned a B on his own over the first semester. Her second semester class was full, so he enrolled in the ESP workshop in order to be allowed in her class the second semester. He raised his grade to an A over the second semester with ESP. Another student was making a C while participating in the ESP workshop. Feeling that the workshop was taking too much of her time, she dropped out of ESP and her grade subseqently fell to a D. The same instructor observed that dropping out of ESP did not affect the grades of two students who were scoring 99's and 100's, but their depth of understanding seemed to decrease. Overall, this instructor rated the ESP workshops as providing only benefits. She noted that, given the responsiveness of the ESP students and their 50 percent return rate for the second semester of calculus, she looked forward to a stimulating second semester.

A second instructor requested an ESP section after learning about the depth of understanding displayed by ESP students and the quality of their questions. Halfway through the semester, she was impressed with the success of most ESP students. When asked if they would again teach sections with attached ESP workshops, all the instructors answered with a resounding "YES!"

OUTCOMES

Both informal and formal sources of data attest to the efficacy of the Emerging Scholars Program in supporting targeted students' academic success.

Informal Observations

Students enter the program planning to major in mathematics, engineering, science, or medicine. From the first day in the workshops, they visit and joke with each other and the TAs. They cooperate in small groups. They complain about the work load and time involved. Yet they attend diligently to the worksheets, take pride in their correct solutions to worksheet problems, and earn grades consistently higher than those of non-ESP students.

Students have shared the following comments:

- "After the workshop, I do not have to spend much time on my homework."
- "I work so hard in here that my head hurts."
- "I thought I did not do well on my last test and I made an A!"

Student after student has stated that while the work is hard, they value the ESP experience because it increases their understanding of mathematics.

What do former ESP students say? Former ESP students are enthusiastic about the benefits of the program.

- "Being a part of an honors-type program with an exclusive number of people makes me feel exclusive and special. I take pride in informing others that I am a part of the program."
- "It wasn't until the Emerging Scholars Program that I really learned calculus ... I kind of got the 'big picture,' if you

will, that allowed me to understand mathematical logic. It feels great to finally understand the derivation of equations that before I had taken on faith alone."

- "You end up learning from each other and improving each other's skills."

- "Emerging Scholars has given me the opportunity to perform to my potential ... The fact that the problems are more difficult is less intimidating because there is someone there to help you do them."

- "Learning together is fun."

- "Being a student in the Emerging Scholars Program makes a large university which by some is characterized as being cold seem more personal. People care about how you are progressing in your classes and you don't feel isolated in the large classroom."

- "I was in Emerging Scholars the first semester, but I decided to leave the second semester because my course load was too heavy. After two weeks in (the second semester of) calculus, I decided to return to the program. I just did not realize what an asset the program was. The extra hours of work allow us to better comprehend the topics introduced in class."

- "By brainstorming and working together, we figure out what's going on and are able to handle problems from the homework on our own."

What happens after ESP? There is no formal follow-up of ESP students, but several professors have become involved informally in various ways with these students after they have completed the ESP workshops. Instructors report the following.

- Former ESP students have enrolled in problem-solving courses specifically

designed for prospective secondary education teachers. The ESP students sit in the front row and study together.

- A number of former ESP students have been chosen to attend the Summer Mathematics Institute at the University of California, Berkeley. The institute serves promising minority students in mathematics who have completed their sophomore year. For some it is their first introduction to rigorous mathematics.

- The Department of Mathematics now offers advanced courses in linear algebra, number theory, and algebraic structures directed toward former ESP students.

Quantitative Data: How Successful Are the ESP Students?

Jackie McCaffrey's report of quantitative evaluation data supports the efficacy of the Emerging Scholars Program for increasing the academic achievement of students of color in mathematics. A principal aim of the Emerging Scholars Program is to increase the numbers of underrepresented minority students at UT Austin excelling in calculus and completing degrees in mathematics or closely related majors. Historically, even well-prepared minority students have fared badly in UT's calculus program. As a point of reference, fewer than one third of African American and Hispanic students who took calculus in the five years prior to the program's inception earned grades of A or B. Only one-half of those who were well prepared (as measured by a math SAT of 600 or above) earned such grades. In contrast, approximately 80 percent of the African American and Hispanic students who have participated in ESP since its inception in 1988 have earned grades of A or B in calculus. An evaluation conducted in Fall 1993 suggests that the program's effect on ESP students' calculus grades is nearly one full grade point.

Sixteen charts and graphs summarizing the data analyses may be requested from the authors. Briefly, these data demonstrate that:

1. As a group, ESP students outperformed non-ESP students in first- and second-semester freshman calculus over five years of program implementation.

2. This achievement difference is maintained over varying levels of mathematics preparation as indicated by SAT scores.

3. Students who participate in Emerging Scholars persist in a scientific or technical major at higher rates than other UT Austin students majoring in science, mathematics, or engineering. African American and Hispanic ESP students' persistence in a science, mathematics, or engineering major was measured by comparing their total attrition rates to those of other first-time freshmen from the same ethnic background in the College of Natural Sciences and the College of Engineering. The data support the efficacy of ESP for retaining students of color in technical majors.

4. ESP students further demonstrate lower attrition rates compared to the general first-time freshman cohort at UT. Attrition rates for ESP students entering 1988–1992 have been compared with attrition rates of first-time freshmen cohorts entering in the fall semesters from 1983–1991 as reported in the latest flow analyses from the Office of Institutional Studies at the University of Texas. Average progression rates historically have remained fairly stable over time.

5. A high percentage of ESP students graduate with grade-point averages that are competitive for graduate school admission and employment in a technology field. Of the twenty former ESP students who have graduated from the university, thus far 75 percent completed their undergraduate degrees with a cumulative grade-point average of 3.0 or above.

RECOMMENDATIONS FOR SUCCESSFUL PROGRAMS

According to Ms. McCaffrey, successful programs have several aspects in common:

• Successful programs are institutionalized and supported through continuing internal resources. External funds, such as grants and contracts, tend to disappear and leave programs stranded. A program supported as a budget line item has a much better chance to survive. The program at UT is funded by the Mathematics Department and the Dean of Natural Sciences as part of the general instructional budget.

• Successful programs are run by key faculty. Programs led by poorly respected faculty and faculty outside the mainstream encounter difficulty in gaining the needed support of academic faculty and staff. As an example, Dr. Armendariz, who coordinates the Emerging Scholars Program at UT, chairs the Mathematics Department.

• Successful programs are tailored to meet the institution's needs. Programs that have attempted to copy directly from others rather than adapting ideas to their situation experience less success.

• Successful programs are integrated rather than isolated. Communication must exist among departments, support services, and the program. Support services are essential for students who have special issues or needs. A program in isolation cannot meet existing student needs nor adjust to changing student needs. At UT, the Mathematics Department and the Dean of Natural

Sciences collaborate on the Emerging Scholars Program. Additional academic departments and offices recognize the program and refer targeted students.

Student and instructor comments as well as grade and retention data attest to the success of UT's Emerging Scholars Program in supporting the mathematics achievement of students from underrepresented groups. The ESP represents one model that can be adapted to other institutions, with the above caveats, to accomplish similar goals. Within the context of this book's framework, it is important to keep in mind that ESP focuses on the instructional component of freshman calculus with the multicultural goal of improving diverse students' mathematics achievement. In our view, raising academic competence constitutes a critical approach to empowering students of color and to promoting social equity.

Acknowledgment
The authors wish to thank Jacqueline McCaffrey for permission to use the quantitative data and charts compiled as part of the evaluation of the effectiveness of the Emerging Scholars Program. The authors also thank James Epperson for permission to use his worksheet construction guide as well as the sample worksheets.

WRITING WORKSHEETS[*]

ESP Teaching Assistant Training Program

by James A. M. Epperson

One of the important tasks as a workshop leader is writing worksheets. The following points should be kept in mind when writing a worksheet.

Goals

1. Challenge the students.
2. Relate the worksheet to the material covered in lecture.
3. Make the worksheet interesting for both you and the students.

Structure

1. Begin the worksheet with a routine problem to serve as an "icebreaker" and confidence booster.
2. Continue the worksheet with problems of varying difficulty. Putting them in order of difficulty is not always the best idea. Students soon realize this and tend to work them in order. It can then be disappointing for you when they are unable or unwilling to solve the "interesting" problems at the end of the worksheet.
3. Finally, it is ideal to have at least one extremely challenging problem per worksheet. It is important to give them the opportunity to choose to work such a problem. Since the problem should take more thought, it also paces the students and allows others to catch up.

Types of Problems (*Treisman*)

1. old chestnuts–problems which often appear on tests but rarely in the homework.
2. monkey wrenches which uncover the students' misunderstanding of certain fundamental concepts.
3. problems that pass on a knowledge of "street mathematics" or those tricks and short-cuts not explicitly taught.
4. problems which expose examples and counter-examples to deepen their familiarity with the theory.
5. problems to improve their facility with mathematics language.

Alternatives to Worksheets

1. Sometimes innovative games can take the place of a worksheet. At UT, we have used a Jeopardy game with categories that deal with mathematics.

---

*ESP Worksheets used by permission of James Epperson.

2. After exams (which are administered during lecture) schedule a guest speaker instead of having a worksheet. The guest speaker could be someone from industry or business, for example, who uses mathematics extensively in his/her work. The best resource and probably the optimal way to enhance a student's feeling connected to the mathematics department is to have someone from the department as a guest speaker. The faculty member should discuss their background, how they became interested in mathematics, their research (or whatever is comprehendable given the students' level), and/or their life as a mathematician.

3. If it is not possible to schedule a guest speaker after an exam, any activity that would broaden the students' view of mathematics as a discipline or would enhance the social identity of the students as a group is preferred to having a worksheet.

Miscellaneous

1. Useful sources for writing worksheets are: *Calculus*, Michael Spivak; *Mathematical Methods in the Physical Sciences*, Mary Boas; Shaum's Ou dine Series in Advanced Calculus; other calculus books; elementary analysis books; worksheets from other universities.

2. *Remember* to keep *your* students in mind when writing worksheets. It is generally not a good idea to simply copy worksheets from other universities. They are a great resource, but only you know your students. At times worksheet problems are written with the weaknesses of a particular student in mind or a special topic that is non-standard in most courses, so the latter would not be appropriate for all classes.

3. Try to avoid problems that are either too theoretical, too straightforward, or too mechanical in nature.

4. In addition to worksheets, providing difficult practice exams which you may have them solve during workshop or at review sessions held outside of class time are an indispensable supplement to the worksheets.

WORKSHEET 1

1. Find the following limits if they exist. <u>Do not use</u> L'Hôpital's Rule.

a) $\lim\limits_{x \to \infty} \dfrac{3x^2 - 5x}{5x^2 + 2x - 6}$ b) $\lim\limits_{x \to \infty} \left(\dfrac{2x - 3}{3x + 7} \right)^4$ c) $\lim\limits_{x \to \infty} \left(\sqrt{x^2 + x} - \sqrt{x^2 + 1} \right)$

d) $\lim\limits_{x \to \infty} \left(\sqrt{x^2 + x} - x \right)$ e) $\lim\limits_{x \to \infty} \sqrt[8]{x^2 + 1} - \sqrt[4]{x + 1}$ f) $\lim\limits_{x \to \infty} \dfrac{1}{\sqrt{2\pi\sigma^2}} \displaystyle\int_{-x}^{x} te^{-\frac{1}{2}\left(\frac{t}{\sigma}\right)^2} dt$

g) $\lim\limits_{x \to \infty} \dfrac{1}{\pi} \displaystyle\int_{-x}^{x} \dfrac{1}{1 + t^2} \, dt$ h) $\lim\limits_{x \to \infty} \left(x - \sqrt{x + a} \, \sqrt{x + b} \right)$ (a, b, $\sigma > 0$ are constants)

2. The following are indeterminate forms for limits.

$$\dfrac{0}{0} \qquad \dfrac{\infty}{\infty} \qquad \infty - \infty, \quad 0^0, \qquad \infty \cdot 0, \qquad 1^\infty, \qquad \infty^0$$

Give examples of functions with the given limits and indeterminate form. *(e.g. For part (a) choose f (x) so that it has limit 0, then choose another so that it has limit ∞, etc.)*

a) $\lim\limits_{x \to \infty} f(x) = \left\{ \begin{array}{c} 0 \\ \infty \\ \pi \end{array} \right. , \left(\dfrac{0}{0} \right)$ b) $\lim\limits_{x \to \infty} f(x) = \left\{ \begin{array}{c} e \\ 1 \\ 0 \end{array} \right. , (0^0)$ c) $\lim\limits_{x \to \infty} f(x) = \left\{ \begin{array}{c} 0 \\ \infty \\ 1 \end{array} \right. , \left(\dfrac{\infty}{\infty} \right)$

d) $\lim\limits_{x \to \infty} f(x) = \left\{ \begin{array}{c} 0 \\ \infty \\ 2 \end{array} \right. , (\infty - \infty)$ e) $\lim\limits_{x \to \infty} f(x) = \left\{ \begin{array}{c} e \\ \infty \\ 2 \end{array} \right. , (\infty \cdot 0)$

3. Indicate the indeterminate form for the following. <u>DO NOT EVALUATE THE LIMIT!</u>

a) $\lim\limits_{x \to 0} (\cos x)^{\frac{1}{x}}$ b) $\lim\limits_{x \to 0} \left(\dfrac{1}{\sin^2 x} - \dfrac{1}{x} \right)$ c) $\lim\limits_{x \to 0} (e^{3x} - 5x)^{\frac{1}{x}}$

d) $\lim\limits_{x \to \infty} \dfrac{3x^2 - x + 5}{5x^2 + 6x - 3}$ e) $\lim\limits_{x \to \infty} x^x$ f) $\lim\limits_{x \to \infty} \dfrac{1}{x} \displaystyle\int_0^x f(t)\, dt$ ($f(t)$ is continuous)

g) $\lim\limits_{x \to \infty} xe^{-x}$ h) $\lim\limits_{x \to \infty} x^{\frac{1}{x}}$ i) $\lim\limits_{x \to 0} (1 + x)^{\frac{1}{x}}$

4. Let

$$f(x) = \begin{cases} e^{-\frac{1}{x^2}}, & x \neq 0 \\ 0, & x = 0 \end{cases}$$

Prove that $f'(0) = 0$ and $f''(0) = 0$. (*Hint: Need to we the definition of the derivative.*)

5.

  a) Graph $f(x) = x^{10}$ and $g(x) = e^{\frac{x}{10}}$, $0 \le x \le 2$.

  b) Despite the impression you get from (a), show that for large enough x, $g(x) > f(x)$.

  c) Show that for large enough x, $x^n < e^x$ and In $x < x^{\frac{1}{n}}$, where n is any fixed positive integer, no matter how large.

6. Which indeterminate forms allow use of L'Hôpital's Rule? For each of the forms listed in problem (2), explain how to get them into the form(s) necessary for L'Hôpital's.

WORKSHEET 2

1. Find the volume of the solid formed by revolving the region bounded by $y = e^x$, $y = 0$, $x = 0$, and $x = 1$ about the x-axis using: (a) disc method; (b) shell method.

2. Find the arclengths of the graphs:

   a) $f(x) = \frac{2}{3}(x-7)^{\frac{3}{2}}$ on $[7, 14]$;   b) $f(x) = \frac{2}{3}(x-6)^{\frac{3}{2}}$ on $[6, 12]$;

   c) $f(x) = \frac{2}{3}x^{\frac{2}{3}}$ on $[0, 3]$;   d) $f(x) = \frac{1}{4}x^2 - \frac{1}{2}\ln x$ on $[1, 2]$.

3. A right circular cone is generated by revolving the region bounded by $y = \frac{hx}{r}$, $y = h$, and $x = 0$ about the y-axis. Verify that the lateral surface area of the cone is $S = \pi r \sqrt{r^2 + h^2}$.

4. A sphere of radius r is generated by 2 revolving the graph of $y = \sqrt{r^2 - x^2}$ about the x-axis. Verify that the surface area of the sphere is $4\pi r^2$.

5. For the following, *set up* the integrals which represent the volume using the shell method *and* disc method (i.e., set up the integrals two ways). Decide which integral would be easier to calculate (but don't do it!).

   a) the region bounded by $y = x^3 - 3x^2 + 2x$, $x = 0$, $x = 1$, $y = 0$ rotated around the y-axis;

   b) the region bounded by $y = \cos(x^2)$, $x = 0$, $x = \sqrt{\pi}$, $y = 0$ rotated around the y-axis;

   c) the region bounded by $y = \cos x$, $y = \sin x$, $x = 0$, $x = \frac{\pi}{4}$ rotated about the x-axis;

   d) the region bounded by $9 - x = (y - 3)^2$, $x = 0$ rotated about the x-axis.

6. Find the volume left over after a sphere of radius R has a hole of radius $\frac{1}{2}R$ drilled through the center.

7. Marcellus and Albert were working out at the Geometrically-Ideal Super Gym where all the dumbbells were constructed according to the model shown below.

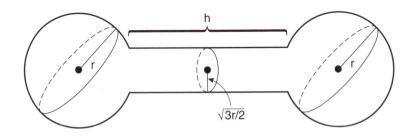

   a) Find the volume of the dumbbell pictured above.
   b) Suppose that they needed a dumbbell suitable for bench-pressing 200 pounds and $h = 4$ feet, what should the density of the material used to make the dumbbell be?
   c) Ramiro joins the group and wants to sketch funny pictures on the dumbbells; how much drawing space does he have on the dumbbell shown above?

8. Show that the arc length integral gives the expected result for a linear function $f(x) = mx + b$, $a \le x \le c$.

CHAPTER 9

Multicultural Science: Focus on the Biological and Environmental Sciences

Judith W. Rosenthal, Ph.D.
Professor, Biological Sciences, Kean College of New Jersey
Union, New Jersey

Editor's Notes:

Judith Rosenthal's chapter speaks to the assumption that all groups have the same underlying ability and may differ in preferred modes of acquiring and expressing competence. She believes that the goal of multicultural science is to provide equitable educational opportunity for all students and that such science takes into account the influence of culture on what is studied, how it is studied and by whom.

Rosenthal examines the scientific "culture" as one reason for resistance to multicultural science. She also argues that the traditional college science classroom does not spark interest in the sciences for many of today's students. Infused content and a variety of instructional strategies have potential for rekindling the interest of students in science.

Rosenthal acknowledges that initiating course transformation may be challenging for many faculty who may lack the time, resources, and knowledge base. Her many suggestions provide useful insights and guidance to faculty. The topics she addresses regarding multicultural course change touch all four components of the model.　　■

MULTICULTURALISM: THE GOAL OF SCIENCE EDUCATION REFORM

Though never stated as such, the underlying goal of recent efforts to reform science education is truly multicultural: to make science accessible to all students. Consider the following quotes that have been taken from some of the most widely circulated reform documents:

> The Nation should adopt the goal that all children born today, from all backgrounds, have a quality education, including mathematics and science education, and the opportunity to participate in the science and engineering workforce to their fullest potential. (*Changing America: The New Face of Science and Engineering*, 1989, p. 3)
>
> Liberal education in the sciences must be provided to all students, ranging from those exhibiting high levels of achievement and interest to students with weak precollege preparation in science and fear of mathematics and science learning. Such problems are exacerbated for both minorities and women because they are already encumbered by many social and eco-

nomic biases and stresses. (*The Liberal Art of Science*, 1990, p. xiv)

Two of the best-known reform efforts—Project 2061 (at the school level) and Project Kaleidoscope (at the undergraduate level)—have similar orientations. The recommendations of Project 2061 constitute

> a common core of learning in science, mathematics and technology for all young people, regardless of their social circumstances and career aspirations. In particular, the recommendations pertain to those who in the past have largely been bypassed in science and mathematics education: ethnic and language minorities and girls. (*Science for All Americans*, 1989, p. 20)

Likewise, the first goal of Project Kaleidoscope is

> to increase the number, quality, and persistence of individuals in careers relating to science and mathematics, and educate citizens to understand the role of science and technology in their world. (*What Works*, Vol. One, 1991, p. ix)

Clearly, the scientific community has begun to recognize the multicultural nature of today's students; nonetheless, multicultural science has received scant attention. Even the above-quoted reform documents give only oblique reference. Meanwhile, no one is really certain how to achieve the goals of science education reform, and there are no studies proving that any one approach or remedy is more effective than any other. We only have various hypotheses about what works. As will be argued in this chapter, there are, however, numerous reasons why a multicultural approach to science education should not be overlooked.

DEFINING MULTICULTURAL SCIENCE

Except for a handful of articles, little has been published about multicultural science, and there certainly is no consensus as to its exact meaning (e.g., Atwater, 1993; Atwater & Riley, 1993; Case & Lau, 1991; Hodson, 1993; Mason & Barba, 1992; Middlecamp, 1995; National Science Teachers Association, 1991; Persell, 1994; *Science for All Cultures*, 1993; Stanley & Brickhouse, 1994). Therefore, before attempting to arrive at some kind of definition of multicultural science, it is perhaps worthwhile to take a step backward, to begin with the broader perspective: what is meant by "multicultural education."

According to Bennett (1990, pp. 11-13), multicultural education has four overlapping features. These include:

1. The movement toward providing all students with equitable educational opportunities while maintaining standards of academic excellence

2. Integration into the traditional curriculum of multiethnic and global perspectives so that the points-of-view, contributions, and achievements of individuals and societies other than white Anglo-Europeans are considered and valued

3. The process by which an individual comes to recognize his or her own culturally determined values and beliefs and can set them aside so that issues and situations can be considered from alternative perspectives

4. A commitment to "combat racism and other forms of discrimination" by appreciating cultural diversity and through the development of "appropriate attitudes and skills."

Bennett's first characterization of multicultural education—as a movement to provide equitable educational opportunities to all students—is precisely the goal of science education reform. Curriculum change and cultural (self-)awareness—Bennett's second and third aspects of multicultural education—are a means for achieving this goal. And finally, by attending to Bennett's first three features of multicultural education, the fourth—combatting racism by developing appropriate attitudes and skills—should be a natural outgrowth.

Based on this analysis of multicultural education, we might postulate that any definition of multicultural science should take into consideration a wide range of issues such as:

- presenting scientific information in a way that appeals to the diverse learning styles of today's students

- transforming the curriculum so that science will be viewed, at least in part, from a nontraditional perspective

- making entry-level science courses interesting and relevant to the lives of all students so that they will want to continue studying science or at least retain an interest in science upon completion of what is often their last formal science course

- helping students make connections between what is learned in a science class and events that occur in their own lives and in the lives of people around the world

- bringing to awareness the relationship between culture and science

- meeting the linguistic and cultural needs of a growing population of immigrant and refugee students who are simultaneously learning English as well as science

- addressing the ambiguities inherent in scientific knowledge as well as the limitations of the methods of science.

Keeping all of this in mind, a broad, working definition of multicultural science might be as follows:

> Multicultural science is the presentation of scientific information in a way that is interesting and accessible to diverse students. It takes into consideration the influence of culture on what is studied in science, how it is studied, and by whom. Multicultural science enables every student to attain a fundamental understanding of both the methods and content of science which can then be used in making personal, societal, and global decisions.

WHY RESISTANCE TO MULTICULTURAL SCIENCE?

While the social and behavioral sciences have more readily and rapidly embraced the concept of a multiculturalism, the sciences are only beginning to move in this direction. Discussions of multicultural science create some unease among science educators. The reasons for this reaction touch on the intrinsic nature of science—both its culture and how graduate students and future scientists are trained—as well as the multiple responsibilities already confronting science instructors.

First, when today's science faculty received their graduate training, they studied SCIENCE. In other words, obtaining a master's or doctorate in chemistry, biology, physics, or another "hard" science involved course work and considerable research. The methods of science were unquestioned by most; matters of diversity, gender, and ethnicity were of little or no concern, nor were social, political, economic, and ethical implications. A graduate education dealt with "pure" scientific information, and research investigations were carried out under controlled conditions, sheltered from "outside" influences. College teaching was secondary—learned on the job—with graduate students and new faculty members generally mimicking the methods used by some of their previous instructors. Indeed, only recently have some graduate science departments begun to organize special seminars and training courses to provide their students with the opportunity to learn about and discuss instructional strategies, classroom management techniques, and how to interact with and teach an increasingly diverse undergraduate population.

Second, given the belief system underlying modern-day science, the concept of multiculturalism may seem a bit redundant. Traditional science teachings promote the idea that science is based on objective observations and is therefore culturally neutral. Indeed, the methods and findings of science are considered universal: any scientist in any part of the world should obtain similar results and draw similar conclusions if he or she begins with the same hypothesis and uses essentially the same methodology. Consequently, the theories, laws, and principles of science are as valid and applicable in the United States as they are in Kenya or Thailand. According to many scientists and science educators, it is precisely these qualities that make science different from and superior to all other "ways of knowing." And, for precisely these reasons, a traditional science educator would argue that science is inherently universal, global in perspective, and that there is no need to jump on the multicultural "bandwagon." However, such a point of view neglects the powerful influence that culture has on every aspect of science (a theme that will be discussed later in this chapter).

A third reason why science faculty have remained outside the multicultural movement concerns time pressures. Besides teaching, advising students, serving on committees, and carrying out research, science instructors must keep up with the literature in their particular fields of interest. In some areas of science—such as molecular genetics and biotechnology—the rate of discovery and new developments is explosive. In addition, the most widely read scientific journals, such as *Nature* and *Science*, as well as those in each scientific sub-specialty rarely contain information on educational strategies. In fact, unless a college or university emphasizes excellence in teaching and encourages faculty from all disciplines to participate in development and training activities, then the laws of inertia guarantee that science instruction will remain static.

Fourth, on some campuses the faculty have reached the saturation point with educational innovations. They already have been asked to incorporate critical thinking activities, gender issues, writing across the curriculum, computer usage, outcomes assessment, cooperative learning groups, global perspectives, and a host of other changes into their existing courses. They are frazzled from trying to balance coverage with instructional change; mention multiculturalism, and they are ready to balk. Nevertheless, many of the "activities" just listed are of considerable value in a multicultural science classroom.

Finally, science as traditionally taught has mainly attracted and retained those students who are "younger versions of the science community itself" (Tobias, 1990, p. 11). Welcoming women, minorities, individuals with disabilities, and other nontraditional students to the sciences as well as actively recruiting science majors are relatively new phenomena. Undoubtedly, a multicultural approach to science education can enhance these efforts without detracting from them.

While scientific discoveries may bring about social revolutions, science educators are relatively conservative and slow to change how they teach. For example, science faculty, when compared to their peers in education, the humanities, and the social sciences, rely more on lecturing and less frequently use student-centered pedagogy. They also are less likely to attend workshops to increase cultural/ethnic awareness and more likely to express dissatisfaction with the quality of their students (*Undergraduate Science Education,* 1992). Clearly, findings such as these conflict with the goals of science education reform and provide all the more reason to argue for the implementation of multicultural science education.

THE NEED FOR MULTICULTURAL SCIENCE

A multicultural perspective may be one of the most cost-effective ways to rekindle student interest in science. Changing some aspects of what we teach and how we teach does not demand big budgets, outside funding, nor new and improved laboratory equipment and science facilities. What multicultural science does require is instructors who are willing to increase their awareness of how culture affects science and who are sufficiently flexible to rethink the traditional curriculum and to seek out alternative examples, materials, assignments, and methods of instruction.

During the last twenty-odd years, while the undergraduate population has become more diverse—ethnically, linguistically, and culturally—the proportion of students majoring in the sciences has declined steeply (Green 1989; *Science and Engineering Degrees,* 1992). Yet, today's job market demands scientifically and technologically competent employees, and citizens on a daily basis must make scientifically informed decisions related to matters such as personal health, the siting of a garbage incinerator in their neighborhood, and the

significance of a DNA fingerprint presented to a jury. Science has descended the ivory tower and today permeates almost every aspect of our lives. It no longer remains the exclusive domain of a highly educated, scientific elite. Everyone—regardless of gender, race, preferred learning style, native language, and previous schooling experience—needs some fundamental understanding of what science is and how it affects them and the rest of the world.

Providing science education to all students assumes that each and every one is capable of learning and doing science. This assumption does not imply that every student will want to become a science major and pursue a career in the sciences; nor does it mean that all students will exhibit the same level of achievement as that of the Westinghouse Science Talent Search winners. However, it does signify that every student can achieve basic scientific literacy if science is made accessible to students of varying abilities and levels of interest and if instructors are willing to eliminate any stereotypes they have about who can and who cannot succeed in science.

Recent studies (Lipson & Tobias, 1991; Seymour, 1992a, b; Tobias, 1990) indicate that many of today's students find their experiences in the science classroom less than ideal. Even "good" students who are interested in science, who enter college intending to major in science, and who earn high grades in the sciences often get "turned off," lose interest, and switch to other disciplines. They discover an incompatibility between their preferred ways of learning and how their professors teach, and they are unwilling to tolerate traditional science classroom practices. Some of the reasons these students give for leaving science include the competitive environment, the lack of community in the classroom, the unapproachability of faculty, and the emphasis on coverage rather than genuine understanding of the information presented to them.

As stated in Project Kaleidoscope's *What Works: Vol. One* (1991, p. xiv), "Courses labeled *introductory* turn out to be terminal." In other words, for many students, both intended science majors and non-science majors, their first college science course often becomes their last. Whether they receive good grades or bad grades, many find the experience alienating and unpleasant, and they will not take any more science courses than those required. Think of it this way: Unless they are science majors, how many students do you know who choose to fill their electives with additional science courses? Art, psychology, history, literature, business, economics, computer science, and sociology electives, yes; chemistry, physics, and biology electives, almost never.

THE MANY CULTURES OF THE SCIENCE CLASSROOM

Although we rarely think about it, the science classroom is truly multicultural. The cultures of the students and teacher as well as the cultures of science and the academy influence not only the content of the course, but also the teaching and learning processes, interactions between the instructor and students, verbal and nonverbal forms of communication, and observable behaviors.

Contrary to what most of us have been taught, science itself cannot be culture-free because it is practiced by humans, and humans—depending on where they are raised and socialized—bring to their endeavors culturally influenced values and beliefs (Gordon et al., 1990; Harding, 1993; Kelly et al., 1993; Maddock, 1986; Rosser, 1990; Selin, 1993a, b; Stanley & Brickhouse, 1994). Culture molds and shapes every aspect of science research and teaching. For example, modern-day, Western science begins with the premise that through observation and investigation we can learn why things happen in the world around us. With the knowledge thus attained, we can then predict, possibly modify, or even change the course of future events. Progress will take place, and the quality of human life will improve. Science, therefore, not only allows us to understand nature but also to control it (Samovar et al., 1981).

This description of science, which many people take for granted as being fundamentally true, ignores the fact that other cultures, generally non-Western, have alternative value and belief systems (Anderson, 1988; Sitaram & Cogdell, 1976). For example, in some Asian cultures, people seek the truth by spiritual means. Or, many Native Americans believe that humans should live harmoniously with nature, without exploiting or attempting to control it. From these points of view, much of what today's Western scientists take for granted as being logical and important, may not be nearly so obvious. This is especially true for those individuals raised, socialized, and previously schooled in other cultures and other parts of the world.

Just as researchers bring their cultural biases to their investigations, so do those of us who teach science. We bring to the classroom—in our attitudes toward and expectations about students, in our assumptions about students' prior knowledge, in our convictions about what is and is not important to teach—an entire way of thinking that is culturally determined and that is reinforced by the society in which we live as well as by the academic and scientific communities. When we teach, we are not just transmitting to our students scientific information, concepts, and facts; simultaneously, we are communicating to our students an entire belief system about which we are often unaware. Only when we become conscious of how strongly culture influences all that we do, as scientists, researchers, and teachers, can we even begin to envision what is meant by multicultural science.

A MULTICULTURAL SCIENCE CURRICULUM

Banks (1991) has identified various ways by which the mainstream or traditional curriculum can be made multicultural. The "ethnic contributions" or "additive" approaches are the easiest for most instructors to implement. For example, in an introductory science course the achievements of an African American scientist such as Walter E. Massey (a physicist and former director of the National Science Foundation) would be discussed. Students might be required to write a short paper about Barbara McClintock as an example of a successful female geneticist and Nobel Prize winner, or they might read and discuss one of Selin's (1993a, b) recent articles on *Science Across Cultures*. Instructors seeking ideas along these lines are referred to the special sections in *Science* on minorities[1] (Nov. 13, 1992, and Nov. 12, 1993) and women[2] (March 13, 1992; April 16, 1993; March 11, 1994).

For the teacher, the primary advantage of making a course multicultural via the "ethnic contributions" or "additive" approaches is that the objectives and content of the "core" course do not have to be altered. As for the students, they do receive exposure to some nontraditional aspect(s) of science. However, additive and contributions approaches have several disadvantages. First, add-ons are more likely to be eliminated when the instructor is pressed for time. Second, in the minds of the students (and the instructor) the additional information will always remain outside what is viewed as "normal" science. Thus, students gain the impression that add-ons and contributions have less value or importance than other parts of the course. As

Banks points out, such information is viewed as an appendage. It is not an integral part of the basic curriculum, and the analysis of the add-on material reflects the values and belief system of mainstream society.

For reasons such as these, Banks (1991) supports the "transformation" approach which changes the basic assumptions of the curriculum and allows students to study events and concepts from several ethnic and cultural perspectives. Taken one step further, the transformation approach becomes the "social action" approach which requires that students "make decisions and take actions related to the concept, issue, or problem they have studied" (Banks, 1991, p. 24).

Certain subjects in science are much more amenable to transformation and social-action approaches than are others. While the steps of cellular respiration or photosynthesis may not readily lend themselves to multicultural analysis, many health and environmental issues do.

SOME EXAMPLES OF CURRICULUM TRANSFORMATION

For example, the topic of AIDS arises in most introductory biology courses (as well as in more advanced immunology and human physiology classes). The majority of students are interested in and concerned about AIDS in terms of their own sexuality and health. The media bombard us with warnings about practicing safe sex, and the nightly news brings into our homes the most recent figures on the number of infected individuals in the United States (and in other countries around the world) as well as the latest developments in terms of treatments and cures. The World Health Organization (as reported in Merson, 1993, p. 1266; also see Palaca, 1991) estimates that as of mid-1993, 13 million young people and adults had become infected with HIV. About 2 million adults had developed AIDS, and most had died. Another 1 million children had been infected prenatally by HIV.

Nevertheless, on a worldwide basis AIDS does not rank as a major killer. While the AIDS epidemic is frightening and demands urgent attention, from a global perspective, it still affects relatively few individuals and is a very new disease. In contrast, malaria has been taking lives for centuries. Today, it is estimated that there are 270 million new cases of malaria every year resulting in approximately 2 million deaths annually; 2.1 billion people, or approximately 40 percent of the world's population, live in malarious areas (Hoffman et al., 1991; Rosenthal, 1991). Yet here in the United States we rarely hear anything in the news about malaria nor are we overly preoccupied with its prevention or cure (Marshall, 1990, 1991).

Why aren't U.S. citizens particularly concerned about the millions infected with and who die from malaria in any given year? Why isn't money being poured into malaria research? Why do we focus our attention and resources on some diseases like AIDS and not on others, such as malaria?

Comparing AIDS and malaria provides the opportunity for genuine curriculum transformation. In order to answer the above questions, students need to learn about the biological basis and mode of transmission of malaria and AIDS and about previous and current efforts to prevent, control, and cure these diseases. They would discuss the special problems that are associated with parasitic diseases like malaria and compare them to a virally and sexually transmitted disease such as AIDS. With this essential, scientific information in hand, students could then begin to confront the related issues of who (which countries, which organizations) has the money, resources, and know-how to carry out basic health research and who decides how that money is spent. Attempting to answer these questions, students would have to deal with the social, political, economic, and ethical issues that govern seemingly scientific problems. Certainly, they would become much more aware of the inequities in the delivery of health care and medical services on a worldwide basis (for example, rich vs. poor; nationally vs. globally; developed vs. less developed countries). The cost of disease, not only financially but also in loss of human life and talent, must also be considered. By looking at and comparing AIDS and malaria, students would learn not only some basic science but also would come to view a science/health issue from a global, multicultural perspective.

Other topics of this type that lend themselves readily to curriculum transformation include:

- Tuberculosis: This major leading cause of death around the world had almost disappeared in the United States but is now making a comeback (Altman, 1992a and 1992b; Bloom & Murray, 1992; Rosenthal, 1992; Weiss, 1992). Why is this happening and what are the implications?

- Until recently, women and ethnic minorities were often excluded as subjects from major medical studies (Marshall, 1994). Why did this happen, and what are the implications in terms of the validity of the research findings and equitable health care?

- How can we reconcile the spending of thousands of dollars on reproductive technologies so that a given couple can have a biologically related child when on a worldwide basis there is a population crisis?

Instructors also can infuse many of today's environmental concerns—such as acid rain, ozone depletion, the greenhouse effect, and tropical deforestation—into traditional science courses (including biology, ecology, environmental studies, and chemistry), encouraging students to analyze such issues from a multicultural perspective. After selecting a specific environmental topic, students might begin—either in small groups or by means of a class discussion—to brainstorm, writing down all that they already know about the selected subject (what it is, what causes it, where—in what part of the world—is it a problem and for whom, who is affected and how, and what is being done to correct the problem and by whom). With the collective wisdom of the class, a fairly accurate picture will emerge which can be clarified and refined by appropriate readings, relevant videos, and other instructor-guided activities. As a result of such an exercise, students will be sufficiently informed to be able to consider the environmental issue from a variety of points of view: that of native or indigenous peoples; of government officials and/or industrial leaders of the affected nation, and from the perspective of environmentally concerned U.S. citizens.

Such an analysis will help bring to awareness just how strongly the culture, values, and beliefs of different groups of people affect how they perceive and react to environmental "problems." Students will also discover why there are no easy answers, nor quick technological fixes, to environmental issues.

While multicultural curriculum transformation may be applied more readily to the biological and environmental sciences, the fields of chemistry and physics should not be overlooked. Although the emphasis in the latter may be more quantitative and problem-based, it is still possible to add a multicultural dimension to the standard introductory chemistry or physics curriculum.

For example, a chemistry course may begin with the topic of units of measure and interconversions between the British and metric systems and the *Système International*. Similarly, students will be expected to understand temperature measurement using degrees Celsius and Fahrenheit. Rather than relying solely on textbook problems, the students themselves can provide examples from their everyday experiences, especially if they have grown up in different countries. Before coming to the United States, were they accustomed to buying gasoline by the gallon or liter, or fruit by the pound or kilo? In what units were speed limits posted on major highways? Did the newspaper in their native language provide the daily temperature readings in degrees Fahrenheit or Celsius? The students in the class could practice the unit interconversions using their own examples. Another topic in chemistry—that of energy transformations—presents many possibilities. Students could compare and contrast energy sources in various countries for cooking, or for the production of electricity, or for long-distance travel. Advantages and disadvantages; cost, benefits, and risks; and government regulations (or lack thereof) could be brought into any of these discussions.

In physics, when studying the concept of sound production and sound waves, students might bring to class the musical instruments and/or recordings of music typical of their cultures. By demonstrating how the instruments work and by listening to the recordings, they could then discuss the similarities and differences between the musical instruments and the sounds they produce. Likewise, when electricity is the topic of study, the class could discuss why, when traveling around the world, one needs electrical plugs with different prong configurations as well as adapters for differences in voltage and for alternating currents. What may happen—and why—when the unsuspecting traveler tries to plug in his or her hair dryer or laptop computer.

The instructor who succeeds in transforming even a small part of a traditional science curriculum cannot help but instill in students an appreciation for the diverse cultures of the world—both past and present—and of the contributions made by individuals and societies similar to and different from our own. What better way exists in a science class to fulfill Bennett's fourth aspect of multicultural education, that of helping students to respect and understand other cultures and peoples?

Banks (1991) further recommends that curriculum transformation include a social-action component. With so many controversial and unresolved issues in the sciences, students can easily get involved and exert their influence. After researching a topic and formulating what they consider an appropriate course of action, they can write letters to the editor of the local newspaper or to government officials. They can start a campaign to eliminate the use of styrofoam cups and plates in the cafeteria or begin a campus recycling project. They can explore the activities of and perhaps join organizations such as the Audubon Society or the Nature Conservancy. Social-action projects can be as small as making a personal commitment to recycle or as large as organizing a campus-awareness day on topics such as reforesting the earth or renewable energy sources. What is most important is that students come to recognize that the science they are learning in class has relevance to their lives and to the lives of people around the world. At the same time they will discover that resolving scientific, medical, and environmental problems often requires making tough choices, for which there are pros and cons, benefits and risks.

INITIATING CURRICULUM TRANSFORMATION

Making the science curriculum multicultural does not mean watering down the content. Nor does it require that every topic in the course be analyzed from all possible perspectives. Rather, at least one theme should be discussed from alternative points of view, and this information must be meaningfully incorporated into the course.

Many of us already have an untapped wealth of information of this type readily available in our classes: our students who grew up in other countries and cultures. Often, they will gladly share contrasting perspectives on topics we tend to discuss from our own ethnocentric position. Having a map of the world present in the classroom enhances discussion and learning. Many students are weak on geography; a map will help them identify the countries from which their classmates come as well as the regions of the world affected by particular environmental and health problems.

For the instructor who is getting started in science curriculum transformation, one of the major challenges is finding appropriate reading assignments and videos. A staff member of the instructional resource center on campus may be able to provide valuable suggestions for AV materials. In addition, public broadcast television has produced many programs on relevant and timely health, science, environmental, and medical topics. A catalog of recent PBS Videos (1320 Braddock Place, Alexandria, VA 22314) is available by calling 1-800-344-3337.

As for reading materials, the science section of the Tuesday edition of *The New York Times*, the *State of the World* which is issued on a yearly basis by the Worldwatch Institute (1776 Massachusetts Ave., N.W., Washington, DC 20036), some articles in journals such as *Science* and *Scientific Amer-*

ican as well as articles in popular magazines like *Time* and *Newsweek* provide a wealth of information. Even the local newspaper should not be overlooked. Instructors will find it helpful to collect articles on the same topic in a folder (always jotting down the source of the article, date, page numbers, etc.). Creating files of articles on topics currently being taught and on topics which might be taught at some future date ensures that information and references will be available on a wide range of themes whenever they are needed.

WHAT IS REALLY KNOWN ABOUT HOW STUDENTS LEARN SCIENCE?

As described in Chapter 1 of this book, the college population is increasingly diverse, and we are now teaching more females, minorities, students with disabilities, immigrants, refugees, and more non-native English speakers than ever before. While the student body has changed, science instruction, for the most part, has not; the lecture/lab format still predominates.

As for the effectiveness of lecturing, Fisher et al. (1986, p. 280) refer to the "most interesting assumption made by teachers." It goes like this: "I said it, they heard it, they read it, therefore they know it." Clearly, if learning were so simple, most of our students would end up with A grades. All they would need to do is listen to their teachers and read the assigned pages in the text. In the sciences, a few "good" students do seem to learn this way; however, the majority do not. Instructors often view the latter as poor students, unfit for further study of the sciences. Perhaps we should be embarrassed to admit how quickly we pass judgment on our students when many of us who teach science do not have the slightest notion how students grasp the concepts that we try to explain to them.

Concerning the laboratory component of a science course, we have little evidence of its effectiveness for all students. Edmondson and Novak (1993) recently investigated the attitudes of students carrying out laboratory work in an introductory college biology course. About one third of the students took the approach of "Think as little as possible" (since I am not going to understand it anyway); another third favored "think procedurally" (just follow the instructions very carefully in order to complete the task at hand). Only the remaining third addressed their laboratory work with the attitude we would like all our students to take, "think meaningfully" (try to understand the significance of the laboratory exercise and relate it to information presented in the lectures and text).

We also know little about the prior knowledge that our students bring to our classes. In spite of what some instructors believe, students do not enter our courses with empty heads waiting to be filled by our words of wisdom. Elementary school children as well as college students already have formulated explanations to describe and explain what happens in the natural world. In fact, students are very reluctant to give up these beliefs in spite of what they are taught, observe, and experience in formal science courses (Fisher et. al., 1986; Kessler & Quinn, 1987; Meyer, 1993; Soyibo, 1993). For example, many students believe that respiration and breathing mean the same thing, that all fruits taste sweet, and that fertilizer is "plant food." No matter how ridiculous such preconceived ideas, misconceptions, or naive theories may seem to the scientifically trained individual, students find them satisfactory explanations. (For an excellent video demonstrating just how ineffective science courses are in terms of eliminating misconceptions, readers are referred to "Private Universe," an 18-

minute color video produced by Pyramid Film and Video, Santa Monica, CA; 1-800-421-2304.)

Actually, students can do very well in science classes without relinquishing such alternative beliefs. How is this possible? By compartmentalizing what they genuinely believe from what the teacher wants them to learn and expects them to give back on exams. Students can become "masters of maintaining parallel ways of knowing" such that what they learn in a science course never becomes integrated into their own experience or way of knowing the world (Edmondson & Novak, 1993, p. 555).

The key to successful science instruction then becomes teaching in ways such that students "meaningfully integrate into their existing conceptual frameworks" (Edmondson & Novak, 1993, p. 548) the subject matter they are being taught. Since we are not certain how this process occurs, we must use a variety of approaches to connect the information presented in class to students' prior knowledge and experiences. Students must do more than listen, memorize, and mindlessly follow laboratory instructions. They must become active participants in the learning process, for example, discussing or writing, in order to clarify and organize their thoughts, putting the newly acquired information into their own words. By keeping a journal or by doing short, in-class writing assignments, students can summarize what they have learned and explain how that information relates to their lives or to society as a whole. Instructors might permit students to select topics to be studied or problems to be investigated. Visual aids, overheads, model-building activities, computer simulations, as well as cooperative learning groups should be used on a regular basis, thereby increasing opportunities for students with diverse learning styles to take in and process the new information.

How students acquire knowledge—or their learning style—is biologically based yet strongly influenced by the environment in which each student is raised (Anderson, 1988; Bennett, 1990; Border & Chism, 1992; Claxton & Murrell, 1987; Green, 1989; Haukoos & Satterfield, 1986; More, 1987; Reyhner, 1992; Shade, 1989). The socialization process, previous schooling experiences, and the values and worldview of the culture in which a person grows up strongly affect how he or she organizes and conceptualizes information.

Learning styles not only affect the acquisition of knowledge; they also influence students in their selection of a major. Students gravitate to those courses and disciplines most compatible with their preferred learning styles (Kolb, 1981). This tendency may in part explain why numerous efforts and programs to increase the participation of women and minorities in the sciences have not been particularly successful (*Science and Engineering Degrees*, 1992; Sims, 1992; *Undergraduate Science Education*, 1992). Introductory science, as traditionally taught, favors the competitive/field independent/analytic/sequential learner. Yet, a growing number of today's students are cooperative/field dependent/global/simultaneous learners. In a multicultural science classroom the teacher tries to present information in a variety of ways so that students—regardless of their preferred learning styles—will increase their knowledge and skills. For example, field-dependent learners might find a class less confusing if the instructor begins with an overview of a topic before dwelling on the details; the subject matter might seem more interesting if the teacher starts with a catchy topic (e.g., cancer) before getting down to the basics (cell structure and division).

Properly coached, students can modify and expand their learning style repertoire. So, if we can "hook" them on science at the introductory level through nontraditional forms of instruction, we can help them to develop the skills they need to succeed in more advanced and traditionally taught science courses.

THE GROWING NUMBER OF NON-NATIVE ENGLISH-SPEAKING STUDENTS

The need to diversify teaching strategies becomes increasingly important as the number of non-native English-speaking students grows. For many years, we have all been aware of the presence on campus of international students. At the undergraduate level, the number of these students has been growing slowly and steadily (+12.5%) from 208,000 in 1980 to 234,000 in 1991 (*The Chronicle of Higher Education Almanac,* Aug. 26, 1992, p. 11, and Aug. 25, 1993, p. 13). However, at the graduate level, international students are now earning large percentages of the master's and doctorates awarded in many fields, especially in engineering, business and management, and the sciences (*The Chronicle of Higher Education Almanac,* Aug. 25, 1993, p. 16). For example, in 1991, non–U.S. citizens with temporary visas earned 24.3 percent of the doctorates in the life sciences and 35.2 percent in the physical sciences. Asia is the largest source of international students with China, Japan, Taiwan, India, and the Republic of Korea topping the list.

There is, however, another population of non-native English-speaking students—immigrants and refugees—which is growing exponentially. Consider the following: Between 1980 and 1991, the undergraduate population as a whole increased by 17.8 percent while the number of Hispanic undergraduates rose from 438,000 to 804,000 (+83.6%) and that of Asians from 253,000 to 559,000 (+121%) (*The Chronicle of Higher Education Almanac,* Aug. 26, 1992, p. 11, and Aug. 25, 1993, p. 13).

Although many Asian students major in and have done very well in the sciences, they represent only a small percentage of the students awarded bachelor's degrees in the physical and biological sciences. For example, Asian students earned only 5.8 percent of the physical and 8.5 percent of the biological sciences baccalaureate degrees awarded in 1990 (*Science and Engineering Degrees,* 1992). And, in spite of the hoopla in the press about this "model minority," there was a 16.3 percent decrease between 1985 and 1989 (*Undergraduate Science Education,* 1992, pp. 3–15) in the number of Asians planning to major in the sciences.

Meanwhile, the number of Hispanic undergraduates is growing rapidly and far exceeds that of Asian undergrads. However, Hispanics rarely major in science. In 1990, Hispanics earned 3.2 percent of the bachelor's degrees in the physical sciences and 5.6 percent in the biological sciences (*Science and Engineering Degrees,* 1992).

Few Asian and Hispanic students obtain their doctorates in the sciences. For example, of the doctorates earned in the life and physical sciences in 1991, Asians (U.S. citizens or with permanent visas) were awarded 6.5 percent and 8.1 percent respectively, and Hispanics (U.S. citizens or with permanent visas) 2.5 percent and 2.6 percent (*The Chronicle of Higher Education Almanac,* Aug. 25, 1993, p. 16). Clearly our educational system in the sciences is having much more success with international graduate students than with immigrant and refugee undergraduates. Although instructors often cannot distinguish between these populations (Cheng, 1993), there are major differences.

International students have been described as the "créme de la créme of their countries" (Holden, 1993, p. 1770). Their academic preparation is outstanding, they are willing to work hard, and often bring along their own financial support. They also are already somewhat proficient in English as demonstrated by their scores on the TOEFL exam (Test of English as a Foreign Language). In addition, most international graduate students have had the benefit of receiving their undergraduate education in their native language and in familiar surroundings.

In contrast, political and economic problems in their homelands bring immigrants and refugees to the United States. And, unlike the international students, their level of education and previous study of English are quite variable. Kinsella in Chapter 7 describes in detail the diversity among these students.

Only a few publications address the issue of teaching science to college students who are still learning English (Case & Lau, 1991; Rosenthal, in press; Rosenthal, 1993a and 1993b; Rosenthal, 1992–93; Sutman et al., 1986), and, as a result, there are many misconceptions about science instruction for ESL students. One such misconception is that the technical and scientific words make the discipline particularly difficult for non-native English speakers. If anything, the vocabulary of science is "foreign" to both native and non-native speakers of English and is equally as problematic for both groups.

However, several other aspects of the English language apparently cause problems in science classes for many non-native speakers. One is understanding the complexity of the sentence structure found in science texts (which are written at very high reading levels). Another is that many everyday words in English have alternative and very precise scientific meanings. Consider the following examples: *Volume* may refer to the loudness of sound, to a book, or to a three-dimensional space. A *fluid*, to most people, is a liquid, wet to the touch; however, scientifically, a *fluid* can also refer to a gas. Many ESL students encounter difficul-

ties when they try to express in English (either verbally or in writing) what they know and have learned. This situation is compounded when given strict time limits, such as during a test. Another problem experienced by ESL students in science classes is understanding the language of their professors during lectures. Faculty members inadvertently use complex sentences (e.g., separating the subject and verb by a series of dependent clauses); they use vocabulary words not known to many students who are still learning English. The native English speaker automatically and unconsciously understands most of the language of the classroom and can, therefore, focus specifically on the course content. However, the non-native speaker must first break through the language barrier before attempting to comprehend the new subject matter. When you consider that students typically enroll in several courses and simultaneously are learning several new subject areas, the enormity of the challenge for ESL students becomes readily apparent.

Nevertheless, for some students of limited English proficiency, science is an especially attractive major. Compared to courses in many other disciplines, science requires fewer books to be read, little or no class discussion, few long papers to be written, more hands-on and laboratory activities, and more objective than subjective testing. The mathematical basis of many science courses also reduces linguistic barriers to learning.

EVALUATING STUDENT ACHIEVEMENT

One of the difficulties in testing a multiethnic and multilingual population is that students bring very different strengths (and weaknesses) to the testing process (Ballard & Clanchy, 1991). For example, many ESL students find multiple-choice tests, which are frequently used in the sciences, to be particularly difficult. First, a multiple-choice exam requires considerable reading when little time is available; second, the differences between the answer choices are often extremely subtle or may involve double negatives and other complex sentence structures. Third, many students schooled outside the United States lack familiarity with multiple-choice exams; they are accustomed to writing essays and find multiple-choice tests especially picky (and tricky). Nevertheless, essay questions present other problems for ESL students who may know the information but lack the words in English or the organizational skills to explain their thoughts clearly in writing.

Students, regardless of their ethnicity and language proficiency, show a wide variety of reactions to evaluation procedures. While some achieve better under pressure, others become anxious and forget much of what they have learned. A student who can research a topic and make an oral presentation to the class may fall apart during a timed, multiple-choice test. Another student may be all thumbs when working in the laboratory, yet can analyze data and accurately draw conclusions. To equitably assess students, the instructor of a multicultural science classroom may need to be a bit creative. In other words, grading will no longer be based on the average score of the three or four timed tests of identical format. Taking into consideration the size of the class, how much time and energy the instructor is willing to devote to the assessment process, and the nature of his or her students, the faculty member can combine a variety of assessment procedures that will tap into some area of strength for each student. These strategies might include:

- tests with several types of questions (essay, multiple-choice, matching, problem-solving, fill in the blanks, etc.).

- written assignments that can be revised several times until a satisfactory grade is earned. (The critiquing can be done by the instructor or by peers.)

- the option of taking a test or, instead, writing a paper on an assigned topic.

- removing time limits during testing and/or making tests open-book or take-home.

- small group projects in which the members of the group each receive the same grade for the project as a whole and, in addition, each member of the group receives a second grade based on his or her specific contribution. (For example, the topic of the greenhouse effect could be divided among a group of three students. One student would research what is meant by the greenhouse effect and what are its causes. Another would investigate the problems that might be caused by the greenhouse effect and the regions of the world that will be affected. The third group member would analyze the pros and cons of various recommendations on how to reduce or prevent the greenhouse effect. After pooling their findings, the group could make an oral presentation to the class or prepare a written report. Each member of the group would receive two grades, one evaluating the project as a whole and the other for the specific contribution made by the individual student.)

For the instructor who is accustomed to giving the same multiple-choice tests semester after semester, the kinds of assessment strategies mentioned above do require additional work and effort. The reward, however, is in finding out that if allowed to demonstrate where their abilities lie, all students in some way are capable of learning and achieving in a science class.

CONCLUSIONS

Little by little, a multicultural approach can be phased into a science course. Making the necessary changes in the curriculum, widening one's repertoire of teaching strategies, trying out innovative assessment procedures, and paying more attention to the classroom atmosphere and dynamics can be initiated gradually by the individual instructor. Feeling comfortable with a less traditional form of science instruction invariably takes time. For many instructors the major obstacle is broadening the curriculum; for others, it is giving up lecture time to allow for alternative types of activities and a more student-centered pedagogy.

The growing diversity of our undergraduate population argues strongly for multicultural education. With it, diversity becomes an asset and a source of enrichment to the course, not an annoyance to the instructor nor a handicap to the learner.

In the sciences, we must begin to pay greater attention to the learning styles, linguistic needs, and culturally influenced belief systems of our students. This need is especially critical in introductory courses which often determine potential majors' decisions to remain in science and also the final impression of science that many students take with them from college. We cannot keep teaching as if all students had the same background and upbringing, the same educational experiences, and as if they all learned in the same way. They don't, and we know it.

Conventional science instruction has not worked well for many minority group members nor has it served the traditional undergraduate population particularly well. We can continue blaming the high schools for inadequately preparing students in the sciences and math; we can criticize the government for underfunding science education; we can grumble about the out-of-date equipment and laboratories at many colleges and universities; we can complain about today's students because they are different from those we taught twenty-five years ago, and we can fuss about the graduate teaching assistants whose proficiency in English may be inadequate for the job they are required to perform. Or, we can recognize that our society as well as our students have changed dramatically and that whatever the source of "the problem," one effective solution that can be readily implemented is multicultural education. Multicultural science may not be the only way to jumpstart student interest in the sciences, but it is a reasonable place to begin.

ENDNOTES

1. Minorities in science: The pipeline problem (1992, November 13). *Science, 258,* 1176–1235.
   Minorities in science '93, Trying to change the face of science (1993, November 12). *Science, 262,* 1089–1135.
2. Women in science (1992, March 13). *Science, 225,* 1365–1388.
   Gender and the culture of science, Women in science '93 (1993, April 16). *Science, 260,* 383–430.
   Comparisons across cultures, Women in science '94 (1994, March 11). *Science, 263,* 1389–1393.

CHAPTER 10

The Humanities

Jackie R. Donath
Assistant Professor
California State University, Sacramento

Editor's Notes:
The emergence of cultural diversity or plurality as a viable perspective in the Humanities has challenged its more limited and traditional canon. The resultant controversy has already produced new courses and curricula which demonstrate that the Humanities offers a rich milieu to further the goals of multiculturalism.

In her chapter, Jackie Donath discusses the debate with a particular focus on Humanities classes. She believes that Humanities courses are logical places to model more humane learning environments, where mastery of subject matter is combined with an intellectually expanded exchange of contextual information about human cultures and experience.

Donath addresses the levels of infusion noted in our model, giving specific examples of additive and transformed courses and also providing information on useful references and resources. She examines each component of the model—content, instructional strategies, classroom dynamics and evaluation and assessment—from the perspective of the Humanities. Donath presents some principles that should be helpful to faculty wishing to make progress in multicultural course infusion in the Humanities and other academic areas. ■

What the past decades of social change, what the research and pedagogy that is derived from them have taught us is that the extraordinary diversity in the historical experience of people in this country can not be represented by "a tradition," a narrow canon, however resounding the names that constitute and recommend it. Nor should the fact that our culture draws upon many diverse and sometimes conflicting traditions be troubling to us. To dream of creating a "common language" we must begin, with joy, at our common diversity.
—Paul Lauter (1991, p. 255)

The Humanities is a broad and inclusive area of study, encompassing the basic humanness of the species and the various ways in which that humanness is expressed in different cultural settings, across time and space. The subjects and insights which the Humanities offer us provide a rich milieu for furthering the goals of multicultural education. Through the Humanities, students can obtain knowledge, understanding, and appreciation of the contributions and perspectives of various groups. Within the disciplines of the Humanities, students can experience how the threads of common human experience and the uniqueness of individual perspectives are richly intertwined. Traditionally, the Humanities have been seen as an area in which the universals of human experience are the primary focus. In this context, the elements of human nature and behavior which seem to remain constant through time and across cultures are given emphasis.

Such a method might appear workable, at least on the surface, when addressing a seemingly stable cultural pattern (like "Western" culture) or the cycles of a culture's history. However, culture(s) of the past can only be imperfectly and superficially understood in the present, and the lessons of the past are only of value if we examine them in their complexity. Events, behaviors, values, attitudes, even material artifacts, can only be really understood in culturally and historically specific ways.

Historically, as a central component of a liberal arts education, the Humanities is often an arena in which concerns about commonality and difference appear as pedagogical and epistemological categories in curricular discussions, such as the future of traditional Western texts and themes; the circumstances and details of including "non-Western" cultural materials; the importance of recognizing and discussing American pluralism or multiculturalism; and the need to treat categories of experience such as gender, race, class, and so on, as significant elements of culturally constructed human identities.

In response to these sorts of issues, Trend (1992) calls for recognition of, and concern for, a pedagogy of culture, with teachers (among others) as "cultural workers," examining and analyzing the mecha-

nisms which create and transmit culture, and acting on their insights in order to broaden and enlarge the "conventional definitions of art, literature, taste, 'quality,' and school itself to examine them within the fullest contexts of daily experience" (p. 2). While Trend's overtly political agenda can be off-putting, his description of the need for, and the functions of, a self-conscious cultural pedagogy is compelling.

Cultural pedagogy requires acknowledgment of the constructed nature of cultural institutions and narratives of all sorts, and the analysis of their transmission and reception within both specific historical contexts and across a wide range of circumstances. In his call for a praxis of "cultural work," Trend sees the possibility of a positive breakdown of the unnecessary and artificial boundaries between academic disciplines, students, and teachers, and what we might call "professional" scholars and "amateur" learners.

In American higher education, institutions have attempted to respond to the challenges of the changing boundaries of scholarship and the changing needs of society by diversifying the curriculum (see Chapter 1). The expansion of the materials and subjects which may be considered academically legitimate is not an easy or gentle process. The explosion of the canon of the Humanities has been a controversial, and for many, a painful process. Disagreements abound about what constitutes an education, what is worthy knowledge, and what should be the purposes and expectations of institutions of higher learning.

Decentralization and the dismantling of traditional social and intellectual hierarchies is often perceived as a threat by those, like Dinesh D'Sousa, Lynne V. Cheney, and the late Allan Bloom among others, who appear to have vested interests in the actual or perceived influence of Western thinking and power. Multiculturally infused Humanities offer a new sort of synthetic paradigm which encompasses acceptance of the complex and contested qualities of human experience, without resorting to a slippery and mushy sort of "common culture" line, of the sort suggested by Diane Ravitch for California public school history texts. Her texts of choice would promote the idea that different ethnic groups "competed, fought, suffered, but ultimately learned to live together in peace and even achieved a sense of common nationhood" (Waugh, 1990).

Infusion can offer the Humanities a model which includes both theoretical and methodological concerns and avoids the pitfalls of a simplistic approach to the complexities of human experiences and expressions. Infusion includes mechanisms for addressing complex issues of intellectual distance and academization in ways which enrich and influence both instruction and content. In addition, consideration of multiculturalism as diversity and difference allows an expansion of the knowledge bases and pedagogical tools available to students and teachers of Humanistic subjects—whether they are found in "traditional" disciplinary configurations or are attempting interdisciplinary syntheses.

Like the Roman god Janus, the Humanities can simultaneously look to the past and the future, offering perspectives and information which resonate in the present-day lives of students. Multicultural infusion in the Humanities allows instructors to present students with an integrated and coherent sense of what it means to be human; ways to understand and connect the similarities and differences of human experience; and ways to respond to the needs of diverse populations of learners. In doing so, university Humanities courses can meet the worthy goals of the Engaging Cultural Legacies Project of the American Association of Colleges by helping students to

address the complexity that is part of their cultural inheritance; the disparate and often conflicting sources of their traditions; the values, commitments, questions and tensions that are intrinsic to any rich tradition; the difficulties of framing judgments that draw on inherited values. (Association of American Colleges, 1989, p. 2)

CONTENT

American culture has traditionally considered interest in the arts, music, and literature as frivolous and bordering on the trivial, to be taken up only after, or as a secondary adjunct to, the important, practical, pragmatic knowledge and skills necessary for physical or financial survival. Even in the nineteenth century, when the nation began to cast about for a usable and unifying past, and to yearn for the legitimation which tradition confers, American artists in a wide variety of media turned to the styles of the "old" world in which to express their often original, "new" world ideas. It is really only relatively recently that Americans have begun to consider the importance of art, music, and literature as expressors of, and clues to, the values, attitudes, beliefs, and behaviors of citizens of this nation and people living in other places and times.

Interdisciplinary courses in Humanities often combine history and philosophy with discussion of the creative branches of human expression, such as literature (drama, poetry, and the novel), music, fine arts (painting, sculpture, architecture, and related genres), and occasionally dance.

In this form, the Humanities class is really a uniquely American invention. While educators and philosophers have long argued for the importance of interdisciplinary connections in cultural studies, and a good deal of contemporary political, corporate, and social rhetoric acknowledges the interdisciplinary and global nature of human experiences, the barriers between academic disciplines have remained, for the most part, steadfast. New subject areas, often spin-offs of "parent" disciplines, or multidisciplinary mutations, have been forced to find their own turfs rather quickly, and to defend and justify them, intellectually, politically, and curricularly.

The peculiar bipolarity of many college curriculums—in terms of the administratively fragmented nature of discipline-centered knowledge on the one hand, and the desire and need for some sense of an orderly, integrated pattern to the curriculum and the world outside the University, on the other—may be particularly problematic for teachers and courses in the Humanities, because of their multidisciplinarity. How might these conflicting requirements—the need for discrete, specific, discipline-based knowledge, and the desire to make connections and understand commonalties in the world of human experience—be resolved in ways which facilitate the infusion of multicultural materials?

Ira J. Winn, in an article entitled "An Ecological Approach to Multiculturalism" (1993), has pointed out some of the problems which arise when the interconnected nature of learning, knowledge, and experience is ignored:

> ...piece-meal approaches to problem-solving segregate knowledge rather than integrate. The proverbial forest is overlooked for the trees. The attempts to introduce multiculturalism into the curriculum as one or several special courses may turn out to be just such an example; they will function little better than the now moribund Western civilization courses which were so long entrenched in so many universities and schools. (p. 119)

What Winn suggests as central to issues of multicultural infusion and balanced curriculum is a deeper, more considered discussion of what sorts of knowledge are most worthy (although he does not fully develop the implications of *that* question), and how people learn. His arguments and suggestions, although framed by concern with issues of a "core curriculum," certainly have relevance to issues of multicultural course content in the Humanities. I have extracted several of his relevant points below:

- In a world where everyone gets a piece of the curriculum pie, eventually all go hungry.
- The development of a civic and planetary consciousness is a vital goal for education.
- Core studies...must not be limited to books and readings.
- Any...curriculum of great worth must aim at lifelong learning. (pp. 122–124)

This "ecological" approach to curriculum planning and concern with an authentic infusion of multiculturalism into college courses is a thought-provoking one. Winn's ideas can provide an organizational structure for discussing multicultural infusion from both a content and instructional perspective, and so I have converted them into "principles" which might guide instructors who are engaged in or contemplating multicultural infusion in the Humanities.

Slicing the Pie: The Principle of Additive Infusion

Winn's pie analogy suggests the problems inherent in offering students information in discrete bites which touch base with various groups or subjects without offering an overarching sense of organization or direction. At this level of additive multicultural infusion, to use James A. Banks's term (1991), the curriculum is basically unchanged. Adding cultural content, themes, or concepts at this level does not challenge the canon or structure of the curriculum in any substantive way. In fact, as Kitano noted in Chapter 2, the selections made of people, events, and themes often act to reinforce or illustrate the values of the dominant culture rather than accurately representing those of different cultural groups.

However, to extend the pie analogy, one cannot reasonably expect to consume an entire pie at one sitting, and sharing the pie—moving a course from an exclusive perspective to a more inclusive one—is a matter of process as much as product. Instructors who are beginning to infuse their classes must begin somewhere. So it may be that any level of infusion, no matter how simplistic, is a reasonable preliminary goal, as long as the instructor (and students) realizes that lip service to the contributions of different groups or the addition of a unit of multicultural content in a course is not completely addressing the goals of multicultural education.

Instructors beginning at an additive level of infusion might easily begin the process by changing the reading material, lectures or assignments in a class. One might change to a basic text which incorporates material about ethnic minorities and women. With the topicality of multiculturalism in higher education, publishers are changing even basic Humanities texts to reflect new scholarship and new educational goals. If an appropriate new text is unavailable, or such a change seems too daunting, addition of an excerpt from a book or an article which includes information on the contributions of a minority group or women to the subject-area would be a manageable start. Changing a lecture or two by choosing examples from the experiences or contributions of underrepresented groups would also be a fine beginning in multicultural infusion, and could highlight

the importance and universality of a course's themes and concerns. Finally, a simple and "painless" variation, particularly from an instructor's point of view, is to make a change in the assignments given to students. Requiring students to search for, or research, a work of art, event, or artifact which reflects either their own ethnicity or perspectives or experiences which are different in some way, is a simple, nonthreatening way to begin to add diversity to a class and takes pressure off the instructor to be the source of all knowledge.

University instructors might accomplish the goal of preserving and extending diversity in American society with an inclusionary model, drawing on the methods and insights of ethnic studies. Based on recognition and acceptance of cultural diversity, this level of infusion can help students to understand their own particular cultural backgrounds and the cultural inheritances of others.

Ethnic studies, as a discipline, arose in the 1960s as minority groups pressured public schools and universities to provide these groups with instruction in their languages and cultures and to integrate previously monocultural curriculums. As time passed, many of these programs expanded their goals to include promotion of attitudes of respect and understanding toward these languages and cultures as ways to appeal to students of various ethnic backgrounds and to prevent the ghettoization of ethnic studies materials and insights.

College and university instructors who are just beginning to explore multiculturalism might also do well to investigate the curriculum guides and instructional suggestions which have been developed for elementary and secondary teachers over the past decade. While geared to younger students, many have information and concepts which are valuable for undergraduates and their instructors.

For example, in 1986, the American Association for Colleges of Teacher Education (AACTE) published *Multicultural Education and Ethnic Studies*, which included an analysis of accreditation standards for multicultural education and a very useful annotated bibliography of multiethnic books and materials. James Banks, of course, has written a number of texts to help teachers infuse their curricula. Banks is the author of a useful philosophical and theoretical text entitled *Multiethnic Education: Theory and Practice* (1988), which is a significant resource for instructors who may be interested in strengthening their understandings of the foundations of multiethnic education. His *Teaching Strategies for Ethnic Studies* (1991) offers materials, strategies, and ideas for teaching about a number of ethnic groups. This book also provides rationales, goals, concepts, and information on current trends in infusing ethnic content in the curriculum. Banks describes his ideal of "ethnic literacy," and discusses how teachers in most subject areas might develop units on cultural differences which could be integrated into their regular lesson plans (pp. 53–92).

Another scholar of teacher education, Ricardo Garcia, has developed a very useful model of the ethnic studies approach which has a good deal to offer instructors in the Humanities who wish to begin to include materials from different ethnic groups into their courses. In his book *Teaching in a Pluralistic Society* (1991) he defines the goal of the ethnic studies model as the increase in knowledge about different ethnic groups in order to encourage better understandings about people in the group. He asserts the model's applicability as a conceptual framework to any human group. However, he also sounds a cautionary note, reminding teachers that using his model demands that one understand "the difference between teaching an experience and teaching about

an experience" (p. 142). Ethnic group experiences need to be considered from both an insider's and an outsider's perspective(s), and that is where the subjects and insights of the Humanities can offer both significant pedagogical and methodological resources. A group's self-defined music, literature, art forms, language, religion, and historical understandings give students insight into the insider's point of view. By investigating the perceptions and experiences of others who have had contact with the group being studied, students can view the group from the outside. A group's worldview can be experienced and understood through its humanistic expressions, especially when treated with care and sensitivity.

In *Multicultural America; A Resource for Teachers of Humanities and American Studies* (1993), Betty Ch'maj and her colleagues have collected a number of syllabi of just this sort. They are divided into groups according to what she describes as "deliberate 'ethnic' emphasis," and "deliberate 'American' emphasis." The syllabi also include a group which illustrate "transforming 'basic' or 'mainstream' courses," which are suggestive of both practical and philosophical matters which must be the concerns of instructors who want to move the multicultural infusion of their classes to a more comprehensive, "transformed" level (pp. v–vi). Mariette Sawchuk has also included several useful sample syllabi for undergraduate liberal arts classes in her *Infusing Multicultural Perspectives Across the Curriculum* (1992). This work includes a questionnaire to assess faculty needs and suggestions for student evaluation questions.

Civic and Planetary Consciousness: The Principles of Transformational Infusion (Universality and Continuity)

Ira Winn's injunction that education must be grounded in civic and planetary consciousness is suggestive of the Humanities concern with both what James Axtell called "society over time," and "the functional whole" of culture (p. 6). While an additive or "inclusive" phase is a likely starting point on a journey to multicultural infusion, such an approach carries with it at least an implication, and often the perpetuation, of a belief that groups who have been traditionally underrepresented in the curriculum are not really integral parts of either society or the world of knowledge.

A transformational plan is fundamentally different from an additive approach, because it challenges and changes the basic paradigms of disciplinary content; it attacks the subject's canon, exposing unspoken assumptions of worthiness and presenting both diverse perspectives and critical materials. Central to this approach is the instructor's recognition of the socially constructed nature of knowledge, and a commitment to evaluation of course content with that understanding firmly in place. And yet, one must try to present a coherent and rational course of study to students.

A central problem in achieving this goal is that there is no longer a consistent or dominant model for describing or teaching what colleges and universities generally refer to as "our common cultural heritage." The definition of who "we" are and what is "ours" is at the heart of the battle over curriculum reform. And in many ways, that part of the battle is at once the most hard-fought and the most specious.

The discussion may be moved into course content by looking for guidelines in works which are concerned with curricular reform. One fine preliminary source is Betty Schmitz's *Core Curriculum and Cultural Pluralism; A Guide for Campus Planners* (1992). Her text includes a compilation of the stated goals of a number of core Humanities programs which participated in the Association of American Colleges'

(AAC) Cultural Legacies Program. What is most significant and useful about the list is the ways in which the different institutions tried to define the relationship between student learning and course content. They range from Earlham College's, "To help us overcome provinciality and transcend our own narrow sphere of experience," to the University of Wyoming's goal, "To help students identify, explore and evaluate concrete examples of their own cultural heritage and elucidate links between this heritage and other times and places" (p. 11). What is remarkable about even the short list in this volume is that it reveals how important it is to have a purpose in mind *before* (and when) tackling curricular changes. *Core Curriculum and Cultural Pluralism* offers a number of useful insights, practical suggestions, and sample syllabi and programs which were attempts to somehow reconcile the needs of "coreness" and pluralism.

Courses in the Humanities may be able to mediate this contested dialectic by emphasizing the integrity, continuities, and universalities of cultural life and expressions. The principles of continuity and universality connect all people, as individuals and in cultural networks, across time and space, and in the past, present, and future. Consideration of cultural integrity demands that every generation evaluate its cultural inheritance within the contexts of past and present events and to make value judgments about the present and the future in terms of continuity and universality. As the "praxis" section of the special issue of *Liberal Education* on "Engaging Cultural Legacies" (1991) makes clear, these ideas and principles are compatible with multicultural concerns as well as the basis for practical pedagogical and content-concerned strategies. As a matter of fact, Claire Gaudiani, President of Connecticut College, has suggested that they are strategically intertwined and central to the teaching of civic virtues. According to Guadiani, courses in the Humanities should be organized in ways which lead to the investigation and identification of these virtues in the context of what she calls "citizenship in the global community," and facilitate their transmission and practice:

> our pursuit of knowledge must include learning about the virtuous behaviors of other cultures.... Multiculturalism in pursuit of civic virtue might blunt the pernicious impact of ethnocentric particularism on the one hand and racial or ethnic stereotyping on the other.... As students discover that many cultures prize the same commonly acknowledged virtues, they establish common ground with those citizens. As they find distinctive and shared virtues, students may be less likely to participate in interracial or intercultural hatred or be victims of empty filiopietism that can bring only disappointment. (*Engaging Cultural Legacies*, p. 15)

In the "new," expanding universe of humanistic subjects, responsibilities, and concerns, how might instructors "reform" their classes to improve their "inclusiveness"? Several essays in Betty Ch'maj's *Multicultural America* (1993) provide both useful insights and helpful models. For example, Sherry Sullivan, Department of English, University of Alabama at Birmingham, reveals both the problems and the pleasures which accompanied her work to transform a survey class in American literature. She began with something of an additive change, placing works by diverse writers at the center of her course, but also retaining traditional texts which she felt would work with her new selections. What I found striking and encouraging in her experience was that the first change led her to modify her course in other ways; an additive change transformed her course inclusively as she reconsidered matters of presentation and organization, course

goals, and teaching practice (p. 201–206). Professor Sullivan's experiences suggest that transformational infusion might follow "naturally," once additive infusion is begun and faculty commitment and knowledge base grows.

Generally, Humanities classes seem to be organized in one of four basic ways, and each can be "transformed" by including multicultural materials and perspectives, while at the same time emphasizing the continuity and universal nature of many aspects of human experience.

The Cultural Epoch Approach

This approach is traditionally organized around an historical approach to great periods of human activity, often according to Western cultural perspectives: Greece and Rome; the Renaissance; the medieval period; the Enlightenment. These eras are discussed primarily in the context of their social, intellectual, and cultural histories. In classes of this sort, multicultural material could be easily incorporated by widening the area of investigation to include non-Western European cultures of the time. Many of the most recent texts created for Humanities survey courses include such information on previously neglected places and populations.

In addition, while this approach appears to emphasize history, other disciplines including music, literature, architecture, and the visual arts are also incorporated to introduce the ways in which ideas and ideals are expressed and communicated in different periods. Here again even a modest shift in primary materials offered to students—travelogues of trips to the Far East, journals of nuns, examples of artworks from Africa—would infuse the course with multicultural information while opening a dialogue with the ideas and experiences of European cultures.

The Great Themes Approach

Somewhat similar to the cultural period approach, a great themes class is concerned with universal questions which can, of course, cross cultural boundaries: questions about Nature, Beauty, Free-Will, and so on. In some ways, this approach is more easily adapted to the goals of multicultural infusion, because thematically organized studies, by their very natures, need not be concerned with a single historical period or locale, but may range freely across time and space in search of materials which respond to the issue under investigation.

For example, Trenton State College has a four-course Humanities core, whose first component is a class entitled, "Humanity: Ideas and Ideals." The course is centered on examination of theories, concepts and interpretations of human nature, and includes *Siddhartha, The Koran, The Varieties of Religious Experiences* and readings of Native American mythology—Dante, Buber, and Milton (Association of American Colleges, 1989, pp. 42–44). A somewhat similar approach is part of CUNY-Queens College "World Studies" core of four courses which are team-taught by professors of humanities and social sciences. One of the courses of the sequence, "Ancient Worlds," focuses on the ways in which early civilizations around the globe created themselves through their myths, texts, art, and artifacts. Another, entitled "Encounters Between Civilizations, 1500–1900," examines the political, social, economic, artistic, and technological changes which took place as different cultures came into contact and shaped what would become the modern world (Association of American Colleges, 1989, pp. 48–49).

The Great Works Approach

At the center of much of the controversy in diversifying humanities course content is the historical importance of courses which emphasize the reading and study of "major" texts. Paul Lauter (1991), for one, sees "the question of the canon" as vital. He defines the canon as "the set of literary works, the grouping of significant philosophical, political, and religious texts, the particular accounts of history generally accorded cultural weight within society." According to Lauter, not only does the definition of the canon influence curriculum and research, "it also helps to determine precisely whose experiences and ideas become central to academic study" (p. ix.).

In *Canons and Contexts*, Lauter sees efforts to change the canon as having far-reaching implications: "Canons do not, after all, exist in the sky; rather they are made manifest in particular social and educational practices...." (p. 149). As a matter of fact, canonical criticism has led to revelations about institutional and social power structures. The process of trying to expand the curricula,

> allowed many to discover—the deeply racist, patriarchal, heterosexist assumptions that actually shaped such seemingly innocent documents as reading lists, book order forms, and literary histories. Similarly, practical efforts to change institutional hiring procedures and priorities revealed the power equation implicit in seemingly neutral, meritocratic criteria. (p. ix)

Lauter's definition of the canon and its implications can certainly be broadened to include non-literary texts, and his arguments lose none of their validity when applied to works of art by non-hegemonic groups. Broadening the universe of "texts" to which students are exposed in any Humanities class is clearly a goal of multicultural infusion, and acknowledging the impact of belonging or not belonging to the canon is a fine place to begin to confront, with students, how works of art are valued and devalued.

The Multimedia Approach

Humanities courses occasionally seem to take a fourth general approach, one which emphasizes the creative process in itself, and directs student attention to technique, artistic intention, and aesthetics. Often such courses are less interested in the "texts" which artists produce, whether buildings, books, or baubles, than in the artist, and his or her methods and purposes. This approach is common to introductory Humanities methodology courses whose goals are to help students recognize and understand the relationships of form and structure across the arts, and to differentiate between the purposes and intents of artists in different genres. More than some of the other approaches, this sort of course may easily incorporate the work of non-hegemonic artists, and then discuss how cultural matters may affect an individual's aesthetic and personal production. Particularly in this sort of course, however, some formal discussion of cultural biases and the often hidden political and cultural nature of aesthetic values will also be necessary.

This fourth general organizational pattern may be as much about instructional method as content, and so may provide a link between these principles of content and two other Winn-based ideas which have resonance in terms of classroom life: (1) instructional strategies and classroom dynamics and (2) student assessment.

INSTRUCTIONAL STRATEGIES AND CLASSROOM DYNAMICS

One might argue, with some success, I think, that for the past twenty or so years, the Humanities and its constituent disciplines have been in a state of perpetual upheaval. In part, this is because they are centrally concerned with matters of history, art, and values, and there are new developments in these areas every year. Some of the changes are also the result of the increasingly interdisciplinarity of academic life. Humanistic scholars are engaging in the study and use of an ever-expanding repertoire of artifacts, documents, and theoretical perspectives, and in addition to epistemological changes, this expansion has potential pedagogical impact as well.

The Classroom and "Real" Life: The Principle of Cultural Relevance and Reference

A point in Ira Winn's ecology of the Humanities, which I am identifying as my third principle, is his call to integrate the visual and performing arts into the curriculum. The Humanities must expand its definition of the arts to include popular as well as elite expressions. Doing so certainly proves the relevance of the subject, but use of the popular also improves the ability of the student and instructor to come to shared points of reference in discussing the material under investigation, no matter what organizational approach the class employs.

In the modern Humanities classroom, popular culture materials are most often used as casual and suggestive examples, emphasizing their formulaic and diffuse nature. On one level, that is certainly acceptable, as the popular arts are, after all, generally stereotypical and limited, and since they are familiar to students, allusion to a particular work or image may be all that is necessary to make a point. However, to treat the popular as trivial is to miss a significant opportunity to exploit a strand of culture which students have in common. As a matter of fact, it may certainly be argued that an American student's cultural environment is almost completely made up of popular artistic products transmitted to him or her as a member of a mass audience.

Winn also argues that contemporary education cannot consider itself successful if it does not provide students with critical skills as consumers of the arts and mass media. As a part of the development of "culture studies," the effects of mass communications have become the subjects of a new sort of intellectual examination, one which, in the words of David Trend (1992), is an "amalgam of reader response and resistance theories," and which emphasizes individualized uses and media literacy (p. 63). Using popular and mass cultures as integral parts of a class permits the instructor, and, by extension, the students, to connect personal, social, theoretical, and practical issues with materials which are familiar, and therefore powerful. As a matter of fact, use of the mass media in particular, as conduits of popular works of art, offers lessons on the ideological implications of media practice (both commercial and non-commercial). David Trend sees the use of mass media in the classroom as an opportunity to "describe the way values are conveyed both directly in the specific content of works and indirectly through the 'structured absences' that systematically exclude certain viewpoints" (p. 65).

The multicultural Humanities class requires the development of strategies and techniques which mirror, in a more positive fashion, the direct and indirect model of the mass media. By this I mean not only that course content should directly and explicitly promote cultural learning, but the classroom environment itself, should acknowledge and accommodate cultural pluralism, at least implicitly. Jane Tompkins put it well when she remarked, "I have come to think that teaching and learning are not a preparation for anything, but the thing itself.... The classroom is a microcosm of the world; it is the chance we have to practice whatever ideals we may cherish" (1991, p. 26).

The classroom in which everyone is expected to fit the same "old" mold will undercut even the most diverse and infused curriculum. An under-discussed subtext to the curricular debate is the issue of the process by which people with different perspectives interact—with one another and with the course materials. To improve the relevance of the classroom experience and to provide different students with reference points in classwork may require instructors to modify what Geneva Gay has called the "'what' and 'how' of teacher talk" (Diaz, p. 47). Professor Gay makes several specific suggestions for modifications in classroom dynamics and practices which reflect a sensitive understanding of students' cultural backgrounds (p. 49), including the following, which I have annotated:

- "...asking students to summarize points previously made, to restate another's point of view, or to declare their personal preferences on issues under discussion...." This allows the instructor to broaden the universe of examples, making them culturally pluralistic, while minimizing the feeling that a student must perform a high-profile task.

- "Minimizing teacher talk through the use of more student-focused and active learning strategies, such as small group tasks, simulations, role playing, dramatic readings, and cooperative learning." Cooperative pair, team, or group arrangements, if monitored and structured, can have a significant impact on the classroom climate. Such experiences give students a measure of control over both classroom discourse and the management of the learning process. Be sure to structure such groups so that membership and leadership roles are balanced across ethnic and gender groups (do not leave such elements to chance). Helping students learn how to interact in positive and effective ways in the relative safety of the classroom is an important first step in modeling for them how to function in a multicultural society.

Another active-learning technique with high potential in the Humanities is the case study method, which has, in the past several years, moved from its origins at the Harvard Business School into use in a variety of disciplines. One benefit of the case method is that, depending on the case, the principles under investigation in the course can be tied to real-world experiences and problem-solving. Helpful introductions to the method, which illuminate both its strengths and weaknesses, include Roland C. Christensen's and Abby J. Hansen's *Teaching and the Case Method* (1987) and Nancy Lyons's "Teaching by the Case Method" (1989).

- "Asking more divergent, high-order cognitive and affective questions that allow all students the chance to respond, and accepting their affective reactions as legitimate contributions to the learning process." Faculty have an opportunity in the classroom to help students by drawing out their opinions and preconceptions and illuminating the role which personal experience plays in interpreting events, and by extension, course content. Even while (necessarily) acknowledging the validity of a student's emotional reaction, an instructor can help a student understand the perceptions which shape it. In this way, invisible structures become visible, and the instructor is able to manage discussion and control classroom behavior by modeling what Paul Palmer has called "respectful listening and faithful responding" (1983, p. 27).

In a very informative and helpful article entitled "Bridging Emotion and Intellect: Classroom Diversity in Process" (1993), Jane Fried suggests that this sort of modeling essentially changes the ways in which classes are taught, by balancing discipline-specific knowledge with discussions of how such knowledge is legitimated and transmitted, and changing the role of the instructor from authority to facilitator. From Fried's point of view, "the professor, therefore, becomes responsible for teaching students three sets of skills" (p. 126), which are, in my opinion, particularly relevant to a multiculturally infused study of the Humanities.

The first skill is the ability to separate facts from cultural assumptions and beliefs about those facts. Assignments and discussions must encourage students to recognize and analyze their own beliefs and assumptions about course materials. In this way, students will begin to realize that facts and their interpretations exist in interactive relationships with one another, and that all facts and experiences are arranged and presented within a frame of reference, often cultural, which affects our understandings and interpretations.

A second skill which teachers of the Humanities should help their students develop is one which allows the consideration of different perspectives. Developing a classroom environment of respectful listening and faithful responding is one way to begin weaning students from their previous training and subsequent expectations that the instructor will provide them with the Truth. Instructors need to help students compare and contrast points-of-view, and to constructively analyze different perspectives without losing a sense of the possibility of a multiplicity of valid outlooks on any experience or artifact. It is, after all, that very sense of variation which characterizes and enriches human experience.

Perhaps the most difficult and important skill to be cultivated in a Humanities classroom is the ability to distinguish the personal from the intellectual. Facts, feelings, and opinions are difficult to separate from one another. According to Jane Fried,

> In order to create multicultural understandings, it is necessary that students learn to…think and speak in both realms, that of logic and fact, and that of beliefs, values and personal experiences, [and] they will begin to learn when it is appropriate to challenge and disagree and when it is appropriate to understand, accept, and self-disclose. (p. 127)

The multiculturally infused classroom must provide students with the opportunity to practice discussing difference in a validating context which rejects the search for a single correct answer in favor of recognition of the students' rights to explain and discuss their perceptions and experiences, so long as that right is extended to others who may offer differing, and even contradictory, knowledge and interpretations. Humanities classes are logical places to model more humane learning environments, which expand the process of education from specific subject mastery to an intellectually expanded (and expanding) exchange of contextual information about human experience and expressions. As Jane Fried so eloquently put it, "Once people have learned to listen respectfully and acknowledge context, it becomes very difficult for them to return to cultural encapsulation" (p. 128).

ASSESSMENT AND EVALUATION

One of the most difficult and often unpleasant parts of a teacher's responsibility is the process of placing a value on the educational experience and assigning student grades. In a multiculturally infused class,

this matter becomes even more problematic, because the process of infusion can alert the instructor to differences in learning styles, and such styles certainly may require different methods of evaluation and assessment, as well as a wide range of learning experiences. Evaluation, then, is a broader and more complicated process than simply testing and grading.

The Principle of Life-Long Learning

In his arguments for an ecological approach to multiculturalism, Ira Winn's last point is that a curriculum should be judged by its ability to turn learners on to great issues, certainly a worthy goal for instructors in the Humanities. In addition, instructors need to have a clear sense of their goals for each course, and begin to develop some means to assess whether individual students meet the instructor's objectives, and for that matter, whether the course itself, as it is taught, is in alignment with the stated course goals. In this regard, it is imperative that instructors include some written statement of their goals in the class materials given to students. Course objectives should be stated in operational terms which include both the type of behavior and kinds of situations in which that behavior will be evaluated.

Usually the syllabus is a likely place to document this information. One must be certain not to fall into the trap of using catch phrases or buzzwords when defining the tasks or skills on which students will be evaluated. For instance, one of my particular favorite phrases, which had a place of honor on my syllabi for years, was the phrase "read and analyze critically." But what exactly that involves, and how a student will be able to prove that skill, become important questions which must be clearly answered and rationalized before any evaluation can be undertaken. For instance, in a course involving works of both visual and literary art, critical analysis might include the ability to recognize the assumptions and intentions of the artist; the ability to apply aesthetic or formalistic criteria to works under consideration; and/or the ability to detect culturally specific elements in the works examined. Instructors must begin to develop a strong and arguable sense of what is significant and important in the material they offer in each class, not just in terms of their disciplines, but in terms of what the course materials and the experience in the classroom offer in the way of enhancing a student's life, both in the present and in the future.

For example, teachers are beginning to realize, I think from experience, what research reveals, that a testing situation is also an ideal learning situation, and so test-making and grading is an area which deserves some consideration from a pedagogical standpoint. One must also realize that test-taking as a skill is, to a great extent, an artificial, culturally specific experience, and instructors interested in transformational multicultural infusion will need to transform their testing methods in recognition of cultural difference. We must be vigilant in examining our grading tools for instances of gender, racial, ethnic, and class biases. In addition, we should consider testing as just one of a variety of evaluative devices at our disposal; just one step in the process of education occurring in our classrooms, a process that includes skills and abilities in addition to content-centered knowledge, and not simply use testing as an end in itself.

On what bases then, might we begin to evaluate both our students' performances and our own? Against what sorts of scales shall we measure our progress toward transforming our courses in terms of content, instruction, and assessment? For me, three basic principles seem to offer the best guidelines for evaluation and assessment: the principle of individualization, the principle of motivation, and the principle of progress.

The Principle of Individualized Instruction

This principle emphasizes the importance of an awareness of, and adaptation to, the backgrounds, needs, and interests of students. In the case of the Humanities, this principle may be illustrated by the changes I have made to my courses since I came to a painful acceptance of the reality of teaching in General Education. Rather than continuing to bemoan the casting of my pearls of wisdom before intellectual swine, I began to search for ways in which I might make my classes relevant to accountants and nurses and social workers.

One change I made was to widen the range of choices of topics on which students might write: I often allow students to generate their own topics within the confines of the course goals and the forms of various projects—not everything must be a research paper. Similarly, in evaluating a student's work, I have tried to individualize my comments and reactions to the student's theme and critical points and to get away from generic annotations about punctuation, although, candidly, I still try to give grammatical pointers.

The Principle of Motivation

Again, in response to my experiences in General Education, I have begun to realize that students are seldom interested in mastering Humanities subject matter as an end in itself. And even a behavioral goal, such as developing one's abilities for critical thinking, has little to recommend it from a student perspective. However, it is quite clear that students work harder and accomplish more when the tasks they are assigned have some significance for them. Guided by the principle of motivation, then, an instructor should make the meaning of the course's objectives quite clear, and, through examples and opportunities, allow students a number of ways to practice and understand them.

Motivation seems to result from active participation. Students must be assigned a number of concrete, definite tasks, beyond the "read the next chapter" sort. Instructors should spend some time thinking about and assessing the relationship between class meetings, course assignments, and the course's specific objectives. A successful course will include specific tasks usable both in and out of class which will give students the chance to replace passive listening to the instructor with activities which build toward mastery. Often students think familiarity is mastery, until they receive an exam grade and have no incentive or opportunity to remedy their misunderstandings. Use of peer reactions to written or oral work, journals, and instructional- or pre-tests and writing assignments are all devices which can help provide motivation and encouragement to students while there is still time to clarify points of confusion or improve study habits and performance.

The Principle of Progress

Particularly in the Humanities, students complain that the course is irrelevant to their career goals, skills, or intellectual abilities. Or that the class really did nothing for them. In some cases, this criticism may be valid, but often this judgment is made simply because there is no material evidence of improvement. Pretesting is one way to provide such information, as is a course portfolio, in which the student collects work done over the term. It may be that our emphasis in testing needs revisiting in some way that allows us to evaluate change or progress as well as to assign grades. In the Humanities and in multiculturally infused Humanities, in particular, interest in affective instruction and outcomes requires developing a way to help bring individuals to realize their own values and attitudes, and how they contrast with, deviate from, or are reinforced by, those of other individuals and societies.

Evaluation and assessment are areas of instruction which must be considered in the context of the goals of multicultural infusion. Examination of our work and its objectives may lead us to enlarge the instructional tools at our disposal. Assessment of our instruction and evaluation of our students' work should function to enhance and maintain our sense of the order and meaning of a specific class and the general purpose of the humanistic enterprises of which we are a part.

CHAPTER 11

Integrating Race and Gender into Introductory Economics

Robin L. Bartlett
Professor of Economics
Denison University,
Granville, Ohio

Susan F. Feiner[1]
Visiting Associate Professor of Economics and
Women's Studies, University of Southern Maine,
Portland, Maine

Editor's Notes:

Robin Bartlett and Susan Feiner present a compelling rationale for integrating race and gender issues into introductory economics courses to "balance" the content. The current status of multicultural content integration in economics textbooks suggests a dismal picture. Content analyses demonstrate the virtual exclusion of information and examples regarding women and people of color. Where such information does appear, it is frequently stereotypical or blatantly inaccurate. To promote change, the authors share three concrete examples developed by faculty members who have participated in their workshops designed to support course transformation in higher education.

While the authors focus primarily on race and gender issues as content, they argue persuasively that such content intrinsically creates opportunities for higher level cognitive skills, including analysis and critical thinking. The three examples integrate issues of race and gender with inclusive instructional practices such as cooperative learning and case method. Creating balance in introductory economics courses as illustrated by the examples enables faculty to address a variety of multicultural goals. The transformed content and inclusive instructional strategies better motivate diverse students and women to pursue economics. Additionally, they enhance students' knowledge concerning the new scholarship; provide diverse perspectives; promote understanding and valuing of diversity; and encourage the critical thinking necessary to produce social change. ∎

The movement to produce a race- and gender-balanced economics curriculum has important support both inside and outside the community of academic economists in the United States. The National Science Foundation funded a program titled "Improving Introductory Economics Education by Integrating the Latest Scholarship on Women and Minorities," and that project has now been renewed for two more years.[2] In 1991 and again in 1993 the American Economic Association Committee on Economic Education has elected to include a panel on race and gender balance as part of their scheduled contribution to the annual meetings of the American Economic Association.[3] And the work of The Committee for

Race and Gender Balance in the Economics Curriculum[4] received a great deal of attention in the profession for its publication "Guidelines for Recognizing and Avoiding Racist and Sexist Biases in Economics: Problems, Issues and Examples" (May 1991).

It is not unreasonable to wonder why economists, after decades of near silence on these issues, are now interested in them. In the first part of this chapter we discuss the motivations leading economic educators to integrate race and gender issues into the introductory course. In the second we present an overview of the current state of the introductory economics curriculum to lend weight to our contention that the curriculum itself contributes to the low levels of interest in economics evinced by women and students of color. Finally, for those who find themselves persuaded by the first and second parts, we offer a sampling of "how to" examples developed by the participants in the first (1993) National Science Foundation summer conference.[5] It is our hope that this essay will demonstrate the intrinsic merit of the balancing project while offering practical suggestions for teaching economics from a perspective which acknowledges and appreciates diversity.

WHY SHOULD WE CARE ABOUT BALANCING THE ECONOMICS CURRICULUM?

The Profile of the Economics Profession

In 1989 the U.S. citizens who were members of the American Economic Association were overwhelmingly White men. Of the 12,000 members only 1,600 were female and only 125 were African American. This demographic homogeneity of economics will only change when more women and people of color attend economics graduate school and earn doctoral degrees. This, in turn, can only happen if more members of these groups major in economics and choose to go to graduate school. Yet there will only be more economics majors from these historically underrepresented groups if more students from these groups find the experience in introductory economics sufficiently interesting to motivate them to continue in the discipline. Thus, attention to race and gender balance in the economics curriculum finds a logical beginning in the introductory sequence (hereafter introductory economics refers to both micro and macro principles).

There are reasons for wanting to increase attention to race and gender issues in the introductory class which go beyond the desire to draw nontraditional students into the economics profession. Every year in the United States there are close to one million college students enrolled in introductory economics courses. Yet, each year only 32,000 students graduate with the Baccalaureate degree. So a large proportion of introductory students do not go on to take further classes. Ironically, some of the voices most opposed to discussing the economic status of women and minorities suggest that these topics can be left out of the principles sequence because they are taught in upper-level courses.

Courses which neglect topics relating to race and gender, while perpetuating stereotypes (see later where we discuss the content of the current curriculum) convey two unfortunate messages. First, silence on the subjects of race and gender leads to the impression that these pressing public policy issues are not fundamentally connected to economics (or the economy) despite the fact that academics and the public are aware of the crucial role economic relationships play in the creation, perpetuation, and resolution of problems of inequality. Second, the unfortunate reliance on stereotypical roles for women and people of color gives the impression that economics uniformly endorses the status quo. Third, the "unbalanced" introductory curriculum also conveys a false sense of the intellectual homogeneity of the economics profession (Moseley, Gunn, & Georges, 1991). The first problem noted above certainly warrants the attention of all interested in access to and equity in post-baccalaureate education. We believe that the second and third issues noted above raise serious questions about the role of introductory economics education in the undergraduate curriculum.

Introductory Economics and Critical Thinking

An important component of the drive to revise economics, especially at the introductory level, is connected to the view that economics education can contribute to the development of critical thinking skills. To see this connection it is useful to refer to Bloom's Taxonomy of Educational Objectives for the Cognitive Domain (Bloom, 1956).[6] This taxonomy, described in Chapter 5, is an appealing heuristic device because it enables us to present "learning" goals to students in ways which they can understand and which are not intimidating. Planning an introductory economics course with explicit reference to Bloom shows students how they must move from relatively simple cognitive skills to relatively more complex ones in order to make informed judgments about economic policy questions.[7] For example, the simplest cognitive tasks require students to define terms, describe concepts, and list facts. These tasks fall under the heading of "knowledge." However, simply knowing the definition of gross national product (GNP) does not imply that the student can offer an analysis of why GNP grows unevenly. For students to be able to demonstrate their command of concepts related to changes in the rate of growth of GNP, they would need to perform tasks linked to comprehension, application, analysis, synthesis, and evaluation.

In economics education many courses, and especially the introductory courses, stop at the level of application. At this level students demonstrate that they can manipulate basic tools (shift supply and demand curves); compute changes in the value of certain economic variables (the consumer price index); predict the effect of a policy change (what happens to employment if taxes are cut), or solve numerical problems (given some data, what is the price elasticity of X?). But work stressing these tasks does not necessarily help students in the very important critical thinking skills of analysis and evaluation, skills which are crucial to the discussion of the economic status of women and people of color.

The connection between critical thinking—analysis and evaluation—and the economic status of women and people of color is quite direct. *Informed* discussion or judgments on these issues requires a command of higher-order thinking skills. Consider first the cognitive tasks involved in analysis: differentiation, identification, illustration, separation, and selection. Students working at this level would be able to distinguish between the causes and effects of poverty or infer the effects of alternative economic policies on income distribution. We pose the rhetorical question: How could any educator reasonably suppose that students can sort through competing policies for welfare reform, homelessness, urban revitalization, or occupational segregation if they have not practiced "analysis"?

Consider too the role of evaluation, a critical thinking skill which is central to the process of integrating the topics of race and gender into introductory economics. Evaluation involves appraisal, comparison, criticism, justification, defense, and interpretation. Integrating material on the economic status of women and people of color helps students develop these higher-order critical thinking skills since this material *is* controversial. Almost every statement, short of a recital of "facts" about differential unemployment rates, or income levels, can be *both* criticized and defended. Despite the recent hegemony of neoclassical perspectives, economics is characterized by alternative paradigms,[8] and every interpretation touching on the economic status of women and people of color is paradigm-dependent. In short, the topics of race and gender provide an excellent vehicle for developing critical thinking since evaluation is demanded by the multiple perspectives which exist within economics.

Economics Education and Citizenship

A large number of issues in the public policy arena concern the economic status of people of color and women of all ethnic backgrounds. Neglect of these issues raises the possibility that the economics curriculum is not contributing as much as it could to the education of citizens. As Professor Robert Solow correctly notes, "The future is likely to be full of important analytical and policy questions centering on the absorption of minorities, the role of women in the labor force, and the relation between family and work. Progress in teaching is thus very important" (Solow, personal communication, 1990). As we will show, none of the currently available textbooks or supplemental curricular materials[9] address these issues in a manner appropriate to the introductory level, nor do they encourage the discussion of topics relating to these themes. Faculty currently teaching introductory economics who want to equip their students to intelligently assess the competing economic and social policy approaches to questions of race and gender need to integrate the findings of

the new scholarship on race and gender into their introductory courses. As Dr. Alice Rivlin[10] observes, "the failure of economics generally, and introductory courses in particular, to focus on race and gender issues is anomalous since many of the major public policy issues in economics…will necessarily revolve around race and gender" (Rivlin, personal communication, 1990).

A quick perusal of many college and university catalogues reveals that the introductory economics sequence meets both social science and general education requirements. When economists are asked to provide a rationale for this, a frequent response references the close connection between the study of economics and the assessment of economic, political, and social policy. Yet, as currently structured, the introductory economics curriculum offers little instruction on these pressing matters.

PROBLEMS WITH THE TRADITIONAL INTRODUCTORY CURRICULUM

Despite the importance of issues relating to diversity and the economy, economics courses at all levels (primary, secondary, and college) are taught with curricular materials which largely ignore, distort, or present very one-sided views of the economic circumstances of women and minorities. These problems can be most easily presented within the framework provided by "The Guidelines for Recognizing and Avoiding Racist and Sexist Biases in Economics" (see Appendix A). These Guidelines[11] identify three general types of biases likely to appear in economics: (1) defining economic problems, (2) review of previous research, and (3) marginalizing minority and female experiences. Before turning to examples illustrative of each category, some brief attention to the quantity of coverage in introductory textbooks is in order.

Quantitative Analysis of the Textbook Treatment of Race and Gender

The lack of attention to topics directly related to the economic status of women and minorities is quite dramatic. An examination of introductory economics texts found that on average the typical textbook, which has 800 pages, had only 14.25 pages on which there appeared some reference to women or minorities. This figure represents 1.71 percent of the total pages in these books (Feiner, 1993). When one considers the centrality of problems relating to race and gender, as well as the attention paid to these problems in debates over social policy, the silence of these textbooks seems quite amazing.

Qualitative Analysis of the Textbook Treatment of Race and Gender

Qualitative analysis also uncovers some serious problems. For example, racial or sexual biases in economics research or teaching are present when topics relevant to women and minorities are ignored while other topics are treated at length. In one text (Ruffin & Gregory, 1990) none of the eleven examples presented to illustrate labor markets specifically discuss the labor-market experiences of women or minorities. In this text, of the seven examples used to illustrate income distribution and poverty, only one refers to the unique circumstances of women and minorities.[12]

Another type of bias can arise when the authors of economics textbooks choose not to present the results of previous research. Unlike most other textbooks in either the social or applied sciences, the majority of economics textbooks offer only limited citations to prior research, and virtually none of the introductory textbooks currently on the market offer suggestions for further reading. In the few cases where prior research is cited, there is an alarming tendency to cite only that research which supports the author's point of view. In short, economics textbooks make almost no effort to expose students to the array of theoretical and empirical work on topics relating to the economic status of women and minorities. Instead, they rely exclusively upon arguments which support the conclusion that discrimination cannot coexist with competitive market structures, despite the fact that countless studies document the existence of discrimination. We have not yet found the economics textbook which distinguishes between direct and indirect evidence for discrimination since traditional economic theory only debates the extent to which indirect evidence is actual proof of discriminatory behavior.[13]

A third type of bias in introductory economics textbooks concerns the tendency to marginalize the experiences of women and minorities. Problems in this category most clearly raise the issue of balance. The tendency to exclude women or minorities from the general discussion, or to make inferences unwarranted by the data, produces a vision of the economy which obscures the range of experiences. Such exclusion also disguises the multiplicity of explanations for observed differences. The treatment in Miller (1991) contains two examples of arbitrarily excluding minority and female experiences from the general discussion. This omission is especially ironic since in his introduction the author remarks "nothing makes students pay attention more than the real world. The *Issues and Applications* chosen to end each chapter bring the real world of economic applications to the student" (Miller, 1991, p. xxii). Yet of the 37 issues and applications sections, only three (pp. 179, 752, 825) refer to the economic status of women or minorities (and two of the three contain inferences not warranted by the data) (Feiner, 1993, p. 151).

A related problem concerns the uncritical use of conceptions of genetic inheritance handed down by the now discredited schools of eugenics, Social Darwinism, and sociobiology. One textbook offers this explanation for differential academic success rates: "Some people are born with either better or worse bodies, minds, or nervous systems than other people. Environmental factors cannot be counted on to cancel out such differences. More often, perhaps, they reinforce them, as when bright students go on to college and less-bright ones drop out of high school" (Bronfenbrenner, Sichel, & Gardiner, 1990, p. 809). And another reports that

> Some people have different mental, physical, and aesthetic talents. Some individuals have had the good fortune to inherit the exceptional mental qualities essential to entering the relatively high-paying fields of medicine, dentistry and law. Others, rated as "dull normals" or "mentally retarded" are assigned to the most menial or low-paying occupations or are incapable of earning income at all. Some are blessed with the physical capacity to become highly paid professional athletes. A few have the aesthetic qualities prerequisite to becoming great artists or musicians. In brief, native talents put some individuals in a position to make contributions to total output which command very high incomes. Others are in much less fortunate circumstances. (McConnell & Brue, 1990, pp. 729–730)

One need not have expert knowledge about occupational segregation to recognize that the professions singled out to demonstrate inherited exceptional mental qualities are those dominated by White males, while the "dull normals" or "mentally retarded" are employed in occupations traditionally reserved for people of color

and women. Given the prevalence of examples like these in principles of economics textbooks, is it any surprise that minorities and women rarely take courses beyond the required introductory sequence?

SUGGESTIONS FOR BALANCING THE INTRODUCTORY ECONOMICS CURRICULUM

The last two decades have witnessed an explosion of scholarship concerning minorities and women. This scholarship has had a significant impact on teaching and research in all the disciplines of the social sciences, and it has influenced research and empirical work in some of the natural sciences as well. Although there has been considerable work in economics on these topics, none of the newly developed research methodologies, the often debated empirical findings, or the interdisciplinary foundations of this work have yet found their way into courses in introductory micro or macroeconomics. The final sections of this chapter provide a framework for understanding the impact of balancing introductory economics on the curriculum and three well-developed examples of a balanced approach to race and gender.

How Would a Balanced Course Be Different?

The new scholarship on minorities and women refers to the numerous studies, from various disciplinary and interdisciplinary perspectives, on the causes and consequences of the unique social experiences of females and people of color and seeks explanations for the persistent marginalization of these experiences. Traditional economists often equate this new scholarship with scholarship on race and gender differences in the labor market (Amsden, 1980; Brown, 1987; Cain, 1966; Fuchs, 1988;

Goldin, 1990; Lloyd & Niemi, 1979; Lloyd, Andrews, & Gilroy, 1979; Smith, 1980; Smith & Ward, 1984; Trieman & Hartman, 1981; U.S. Commission on Civil Rights, 1988, 1990). Although the latter is a subset of the former, the new scholarship on race, gender, and economics cannot, for example, be reduced to debates over the extent of "imperfections" in labor markets. Instead, the new scholarship on women and minorities recognizes that race and gender are potentially relevant to the majority of topics taken up by economists. Consequently, the new scholarship insists on the validity of race and gender as categories *of* analysis and thus transcends the traditional economic view of race and gender as special categories *for* analysis.

While most economics textbooks (and presumably many economics professors) apply traditional economic methodologies to a few of the problems confronting women and minorities in the economy, none of the available introductory economics textbooks draws on the interdisciplinary, intellectually diverse contributions of the new scholarship. Few economics professors currently teaching introductory economics, and few of those currently writing introductory economics textbooks, have been systematically exposed to this material (Feiner, 1993; Feiner & Morgan, 1987).[14] Consequently, undergraduate introductory economics courses inadvertently neglect the many new developments in economics which explicitly incorporate the variables of race and gender (Bartlett & Feiner, 1992; Conrad, 1992; Shackleford, 1992).

While ignoring the developments in the new scholarship on women and minorities, the curricular materials currently available barely touch on the recent work which attempts to explain the observed differences between Blacks and Whites, males and females. Work in this area spans the political, ideological spectrum with Sowell

(1981, 1983) and Williams (1987) typifying the conservative approach; Bergmann (1986), Blau and Ferber (1986), and Fuchs (1988) typifying the classical liberal approach; and Amott and Matthaei (1991), The Union of Radical Political Economics (1978, 1984, 1985), and Edwards, Reich, & Gordon (1975) typifying radical approaches to labor market phenomena. Each perspective puts forward its own explanation of why different groups earn less, work less, and work in different occupations. The starting point of the movement to balance the economics curriculum is the recognition that race and gender balance in introductory courses requires that each of these views be treated fairly. But this is only the beginning. Integrating the new scholarship on the roles of race and gender in the economy goes beyond ideology or politics to examine the content, methodology, and pedagogy of the economics discipline.

The new scholarship rests on interdisciplinary methodological foundations which enable us to ask more inclusive questions while developing alternative models. Students of the new scholarship would ask questions like these: "How will theories of behavior or statistical findings change as race and gender become primary categories of analysis?" "How well will the theory describe and predict the economic behavior of non-dominant groups?" (Blier, 1984, 1986; Harding, 1986). Many economists have taken up these questions (Amott & Matthaei, 1991; Bartlett, 1985; Bartlett & Feiner, 1992; Bell, 1975, 1984; Beneria & Roldan, 1987; Beneria & Stimpson, 1987; Bergmann, 1983, 1987; Blaxall & Reagan, 1976; Boulding, 1970; Brown & Pechman, 1984; Dixon, 1970, 1977; Dunbar, 1984; Feiner & Roberts, 1990; Greenwood, 1984; Malveaux & Simms, 1986; Matthaei, 1982; McCloskey, 1985; Nielson, 1990).

Even a cursory survey of this burgeoning literature reveals the wealth of methodological approaches fostered by the new scholarship. In this way the *social diversity* recognized by the new scholarship is mirrored by the *diversity of methods* employed for solving problems and addressing issues. Thus the new scholarship in economics is grounded in and draws upon important critical discoveries in both the experimental and social sciences (Blier, 1984, 1986; Brighton Women in Science Group, 1980; Bronstein & Quina, 1988; Gilligan 1982; Harding, 1987a,b; Harding & O'Barr, 1987; Hardy, 1981; Hubbard, 1990; Keller, 1985; Lewontin, 1984; Nielson, 1990). As a result, training in the new scholarship in economics will permit both professors and students to ask important questions about the most fruitful ways to go about constructing a more inclusive picture of economic reality.

Inclusivity is an important educational goal. For economics instructors who value this goal, the new scholarship on race and gender provides an important vehicle for moving this project forward. Indeed, as one noted economist recently commented:

> ...we might be able to learn something more if we opened our eyes and ears and listened a little more to the subjects who populate the economies we study, the people who actually do the things we theorize about. (Blinder, 1990, p. 297)

Integrating Race and Gender Content into Introductory Economics: Three Examples

During the 1993 faculty development conference funded by the National Science Foundation, 45 economics professors from community colleges, four-year colleges, and research universities from across the United States came together for six days, (May 22 through May 27, at the College of William and Mary, Williamsburg, VA) to revise their introductory economics courses to include content relating to the economic status of women and people of color. Through participation in presentations, hands-on demonstrations, role playing, and small group working sessions we were able to generate eight examples for teaching economics in which race and/or gender figure prominently. In the volume *Integrating Race and Gender into Economics 101* (Bartlett, forthcoming) each of the examples is fully developed to include suggestions for further reading, lecture outlines, questions for class discussion, and ideas for active learning, as well as sample examination questions and homework assignments. To give readers a sense of the type of work which has been produced, we provide an abstract of three of the examples below.

Gender and race and the decision to go to college. This example was developed by Louise Laurence (Towson State University) and Robert Moore (Occidental College). As the title suggests, this material combines the gender and race neutral concepts of "opportunity cost" and "returns to human capital" which are standard topics used throughout the introductory microcourse, with information on how these opportunity costs and returns to human capital may be affected by race, gender, and social norms. In mainstream economics courses "the economic way of thinking postulates that individuals make decisions by comparing the costs and benefits of various choices. One choice of particular interest to students is the decision to go to college" (Laurence & Moore, in progress). Laurence and Moore have structured this example so that it can be used in up to three different contexts, depending on how the instructor wishes to organize the course.

In the first instance this material can be used in the portion of the course discussing human capital. Faculty would begin by developing the standard human capital model which does not make the gender or race variables explicit. Then students are introduced to gender differences in the decision to go to college. Class work and discussion center on the explanation for the dramatic increase in the percentage of women attending college from 1950 to 1988 coming out of the basic human capital model. Students also consider how the model can be modified to account for both "traditional" and "nontraditional" female career paths. An approach is taken for analyzing the decision to attend college by an "average" African American male. Many will find the case study approach (see Chapter 4 in this volume) developed by Laurence and Moore to be of special interest. Here they present the circumstances surrounding a recent contested divorce in which the wife sought compensation for her investment in her husband's medical degree. Newspaper reports of the proceedings bring this topic alive very quickly, and students are sure to find this material thought-provoking.

The exercises which accompany the text of the example comprise a variety of approaches to learning. Most involve active participation of the students, relying on cooperative learning structures (see Chapter 7). All group members need to know how to explain the answers produced by the group since the specific person responsible for giving the answer will not be known in advance. This attention to the knowledge of all group members can be itself a multicultural experience. Taken together we see that the assignments call on a variety of learning styles and different competencies (mathematical, graphical, verbal). The assignments require students to construct graphs, manipulate data by transferring it from tabular form to graph form, illustrate changes in economic outcomes, and justify various policy and social outcomes. Thus the assignments move through the cognitive tasks outlined by Bloom.

The labor supply decision: differences between gender and races. This example was developed by Margaret Lewis (College of Saint Benedict) and Janice Peterson (State University of New York at Fredonia). Lewis and Peterson (in progress) make the case that a discussion of labor supply decision making should not be left until the end of the course or omitted altogether. They offer a persuasive argument for including this material as part of the usual discussion of "the theory of individual choice." This placement of material relating to how people decide the amount of time to devote to paid employment offers the advantages of both theoretical consistency and increased relevance to students who will, after all, be spending most of their lives working.

Professors of economics can easily use the material developed by Lewis and Peterson to teach both the "labor/leisure" and "market/non-market" approaches to the labor supply question. The authors begin with an overview of the standard theory. Then students are asked to assess the theory in light of data on women's labor force participation rates. Class discussions of the orthodox "labor/leisure" are sure to uncover some differences of opinion as to the veracity of that framework. Consequently students are introduced to a labor supply model which considers the value of time spent on paid market work in relation to the value of time spent on unpaid work in the household. Based on their familiarity with these models, student assignments provide a foundation for analyzing labor force participation data provided in tabular form by the authors. These exercises help develop quantitative skills as students move between tables, graphs, and words.

Students quickly engage in higher-order thinking skills in the assignments designed for this example. Once they understand these two models they move to an analysis of how each model identifies different causes for the observed changes in women's labor force participation over time. Suggestions are offered for group work dealing with the various factors "pushing" and "pulling" women out of the home and into the labor market. Students are then asked to determine the extent to which the behaviors predicted by these models explain the differences in labor force participation rates across different demographic groups: African American women; Asian American women; Hispanic women; and Native American women. Extensive suggestions for background reading are offered and study and discussion questions are posed. Additionally, the authors wish to provide assistance to professors who encounter problems of stereotyping and intolerance among their students when they integrate this material. A highlight of this example is its extensive presentation of relevant data in conjunction with a comprehensive list of sources of further information concerning the labor force participation of American women from all ethnic and racial backgrounds.

How "natural" is the natural rate of unemployment? This example, authored by Robin Bartlett (Denison University) illustrates a way to integrate race and gender topics into macroeconomics classes. Concepts relating to employment, the labor force, and types of unemployment play a major role in all courses in macroeconomics. Unfortunately, most introductory textbooks do little more than present data on the rates of unemployment by race, sex, and sometimes age. This example will allow professors of economics to explore these important issues while drawing out the implications of economic policies for diverse groups in the economy.

Bartlett (1985) begins by developing standard definitions of key terms like "labor force," "structural unemployment," and the "natural rate of unemployment." These

terms are then linked to economic performance through the development of the concept of inflation. With standard tools in hand students are then shown the relationship between inflation (sustained rise in the consumer price level in this example) and the rate of unemployment. The discussion then turns to the role of policy. Students are given a brief overview of recent macroeconomic history to set the stage for the Federal Reserve's switch of policy targets from the rate of interest to the rate of growth of the money supply.

Students are next presented with data on the relationship between inflation and unemployment in the period 1972 through 1984. They are asked to use these data to construct the appropriate aggregate "Phillip's Curve." Upon completion of this task students are asked to determine the costs and benefits of Federal Reserve policy. Initial inspection shows that the cost of the policy was an increase in unemployment of only 2.5 percent, while the benefit of the policy was a decrease in inflation of fully 10 percent. The class is now ready to offer a preliminary assessment of Federal Reserve policy.

Next, students receive annual data on the rate of inflation; African American male and female unemployment; and European American male and female unemployment so that they can disaggregate the rate of unemployment by race and gender. As everyone experiences the same rate of inflation, students can now construct race and gender specific "Phillip's Curves." Using overhead projectors the various relationships can be counterposed to each other so that students can directly compare the changes in the unemployment of White males and that of other groups. Data are available which enable students to compare 1) all male and all female unemployment rates (graphed against the consumer price index or CPI); 2) European American male and African American male unemployment rates (graphed against the CPI); 3) European American men and European American women (graphed against the CPI); 4) European American women and African American women (graphed against the CPI); and 5) African Americans and European Americans (graphed against the CPI). The results give cause for discussion. Students discover that the impact of the Federal Reserve policy switch on, for example, African American men was to increase their unemployment from between 11 and 12 percent in 1979 to over 20 percent in 1983, and then to 16 percent in 1984. The comparable numbers for European American men are 4 percent in 1979, between 8 and 9 percent in 1983, and 6 percent in 1984. Students are then asked to assess the claim that "economic policy is 'one size fits all.' "

CONCLUSION

In the introductory essay to this volume, Kitano suggests that there are six intended outcomes of incorporating multicultural content and strategies (Chapter 2). The examples sketched above clearly reveal that incorporating the topics of race and gender into introductory economics in a critical, transformative way permits instructors to achieve most of the outcomes.[15] First, each example contains a varied set of student/teacher interactions which foster skill/content acquisition by students with a variety of learning styles. In both content and perspective these examples provide an alternative to the "blame the victim" attitude which is transmitted when economic analysis fails to attend to race and gender differences. These examples expose students to information which may help them recognize the structural aspects of social existence which both enhance and limit their life options, and the options of others. This lesson is surely a valuable one of multicultural

integration. And every one of these examples questions received social portraits of women and people of color and so requires students to think about both the sources and effects of these stereotypes. Thus these examples, as suggested by Rosenfelt in Chapter 3, considered either individually or as a group, will help students understand the situated nature of all perspectives.

Finally, these examples create a variety of contexts for talking about issues of equity and fairness in economic outcomes. Again, the authors of the examples have paid considerable attention to "setting the stage" so that all students feel safe to express their opinions on these matters. The contrast with the usual approach to equity in economics courses is stark. While many texts simply ignore questions of equity, the majority of texts broach equity issues while discussing "positive" versus "normative" economics. This basically exclusionary approach makes it all too easy to shove equity off into the taboo region of subjectivity (Feiner & Roberts, 1990). In the three examples presented in this chapter, however, we find attention to the reality of competing notions of fairness, equity, and economic justice. Thus instructors of introductory economics who are motivated to bring material relating to the economic status of women and people of color into their courses can be assured that their efforts will enhance student comprehension of key economic topics while promoting the tolerance and empathy needed by citizens in a pluralistic, democratic society.

ENDNOTES

1. The authors are Professor of Economics, Denison University, Granville, Ohio, and Associate Professor of Economics, University of Southern Maine, Portland, Maine, respectively. They gratefully acknowledge the support of the National Science Founda-

tion Division of Undergraduate Education, Undergraduate Faculty Enhancement under grants 91-54159 and 93-54006. Professor Feiner also wishes to acknowledge the support of The Center for the Study of Women in Society where she was Scholar in Residence during the period when much of this paper was written. Professor Bartlett gratefully acknowledges the support and encouragement of the Department of Economics at Denison University and the Procter and Gamble Corporation, which helps sponsor staff research.

2. The 1993 faculty development conference was held at The College of William and Mary, Williamsburg, VA, from May 22 to May 27. The 1994 faculty development conference was held at Denison University, Granville, OH, from June 10 to June 15. The final faculty development conference to be funded under these grants is scheduled for Wellesley College, Wellesley, MA, from June 15 to June 20.

3. Panel titles are *Alternative Pedagogies and Economic Education (1992)* and *Integrating Race and Gender Issues into the Introductory Course (1995)*. We are pleased to report that the papers presented on these panels are included in the papers and proceedings volume of *The American Economic Review* for that year.

4. Committee members include: Susan Feiner, chair; Robin Bartlett; William Baumol; Barbara Bergmann; Charles Betsey; Robert Cherry; Robert Eisner; Marianne Ferber; Donald McCloskey; Paul Samuelson; Robert Solow; Lester Thurow; and Rhonda Williams.

5. We thank the Department of Economics at The College of William and Mary, Williamsburg, VA, and the Department of Economics at Denison University for their support and assistance.

6. This taxonomy presents a hierarchy of six educational objectives: knowledge (knowing facts); comprehension (grasping the meaning); application (applying the concept to new situations); analysis (breaking down into parts); synthesis (combining parts to form a new whole); and evaluation

(comparing items based on defined criteria). Knowledge-level tasks include defining, describing, naming, and reproducing. Among comprehension tasks are defending, distinguishing, giving examples, and summarizing. Application includes computing, demonstrating, solving, and using. At the analysis level, students might diagram, illustrate, separate, and subdivide. Synthesis might involve categorizing, composing, creating, and reconstructing. Evaluation tasks include appraising, concluding, criticizing, and justifying. We use Bloom to illustrate one interpretation of the development of critical thinking. Other learning models are also helpful. However, we have found Bloom to be especially useful for discussing intellectual growth of students.

7. For an example of how to design and evaluate a course around the various stages of Bloom's taxonomy, see Bartlett and Miller (1981).

8. The volume *Race and Gender in the American Economy: Views from Across the Spectrum*, 1994, edited by Susan Feiner, makes these debates fully accessible to introductory economics students. Unlike any other readers in economics the focus of this collection is on race, gender, and ethnicity.

9. Two exceptions to this are the Feiner volume, mentioned above, and the Bartlett volume in progress, *Integrating Race and Gender into Economics 101*.

10. Dr. Rivlin is the first and only woman to serve as the President of the American Economic Association in its 100 plus history.

11. The Guidelines are available upon request from the chair of that Committee, Susan Feiner.

12. This example is a discussion of comparable worth. We were distressed to find that Ruffin and Gregory could find only one reason for supporting comparable worth, yet they were able to develop in great detail four reasons to oppose it (1990, pp. 694–704, 713–722).

13. See the essay "Loaded Die in the Labor Market," by William Darity Jr. in Susan Feiner, editor, *Race and Gender in the Ameri-*

can Economy: Views from Across the Spectrum, Prentice-Hall, 1994, in which the relevance of this comparison is discussed at length.

14. We are pleased to report that Robert Cherry (Brooklyn College) and David Colander (Middlebury College), authors of introductory economics textbooks, have been active participants in the NSF funded faculty development programs.

15. These are: (1) support diverse students' acquisition of subject matter, knowledge, and skills; (2) help students acquire a more accurate or comprehensive knowledge of subject matter; (3) encourage students to accept themselves and others; (4) understand the history, traditions, and perspectives of specific groups; (5) help students value diversity and equity; and (6) equip all students to work actively toward a more democratic society.

Appendix A
Guidelines for Recognizing and Avoiding Racist and Sexist Biases in Economics: Problems, Issues, and Examples
Prepared and Adopted by
The Committee for Race and Gender Balance in the Economics Curriculum
May, 1991

Gender and race bias in economics teaching and research must be watched for and guarded against. This document seeks to help all members of the profession, including teachers, researchers, grant officers, research consumers, and publication editors, to recognize and deal with problems of gender and race bias. This document identifies three interrelated dimensions of economics in which bias may inadvertently occur. These are: **I)** the definition of economic problems; **II)** the review of previous research; and **III)** the use of examples or discussions which marginalize the experiences of women and minorities. The problems are closely linked and reinforcing, and often curricular materials and professional research suffer serious shortcomings in each of the areas at the same time.

These guidelines identify the most serious types of problems in each area and provide examples related to Women, African Americans, and Hispanics. The list is clearly not exhaustive, and readers are invited both to identify and share additional problems and to recommend solutions.

Unless economists make an effort to correct these biases they are likely to continue. A profession-wide effort to address problems of race and gender bias has precedent in other social science disciplines and in many of the physical sciences as well. To prevent race and gender bias, teachers, textbook authors and researchers must understand that the ways in which we select subjects for study, frame questions, and choose illustrations affect both the analysis and the learning process. To help economics professors improve the balance of their courses, suggestions for further reading are included on page four of this document.

The Committee for Race and Gender Balance in the Economics Curriculum

Chair, Susan Feiner, Department of Economics, Hampton University, Hampton VA 23668 (804)-727-5862; Robin Bartlett, Denison University; William Baumol, Princeton University and New York University; Barbara Bergmann, American University; Robert Cherry, Brooklyn College; William Darity Jr., University of North Carolina; Robert Eisner, Northwestern University; Marianne Ferber, University of Illinois; Donald McCloskey, University of Iowa; Paul Samuelson, Massachusetts Institute of Technology; Robert Solow, Massachusetts Institute of Technology; Lester Thurow, Massachusetts Institute of Technology; Rhonda Williams, University of Maryland.

I. DEFINING ECONOMIC PROBLEMS

A. Gender and Race Blind Social Theory

Definition: Considering an economic situation in which gender or race are significant variables, but the gender/race variable is not explored or incorporated into the theory, interpretation, or analysis.

Example 1: Assuming that all wage differentials are due to human capital differences and that race and/or gender have no independent influence.

Example 2: Failure to consider, in a study of the benefits of union membership, the fact that blacks have historically been prevented from joining unions. Ignoring this point suggests that perhaps such blacks voluntarily choose non-union jobs.

Example 3: Failure to note that attempts by employers to avoid hiring "illegal aliens" may prevent Hispanics, especially first generation workers who are primarily Spanish speaking, from entry-level positions needed to become part of mainstream America.

Example 4: Analysis of economic inequality in a society that does not refer to both race and sex inequality.

Example 5: Assuming that employers disregard the race and gender of applicants in hiring and promotion.

B. Significant Topics Ignored

Definition: Cases in which topics of particular significance for white women, women of color and minority males are ignored while similar or related problems of relevance to white males are addressed in length.

Example 1: Insufficient research on the values of housework, on the relation between housework and market work,

and on discrimination in the labor market.

Example 2: Failure to explore the labor market disadvantages stemming from ghetto residence.

Example 3: Failure to explore possible market failures in the child care industry.

C. Selective Treatment of Topics

Definition 1: Cases in which aspects of a topic of special significance for the majority race or for males are taken to cover the entire topic, while aspects of special importance for minority males and females and white women are underemphasized or ignored.

Definition 2: Cases in which an issue is formulated for either men or women, blacks or whites, but this limitation is not explicitly noted.

Example 1: Focusing on the effect of the father's socio-economic status on the occupational achievements of the son while ignoring the effect of mothers' and fathers' labor force status on the labor force participation and occupational attainments of daughters and sons.

Example 2: Consideration of the benefits to consumers of free trade without discussing the uneven racial impact of the shifts in manufacturing which are likely to follow.

Example 3: Discussions of motivating work effort in the poor without reference to the fact that many poor people are single mothers who would require child care.

Example 4: Assuming that the adjustment of women to work depends primarily on their household situation, while the work adjustment of men is largely unaffected by family circumstances.

Example 5: Looking for the effects on wages of interruptions of careers for women without investigating these effects on men's earnings.

D. Pejorative or Stereotypical Labeling or Conceptualization

Definition: Implicitly ignoring the possibility of non-conventional gender roles or high status positions for members of a minority race; downgrading the value and skill of the work they typically do.

Example 1: The tendency to ignore unpaid domestic labor when studying work, and the failure to discuss the value of housework when discussing GNP.

Example 2: Referring mainly to men when discussing work and careers, while referring mainly to women when discussing housework and family responsibilities.

Example 3: Placing discussions of race and gender inequality under the heading "market imperfections," and then ignoring their effects.

Example 4: Failure to use examples of women or minorities in respected professions.

Example 5: Referring to secretarial jobs or child care workers' jobs as having low skill requirements.

Example 6: Discussions of the problems of female-headed households in which the absence of a male adult is automatically assumed to be a problem in itself and not a problem of inadequate earnings.

II. REVIEW OF PREVIOUS RESEARCH

A. Failure to Mention That Samples Are Single-Sex or Single-Race or Have Highly Unbalanced Sex or Race Ratios

Example 1: Citation of a study demonstrating a positive association between position in job hierarchy and work sat-

isfaction, while failing to mention that the study sampled men only.

Example 2: Summary of results of previous research on occupational mobility, without indicating that nearly all studies cited are of white males only.

Example 3: Citing the results of a study without mentioning the sex or race composition of the sample upon which the study is based.

B. Methodological Weaknesses of Previous Research Ignored

Definition: Reference to studies which cast women or members of racial minorities in an inferior light, without criticizing the methods used by these studies or challenging their findings.

Example 1: Uncritical citation of studies purporting to find sex differences in the fear of success and in industrial productivity.

Example 2: Mentioning racial differences in educational attainment without discussing the effect of either school segregation or primary school tracking on minority achievement.

Example 3: Discussing educational attainments as a variable explaining income differences but failing to mention the gender and race biases of standardized tests which influence educational opportunities.

III. MARGINALIZING MINORITY AND FEMALE EXPERIENCES

A. Arbitrarily Excluding Women or Minorities from the General Discussion

Example 1: Defining the man in a family unit as "the head" and using only variables relating to him to characterize the family.

Example 2: A study of job search incentives which does not discuss differences in incentives among races.

Example 3: Describing entrepreneurial success stories without mentioning blacks because they are relatively fewer.

B. Inferences Unwarranted by the Data

Definition: Improper extrapolation from data to conclusions with biased implications for women or members of racial minorities.

Example 1: Discussions of gender-linked occupational segregation couched exclusively in terms of individual choice.

Example 2: Discussions of the growth of the underground economy or the underclass which ignore the problems created by the changes in the urban economy.

Example 3: Discussions which cite the rising proportion of women and minorities in the labor force as an impediment to productivity growth without noting that these groups have not had the opportunity to learn by doing.

Example 4: Assuming, without empirical proof, that women are less productive than men in paid labor due to "their" child care responsibilities.

Example 5: Studies of occupational mobility which sample males only, based on the assumption that male experiences can be generalized to the entire population.

C. Reliance on Unscientific Concepts of Genetics and Biology

Definition: Cases in which observed differences between males and females and members of minority groups are attributed to individual level biological and psychological differences, while social influences correlated with gender and/or race are ignored.

Example 1: Attribution of lower aspirations for bureaucratic promotion and advancement among women and members of minorities to general sex or race differences, ignoring differences in opportunity structure.

Example 2: Discussions which refer to achievements of parents (like "success") and suggest that biological inheritance explains the economic success of the children.

Example 3: Treating as a problem that black women are increasingly having children outside of marriage, while ignoring this problem in whites.

Example 4: Assuming that, after accounting for human capital differences, minorities and women are less productive.

Example 5: Assuming that children will have to be nurtured by the female parent for biological reasons.

CHAPTER 12

Multicultural Infusion in Teacher Education: Foundations and Applications

Geneva Gay
Professor of Education and Faculty Associate
Center for Multicultural Education, University of Washington, Seattle

Editor's Notes:

Rather than focusing on individual course change, Geneva Gay provides a framework for multicultural transformation of teacher education programs as a whole. She argues with passion that teacher preparation programs must be designed to correct four current sociocultural realities: the growing dissimilarity between teachers and students in cultural background; teachers' and students' ethnic and cultural isolation; the continuing achievement disparities among ethnic groups; and the Eurocentric perspective of traditional teacher preparation programs.

Gay further clarifies that teacher education can embrace multicultural education as both a specialization and as the "infusion" of content and strategies across all courses. She then analyzes the literature on competencies needed for effective teaching and learning in a diverse society and ties these competencies to content, structure, and processes for multicultural teacher preparation. In so doing, she implicitly considers all six multicultural goals listed in Chapter 1: supporting diverse students' acquisition of knowledge; exposing all students to the new scholarship; encouraging acceptance of self and others; acquiring culture-specific knowledge; instilling a valuing of diversity; and developing skills for social change.

Gay offers specific suggestions for both specialized multicultural and infused program strands in terms of admission requirements, foundational and subject matter content, field experiences, and exit criteria. In short, she prescribes total program modification as a vehicle for transforming teacher preparation to meet the needs of today's children and youth. ∎

Teachers play a pivotal role in determining the quality of opportunities, activities, and outcomes students experience in schools. How teachers were taught significantly influences how they teach. Thus, modeling is a powerful tool in professional development. These facts provide some instructive lessons for how issues of ethnic and cultural diversity should be addressed in teacher preparation programs. Two positions frequently adopted in the past need to be abandoned. One position assumes that teachers can effectively implement multicultural education despite receiving little exposure to cultural diversity in their professional preparation programs. The second notion is that incidental, fragmented, and infrequent exposures to cultural diversity and multicultural education constitute sufficient preparation.

Rather, multicultural philosophies, issues, content, materials, and techniques need to be incorporated in deliberate, systematic, and substantive ways throughout the entire structure of teacher education programs. This chapter details an approach to implementing multicultural infusion in teacher preparation in a comprehensive manner. The chapter begins with an overview of sociocultural developments that substantiate the need for multicultural education to have a significant presence in teacher education curricula. An argument for multicultural education as a subject matter for infusion and for specialization is advanced. The chapter then discusses competencies critical for teachers in a multicultural society and describes the content, structure, and process essential to multicultural education infusion and specialization in teacher preparation programs.

SOCIOCULTURAL DEVELOPMENTS AND THEIR IMPLICATIONS FOR INFUSION

Three current and emerging sociocultural realities about teachers and students underscore the importance of and need for infusing multicultural education into teacher preparation programs. A fourth illuminates the difficulty of achieving the goal of *infusion* in practice. Embedded in each of these developments are significant implications, challenges, opportunities, and potential obstacles to multiculturalizing teacher education.

Widening Gap Between Students and Teachers

The first of these sociocultural realities is the growing dissimilarity between the teaching force and student population in the United States. Teachers currently in the profession are increasingly White, female, middle-class, highly educated, middle age, monolingual, Protestant, and Eurocentric (National Education Association, 1992). The declining number of teachers of color (from about 12 percent in the 1970s to approximately 8 percent in the 1990s) means that whatever positive effect their ethnic presence may have had as significant players in diversifying the learning environment is lost. This role and responsibility now must be performed by European-American teachers. Zimpher and Ashburn (1992) describe the average preservice teacher education student as:

> typically a female from a small town or suburban community who matriculates in a college less than one hundred miles away from home and intends to return to small town America to teach middle-income children of average intelligence in traditionally organized schools. Specifically, 76 percent of the students are female and 91 percent are white; nearly half speak no language other than English...less than 7 percent [are] people of color or of international descent...and over 75 percent...[want] to return to their suburban or rural home towns to teach. (Zimpher & Ashburn, 1992, p. 41)

Teacher education faculties mirror this profile. Surveys conducted by the American Association of Colleges for Teacher Education reveal that 91 percent of education professors are White, over 70 percent are White males, and most of them come from lower middle-class socioeconomic backgrounds (Zimpher & Ashburn, 1992). In other words, teacher preparation programs can be characterized as White, middle-class, female (and increasingly almost middle-age) students being taught by White middle-class male professors employing a Eurocentric middle-class framework to go out and teach White middle-class, suburban students. This focus systematically excludes massive numbers of students, and most frequently those who are in greatest academic peril in K–12 classrooms. It perpetuates a vicious cycle of frustration and failure for both students and teachers. Because society and schools are increasingly multicultural, monoracial teachers whose professional education is monocultural simply are not adequately prepared to meet the educational needs of ethnically, culturally, and socially diverse students (Bennett, 1988).

These differential demographic growth patterns between students and teachers generate profound implications and challenges for reforming teacher education. Yet the disparities are not fully recognized or accepted by the governance bodies that have regulatory power over teacher education programs. Gollnick (1995) reports that only 21 states have some kind of regulations concerning the inclusion of multicultural education in approved teacher preparation programs. Even fewer (14) report multicultural requirements for licensure.

Ethnic and Cultural Isolation

A second reality that underscores the need for multicultural education in teacher preparation programs is this country's continuing segregation along racial, social class, ethnic, and residential lines. Most students and teachers live in ethnic and cultural enclaves relatively isolated from each other. This isolation and separation produce some major social consequences and curricular implications for teacher education. Because *substantive* and *sustained* interactions across

ethnic and cultural groups in the United States are minimal and selective, myths, stereotypes, prejudices, and fears are perpetuated.

Smith's (1990) General Social Survey on "ethnic images" supports this view. The survey reveals that racial minority groups continue to be rated more negatively than Whites on such criteria as patriotism, wealth, industry, intelligence, nonviolence, ingenuity, and self-support. No ethnic group scored higher than Whites on any of these characteristics. The sequential rating of groups in the study, from top down, were Whites, Jews, Asian Americans, Latinos, and African Americans. The latter two groups were consistently rated at the bottom of the scale. The study also found a reverse correlation between negative ethnic images and desirable social distance among groups. That is, the stronger the negative attitudes, the more social distance participants wanted between themselves and other groups with respect to such issues as living in integrated neighborhoods, school desegregation, affirmative action, and interracial marriages. This pattern was especially pronounced for Latinos and African Americans. When carried to the extreme, these types of racial prejudices lead to acts of ethnic intimidation and hate crimes. While more and more state legislatures are enacting statutes prohibiting crimes of battery, vandalism, and phone harassment, the number of such incidents has increased rather than declined (Donato, 1994).

Because the "cultural sites"—actual and "existential places" where students and teachers live their lives—differ fundamentally, they create some "referential gaps" that can render extremely difficult teaching and learning in ethnically and culturally pluralistic classrooms. Professional preparation of teachers must compensate for this lack of cross-cultural and inter-ethnic group interactions. Instructional success depends largely on how capable teachers are in building meaningful pedagogical bridges across these different cultural systems.

Several authors (Delgado-Gaitan & Trueba, 1991; García, 1994; Giroux, 1993; Phelan, Davidson, & Yu, 1993) refer to the educational needs and related skills for bridging gaps between diverse groups of students and classroom teachers as "crossing cultural borders." Phelan, Davidson and Yu (1993) describe six of these borders that can "impede students' connections with classroom and contexts" and are important for teachers to understand as they "attempt to identify strategies that will enable students to make transitions successfully" (p. 57). The six borders are *psychosocial, sociocultural, socioeconomic, linguistic, gender,* and *structural.*

Before teachers can determine appropriate bridges for connecting and crossing these cultural borders for ethnically diverse students, they must understand the characteristics, intersections, and potential conflict points of their different cultures. Some cultural border crossings will be more difficult than others, depending upon the degree of *neutrality, alignment,* or *compatibility* among them. According to García (1994, p. 184), cultural boundaries are neutral when "sociocultural components experienced by the people on each side of the boundary are perceived as equal." Thus, a higher degree of cultural neutrality exists between the home cultures of middle-class White students and schools as compared to poor Whites and students of color. García explains further that:

> When boundary lines are neutral, movement between cultures occurs with relative ease because the social and psychological costs to the individual are minimal. Alternately, when cultural borders are *not* neutral and separate cultures are *not* perceived as

equal, then individual movement and adaptation across borders is frequently difficult because the knowledge and skills in one culture are more highly valued and esteemed than those in the other. Although it is possible for students to navigate nonneutral borders with apparent success, these transitions can incur psychological costs that are invisible to teachers and others. Moreover, when the psychological consequences of adaptation across borders become too great for individuals to face, cultural boundaries become impenetrable barriers. (1994, p. 184)

The *systematic* inclusion of multicultural education in teacher preparation programs has the potential for building bridges across the cultural borders ethnically diverse students bring to the classroom. Systematic inclusion can also create shared *referential linkages* between students and teachers and prevent impenetrable barriers to effective teaching and learning from occurring (Gay, 1993a).

Achievement Disparities and Cultural Discontinuities

Persistent discrepancies in school achievement among different ethnic groups provide another persuasive argument for multiculturalizing teacher education. The glimmers of improvement heralded by the testing industry as evidence of narrowing the achievement gap between European Americans and students of color are *nonsignificant* gains. The *patterns* of achievement among ethnic groups established decades ago continue largely unchanged. The academic achievement of students of color and students from poverty backgrounds is frighteningly lower than for their White, middle-class peers. For some groups, notably African Americans, Native Americans, Puerto Ricans, and Mexican Americans, the longer they stay in school, the greater the discrepancy in achievement becomes. Some Asian American groups, such as Japanese, Chinese, Koreans, and Filipinos may constitute a partial exception to this pattern (Gay, 1993b; U.S. Department of Education, 1993). Brown (1992) attributes the persistent lack of significant improvements in the academic achievement of some ethnic groups to school systems incorporating "only minor, inconsequential, and noncontroversial elements of reform...that have not impacted the central elements of schools" (p. 6). One of these key "central elements of schooling" is teacher education.

The works of educationists, sociolinguists, and anthropologists, such as Spindler (1987); Au and Kawakami (1994); and Ladson-Billings (1994b) offer another explanation for the continuing disparity in the academic achievement of ethnic groups. They suggest that the culprit is "cultural incompatibilities or discontinuities." Because learning occurs in particular sociocultural contexts, a "misfit" or "mismatch" between the cultural systems of the school and the homes/communities of various ethnic groups can jeopardize the success of the teaching-learning process. Culturally different students—especially those from highly visible, historically oppressed racial minority groups such as Latinos, African Americans, and Native Americans—"have less opportunity to learn when school lessons and other activities are conducted, or socially organized, in a manner inconsistent with the values and norms of their home culture" (Au & Kawakami, 1994, p. 6). When students have to cross one or more cultural boundaries before they can begin to attend to learning tasks, great social, psychological, and academic consequences may be incurred. Thus, developing effective skills for teaching in ethnically diverse and culturally pluralistic classrooms requires that teachers understand the interactions among culture, ethnicity, socialization, teaching, and learning (García, 1994; Hollins, King, & Hayman, 1994; Spindler, 1987).

These ideas, along with learning theory principles of *continuity* and *similarity*, lead to some logical conclusions that support the need to multiculturalize teacher education. The argument can be made that White, middle-class students do well in school because they benefit from *culturally centered or culturally responsive teaching*. The entire educational enterprise—from its structure to its procedures, policies, images, symbols, sanctions, and actions—is grounded in the cultural values, assumptions, beliefs, heritages, content, decorum, and protocols of European Americans. The learning climates, environments, and materials they produce provide cultural validation, affirmation, and support for White students, which, in turn, facilitates learning and achievement of academic, social, and personal development tasks. If the educational process were likewise culturally centered, responsive, or contextualized (Gay, 1993a) for other ethnic groups, they too would experience far greater academic success in school.

Pewewardy (1994, p. 78) defends culturally responsible pedagogy for teaching Native Americans as "providing the best possible education for all children that preserves their own cultural heritage, prepares them for meaningful relationships with other people, and for living productive lives in the present society without sacrificing their own cultural perspective." Asante (1991/92) makes a similar argument. He contends that ethni-centric curricula seek "for the African, Asian, and Hispanic child the same kind of experience that is provided for the white child" (p. 29); that is, for education to "center" them in their own cultural heritages. Other advocates add to this approach to teaching the goal of helping students develop the knowledge and skills to transform society in order to make it more open, egalitarian, and just for people from various ethnic, racial, social, and linguistic backgrounds (Banks, 1993; Gay, 1994).

"Cultural grounded" education empowers students and makes learning easier by ensuring congruence between their home cultures' perspectives and experiences and the curriculum content taught in schools. This *multiculturally centered teaching* contributes significantly toward implementing what Banks (1993) calls "equity pedagogy." To meet these challenges teachers will need "cultural therapy" (Spindler & Spindler, 1993) and skills for being "cultural workers" (Giroux, 1993) or "cultural brokers" (Gentemann & Whitehead, 1983). *Cultural therapy* is "a process of bringing one's own culture, in its manifold forms,…to a level of awareness that permits one to perceive it as a potential bias in social interaction and in the acquisition or transmission of skills and knowledge" (Spindler & Spindler, 1993, p. 28). A *cultural broker* is "one who thoroughly understands different cultural systems, is able to interpret cultural symbols from one frame of reference to another, can mediate cultural incompatibilities, and knows how to build bridges or linkages across cultures that facilitate the instructional process" (Gay, 1993a, p. 293).

Professional Socialization Precedents

The conventional practice of enrolling elementary majors in colleges of education while enrolling secondary majors in liberal arts schools can affect their commitment to and feeling of competence for teaching to and about cultural diversity. The philosophical and pedagogical emphases of these preparation programs direct elementary teachers toward being child-centered and their secondary counterparts content-centered. The focus on children may influence elementary teachers to be more amenable to culturally responsive teaching. Some of the

conceptual principles learned about the "culture of childhood" may transfer to ethnic diversity, even without any conscious and deliberate intent on the part of the teacher. The middle-school movement's emphases on student-centeredness and developmentally appropriate pedagogy (George & Alexander, 1993; Irvin, 1992) may have similar effects for teachers in grades 6–8. In contrast, high school teachers are professionally socialized into a "culture of disciplinary content." This focus can be incongruent with the interdisciplinary, integrative, and humanistic content and instructional emphases of multicultural education. Therefore, high school teachers may find it more difficult to become vested in cultural diversity at both the valuative and functional levels. Implicit in this distribution of course requirements and professional socialization emphases is the idea that elementary teachers teach children and secondary teachers teach subjects. Yet, research tells us that the nature and quality of the interactions that occur between students and teachers is the "site" where real learning happens.

The differences in student-teacher interactions in elementary, middle, and high schools may partially explain why the achievement gap between middle-class European American students and some groups of color increases as they advance through the grades. If these speculations have any merit, then the need to infuse multicultural education into professional preparation is even greater for middle and secondary teachers than elementary ones. The reflections Boyer (1990) provides on the nature of teacher education programs he has witnessed over his twenty-five years or so as a teacher educator further illustrates the need to multiculturalize the professional socialization of teachers. He says:

> I have found [teacher education programs] woefully traditional and almost

100% Eurocentric in perspective.... Not only have many of our programs reflected subtle messages of traditional conceptualizations, but they have been viewed as detached, separate entities through which one can travel without being philosophically touched.... [Improving] teacher education to serve a pluralistic population...require[s] new analyses of programmatic delivery to include procedural reviews, substantive content, intensive synthesis of the human service delivery role of the American teacher, and professional academic endeavors of all kinds. (pp. 244–245, 246)

MULTICULTURAL EDUCATION FOR INFUSION AND SPECIALIZATION

The preeminent current conceptual proposal for how to do multicultural education in K–12 instruction, teacher preparation, and other university programs is *infusion*. Infusion is a very powerful idea pedagogically and a very challenging one operationally. Another conceptual model familiar to educators that can help to illustrate this point is Bloom's (1956) taxonomy of cognitive objectives, a typology of increasing complexity and interrelationship among six intellectual skills—knowledge, comprehension, application, analysis, synthesis, and evaluation. Its basic premise is that every skill on the typology encompasses all of the preceding ones. Thus, *comprehension* (the second-level skill) incorporates its predecessor, *knowledge*. For individuals to do *analytical* (fourth-level) intellectual operations they also must be competent in knowledge, comprehension, and application. Infusing multicultural education into teaching and learning is a synthesis-evaluation task at the top of Bloom's taxonomy. Few teachers and professors of education possess the prerequisite skills in multicultural education needed to translate the theory of infusion into the practice of curriculum develop-

ment and classroom instruction. The rhetoric of infusion is enticing, but attempts at practicing it often are inadequate.

Further complicating these intellectual and pedagogical demands of infusion is the fact that multicultural education is strongly affective- and action-oriented. Consequently, infusion in teacher education requires that some of the existing ideologies, values, assumptions, and instructional practices undergirding the preparation of teachers, as well as its curriculum content, must change. Modifying these deeply ingrained cultural beliefs and associated behaviors to make them multicultural is a challenging task (Brown, 1992; Garibaldi, 1992; Gay 1993a). Two major factors contribute to this difficulty: the questionable competence and conviction levels of faculty in colleges of education and the prevailing pedagogical norms of college teaching. Anything that deviates from lecturing is more an aberration than a rule.

Yet, the inherent nature and intent of multicultural education require more engaging and varied instructional strategies (see Chapter 4). As Cuban (1973) explained so cogently over twenty years ago, "white instruction" will kill the vitality and potentiality of ethnic content. Although his comments were directed to teaching about ethnic diversity in K–12 grades, they are apropos to teacher education as well. He describes "white instruction" as a teaching style that emphasizes acquiring factual information to the virtual exclusion of the analysis of values and ethical issues:

Ethnic content will be drained of its vitality by white instruction as long as the community of students and educators continues to formulate the problem of educational change upon the narrow base of curriculum reform. We need teacher change, not so-called curriculum change. (Cuban, 1973, pp. 104, 111–113)

Thus, if infusion is taken seriously, the curriculum, climate, philosophy, pedagogy, and ethos (underlying value assumptions) of teacher education programs must be revised to reflect the cultures, histories, and heritages of the many ethnic, racial, and social groups in the United States.

Typically, two types of curricula operate in tandem in colleges of education. One provides "general studies," an overview of fields of study; the other offers areas of specialization. The first type of program provides grounding in "universal" or "generic" educational ideas, concepts, principles, and understandings that transcend subject specializations and school levels. Such course offerings as human growth and development, school and society, principles of curriculum development, classroom management, educational philosophy, and performance assessment fall into this category. They comprise the *foundational core* of teacher education.

Specialized programs of study are both school-level and subject-specific. Illustrative of these are teaching elementary school and teaching middle and high school subjects such as English, reading, math, music, and computer science. They represent the *areas of expertise* in which one is licensed to teach. For multicultural education to be genuinely infused into the structural frameworks of teacher education, it must be treated similarly by having a dual presence in the program offerings. Issues of cultural and ethnic diversity must be woven throughout all the foundational cores and areas of concentration offered. In addition, multicultural education must constitute a distinct and visible area of specialization.

Multicultural education is both a substantive and methodological domain. Like other liberal arts, many of its foundations (ethnic and cultural diversity) should be mastered by prospective teachers prior to their professional courses. Its methodologi-

cal dimensions rightfully belong in colleges of education along with learning other pedagogical skills.

Some precedents for this dual approach to infusing multicultural education in teacher preparation programs already exist. Education students learn how to teach reading and writing "across the curriculum" while simultaneously having the option of majoring in reading, language arts, or literacy instruction. For example, the University of Washington in Seattle has a policy that requires certain courses to allocate so much of their time and tasks to developing writing skills. These courses are designated in bulletins and schedules with a "W" or with the notation, "Meets Writing Course Requirements." Students enrolled throughout the university must complete 10 credits of these courses to meet graduation requirements.

A common misconception associated with multicultural education is that "infusion" and "separate area of concentration" approaches are mutually exclusive. The position taken here is the direct opposite. It assumes that these two approaches are natural complements of each other and can readily be accommodated in teacher preparation programs. If colleges of education do not provide both options, they are imposing a restriction upon multicultural education that does not extend to other parts of their curricula deemed essential for teaching students of the present and future. This restriction constitutes a form of academic discrimination and marginalization toward multicultural education in the midst of claims of endorsement and advocacy.

MULTICULTURAL TEACHER COMPETENCIES

The ideas suggested here derive from three assumptions. First, the sociocultural developments discussed above should inform the structure and substance of teacher education programs. Second, the strategies for multiculturalizing teacher education can be applied to infusing the requirements of all areas of study as well as creating a separate area of specialization. Third, infusion demands more than curriculum content revisions. This section identifies several sets of "categorical competencies" that represent the "basics" of multicultural education for teacher education and the foundational anchors of culturally responsive pedagogy. They are "categorical" in that each one encompasses many different kinds of knowledge and skills. Each of these sets of competencies is discussed in three ways: as substantive content; as elements of an area of specialization in multicultural education; and as elements of infusion to be included in other aspects of teacher preparation programs.

Most proponents of multicultural education agree that preparing teachers to work effectively with ethnically and culturally diverse populations and content is a multidimensional process. The key components were identified early in the evolution of the movement during the 1970s. They have remained essentially the same ever since, although refined, renamed, and elaborated somewhat. The most simplistic categories used to identify the "basics" of multicultural education are the *knowledge, attitudes, and skills needed to teach to, about, and through cultural diversity*. These categories have counterparts in suggestions made by scholars and researchers (Dill, 1990; Reynolds, 1989) about what is the essential knowledge base of teacher education in general, even though multicultural education and cultural diversity are conspicuously absent from their analyses and proposals. This knowledge base is comprised of knowledge, skills, and values about subject matter content, general and content pedagogy, curriculum development, characteristics of learners, human growth and development,

the sociocultural nature and functions of schooling, and the morality and ethics of teaching. Implicit in these pivotal foundations of teacher education is the assumption that knowledgeable teachers are not technicians, but professionals able to make reflective decisions based on a range of factors, including the instructional context and student characteristics (Reynolds, 1989).

Multiculturalists use a variety of other labels to identify essentially the same competencies about cultural diversity for teachers. In the early scholarship on teacher preparation for multicultural education, Baker (1974) described these competencies as a series of sequential "stages" of training including *acquisition, development*, and *involvement*. The acquisition stage focuses on acquiring knowledge about ethnic and cultural diversity. The development stage involves adopting a philosophy of education that is grounded in understanding and accepting cultural pluralism as a valuable trait of individuals and society. The involvement stage concentrates on skills needed to place multicultural content in the curriculum and use culturally pluralistic techniques and perspectives in classroom instruction.

The components of Aragon's (1973) three-part model of multicultural teacher education parallels Baker's stages, although the content focus varies somewhat. The first part, *awareness*, is identical to Baker's acquisition stage. The second part, *application of awareness*, involves learning how to analyze school programs, teaching styles, learning theories, and instructional materials for cultural and ethnic biases and equity. The third part of Aragon's model focuses on the *logistics of implementation* and includes using multicultural instructional strategies and methodologies. Implicit in these suggested components of multicultural teacher education are what Sullivan (1974) describes as the "four C's" of professional preparation that are essential to success in culturally pluralistic classrooms. These are *content, commitment, competence,* and *confidence.*

Cooper, Jones, and Weber (1973) identified four sources or frames of reference from which multicultural education competencies and content derive. *Philosophical* sources generate ideas about the values of humankind, the purposes of education, and the nature of learning within the contexts of cultural and ethnic pluralism. *Empirical* sources refer to findings derived from research and experimentation about how to make teaching and learning more effective for students from diverse social, racial, ethnic, and cultural backgrounds. *Disciplinary knowledge* offers information about ethnic groups' experiences and contributions that teachers must know if they are to multiculturalize the various school subjects. *Practical* sources include analyses of the roles and functions of teachers and how these can be best performed with different student groups and school settings.

A major underlying belief of these early proposals for multicultural teacher education was that too many teachers in the profession were inadequately prepared to work well in culturally pluralistic settings. Gay (1977, pp. 56–57) summarized:

> Because most teachers enter professional service with virtually no knowledge of ethnic groups, ethnicity, and cultural diversity, it is fallacious to assume that they will be able to relate well to culturally diverse students and successfully teach multicultural content in the classroom. Therefore…[t]eacher education curriculum must be designed to help teachers acquire knowledge, attitudes, and skills consistent with the principles of cultural pluralism and to translate the philosophy of multicultural education into classroom practices.

More contemporary discussions of what multicultural components should be included in teacher preparation reinforce the need for teachers to have a culturally sensitive educational ideology, some ethnic and cultural literacy, and skills in culturally centered pedagogy. The suggestions of three scholars illustrate the consistency and consensus of this thinking. Gay (1986) suggests that prospective teachers need to understand 1) different theoretical conceptions of multicultural education and their implications for classroom practice; 2) various assumptions and beliefs about the values and benefits of cultural diversity for learning, individual development, and the renewal of society; 3) cultural characteristics, heritages, contributions, and sociopolitical experiences of different ethnic groups; and 4) materials and techniques for doing culturally pluralistic teaching. She labels these categories of competencies as *theory, philosophy, cognition,* and *pedagogy,* respectively.

García (1994) classifies "characteristics of effective teachers of culturally and linguistically diverse students" as *knowledge, skills, disposition,* and *affect.* Knowledge involves being competent in content areas and able to articulate philosophies and beliefs that guide instructional decisions and actions. Skillful teachers use student-centered, process, and experimental approaches to teaching; employ thematic or topical curriculum structures; provide opportunities for active learning; and employ collaborative interactions among students. They have a frame of mind that radiates dedication, creativity, resourcefulness, persistence, and continuous seeking of improvement. Ladson-Billings (1994a) adds to this list high expectations of and a strong affinity with students; caring relationships and personal connections between students and teachers; and commitment to creating a psychosocial environment in the classroom that is conducive to learning for different students.

In other words, effective teachers of ethnically, linguistically, and culturally diverse students are *multicultural activists and advocates* who teach, value, model, and promote cultural diversity in the classroom. Similar multicultural knowledge, skills, values, and advocacy functions are recommended by the National Council for the Social Studies, *Curriculum Guidelines for Multicultural Education* (Banks et al., 1992).

Brauer (1994) provided some insightful thoughts that extend García's disposition and affect components of multicultural teacher education. These emerged from an "exit" task which requires students to develop a "reflection paper" on their learning experiences. While she feels that individuals who have the following attributes will benefit the most from multicultural teacher education, the program itself can and should help to develop these "dispositions":

- Self-awareness, a strong sense of personal identity, and a commitment to personal growth.
- Openness to new ways of thinking and knowing.
- Flexibility and tentativeness in searching for answers.
- Willingness to confront one's own cultural identity, biases, and prejudices.
- Understanding culture as a filter through which our underlying human similarities and connectedness are processed.
- Cooperation and collaboration to create a shared understanding of each other and to respect multiple sources of knowledge.

Brauer's perceptions are similar to those of Ayers (1993), who attributes greatness in teaching to understanding teaching as an intellectual challenge, a moral act, a creative endeavor, and a constantly unfolding, unfinished drama. Therefore, effective teachers have an openness to the new, untried, unique, dynamic, unpredictable, and unexpected. They also are adept in linking their consciousness to their conduct.

Virtually all proponents of multicultural education endorse these competencies, or some variations, as fundamental to preparing teachers to meet the needs of cultural diversity in their classrooms. One such variation is offered by Brown (1992) who adds "personal reflection" to the list. As Brown explains, "teachers must be able to reflect on their own actions, observations, and responses to experiences and to apply these reflections and their academic knowledge to the design and implementation of new approaches to teaching" (p. 11). His suggestions that new knowledge should be used to transform teaching strategies is analogous to Gay's (1990, p. 227) proposal that opportunities should be provided for prospective teachers to "practice translating knowledge about cultural diversity into action strategies for instructional reform." Bennett's (1988) variation includes four main goals that should be the focal points of multicultural teacher education. These are historical perspectives and cultural consciousness; intercultural competence; reduction of racism, prejudice, and discrimination; and successful experiences in teaching multicultural students. Each has knowledge, understanding, skill, and attitude dimensions as well as its own specific content, strategies, and areas of self-awareness. Zimpher and Ashburn (1992) give priority to cultivating values in multicultural teacher education that emphasize appreciating diversity of all kinds, the importance of establishing a caring community among teachers and students, and the value of cooperation and collaboration in learning.

A recent statement made by multicultural education scholar James A. Banks is indicative of the challenge involved in translating general ideas about multicultural substantive and pedagogical content into specific information and actions for teacher education programs. He (1994, p. 5) declares:

> I know it's complicated, but we need to help teachers attain a process for looking at the American experience so that they can raise questions. We won't know all the answers. Teachers need to understand…knowledge…[as] process. Teachers also need skills for teaching ethnic content and working with a multicultural population. They need these skills no matter where they teach because the population is changing and because ethnic content contains dilemmas and conflicts that require skills. Finally, teachers need to examine their own ethnic and cultural history, and their own ethnic journey.

Garibaldi (1992) offers even greater specificity in the skills he considers essential for all teachers to acquire in preparation for teaching multiculturally. He suggests that "teachers of the future will have to be creative and resourceful educational leaders who are independent thinkers, applied researchers, and individuals who can detect flaws in their own instructional practices" (p. 24). Nine specific skills will help make this happen and include understanding:

- a variety of methodological techniques in order to adapt classroom instruction to meet individual needs and cultural styles of diverse students
- the difference between culture and class, intersections between them, and how they may mediate or facilitate teaching and learning
- what and how contextual factors affect the planning and organization of instruction
- how to apply culturally sensitive tools and techniques in monitoring students' academic progress and diagnosing their strengths and weaknesses

- how to facilitate classroom management without creating double standards for culturally diverse students and/or allowing discipline issues to interfere unduly with instructional time
- motivational techniques that are effective with different ethnic groups and individuals
- the cultural dynamics of different ethnic communities through actual field-based and clinical experiences
- how and why various educational philosophies, theories, research findings, and professional writings reflect different cultural orientations, biases, and ideologies
- how to establish coalitions and collaborations between the school and different ethnic homes and cultural communities.

Underlying these suggested competencies for multicultural teacher education is the idea that teachers need to be "reflective practitioners" (Dill, 1990; Reynolds, 1989) and culturally sensitive agents of change (Gay, 1993a; Spindler & Spindler, 1993) and to possess skills for self-renewal (Gardner, 1981). Gardner's (1981) ideas concerning factors involved in the renewal of individuals and societies are directly applicable to teacher preparation for cultural diversity. Motivation, stamina, perseverance, hope, constant striving, and feelings of personal competence are essential to self-renewal.

THE CONTENT, STRUCTURE, AND PROCESS OF INFUSION

Table 12–1 provides a structural outline of how to infuse the substantive components of multicultural education into the curricula of teacher education discussed above. The chart includes features appropriate for the

TABLE 12–1   A Dual Approach to Multicultural Infusion in Teacher Education

Multicultural Specialization	Conventional Program Features	Embedded Multicultural Infusion
1. Admissions Requirements • Interdisciplinary social science/humanities degree or major with emphasis in ethnic and cultural pluralism • Experience with children in ethnic communities and culturally diverse groups	1. Admissions Requirements • Degree or major in subject content area • Experience with children	1. Admissions Requirements • Some courses on ethnic and cultural diversity • Experience with culturally diverse children in ethnic community settings
2. Introduction to Multicultural Education • Scholarship, paradigms, historical perspectives • Cultural characteristics that affect learning opportunities, styles, outcomes for diverse ethnic groups • Culturally diverse philosophies of education • Culturally pluralistic characteristics of society and implications for education • Legal and policy regulations on equity and diversity Issues • Managing multicultural curriculum, instruction, and classrooms	2. Introductory and Foundational Courses • Introduction to teaching • Human growth and development; learning theories; developmental paradigms; diagnosis and assessment • Philosophy of education • School and society • Teachers' legal rights and responsibilities • Classroom management and discipline • Conventional Program Features	2. Introduction to Teaching in Ethnically and Culturally Pluralistic Contexts • Culturally responsive teaching • Ethnic and cultural variations in developmental paradigms; sociocultural theories of development; ethnic learning styles; culturally appropriate diagnosis and assessment • Relationship between culture, ethnicity, and education • Cultural contextuality of education; pluralizing school culture • Laws, policies, provisions that obstruct or facilitate multiculturalism • Culturally relevant discipline and management principles and techniques • Embedded multicultural infusion
3. Teaching Multicultural Education • Multicultural instructional strategies • Selecting multicultural resources and materials • Designing multicultural curriculum	3. Subject-Specific Content, Methods, and Materials	3. Ethnic and Cultural Diversity in Subject Matter Content, Structure, and Process • Creating multicultural learning climates

TABLE 12–1   Continued

Multicultural Specialization	Conventional Program Features	Embedded Multicultural Infusion
• Multicultural climates for learning • Teaching multicultural education in the content areas		
4. Field-Based Observations, Experiences, Practicum, and Student Teaching in Multiethnic or Cross-Ethnic Schools and/or Classrooms	4. Field-Based Experiences • Observations • Practicum • Student Teaching	4. Observations and Practicum in Multiethnic Schools/Classrooms • Focus on multicultural issues in school culture and climate • Student teaching placements and task assignments in ethnically pluralistic schools and classrooms
5. Exit Criteria: Demonstrated Competency in Multiculturally Appropriate Teaching	5. Exit Competency According to Established Criteria and Supervisory Reviews	5. Successful Completion of Student Teaching Contingent upon Acceptable Performance on Multicultural Criteria Embedded in Regular Performance Appraisal Criteria and Procedures

dual-dimensional infusion strategy suggested earlier (i.e., multicultural education as an area of specialization and as embedded in all other aspects of teacher education). Some common elements of conventional teacher education programs are identified in the center column; the left column articulates parallels of these for a multicultural education specialization. The right column identifies ways in which these standard features can be multiculturalized. The two approaches to the multicultural infusion of teacher education are juxtaposed to demonstrate the similarity and varying degrees of depth and scope between them. All discussions are based on the assumption that how these program elements are implemented in actual practice will be informed by the sociocultural realities identified earlier.

Admission Requirements

For students who wish to specialize in multicultural education, the degree requirements should specify an interdisciplinary social sciences/humanities major or concentration in ethnic and cultural pluralism. The courses should reflect studies of multiple groups and examine a variety of issues related to ethnic groups, such as historical experiences, cultural characteristics, contributions, and expressions, and from multiple disciplinary perspectives.

Experiences with children from different ethnic groups and cultural backgrounds prior to admission to the teacher education program should occur within two or more ethnic communities and in settings targeted for specific ethnic groups. These settings may be child-care programs, youth recreational centers, church organizations, professional associations, and cultural study groups. An applicant might meet this admissions requirement by being a tutor at a Native American Heritage school, volunteering at a center on parenting for teen mothers and fathers of color, or participating in a big brother/big sister program for Latino youths.

In its embedded format the exposure to cultural diversity requirement for admission to teacher education might include having taken some humanities and social sciences courses about at least one ethnic group within the United States other than European Americans. The "experience with children" stipulation would be similar to that of the multicultural education specialization but with lesser magnitude of exposure relative to numbers of diverse groups and time spent.

Foundational Courses and Experiences

The learning experiences that constitute the foundational core of a multicultural education specialization should be comprised of several elements. First should be "introduction to multicultural education." The content should examine key principles, assumptions, theories, and conceptual models; major authors, scholarship, and "language" in the field; and historical evolution of multicultural education to discern how (or if) its directions and priorities have changed over time.

A second element of this core should examine the cultural characteristics of different ethnic groups and how they affect learning styles, opportunities, and outcomes. Specific content components might include the current educational status of diverse ethnic groups; potential points of conflict and compatibility between the cultural values of schools and different ethnic group cultures; communication, relational,

learning, presentation, and performance styles; and ethnic identity development and affiliation. The common questions in all of these analyses should be: How are cultural characteristics expressed in teaching and learning attitudes, expectations, and behaviors? What kind of intervening variables (such as education, social class, gender, age, generation, immigration, ethnic identity, etc.) affect how cultural characteristics are manifested in behaviors? What are the implications of these for classroom instruction?

A third foundational component in the multicultural education specialization should focus on culturally diverse philosophies and theories of teaching and learning. Concepts may include intergroup relations, maintenance bilingual education, Afrocentricity, infusion, situated competence, and culturally contextualized teaching. Other parts of this component might be: 1) culturally diverse characteristics of society and their implications for schooling, such as ethnic populations, employment, and politics; 2) legal, policy, and fiscal regulations and practices on ethnic equity and cultural diversity in education; and 3) managing multiethnic classrooms with a focus on the interaction among curriculum relevance, instructional appropriateness, the learning climate, cultural continuity, and the classroom discipline of ethnically diverse students.

Embedding multicultural education into the foundational cores of existing teacher preparation programs can be accomplished by using culturally pluralistic perspectives, experiences, contexts, and examples to illustrate general educational principles, theories, concepts, and strategies. Some possibilities follow:

- Culturally responsive teaching in multiethnic school settings in introduction to teaching courses.

- Sociocultural theories, ethnic and cultural variations in developmental paradigms, ethnic learning styles, and culturally valid assessment tools and techniques in courses or topics on human development, learning, and performance evaluation.

- The inclusion of ideas and arguments of multiculturalists about equity pedagogy, the transformation of schooling to accommodate ethnic and cultural diversity, and the interactive relationship among culture, ethnicity, educational excellence, and quality living included in courses on philosophy of education.

- The cultural contextuality of the nature and purposes of schooling and what this means for education in an ethnically, socially, and culturally pluralistic society in courses on school and society.

- Historical, current, and future status of students of color in education and different instructional strategies earmarked for various ethnic groups in courses on the history of educational developments and innovations.

- School law courses should include an examination of local, state, and national laws, policies, and provisions that obstruct or facilitate multiculturalism in schools.

- Classroom discipline and management courses should incorporate cultural factors for ethnically diverse student populations and culturally pluralistic instructional settings.

Subject-Specific Methods and Materials

This component of a multicultural education specialization should address elements of professional preparation that approximate the subject-specific content, methods, and materials aspects of conventional preparation programs, or the traditional methods courses. Its subject matter is the substantive content about cultural diversity discussed earlier. The focus should be on identifying, understanding, and practicing appropriate methods and materials for creating, implementing, and evaluating multicultural curriculum designs and instructional strategies. Other kinds of pedagogical skill development should include teaching multicultural education in the content areas; selecting multicultural materials and resources; creating multicultural climates for learning; and multicultural performance appraisal.

Infusing multicultural education into the other teaching disciplines and areas of specialization can take several different forms. Care should be taken to ensure that what is being infused penetrates the core of *significant and mainstream* subject matter content, methods, and materials. For example, if structured academic controversies and concept formation are high status strategies for teaching social studies, then multicultural education should be a key feature of them. For subjects which use "contributors and achievements" as standard content, these individuals and their contributions should be ethnically and culturally diverse. Learning how to teach the scientific method of problem-solving should be demonstrated by using problems and situations that have both scientific and multicultural content. Methods courses in which micro-teaching is a centerpiece should have students doing mini-teaches on incorporating cultural diversity into subject matter topics, themes, and activities. When teacher education students are asked to write research, analytical, and reflective papers, they should address multicultural education issues pertinent to the topics being studied.

Field Experiences

Beginning with initial field observations, students with a multicultural concentration should examine issues in practice they have studied in theory. Early field experiences may focus on how students from different ethnic groups are assigned to curriculum options; classroom observations to discern how various aspects of culturally centered teaching are actualized in classroom practice; techniques that school personnel use to interact with different ethnic parents and communities; and assessment of the multicultural quality of instructional resources and materials. More advanced practicum should provide opportunities for prospective teachers to implement short units on multicultural education; to conduct ethnographic studies of multiracial, multiethnic, and multicultural classrooms; to tutor students from diverse ethnic groups; to do service projects in different ethnic communities; and to participate in exchange programs to observe teaching and learning in a variety of multicultural school settings.

Student teaching experiences should require prospective teachers to do three things. First, student teachers should teach in multi- or cross-ethnic school settings. Multiethnic classrooms would be ideal settings. However, if such settings are not available, then student teachers should practice-teach in classrooms where students' ethnic backgrounds differ from their own. Second, part of the student teaching should focus on a unit covering a concept, issue, principle, idea, or event that is uniquely multicultural. Some possibilities include employment patterns among various ethnic groups; diaspora experiences across ethnic groups; the forms, functions, and effects of racism on different ethnic groups; and common concerns and diverse methods of power, protest, and cultural expressions among ethnic groups in histor-

ical and contemporary times. Third, students specializing in multicultural education should demonstrate skills in infusing cultural diversity into other subjects and skill areas. Examples include how to use multicultural methods and materials in teaching reading comprehension, word attack, or inferring skills. Or using multiethnic population, residential, and employment statistics to teach such math skills as graphing, ratios, percentages, proportionality, and propositional thought.

Evaluation criteria for determining whether a student's performance merits a university degree and a license to teach multicultural education should be stringent and exacting. Criteria should incorporate different dimensions of pedagogy such as facilitating learning activities, interacting with students, designing curriculum, managing classrooms, establishing supportive and exciting learning climates, and selecting and employing materials. Performance in all of these areas should be filtered through multicultural education assessment screens. The intent is to evaluate the abilities of student teachers to translate knowledge and attitudes about cultural diversity into curricular and pedagogical practices.

An embedded approach to infusing multicultural education should require all prospective teachers to spend a portion of each type of their field experiences in multiethnic and multiracial school settings. If, for instance, a program requires sixty hours of first-level observations, then twenty of the hours could be earmarked for ethnically and culturally diverse settings. Multicultural experiences also can be incorporated into regular observational tasks. If preservice teachers are expected to observe parent conferences, school board meetings, disciplinary processes, and certain types of classroom interactions, some portion of each of these can target cultural diversity. Teaching short lessons and units and working with one or a few students on some specific task, problem, or skill should incorporate multicultural content, materials, and perspectives.

The culminating field experience of student teaching can be designed to incorporate multicultural education by assigning prospective teachers to multiethnic or non-White dominant schools. Another strategy for multiculturalizing the experience is to require that multiculturalism serve as a prominent feature of the instructional and related tasks student teachers are normally expected to perform. Indications of acceptable performance in these areas can be discerned by examining the multiculturality of the examples, methods, and materials student teachers apply in their instructional activities.

Multicultural education also must be embedded in the tools and techniques used to assess the performance quality of student-teaching experiences. Elements of cultural diversity and multicultural education should be incorporated into every aspect of the specific criteria to assess student teachers' performances in such areas as curriculum planning, classroom management, providing instructional guidance, relationship with students, and professional development. No student teaching experience should be declared successfully completed until these multicultural criteria are met.

CONCLUDING COMMENTS

A serious battle is being waged to save our children from the devastating effects of under- and mis-education and to ensure the survival of the United States as a prosperous nation. These goals have some new dimensions due to the incredible ethnic, cultural, racial, and linguistic diversity that characterizes U.S. society and schools. We can neither save children nor teach them

well, nor ensure a healthy future for our country if schools continue to ignore multicultural education. Teachers and teacher educators play a pivotal role in these struggles. We have no choice but to multiculturalize professional education experiences if teachers are to be sufficiently prepared to meet these challenges.

Preparing teachers for the demands of multicultural education is a complicated and difficult task. Much of this complexity stems from the dynamic nature of teaching and the skepticism and ambiguity that many teacher educators hold toward cultural diversity. Infusing multiculturalism into teacher education requires both will and skill. We may facilitate this reform agenda by reminding ourselves that teaching is "at its heart, an intellectual and ethical enterprise…intensely practical and yet transcendent, brutally matter-of-fact, and yet fundamentally a creative act…begins in challenge and is never far from mystery" (Ayers, 1993, p. 127).

Gardner's (1981, 1984) comments about human self-renewal and excellence can inspire and motivate teacher educators as they move forward with changing teacher preparation programs to make them more responsive to cultural diversity. Gardner contends that life is a tumultuous affair and a continuous struggle without an assured victory; it requires a never-ending process of human renewal. To engage fully, we "need a hardbitten morale that enables us to face these truths and still strive with every ounce of our energy to prevail" (1981, p. xii). Teaching is somewhat like life. Teaching, too, is a creative, unguaranteed process of continuous discovery, challenge, and re-creation. Teacher education for cultural diversity must be engendered with this understanding and with all of its attendant attitudes, values, and skills.

All of our children deserve excellence in educational opportunities, experiences, and outcomes. Excellence must be both our method and our mission. Unknowing, unskilled, and uncaring teachers cannot deliver educational excellence to culturally diverse students. To ensure their competence and protect the educational rights of all children, we must demand excellence in multicultural teacher preparation programs. Gardner advises us to "demand excellence in every form that higher education takes. We should not ask it lightly or amiably or good naturedly, we should demand it vigorously and insistently" (1984, p. 101). A fundamental component of excellence in teacher education programs is understanding, valuing, and responding with appropriate pedagogy to the cultural diversity that characterizes U.S. schools and society.

Relationships are also an important anchor of excellence. Gardner explains that "In leading, in teaching, in dealing with young people, in all relationships of influencing, directing, guiding, helping, nurturing, the whole tone of the relationship will be conditioned by our faith in human possibilities" (1984, p. 151). Can teachers have much faith and optimism in the human possibilities of students they do not understand and may not value, and whose potentialities are manifested in cultural ways fundamentally different from their own? Probably not. The infusion of multiculturalism into teacher education will make this faith and optimism possible for more culturally diverse students.

Finally, Gardner (1984, p. 154) advises that "If our leaders at all levels are to be capable of lifting us and moving us toward excellence, they are going to have to believe in the people of this nation—a people...capable of greatness and desperately in need of encouragement to achieve that greatness." These words summarize the ultimate challenge for future teachers. They must believe in the value and potential for greatness of a new-age population of students who are racially, socially, ethnically, and culturally different from themselves. To meet this demand and provide the kind of leadership these students require to reach maximum levels of excellence, teachers must be knowledgeable of and skilled in multicultural education. Without such preparation, their leadership potential is minimized, and the likelihood that students will attain the peak of their educational excellence falls to happenstance. Therefore, competency in multicultural education should be a condition of entry into the profession for *all* teachers.

CHAPTER 13

Integrating Transcultural Knowledge into Nursing Curricula: An American Indian Example*

Karine Crow, Ph.D., R.N.
Assistant Professor
Intercollegiate Center for Nursing Education, Spokane, Washington

Editor's Notes:
Karine Crow's chapter applies multicultural course transformation principles specifically to nursing education. However, the information she provides on American Indian culture and on transcultural program and faculty development will be useful to faculty in any discipline. The chapter's expressed purposes are to provide (a) a framework for assessing nursing programs with respect to cultural competence and sensitivity and (b) guidelines for implementing transcultural change. In accomplishing these purposes, Crow offers strategies for achieving the multicultural goals of supporting diverse students' achievement, helping all students acquire a more comprehensive knowledge of the subject matter, encouraging students and faculty to accept themselves and others, and facilitating understanding of the history, traditions, and perspectives of specific groups. The chapter addresses instructional strategies and assessment of students but focuses primarily on transforming content through workshops that bring faculty and student together.

Acknowledging the relatively sparse literature on American Indians, Crow uses examples from this heterogeneous cultural group to illustrate her points. Nevertheless, her assessment framework and guidelines can be used to expand faculty and student knowledge on additional populations. The author's illustrations give readers a glimpse of the richness of American Indian tradition and an appreciation for different world views and ways of knowing. She incorporates her own guideline of employing the language of the client through story telling and metaphor. Transformed teaching is implicit in her respect for students as partners in the educational process; students "bring intrinsic knowledge linked to ancient widsom." Her unique presentation itself constitutes evidence of the need for universities to diversity their faculty and students in order to benefit from different world views. ∎

* The author would like to acknowledge the following individuals for their review of the chapter and comments.
Jacque Dolberry, M.S, RN
Ursula Knoki-Wilson, C.N.M
John Lowe, Ph.D., M.S, RN
Lee Ann Nickols, Ph.D., RN
Judy Parker, Ph.D., RN
Robbie Pauk, M.S.
Cecelia Tall Chief, RN

Obey the Creator
and do good to all.
It is good medicine,
healing your wounds
and easing your pains.
—*Anonymous*

The field of nursing began to consider multiculturalism from a theoretical view during the early 1960s. In 1965, Madeline Leininger established the discipline of "transcultural nursing." She believed that culture dictated both health beliefs and behaviors and health care provision. Her theories gave impetus to nursing's rethinking of health care promotion, prevention, provision, restoration, and evaluation with multicultural groups. Given the increasing diversity in the United States, integration of transcultural or multicultural views into nursing becomes more critical. More recently, Leininger (1990) urged that

This is an era in nursing in which all nurses must expand their worldview and knowledge of diverse cultures. It is time that…transcultural knowledge…be an integral part of nursing education and care practices….No longer can nor should we promote unicultural or narrow ethnocentric knowledge. Nurses must be prepared to function effectively in diverse transcultural contexts. Furthermore, transcultural knowledge is urgently needed for the new evolution of nursing curricula and for a broader base of research and practice. (p. 31)

Despite Leininger's call, many programs still do not reflect transcultural views. "Undergraduate nursing education programs do not purport to prepare nurses with expertise in transcultural nursing. However, if they are to be accountable to

both students and clients, they must address cultural competencies for nursing" (Carpio & Majumdar, 1993, p. 9). Additionally, "lack of cultural sensitivity by health care providers wastes millions of dollars annually, alienates the very people whom nurses purport to help, and results in misdiagnoses, often with tragic and dangerous consequences (Andrews, 1992, p. 7).

This chapter discusses theoretical and practical ways of integrating transcultural or multicultural nursing into the framework and curriculum of a nursing program. The first major section provides a framework for comprehensive transcultural assessment of the program, from the mission statement to three components discussed in Chapter 2: curriculum content, instructional methods, and assessment of student knowledge. The second section offers guidelines for implementing change with a focus on faculty/student workshops. The recommendations allow participants— nurse educators, students, patients/clients/consumers—to celebrate their similar and uniquely diverse learning styles, health care provision, and caring systems.

The term "transcultural" connotes the ideological implication of an equal exchange between groups rather than a one-way communication from the dominant group (as connoted by "cross-cultural"). However, for purposes of this chapter, transculturalism, multiculturalism, pluralism, and diversity will be used interchangeably to indicate multiple worldviews, values, cultures, socioeconomic and gender groups, or gender orientation.

The major ethnic groups that are contributing to the country's diversity include Hispanics, African Americans, Asian Americans, and Native Americans. The smallest literature is available for Native Americans. For this reason, I will use American Indian experiences to demonstrate principles of transcultural nursing and begin with a brief overview of American Indian perspectives. The U.S. government includes Hawaiians and Samoans under "Native Americans." However, for purposes of this chapter, the terms Native American and American Indian will be used interchangeably. While the Native American is being used as an example, many of the suggested patterns of communication, teaching methodologies, cultural beliefs, and practices are applicable to other groups.

The United States has over five-hundred federally recognized Native American tribes and over three-hundred federal reservations. The period between 1950 and 1980 witnessed a 282 percent increase in the number of Native Americans recorded by the Census Bureau (U.S. Department of Commerce, 1983; U.S. Department of Health and Human Services, 1988). The current census estimate is 2 million. It is important to emphasize that each nation or tribal group, such as the Sun Dance-Lakota nation, Kachina-Hopi nation, and Man in the Maze-Pima nation, has its own culture-specific health beliefs and practices (Joe, 1995). Therefore, the principles described in this chapter must be adapted to specific groups.

Most residents of the United States, including Indians, do not fully appreciate the role that American Indian cultures play in our society, particularly in health care. Many medications, curative and caring practices have been derived from American Indian traditional healing and health care practices such as deodorant, toothpaste, aspirin, casts for broken bones, and over one-hundred medications in the pharmacopoeia (Weatherford, 1988).

A FRAMEWORK FOR TRANSCULTURAL PROGRAM ASSESSMENT

A comprehensive assessment of any program begins with an examination of the program's philosophy and mission statement. Subsequently, the major areas for review are curriculum content, teaching methods, and strategies for assessing student knowledge. This section briefly addresses the mission statement and methods of instruction and assessment and examines curriculum in detail.

Philosophy and Mission Statement

A program's mission statement plays a critical role both as a foundation for course content and instruction and as an informal contract with the public regarding the program's philosophy and values. A review of the program's mission statement should include such questions as:

- Do the program's philosophy and mission statement support inclusion?
- Do the philosophy and mission statements consider the diverse ways in which culture, worldviews, and values are expressed?

The following example might be used as a beginning:

> The University seeks to respect and accept the benefits of diversity as expressed through racial/ethnic, gender, cultural, sexual orientation, ability/disability, and socio-economic differences of its faculty, staff, and students. Through the curriculum, programs, and services, the University provides supportive interaction and respect for its diverse population groups and individuals. Opportunities to explore, understand, and appreciate the similarities and differences of all groups and individuals will be provided that all may become increasingly competent in a pluralistic and global society; thereby fostering a climate of cooperation that promotes unity within diver-

sity as it relates to the University and the College of Nursing. (Adapted from a working draft of a statement on diversity for the Intercollegiate Center for Nursing Education, April 1995)

Curriculum

This section addresses both the content and sequencing of transcultural curriculum. In reviewing the curriculum, major questions might include:

- What level of inclusiveness or exclusiveness do the program's curriculum objectives reveal in relation to our pluralistic society?

- Do the modules, teaching plans, or overall framework for the school of nursing include differing and similar worldviews, values, and cultural perspectives?

- Do the terminal objectives for each course reflect diversity?

- Do the written language and linguistics used reflect inclusiveness?

- What threads run through the curriculum?

- What diversity materials are available to teachers and students that facilitate learning?

- Do they provide helpful transcultural information? Or do they reinforce stereotyping?

- Do the bibliographies, textbooks, and required readings reflect transcultural values?

- Is a multicultural assessment tool available for evaluation of the materials?

In short, the major question is whether the material presented provides an openness to more than one perspective. There are as many ways to promote, maintain, and restore health as there are cultural groups. Are stereotyping and bias being acknowledged if exclusive materials are used? For example, bias can occur with respect to assumptions about experience. In the 1960s and 1970s, in teaching documentation of different-colored stools, one color to describe a certain disease process was called "clay-colored" meaning whitish-gray. If unaware that clay-colored in this context refers to whitish-gray, the student, depending on geography or exposure, might think "clay-colored" stools means red, orange, yellow, green, and so forth. An assumption is made that all clay in everyone's experience is colored whitish-gray.

The analysis and evaluation of the outcomes of this review will provide the basis for promotion of critical thinking within the nursing process in relation to cultural competency and sensitivity toward patient or client care. Moreover, it will allow measurable outcomes to be incorporated into the theoretical and clinical practice settings, that is, discussion of multicultural components in case studies, development of culture-specific care plans, and evaluation of culture-specific patient and client care.

The following outline, adapted from Smoyak (1979) and Tripp-Reimer, Brink, and Saunders (1984), can serve as an assessment tool for reviewing curriculum materials. This guide is not intended to be exhaustive, but to offer examples for consideration. Each major topic will be discussed below in greater detail. For additional cultural guides, see Andrews and Boyle (1995); Leininger (1991); Orque, Block, & Monrroy (1983); and Tripp-Reimer (1984).

Beliefs and Worldviews

A concern related to beliefs and worldviews of health and illness within the curriculum is the acknowledgment of diverse perspectives. Does the curriculum explicitly

Curriculum Assessment Guide

I. Beliefs and Worldviews

  A. Health
1. Health definitions
2. Health promotion
3. Health maintenance
4. Health restoration

  B. Illness/sickness
1. Illness/sickness definitions
2. Cause of illness/sickness
3. Diagnosis
4. Treatment
5. Sick role
6. Prevention

II. Values and Values Clarification

  A. Health and illness

  B. Human nature

  C. Family

  D. Information

  E. Language/emotion
1. Verbal
2. Nonverbal

  F. Decision making

  G. Time

  H. Space

III. Customs

  A. Communication
1. Verbal
2. Nonverbal
3. Symbolic
4. Styles of presentation
5. Emotive responses

  B. Decision making

  C. Religion

  D. Food
1. Standard diet
2. Health restricted
3. Illness restricted

  E. Family roles and interactions

  F. Grief

  G. Sick role

IV. Social Components

  A. Family structure

  B. Religion

  C. Politics

  D. Education

  E. Available health systems
1. Cosmopolitan/Western
2. Traditional
3. Health practitioners
    a. Cosmopolitan/Western
    b. Traditional
4. Facilities

  F. Ethnic affiliation

  G. Art

  H. History

  I. Adaptation to physical environment

  J. Culture change/exchange

acknowledge that the worldview and beliefs related to health and illness being taught constitute only one perception? Or are students implicitly expected to accept the presented concepts as the only correct view of heath and illness? Are multiple health definitions, strategies for preventing illness, and ways of promoting, maintaining, and restoring health included? According to Sobralske (1985), American Indians believe that health reflects living in balance or harmony with nature and being able to survive under difficult circumstances. Additionally, behaviors related to indirect communication, time, individual development, and interdependence which enhance harmony with the family, environment, supernatural forces, living and inanimate objects, and community promote balance or harmony (Attneave, 1982).

Depending on culture and experience, illness or sickness may have multiple definitions, meanings, causes, diagnoses, treatments, and preventative measures. Additionally, ways in which the sick role is determined and manifested may vary. What is considered normative in one society may be considered abnormal in another. For example, an individual who hallucinates may be considered a gift because he or she speaks with the spirits. In Euro-Anglo society, a person manifesting the same symptoms is considered to have a biochemical psychological disease called schizophrenia.

Most Native American belief systems incorporate multiple causality of health problems. Multiple causes may include beliefs that

> causes of illness, misfortunes, or disabilities may be attributed to supernatural or natural causes. The supernatural causes may link etiology to witchcraft, spirit loss, spirit intrusion, spells, and various unnatural forces. In the natural category, the causes may be attributed to various disturbances of balance or equilibrium brought on by such actions as breaking a cultural taboo, acculturation, and/or accidents that are not instigated by witchcraft or the harmful wishes of others. (Joe & Malach, 1992)

For example, in reviewing health promotion or restoration, cultural beliefs on meaning and causation provide explanations for a healthy or unhealthy status. One such belief for illness causation is the arrival of European culture, as evidenced by the response of a woman from the Yuma tribe: "Yes…we know that when you come, we die" (McLuhan, 1971, p. 113). Hagey (1984) reported that diabetes and alcoholism are seen as "problems due to white man's food and environment" (p. 268). One Indian leader attributed the problem of diabetes in his ethnic group to extended contact with White men (Hagey, 1984).

It is not uncommon in some American Indian tribes to attribute ill health to the individual's or clan's misuse of power. Power is to be used for the betterment of the whole tribe. When instead, power has been misused for personal or clan gain, statements might be made that "it will come back to them" or "it will come full circle." These predictions imply that the misuse of power has a boomerang effect and that sickness or misfortune will result. The word "sickness" often is used because linguistically some languages have no word or concept for illness.

Knowledge of health beliefs will facilitate appropriate health promotion, prevention, maintenance, and restoration. Questions that may assist health practitioners to assess the individual's understanding of his or her illness and enable them to participate knowledgeably in their patient's care are listed as follows.

In asking questions, cultural sensitivity dictates that health practitioners must avoid direct questions or "twenty" questions because to do so might be experienced as confrontational. Indirect, open-ended questions as well as storytelling with appropriate content to ask the patient or family member would be preferable. For example, "Who would you like to have participate in the decision making? Whom do you want present during your hospitalization or treatment? If extended family members are present, the practitioner should direct his or her questions and comments to the entire group, thereby showing respect for the family.

Values and Values Clarification

Once the client's beliefs and worldview have been established, values related to health and illness provide the basis for the health practitioner's standard responses or actions. In nursing, the individual patient's informed consent constitutes an important

Health and Illness Queries

I. Health

A. Health definitions
- What is health or wholeness?

B. Health promotion
- What does one do to be healthy or whole?

C. Health maintenance
- What do people do to stay healthy and remain healthy if they have become sick?

D. Health restoration
- What caring activities should an individual or others do to help an individual to become well?
- Who helps care for you during this illness/sickness?

II. Illness/sickness

A. Illness/sickness definitions
- What is illness or sickness?

B. Cause(s) of illness/sickness
- What do you think caused your illness/sickness?

C. Diagnosis
- Who diagnoses the illness/sickness?
- What is the normal course of time for the illness/sickness?

D. Treatment
- What treatment is necessary for this illness/sickness?
- Who prescribes the treatment for it?

E. Sick role
- How do individuals decide they are ill/sick?
- What behaviors are exhibited if one is sick?
- How is pain defined and exhibited?

F. Prevention
- How do you prevent this illness/sickness?

concern. Yet, in many American Indian families, the individual is part of a whole, and informed consent may include the immediate or extended family as well as the individual. Even if family members do not live within proximity to the person needing assistance, it is not unusual for the extended family to be telephoned, money collected, and individuals brought to the location for the decision making process to be finalized. The value thus expressed is group rather than individual. When one person is affected, every person is affected. These behaviors express the group value by bringing the entire group's members (extended family) together. In such situations, the practitioner must determine who is the primary decision maker and who serves as spokesperson. The grandmother or an uncle might carry the most weight; but someone else would speak for the group.

The value placed on family thus might be expressed in an Indian family's response to a hospitalized family member. In addition to the immediate family, the extended or incorporated family (individuals who are not blood relatives) might be present during this time. It is important to note that reality conditions might preclude ideal expression of values. The absence of some key individuals might be unavoidable.

The practitioner's understanding of a patient's cultural values and their expression can support health care, and lack of understanding may have detrimental consequences. In one case, the entire extended family (27 members) arrived en mass to the hospital. Their presence disturbed the nurses because they all crowded into the hospital room. The nurses expressed to the family members that their presence in the patient's room was inappropriate because it disturbed the patient, who was in and out of a coma, and because hospital policy limited the number of visitors at any one time. (Unfortunately, too often nurses request hospital security to enforce policy rather than explain hospital rules to family members, creating additional barriers to care.) Finally, at the nurses' insistence, the majority of family members retreated to the waiting room.

When the patient became more aware, he wanted to know where everyone was and indicated by his reaction a feeling of abandonment. His condition began to deteriorate; banishing members of the extended family in large numbers negatively affected his vital signs and progress. This example illustrates how a conflict between the Euro-American nurse caregivers' values regarding care and hospital policy and the American Indian family's values related to space, information, and caring impacted the patient's responses.

Customs

Customs are the behaviors that act out the culture's values. These behaviors include communication (verbal, nonverbal, symbolic styles of presentation), decision making, religion, diet (standard diet, health-restricted or illness-restricted), family roles and interactions, grief, and sick role.

Communication is essential to culture-specific, therapeutic nursing intervention and teaching. According to Knoki-Wilson (1995), words and silence are necessary components in communication. Silence allows individuals to open their consciousness and to know who they are. Then they can choose the healing path. They may choose traditional or Western or blend them together, an integration and use of knowledge as a whole.

It would not be unusual to encounter silence in working with Indian families, for example, when the health practitioner asks if anyone has questions. Silence does not imply lack of understanding. Indian families may not ask questions unless they feel or know they have received all the information offered. Individuals do not interrupt or respond until all the information has been presented. Once the information has been received, a time of reflection is often taken before questions or decisions are made. Such behavior might also occur in the classroom; many American Indian students do not interrupt or ask questions during the class period.

Use of the patient's language or language style is healing. Practitioners can use anchoring words to convey nursing instructions more effectively. For example, in speaking about breast self-examinations, the nurse might say, "Twilight is when we think of ourselves; is nighttime a good time to do a breast self-examination? In other words, we can use language to convey our meaning in ways that may be understood by individuals whose culture, language, symbols, or points of reference (worldview) differ from our own. Even in cultures that use American English, words may carry different connotations. Health practitioners may assist healing with descriptions using metaphors from the patient's background rather than from a medicalized or nursing framework using the discipline's jargon.

Culture conflict may also stem from differences in presentation styles. Many Euro-American nursing professionals value direct eye contact, asking many questions, and being directive in their promotion of health care practices. In contrast, many American Indians are more accustomed to observing, giving indirect or no eye contact, and listening without interruption as a sign of respect to people of knowledge and authority. A "sandwich" approach may be indicated to improve transcultural communication: To build the relationship and establish trust, nursing professionals can take time with the patient at the beginning and end of each encounter to enhance learning about each other (a professional social time). During the visit, the health issues or concerns will present themselves. Reflective or indirect questions as well as stories about similar situations may provide information needed. Pareek and Roa (1980) support this approach, indicating that establishing rapport requires self-disclosure and appropriate sequencing and structuring of questions. The beginning stages for establishing rapport may require discussion of the nurse's family (use of therapeutic I-thou). Questions would be sequenced in a manner such that sensitive questions would not be asked or mentioned until rapport has been established. These principles apply also for faculty working with students.

One example of severe communication conflict in style and presentation occurred when an American Indian went to see a White physician. The physician instructed the client in health-promotion behaviors and referred her to another health professional. In the process, the physician asked many questions without providing time for reflection. The faster the physician talked and fired questions, the quieter the patient became. The quieter the patient became, the louder the physician's voice became to the point where he was yelling at her. Finally, the patient softly reminded him, "I'm not deaf; I can hear you." To which the physician shouted in reply, "How do I know you're hearing me—I can't see your eyes!" Not only had the patient been silent and not interrupting, she had been looking down at the floor. The patient quietly responded, "Your eyes are too strong." Strong eye contact often is interpreted to convey anger, attempt to discipline, and disrespect. In other words, the direct eye contact and playing of "twenty questions" provoked responses that created unexpected culture

conflict and potential barriers to care. To the American Indian client, looking down at the floor or away from the speaker was intended to convey respect and paying close attention to his words. To the White physician, his inability to see her eyes indicated that she was not paying attention.

Social Components

Social components constitute additional aspects of a culture that affect health care and nursing education. Social components include family structure, religion, education, available health systems, politics, ethnic or racial affiliation, art, history, adaptation to the physical environment (topography, climate), and ongoing culture change. Available health systems can be traditional, such as midwives and healers, or Western. Politics and social change forces have influenced the acceptance of traditional health care practices. Until recently, the Indian Health Service discouraged use of traditional healers, healing ceremonies, and other traditional practices. With the development of the National Institute of Alternative Medicine, other healing modalities such as Indian traditional healing and caring practices are being explored.

Cultural perspectives on art and color also can affect health care. Sensitivity to the content of wall hangings, for example, is an important aspect of culturally responsive care. A picture of President Andrew Jackson could offend because of his views of the American Indian and the impact of his policies. Hunting scenes may inadvertently portray the killing of a patient's personal or clan totem or spirit guide, such as the bear, wolf, and so forth. Some groups consider certain colors unhealthy, making the color of a patient's medication important. Patients may refuse medication in colors perceived as unhealthy. Including on an advisory board members of the population being served will assist in the development of a culturally sensitive healing environment and healing modalities.

Adaptations to the physical environment can influence expression of perceptual abilities, important in teaching health care and in ensuring client comfort. For example, individuals accustomed to looking horizontally will view stimuli from that perspective; those accustomed to vertical perspectives will be more comfortable with stimuli that go up and down. City dwellers may feel more at ease with surroundings that are tall and close together. People raised in the countryside with open spaces may experience claustrophobia in the absence of horizontal views and open vistas where they cannot see the sky. The latter may feel confined or hemmed in by closed surroundings.

Sequencing Transcultural Content

Nursing educators also must consider when transcultural nursing perspectives should be introduced into the curriculum and practice settings. Experience has shown that when transcultural concepts are taught and practiced early in the curriculum, fewer issues arise. Students know from the beginning that transcultural sensitivity and knowledge are required, expected, and normative. Many students appreciate an early introduction and express gratitude that their ways and views are being valued. One student came to the author and acknowledged, "Since being in nursing school, you are the first person who pronounced the name of my home correctly."

Inclusion of conceptual and cultural concepts may be incorporated in the basic fundamentals class with patient assessment. For example, many nursing programs use Gordon's model of basic health care needs. In this model, the first need is listed as maintenance and health promotion; cultural values and spiritual principles occur last. To transform the course, the instructor can provide a different sequence. From a transcultural viewpoint, cultural and spiritual needs would be the first area assessed because culture, values, and worldview impact everything about the individual. Culture determines how one promotes, maintains, and restores health as well as who are defined as the healers and caregivers. It influences food selection, preparation, and how one eats. Culture determines how and when we sleep, work, and play, thereby touching all facets of life that affect health.

Culture-specific information can be incorporated in relation to each basic health care need. For example, with regard to maintenance and health promotion, American Indians have a holistic perspective. The world is viewed as a whole; body, mind, and spirit must be considered in health maintenance and promotion. When the body meets the sun in the morning, one runs to meet the sun. The sun is a symbol of the Great Spirit/Creator who brings life and the ability to maintain health and wholeness. The exercise (running) is a physiological response that helps maintain health, and the mind has a sense of well-being when one is physically attuned. The person also is giving back in running. The expended energy is given back to nature within the concept of the individual's kinship relationship with nature. It is not unusual to hear the expression "Here comes my child" in reference to the individual running to meet the creator as represented in the sun (Knoki-Wilson, May 1995, personal communication).

Each health care need can be assessed in a similar manner. With regard to food, certain foods are eaten because they promote health; abstention or moderation occurs with other foods associated with lack of health. An example across cultures in the United States is maintaining and protecting the health of unborn children by eliminating alcoholic beverages and drugs during pregnancy. American Indians have incorporated this idea because the culture values children; children are the future. Posters, videos, and high school presentations focus on the delivery of healthy infants. These media admonish that "An inner voice tells you not to drink or use other drugs" or "Honor the circle, honor the earth, honor your tribe; join the circle and break the cycle of addiction" (U.S. Department of Health and Human Services Public Health Service; Alcohol, Drug Abuse and Mental Health Administration; developed by the National Institute on Alcohol Abuse and Alcoholism for the Office for Substance Abuse Prevention).

Introducing cultural information early in the program and each course and continuing to integrate cultural themes support development of expectations and attention to individual and group needs. For both students and their potential clients, understanding of cultural needs supports the relationship and permits later questioning on more personal topics that otherwise might be considered intrusive. Provision of appropriate, sensitive, competent therapeutic nursing care requires answers to questions such as: What is most important to you? What gives meaning? How do you define who you are? What is your most important source of comfort? of security? How does one maintain wholeness or balance? Information gleaned through such questions provides insight into the essence of the individual. Students must learn to ask indirectly or through story after creating rapport and connectedness in a safe environment.

Assessment of Students

In addition to evaluating the program's mission statement and curriculum for transcultural appropriateness, it is important to review practices used for assessing student knowledge and skills. Are the examinations biased? Two major types of bias to avoid on examinations (and other aspects of instruction) are facial bias and bias toward the dominant culture.

Questions that contain facial bias refer to those that stereotype on the basis of group membership, such as gender, ethnicity, or sexual orientation. For example, does the examination use a name typically associated with a certain group (e.g., Crow) and associate it with a behavioral stereotype (e.g., a question related to alcoholism)? Content containing facial bias is offensive to members of the implied target group and serves to further negative stereotypes among other students. The majority of American Indians do not exhibit alcoholism or laziness. Care should be exercised to ensure that an item covers the material without targeting a specific group or reinforcing stereotypes.

Bias toward the dominant culture refers to assumptions that characteristics and needs of the dominant culture apply to all, or using the dominant group as the standard. This type of bias is more subtle and less easily recognized. For example, an item testing knowledge on dietary issues in relation to intake of calcium and minerals might ask students how to help a family obtain these necessary nutrients. An instructor who lists "a diet including milk" as the only correct option on either a multiple-choice or open-ended examination fails to consider physiologic variations common to other groups, such as the inability to digest milk. Many American Indians and members of other ethnic groups, such as Asians, are lactose-intolerant. The keyed answer should include alternative diets when milk must be excluded as well as reasons for milk exclusion. Since the tested content concerns calcium uptake rather than a single calcium source, the item might list foods the family currently uses, and if calcium is missing, ask the student to determine what foods would serve to provide the needed calcium and minerals. The goal is to avoid the biased assumption that all individuals must be able to include milk products in their diet.

Instructional Strategies

Another area for review, in tandem with the mission statement, curriculum, and assessment of students, concerns teaching theories and methodologies. The evaluation should encourage adoption of teaching theories and strategies that meet the needs of a multicultural classroom. Since culture determines how we learn, different ways of teaching must be implemented to accommodate the diversity of students' learning modes (see Chapter 4 for greater detail). American Indian students may prefer group projects within the classroom setting as a means of decreasing competition, increasing classroom interaction, and creating a more harmonious environment. The goal is design instruction in ways that connect new learning to students' experiences. For example, incorporation of metaphor can be useful in teaching Indian students. With students from families where tracking ability is necessary for survival, one way to frame reading instruction would be to "follow someone's tracks."

In assessing instruction, helpful questions include:

- How might nursing professors provide competent multicultural nursing education when it is virtually impossible to know and understand the intricacies of all the cultures represented by the students?
- How can students be included in teaching about their culture and in relating to peers representing other cultures?
- Can one theory of instruction apply to all students or would an eclectic approach better support diversity and continuity?
- What methods of teaching would best serve my particular situation?

Once faculty and students are aware of these issues, they can begin to engage in change.

GUIDELINES FOR IMPLEMENTING CHANGE

As will be discussed in Chapter 16 in greater depth, change from the familiar, the status quo, produces fear, anxiety, and resistance as well as an opportunity for growth. This section briefly describes aspects of resistance at individual and organizational levels and presents recommendations for implementing transcultural change in programs that prepare health care professionals.

Organizational and Individual Resistance

Supporters of transcultural change commonly encounter organizational or institutional resistance in relation to the adoption of admissions requirements that encourage a more diverse student body. Frequently, the suggestion of alternatives (e.g., portfolios, examples of products, letters of recommendation, trial admissions) to traditional entrance requirements (grade-point average, Graduate Record Exam, Scholastic Aptitude Test) raises the issue of whether standards are being lowered. In contrast, consideration of nontraditional requirements can lead to greater creativity and improving or raising of standards.

Admitting students who do not meet standardized test or grade-point average cutoffs does not mean that students may complete the program without meeting standards for graduation. Such students are merely provided the opportunity to attempt the nursing program. The standardized tests may not reflect students' potential for higher education; rather, scores are influenced by cultural and experiential differences and application of different metaphors and emphases. For example, a student whose family values mathematics achievement and a student whose family values hunting skills for survival may possess equal intellectual capacity. However, their cultures and experiences encourage different modes for expressing their abilities. Students who enter the program with deficiencies in basic skills required for academic success (English, mathematics, writing, reading, and test-taking) need a support system. Additionally, social support can facilitate adjustment to an academic setting and reduce cultural dissonance and discouragement. In the absence of such support, students are being set up to fail, and failure generates additional victim blaming: "They couldn't do it anyway." "We allow everyone to try." "It's not our responsibility if they don't succeed."

Individual resistance to transcultural change efforts also occurs among faculty and students. Some instructors express anger when colleagues begin to question nursing's academic values and worldview. Questioning long-standing tenets of educational philosophy and practice may leave us feeling vulnerable and uncertain of our teaching and clinical skills. Students also may feel threatened when, for the first time, the parameters of their lives are pushed outward and other ways of being and doing become acknowledged as also correct. Resistance occurs particularly among individuals who have grown up with the notion that theirs is the right way and the only way (a belief common among many cultures). They may interpret transcultural teaching as attempts to change who they are, as causing personal identity loss, or as devaluing their culture. However, faculty, students, and organizations need to become aware that the academic culture has forced Euro-American worldviews, values, and teaching methods on American Indian students (and clients) as well as on other nondominant groups.

Recommendations

Recognize that change takes time and planning. Change agents must be prepared to move slowly. Typically, an idea must be introduced in three different ways over eighteen months before individuals begin to "own," accept, and assimilate the idea into their thinking. After an idea is introduced, it must be reinforced in theory and practice. Careful planning of long-term, ongoing programs and goals is essential in introducing the components of transcultural nursing. A major consideration in program development is creating an advisory board representing the groups impacted by nursing education and practice.

Provide faculty development opportunities. Workshops that provide both theory and practice in working transculturally can help faculty "own" the concept that diversity in health and caring for others should form an integral part of the curriculum. Offering quarterly seminars or reading group discussions led by leaders in the field reinforces new ideas over time.

Include students as partners in training and experimentation. Practice sessions with faculty and students support implementation of change in teaching strategies and encourage experimentation with new ways of performing and expressing nursing care. Students may suggest or initiate different methods for teaching content and demonstrating clinical competence. Consistent (e.g., monthly) scheduling for trying innovative, culturally responsive practice provides faculty and students with the freedom to try new strategies without fear of censure or appearing incompetent in an actual classroom or clinical setting.

Providing opportunities for interactions between faculty and students on a less formal basis than the classroom or clinical setting may facilitate communication. Often faculty cannot explain to students from diverse backgrounds the process they have chosen to enable students to arrive at the expected outcome. The students may not be able to articulate the nature of the difficulties they may be experiencing. Miscommunication resulting from this combination may create frustration, defensiveness, and anger. If both faculty and students have access to the same cultural material being presented, dialogue between them could provide breakthroughs for both, allowing the potential for mutual learning and understanding. Students and peers can be excellent teachers and critics in this informal setting.

Additionally, students can serve as a rich source of information about their own cultures and ways of learning; they bring intrinsic knowledge linked to ancient wisdom. Faculty can ask them to explain how their family teaches, describe a personal learning event, or relate how they would explain a concept to members of their culture. Effective strategies for teaching and learning are in some senses culturally determined and passed from generation to generation. Some American Indian groups suggest that everything must be viewed from the perspective of the next seven generations.

Hold faculty/student workshops conducted by experts in the field of transcultural nursing education. Such a workshop might have the following objectives.

The workshop's initial session would encourage participants to examine their own cultural background. People often have little occasion to reflect on their ways of living as having roots in a specific culture or cultures because "this is the way it has always been."

Outline for Faculty/Student Workshop on Transcultural Nursing

I. **Objectives for the Workshop**

  A. Know the definition of the following terms:
    1. Culture
    2. Ethnocentrism
    3. Worldview
    4. Values

  B. Explore own culture of origin, including:
    1. Spiritual and worldview
      a. What gave or gives meaning?
      b. What is emphasized?
      c. What has primary importance?
    2. Success and failure
      a. Who is successful? Who is a failure?
      b. What does success or failure involve?
      c. What determines success or failure?

  C. Define health or lack of health within one's culture
    1. How is health defined?
    2. What causes health?
    3. What are the implications of health?
    4. How is health promoted?
    5. How is health maintained?
    6. Who is responsible for health?
      a. Individual
      b. Family
      c. Community
    7. What activities indicate a healthy community, individual, or family?

  D. Define lack of health or non-health within one's culture
    1. What terms are used?
    2. What causes it?
    3. What does it mean?

4. What were the behaviors and roles of persons with lack of health?
5. Who are the primary and secondary caregivers?
6. Who are the professional caregivers? the lay caregivers?
7. What restorative activities occur?

E. Evaluate teaching and learning
   1. Classroom expectations
      a. What are the students' expectations of the teacher?
      b. What does the teacher expect of students?
   2. How are teaching and learning accomplished in one's culture?
      a. One on one
      b. Apprenticeship/role modeling
      c. Classroom (one teacher with many students)
   3. How is it similar to the nursing academic culture?
   4. How does it differ from the nursing academic culture?

II. **Clinical and Classroom Practice**

When relating to groups and communities, determine the following:

A. Structure
   1. Group/community network: tribe or group; other involved agencies
   2. Nuclear or extended families
   3. Where people congregate
   4. What people consider their most important need
   5. How one becomes acquainted with or becomes a member of group

B. Leadership
   1. Formal leaders of the group or community

2. Informal leaders
3. Leadership styles
   a. Individual
   b. Group
   c. Network
4. What constitutes power and how it is used
5. How decisions are reached
6. How informed consent is achieved

C. Behaviors
   1. Direct intervention
   2. Non-interference, passive forbearance
   3. Suspicious, accepting

D. Health Care Practices and Methodologies
   1. Maternal and child
      a. Differing birthing practices
      b. Differing prenatal and postnatal practices
      c. Differing family and community involvement
   2. Pediatrics
      a. Differing child-rearing practices
      b. Differing expected tasks for different age levels
   3. Parenting
      a. Roles assumed by individuals, family, and community
      b. Responsibilities and practices
   4. Medical-surgical
      a. Biological variations
      b. Differing syncretic, accommodation, and traditional curing and caring practices
         (1) Curing practices would be pharmacological, invasive treatments
         (2) Caring practices would be the supportive practices

Outline for Faculty/Student Workshop on Transcultural Nursing, continued

      (a) Nursing of individual, family, community

      (b) Dealing with responses to illness: body, mind, and spirit

   (3) Accommodation: All people and groups adapt or accommodate different healing methodologies; compare:

      (a) Ways one's grandparents treated common ailments

      (b) Ways parents treated common ailments

      (c) Ways one currently treats common ailments

III. Classroom and Clinical Educational Methods

Determine which style one most commonly uses

A. Styles

   1. Lecture

      a. Provide broad concepts (whole picture/conceptual) or

      b. Step by step (linear sequential/fragmented)

   2. Questioning and answering

      a. Are questions open or closed?

      b. Who questions and when?

      c. Who responds and how (individual, spot lighting, group, etc.)?

   3. Demonstration, observation, and practice

      a. Passive participation by students?

      b. Active?

   4. Combined techniques (group, multimedia, lecture, drama, games, etc.)

B. Setting

   1. Formal or informal?

   2. Authoritarian or collegial?

C. Consistency between instructor's and students' cultural styles

D. Effectiveness of methods or style with the students or community

E. Feedback from students or community regarding methods or style

IV. Guidelines for Working with Diverse Populations

A. One works *with* an individual, family, or community, not *to do something to* or *for* the individual, family, or community.

B. Allow the individual, family, or community to determine their own needs and intervention.

C. Negotiate with the community's formal and informal leaders.

D. Encourage students to meet the community's needs in the clinical component of training.

E. Encourage student projects that meet needs identified by the community.

F. Develop and maintain a bibliography of readings relating cultural considerations to specific topics being taught.

They have not analyzed or evaluated their basic worldviews and values.

One activity to encourage reflection on one's culture is to have participants write down their expectations for students (or faculty) as well as the origins of those expectations. As a second step, participants compare their expectations with what actually occurs in the classroom or clinical setting. Comparing expectations provides the opportunity to examine the degree of convergence between faculty and students, evaluate the extent to which expectations are realistic or should be modified, and discuss how faculty and students could meet each other's expectations. Acceptance, respect, and honoring of each other would be necessary for this dialogical approach to be effective. The dialogue has potential for generating questions that could result in faculty/student research projects.

A major focus of a faculty/student workshop on transcultural nursing would center on culture-specific content important to health professionals. Faculty and students need to understand the structure of the target community or communities, the leadership, and behaviors related to parenting and health care.

For American Indians, therapeutic syncretism, a combined approach to medical practices incorporating both traditional and modern methods, is common (Crow, 1988). Given life in a rapidly changing environment, some "traditional" techniques currently in use differ from those originally employed by ancestors. However, treatment retains the essence of traditional practices. For example, one woman of a tribe used a glucometer to monitor her glucose levels and traditional herbs to maintain them. From a modern medical perspective, she was considered noncompliant in use of prescribed medications and treatment. Yet her behavior was compliant in her maintenance of glucose levels. These types of accommodation, or therapeutic syncretism, as well as traditional treatment approaches, are worthy of investigation to determine efficacy.

A faculty/student workshop should also examine teaching methods for classroom and clinical settings. Do students' and teachers' instructional expectations and strategies match?

American Indian teachers tend to expect that students watch and observe an entire process before asking questions. American Indian preceptors at a community leadership clinical program commented, "Your students ask too many questions. If they would watch and listen, many of their questions would be answered." Or, "The students interrupt; they don't allow the individual to complete the task or the teaching." The preceptors' expectation was to complete the task or statement before receiving questions. They felt the students should see the concept or process as a whole, rather than breaking it down into parts.

Finally, a workshop on transcultural nursing should provide guidelines to both faculty and students on strategies for developing rapport with and involving individuals, families, and communities in their health care.

Approaching a relationship with clients as equal partners is important. Health care professionals work *with* an individual or family rather than *doing something to* or *for* the client. Health professionals must establish relationships with clients based on trust and confidence. If successful, the clients will introduce the health professional to others in the community. In working with American Indian communities, arrangements for health care and negotiations need to be made with the tribe.

Encouraging students to develop projects that help communities meet needs identified by the communities themselves also supports a trusting relationship. For example, students in a senior leadership nursing course had clinicals in a tribal community health department. Part of the course involved writing standards for nursing practice, patient care, and outcomes. One of the needs of the health department was a chart audit. Fortunately, the tribe had enough American Indian nurses to serve as preceptors. The students learned from the Indian nurse preceptors different leadership styles and cultural interventions. Based on their research, their knowledge of standards development and evaluation, and insight on the community shared by the nurse preceptors, the students developed a chart audit which they provided to the community health department.

The workshop should enable the faculty and students to develop a bibliography of readings on cultural practices related to health care. In maternal and child health or obstetrical nursing, important topics might include cultural birthing practices and alternative ways of birthing currently being explored in the United States. For example, different cultures have different preferred positioning or customary body postures for delivery during birth, such as squatting. Cultures may differ in terms of who delivers the baby; who may attend the birth; how much family participation is expected; naming rituals; religious or spiritual rites; traditional foods, exercise, or rituals; and how agencies accommodate these needs.

After the workshop, the faculty must accept and own the information and integrate it into their teaching. Otherwise, nursing education will not progress toward a more global and pluralistic perspective. Successful integration of knowledge of diverse cultures requires that faculty development opportunities be extended over a long period of time. The goal is to create a better, more flexible faculty—instructors who keep their minds free like an eagle

soaring. The bear who went over the mountain "to see what he could see" could only see one side of the mountain at a time. The eagle can see both sides at once (Knoki-Wilson, 1995, personal communication).

CONCLUDING COMMENTS

Cultural understanding requires commitment and time. Superficial understanding of a culture can be as detrimental as no cultural knowledge (Keltner, 1993). The examples in this chapter are intended to illustrate the richness of diversity in worldviews and to encourage in-depth pursuit of cultural knowledge. The reader is cautioned against using the suggestions or examples for stereotyping or making nefarious comparisons. Cultural understanding is not an end in itself. It is only a tool or mechanism to celebrate similar and diverse paradigms as well as our common humanity. Once understanding of worldviews, values, and cultures occurs, honoring, accepting, and providing culturally competent therapeutic care becomes a possibility.

Application of theoretical and practical ways of integrating transcultural nursing into the curriculum and framework of the nursing program allows nurse educators, students, and patients or consumers to celebrate their similar and unique ways. Transcultural program transformation provides the opportunity to promote diversity in nursing education, to increase diverse nursing personnel, and to provide sensitive, competent therapeutic nursing care.

CHAPTER 14

The Community College Curriculum

Desna L. Wallin, Ed.D.
President, Forsyth Technical Community College
Winston-Salem, North Carolina

Editor's Notes:
Community colleges are the major vehicle of entry into higher education for many students from underrepresented groups. Some community colleges have been leaders in multicultural efforts. Given the high percentages of people of color, women and older students among their clientele, community colleges are ideally positioned to implement a multicultural curriculum. Desna Wallin provides examples of different approaches to multicultural change in seven disciplines and services: music, sociology, English composition, biology, American history, technical preparation, and libraries. These examples address different aspects of the course-change model and all of the multicultural goals.

The examples, while drawn from actual community college cases, are applicable to all levels of higher education. They address additive, inclusive and transformed efforts, presenting content from non-dominant perspectives, designing course assignments to broaden student understandings about culture, using peer assistance, and providing assessment choices for students. Wallin also discusses the use of relevant and not readily available resource materials, the evaluation of textbook materials, and removal of barriers in libraries. ∎

Community colleges are the fastest-growing segment of higher education in the United States, and over half of all first-time freshmen enroll in them. As "people's colleges" with open-door access and low tuition, they serve a diverse body of learners many of whom, without community colleges, would have no opportunity for higher education. The comprehensive mission of community colleges includes transfer, vocational/technical, developmental, community service, and economic development functions. This broad mission sometimes gives rise to criticisms that community colleges attempt to be "all things to all people." By the same token, the over 1,200 community, junior, and technical colleges are known for their flexibility and responsiveness.

Community colleges, with their open admissions policies, have proven to be the vehicle of access to the mainstream for millions of immigrants, people of color, women, first-generation college attendees and other groups underrepresented in higher education. Community colleges have empowered thousands of individuals who, without such institutions, would never have had the opportunity for higher education. However, the story of community colleges as champions of diversity has not been entirely successful. Pauline E. Kayes (1992) maintains that

> many community colleges have failed to take seriously that implicit promise of access, equity, and multicultural diversity: some adopt exclusionary policies and practices; others refuse to address and to serve seriously and directly the needs and concerns of women, people of color, and international students because this is not seen as the "mission" of the community college, not the "real stuff" of education, but a fringy, peripheral waste of money. (p. 85)

Ms. Kayes quotes Dr. Zelema Harris, president of Parkland College in Champaign, Illinois, and a great supporter and leader of multiculturalism in community colleges:

> To create a climate of inclusiveness, every community college should not trivialize diversity, but face real issues: the major increases in minority enrollments without concomitant increase in minority faculty and administration; gender and race biased curricula; and the exclusive use of a teaching method, the lecture, which is the least effective way for adults to learn.... Inclusive policies and practices can't be viewed as supplementary or peripheral to the teaching-learning process. Inclusive policies and practices must cut through to the core of that process; from the teacher who teaches to the curricula that is taught, we must develop an educational system that has as its major tenets multiculturalism and gender-balance. (p. 85)

The community college, the people's college, is well positioned to take a leader-ship role in multicultural education. The pages which follow provide a fourfold perspective on multiculturalism in today's community colleges:

1. An overview of today's community college student

2. Four approaches to multicultural infusion

3. A review of the model proposed by Kitano in *Chapter 2* as applied to the community college

4. Specific examples and ideas relevant to infusing the curricula with multicultural perspectives

THE CONTEMPORARY COMMUNITY COLLEGE STUDENT

First, just what does today's community college student look like? We know, for example, that historically, most culturally diverse students enroll in two-year community colleges rather than at four-year degree-granting institutions (Carter & Wilson, 1991). We know also that community college students are approximately 60 percent female, many of them single parents. We know that the socioeconomic level of community college students is, on the average, lower than that of the university student. Approximately 75 percent of community college students qualify for some form of financial aid. They are often older students (the average age of a community college student is 26) who have experienced academic failure at some point in their lives. They are frequently in need of developmental work in math, English, and reading before they are able to compete successfully in college-level courses.

The Department of Education in its Higher Education Enrollment (1993) report shows clearly the enrollment trends at both the community college and the four-year colleges and universities. In 1978, there were

3,800,000 students enrolled in community colleges; by 1991, there were 5,800,000. There were 750,000 students of color enrolled in 1978 or 19 percent of the total; by 1991 enrollment of ethnolinguistically diverse students had reached 1,400,000 or nearly 25 percent of the total enrollees. Contrast those figures with enrollments at four-year colleges where the total multicultural population of 930,000 represented 13 percent of enrollees in 1978 and only 1,500,000 or 18 percent by 1991. Thus, at the present time we see that the 1,200 community colleges in the country enroll almost the same number of diverse students as do all four-year colleges and universities, public and private, combined (some 4,000 plus students!).

Community colleges are the institutions of higher education most accessible to diverse students. With the opportunities community colleges have to provide an education for these students comes a concomitant responsibility to assure that these students—and all students in the community college—experience a strong commitment to multicultural infusion throughout the curriculum, as well as in the services and support mechanisms available to assist in these students' success.

APPROACHES TO MULTICULTURAL INFUSION

Multicultural education maintains that "all students, regardless of the groups to which they belong, such as those related to gender, ethnicity, race, culture, social class, religion, or exceptionality, should experience educational equality in the schools. Some students, because of their particular characteristics, have a better chance to succeed in school as it is currently structured than have students from other groups" (Banks & Banks, 1993, p. 25). While these comments were made in reference to K–12 students,

they are equally appropriate when considering opportunities and barriers for community college and university students. Multicultural infusion is much more than multicultural education alone. "Multicultural infusion is a process, not a product, its aim being to produce culturally affirming classrooms which address the…needs of an increasingly pluralistic society" (Barba, 1993, p. 10).

Banks and Banks (1993) suggest that four approaches to the integration of multicultural content in the curriculum have evolved over the last three decades. They describe the four levels of integration as the contributions approach, the additive approach, the transformative approach, and the social action approach.

Level 1, or the Contributions Approach, focuses on heroes and holidays. Mainstream heroes such as Booker T. Washington, Sacajawea, and César Chávez are added to the curriculum. Similarly, the holidays approach singles out certain days or months—Martin Luther King Jr.'s birthday, Cinco de Mayo, and Black History month are examples (Banks & Banks, 1993). This approach also celebrates cultural elements such as food and dance. Swee Him Toh (1994) in his keynote address to the National Association of Multicultural Educators characterized these cultural elements as the four D's—diet, dress, dance, and dialect.

Level 2 is the additive approach wherein certain multicultural ideas and perspectives are added to the curriculum without changing its basic structure. "The additive approach is often accomplished by the addition of a book, a unit, or a course to the curriculum without changing it substantially. Examples of this approach include adding a book such as *The Color Purple* to a unit on the twentieth century in an English class; the use of the film *Miss Jane Pittman* during a unit on the 1960's, and the addition of a unit on the internment of the Japanese

Americans during a study of World War II in a class on U.S. history" (Banks & Banks, 1993, p. 201). While this approach may be a positive first step, it still usually results in looking at ethnic content from a purely Western perspective.

Level 3 is the Transformative Approach. Unlike the additive approach, the transformative approach requires changing the basic structure of a course. Ideally, it enables students to view concepts and issues from several different ethnic points of view. For example, when students are studying the American Revolutionary War, the transformative approach assures that they view the conflict not only from the colonists' point of view, but also from that of the Americans loyal to Britain, the Native Americans, and the British themselves.

The transformative approach maintains that when studying American music, art, literature, and science, the emphasis should not be merely on the contributions of various ethnic groups to American culture. Rather, the emphasis "should be on how the common U.S. culture and society emerged from a complex synthesis and interaction of the diverse cultural elements that originated within the various cultural, racial, ethnic, and religious groups that make up U.S. society" (Banks & Banks, 1993, p. 204).

Finally, the social action approach, level 4, includes all the elements of the transformative approach, but, in addition, it requires students to act on their knowledge. "Major goals of instruction in this approach are to educate students for social criticism and social change and to teach them decision-making skills" (Banks & Banks, 1993, p. 205).

These four approaches are not necessarily discrete and separate. It is perfectly appropriate for community college faculty to mix and match the approaches in their actual teaching. "One approach, such as the contributions approach, can be used as a vehicle to move to other, more intellectually challenging approaches such as the transformation and social action approaches. It is unrealistic to expect a teacher to move directly from a highly mainstream-centric curriculum to one that focuses on decision making and social action. Rather, the move from the first to higher levels of multicultural content integration is likely to be gradual and cumulative" (Banks & Banks, 1993, p. 207).

A MODEL FOR MULTICULTURAL INFUSION

The model for course infusion presented in Chapter 2 is appropriate and easily adaptable to community college curricula, both arts and sciences and vocational/technical. Like the four levels of infusion suggested by Banks and Banks, the course infusion model developed by Kitano presents progressively more complete levels of infusion, from exclusive to inclusive to transformed. However, in further delineating the elements (content, instruction, assessment, dynamics) and their embodiment in the course syllabus, we have a model directly applicable to higher education. The model provides a blueprint for faculty to check their progress in successfully infusing multicultural perspectives into their curriculum.

The examples of multicultural infusion in the curriculum of various courses taught in the community college that follow will illustrate a full range of integration, from exclusive through transformed. The content, the instructional strategies and activities, the assessment processes, and the classroom dynamics will be at various levels of sophistication. But they have in common a recognition of the importance and a commitment to the necessary effort to make multicultural infusion a reality in the experience of community college students.

MULTICULTURALISM
IN THE CLASSROOM

How does multicultural infusion actually happen? Is it possible to make multiculturalism a part of all curricula? It seems to be easier to see multiculturalism as a part of a history class, or sociology, or literature, than it is to see it as part of math, chemistry, or biology. But infusion implies widespread integration of multicultural concepts and perspectives through the curricula—*all* the curricula.

The examples that follow illustrate infusion in seven different disciplines and services: Music, Sociology, English Composition, Biology, American History, Technical Preparation, and Libraries. The degree of infusion varies.

Music

At the Annual Conference of the National Association for Multicultural Education (NAME) in February 1994, one session centered on participants' expertise in multicultural infusion. During a free-wheeling discussion, an unnamed professor from the New York system relayed his experience with a typical first-year Music 101 course. He taught in Manhattan. He described his classes as a "mini-U.N." Students of every conceivable ethnic and socioeconomic background comprised his introductory courses. What was he asked to teach? An exclusively Western perspective in the great classical tradition. His textbook began with the Middle Ages. Whose Middle Ages? Western European, of course! He was expected to review the established eras of Western music—the Baroque, the Romantic, and so forth. He was to familiarize students with the instruments of the orchestra. He was expected to teach about the string family— violin, viola, bass—with never a reference to the sitar, the zither, or any number of the other stringed instruments not familiar to Western music.

A multicultural approach to introductory music did not mean the exclusion of Western musical traditions and instruments, but it did mean the *inclusion* of non-Western traditions and instruments. How could he accomplish this goal? Surely not with the curriculum materials and textbooks available to him. Rather, he had to create his own text, his own readings, his own examples, a process familiar to those who are committed to genuine multicultural infusion in the curriculum. All too often, existing resources simply will not adequately do the job. This lack of multicultural resources puts a tremendous burden on a knowledgeable music professor, but it asks an almost impossible task of those trained in Western ways who feel a need to infuse multicultural elements into their curricula, and do not have the background or expertise necessary. Consequently they go back to what they know, and the students are the losers.

Another example of multicultural infusion in a music class comes from Donald Roach. He is teaching in a university setting; however, introductory music appreciation is a typical offering in a community college. Roach believes that Western musical traditions should not be demeaned, "but that a greater awareness of all music cultures can evolve to enhance and enrich our appreciation of the cultures of the United States, cultures that reflect the influence of its citizens from all continents" (Roach, 1992, p. 39).

Professor Roach maintains that while students can certainly learn of other cultures through the study of various disciplines, "music seems a national avenue for building knowledge and appreciation of world cultures" (1992, p. 39). He suggests nine learning strategies (pp. 41–42). With a little imagination and creativity, these strategies could be easily applied to other disciplines.

1. "Begin to teach where the students are." Roach suggests that it is reasonable to assume that students are aware of current popular music styles. The instructor can begin by pointing out similarities in rhythm, sound, and instrumentation.

2. "Utilize existing resources on the campus." He is especially enthusiastic about involving international students who are already on most campuses as teaching resources.

3. "Use videotapes, probably the next best musical resource after live performance." He is especially mindful of videos filmed "on location" and the use of authentic native musical instruments.

4. "Assign short papers on a particular musical culture." He then suggests encouraging the student to share that research in an oral presentation to the rest of the class.

5. "Assign small groups to research a musical culture." This strategy has the obvious advantage of asking students to work in teams and thus share their ideas among themselves.

6. "Have students study a composer such as Aaron Copland (USA), Villa-Lobos (Brazil), Tchaikowski (Russia), Vaughan-Williams (United Kingdom), William Grant Still (African American), O-Yo (Japan), Brahms (Germany), and Carlos Chavez (Mexico) to discover how each used the folk music of their own countries in their compositions."

7. "Examine the lives of musical artists or groups for the diverse cultural influences on their compositions and performances." Roach suggests such artists as Harry Belafonte (Jamaica), Segoria (Spain), Louis Armstrong (African American), Woodie Guthrie (USA), Scott Joplin (African American), and Ravi Shankar (India).

8. "Research the folk instruments of a particular culture. This could include the gamelan of Indonesia, the koto of Japan, the drums of Ghana, the mbiora (thumb piano) of Zimbabwe, the balalaika of Russia, the bagpipe of Scotland, the maracas and castanets of Mexico."

9. "Assign individual research projects that require students to study one culture in great detail." He suggests that the students examine not only the music, but also the religion, geography, language, economy, and politics as well.

These two approaches to multicultural infusion in the music curricula have moved beyond the exclusive phase to encompass elements of both the inclusive and the transformed phase. Content is presented through a nondominant perspective and students are asked to reflect upon and assess what they have learned.

Sociology

Professor Bob LaFleur of Clinton Community College (Iowa) has been committed to multicultural education for over two decades. After years of teaching separate courses that brought multicultural education to hundreds of students, he has determined that the separate course is not sufficient. Multicultural infusion—a multicultural thrust to all his courses—had a much better chance of making a genuine change in the lives of students. "We must start," he says, "with the realization we will never fully understand either ourselves or those we might wish to understand" (LaFleur, 1994).

Mr. LaFleur describes his efforts at multicultural infusion: "To effectively infuse Asia studies into the sociology curriculum I began by searching the field for globally oriented texts. There has, for quite some time, been an interest in cross-cultural comparison, but there has not been an equivalent interest in a truly global sociology. Cross-cultural comparison, much as it appears to be open to ideas, opens itself as often to unintended ethnocentrism, simply because of its lack of depth and its failure to grant each understanding in the larger context of the whole of the culture and society it is compared to" (LaFleur, 1994). As part of the infusion process, Mr. LaFleur maintains that faculty development is essential. Without the opportunity to improve their own knowledge and understanding of multiculturalism, no matter how well-intentioned, they cannot educate students with a multicultural perspective. He also maintains that if multiculturalism is truly infused, not just an add-on to a curriculum, multicultural goals must be specifically stated as part of the goals of the course. In his "Principles of Sociology" (1994) course, he includes two supportive multicultural goals as follows:

> To gain insight into the behavior of people of other societies in order to understand our own…to gain a perspective sufficient to relate to the borders of our contemporary reality, borders that no longer neatly coincide with nations— borders that are increasingly global. (from course syllabus, 1994)

Multicultural infusion is most successful when committed faculty members who are well-versed in multicultural perspectives are given the freedom to develop and teach the course as they see fit.

English Composition

Justin A. Odulana of the University of Cincinnati uses a unique strategy applicable to community colleges. In his presentation at the fourth annual conference of the National Association for Multicultural Education on February 11, 1994, Odulana suggests using a mini-project strategy to enhance reading, research, writing, and presentation in a pluralistic and diversified culture.

The mini-project is much like a research paper assignment, but it has an embedded multicultural component. Odulana suggests research methods/elements as topics, but a more easily accessible project would deal with a cultural idea, tradition, icon, and so forth, unfamiliar to the student. An African American, for example, could not choose to write about Martin Luther King, Jr. or the origins of jazz. An Hispanic student could not write about César Chávez. A northern European could not write about Shakespeare or Bach or John Kennedy.

For the project to be most beneficial, the instructor must assure that students seek out a multicultural experience different from their own. Odulana proposes three basic activities for a successful mini-project: 1) select a topic that is not trite or redundant; 2) experience various sources, methods, and styles of research; and 3) decide on a method of presentation of the project to the class through oral report, video, and computer graphics, etc. He follows up the activities by suggesting developmental characteristics that will occur for the learner through such a project: 1) growth and development in an unfamiliar context, 2) interaction with various services of information, and 3) development of the decision making process through having to evaluate the appropriate methods of presentation.

Students will surely benefit from such a creative version of the typical research paper. Faculty can teach all the appropriate research methods and tools, as they would with any research-oriented course. But the added benefit of a multiculturally based topic brings further enrichment to a standard course. The mini-project, thoughtfully done, can offer an opportunity for multicultural infusion in the community college curriculum.

The mini-project exemplifies the course-infusion model. It is exclusive in its reliance on lecture and on the instructor as the purveyor of knowledge. It is inclusive in the assessment choices students have available to them. And it is transformed in that some methods are used that center on the student's experience and knowledge.

Biology

"The curricula of the natural sciences is difficult to infuse with cultural diversity," maintains Stephen Kellogg, professor of biology at Chaffey Community College in Rancho Cucamonga, California. "Beyond covering a sampling of race—or culture—associated genetic diseases, the effort generally is limited to crediting those ethnically diverse researchers who have contributed to the discipline" (Kellogg, 1994, unpaginated).

While a good first effort by any standard and certainly more than most biology teachers would exhibit, it was not enough for Professor Kellogg. He found himself assigned to a room that had recently been remodeled. State-of-the-art audiovisual equipment now was part of the lecture hall where he taught his freshman biology class. He wanted to take advantage of the sound possibilities. He pondered on ways to integrate the music he loved into the biology curriculum. He ultimately decided that he would simply play music as students arrived for class. His account follows:

> It seemed best to start on neutral ground but not pander to popular tastes. I first played a contemporary album of acoustic jazz by Lionel Hampton and the Golden Men of Jazz. The sound level was important, not earsplitting but with a clear presence. I wanted the students to be consciously aware that something unusual was happening; I also decided not to warn them of my new plan. I could hardly wait for

their reaction. Using the programmable CD player, I timed the music to end at the moment class was to begin. On the first day, I walked into class, the music stopped, and I said "good morning" and began the lecture. The students said nothing. They were indifferent. I was disappointed but not defeated.

Each class meeting thereafter I played different types of music, from blues to bluegrass, from Bach to Bartok. Still, there was no reaction. One day I decided to sacrifice my musical standards to force a response; I played music by U2. "Do you like that kind of music?" a young man asked. This meager beginning blossomed into continuing student dialogues. At the end of the term, one student (an avowed "heavy-metal rocker" who had never said a word) asked if I would play "some more of that guy that plays that vibraphone thing." He was referring to Lionel Hampton.

Before each class meeting I now write the name of the composer and/or musical group on the board and prominently display the album cover. One day I played a recording by Kronos String Quartet, *Pieces of Africa*, packaged in a strikingly beautiful African design. The following class meeting a student from Nigeria was wearing an African shirt of much the same design; previously he had worn only western clothing. A coincidence? Maybe, but it occurred to me that perhaps I had stumbled upon a way to bridge some cultural gaps. I asked students to bring music from their home countries—on the condition it not be Euro-American pop, New Age, etc. That term we shared music from Iran, India, Zaire, and the Philippines. (1994)

Applying the course-infusion model, this example is perhaps at best an exclusive approach to infusion. The argument could be made that the music, while a multicultural addition to the curriculum, is just that—an addition. It is certainly not transformative. Nevertheless, Kellogg believes that it has had a beneficial effect on the teaching of biology in a number of ways:

- It provides a topic of conversation for students who do not yet feel comfortable talking about biology.
- It lightens the classroom atmosphere.
- It recognizes and honors the diverse cultural backgrounds of all students. (Kellogg, 1994)

Faculty in biology have unusual opportunities to teach about multiculturalism in a substantive way through the curriculum. Genetics, of course, is the primary discipline in which ethnic differences manifest themselves through concentrations of certain diseases, or specific tendencies based not on geography or nutrition, but on genuine genetic differences. A higher incidence of sickle-cell anemia among African Americans, for example, can be studied in a scientific way. There is a multicultural dimension to biological science that the knowledgeable and sensitive faculty member can use in a positive way to foster wider understanding.

Nutritional habits, eating patterns of various ethnic and racial groups and the results of those patterns on the general health of the group is another way of bringing multicultural perspectives into the biology classroom. For example, it is established that rice-dependent groups, such as the Japanese, tend to have a lower risk of heart attack and similar cardiovascular ailments than those whose cultures include a great deal of meat and animal fat.

In interviews with biology faculty, an overwhelming concern and caution among them is that any such discussions deal strictly with what is a scientific fact or under

serious scientific discussion. Faculty are very much aware of bogus culturally based pseudo-scientific theories that would point to one ethnic or racial group being inferior to another. Faculty have also pointed out that textbooks in the past five years have made concerted efforts to include multicultural perspectives in science. Alert and committed faculty (once again the key to multicultural education), will seek out and use these newer texts.

American History

It is difficult to imagine a more natural—or more difficult—discipline in which to infuse multiculturalism than American history. Appropriately handled by skilled instructors using progressive textbooks, it is possible to provide students with genuine multicultural experiences. For example, teaching Columbus' "discovery" of the "new world" from the perspective of the Native American or the Revolutionary War from the viewpoint of the Loyalists provokes students' thinking.

Martha Bonte (personal interview, February 14, 1994) teaches American history at Clinton Community College in Clinton, Iowa. Many of her students have had—and are likely to have—very limited multicultural exposure. If they are to be well prepared for the world of work, or for transfer to a university where more diversity exists, they need to be a part of a positive multicultural experience. Ms. Bonte lists two imperatives for infusing multiculturalism in the curriculum: 1) the faculty members must be committed to personal and professional development to become multiculturally literate themselves; and 2) careful attention must be given to textbook and reading selections. Through attention to professional development and textbook selection, multicultural experiences can be truly transformative, not merely additive. One textbook she is currently reviewing touts itself as illustrating "the founding of European settlements in the New World with a vignette of seventeenth century Santa Fe, New Mexico…a view of American territorial expansion through the eyes of the Mandan villages of the upper Missouri River in North Dakota, and Reconstruction policies with the experience of African Americans in the Sea Islands of South Carolina" (advertising circular). The textbook summary goes on to say that it makes an effort to cover African Americans, Native Americans, and other multicultural groups from their points of view, rather than that of the Europeans. The narrative takes on the voice of the people involved in the annals of history, and conveys their understanding of events rather than focusing on their "'treatment' by the majority" (Faragher et al., 1994). Such an approach goes beyond representative additives; it infuses a multicultural perspective throughout the classroom experience.

Looking at the course-infusion model, this course, too, is moving from the inclusive to the transformative phase. The instructor is still the primary purveyor of knowledge, but with monitoring to ensure equity in participation. Careful attention has been given to a textbook that is not merely exclusive in its treatment of content; rather, it reconceptualizes the content through a shift in paradigm and presents content through a non-dominant perspective—it is transformed. Furthermore, many different instructional strategies, which include methods that center on student experience, are used. The curricula is moving toward the transformative phase.

Technical Preparation

Technical preparation, or Tech Prep, as it is commonly called, is a national imperative to more closely link the learning of high school students with the needs of a work-

force that is becoming increasingly high tech. Tech Prep involves the careful articulation of competencies and skills learned in high school with those to be learned in a community college technical program. The expectation is that students who are well prepared by their high school experience will move quickly through the community college skills sequence, perhaps being able to skip some of the introductory level courses if the students have indeed mastered agreed-upon competencies while still in high school.

Ideally, the competencies necessary for a specific technical field are determined by a coalition of high school faculty, community college faculty, and business and industry representatives who work in the field. This agreed upon set of competencies is what the student must master in order to be judged capable of entering the workforce in any particular technical/vocational field of endeavor.

Kerber and Folgiani in "Tech Prep: Preparation for Work Force Diversity" cite the 1992 "Report for America 2000" which lists " 'Works with cultural diversity' as a foundational skill and competency for students and workers who want to succeed in the workplace. Specifically, the report specifies that one must work well with men and women who have a variety of ethnic, social, and educational backgrounds. Demonstrating competence in working with cultural diversity involves understanding one's own culture, those of others, and how they differ; respecting the rights of others, making one's own cultural adjustments and helping others do the same when necessary; basing impressions on individual performance, not on stereotypes, and understanding concerns of members of other ethnic and gender groups" (Adams & Welsch, 1993, p. 93).

Tech Prep courses will often emphasize the value of teamwork and have taken a leadership role in advocating and implementing total quality concepts. No study of quality is complete without an understanding of its most successful applications in Japan. The cultural differences between Japan and the United States, their divergent social and economic perspectives, have been the subject of many books. Tech Prep courses, because they are grounded in the global economy, provide an opportunity for multicultural infusion throughout a technical/vocational curriculum. Tech Prep programs offer many opportunities for both inclusive and transformative curricula. The emphasis in Tech Prep on alternatives that focus on student growth and independence, as well as methods that center on student experience, suggest the possibilities for a transformed curriculum.

Library/Learning Resource Center

While the services provided by a library or learning resource center, even when presented through formalized instruction, cannot be characterized as a curriculum, the accessing of information in a library is essential for success in nearly all curricula. Therefore, we include examples of multicultural infusion with the library. Information literacy has emerged as key to occupational and personal success. While many students find libraries to be overwhelming and unfriendly places for a variety of reasons, many minority students have particularly negative experiences. It is, therefore, essential for community college libraries—and librarians—to be truly learning resource centers accessible to everyone.

In describing the new student the library must reach, Downing, MacAdam, and Nichols (1993) describe the contemporary student as "likely to enroll later in life, to return to school after time spent in the workplace, to be Native American, black, Hispanic, Asian, multiracial, female, or non-

heterosexual, to speak English as a second language, to bring a non-Western European cultural perspective, to be at risk for academic failure due to a complex set of economic, social, academic, and cultural barriers inherent in institutions of higher education" (pp. 1–2). Librarians have the responsibility to understand the needs, support the academic development, and provide leadership to move an institution toward being truly multicultural.

Some of the barriers that multicultural students face include "language, technology, limited prior access to libraries, pedagogy designed for the cognitive styles of 'typical' students, and information systems established around unfamiliar conceptual frameworks" (Downing et al., 1993, p. 4). How can librarians reach out to such students? What strategies will help make the library accessible and meaningful? Downing et al. suggest that the most effective strategy to assist multicultural students in becoming comfortable with library materials and processes is through outreach programs.

Probably the most significant change in library use in the past decade has been remote access. It is no longer necessary to have extensive holdings to provide quality service. With a multitude of on-line data bases easily available to academic institutions and individuals alike, with the advent of the information superhighway, with nearly instantaneous international communications via internet, the librarian's job becomes one of facilitator and bridge builder between the technology and the user. However, the proliferation of information available electronically has created new barriers, particularly for those who have not had extensive experience with technology. "If remote system access offers virtually unlimited information resources to the multicultural student, outreach programs are a bridge between student and the library, assuring them the personal and academic support critical to their effective use of information" (Downing et al., 1993, p. 5). Using students to reach students is a proven way to increase both the participation and the comfort level of multicultural students. Peer assistance assumes that in unfamiliar situations, one can be greatly helped by another who is perceived as not being very different from oneself. Someone who has been through similar challenges and becomes successful has much to offer a neophyte. Ethnolinguisitically diverse students, working as peer counselors, advisors, or assistants can help a student with an immediate curriculum-related concern. But more importantly, such interactions can foster a sense of belonging to the larger college community. Peer support is a crucial element in retaining all students, but particularly multicultural students in a community college setting. "As partners in academic support efforts within the library, minority students can help library staff better understand the feelings and needs of the multicultural student community" (Downing et al., 1993, p. 6).

Important peer counselor tasks, for which adequate training and follow-up must be given, are listed and elaborated on by Downing et al. They suggest twelve important functions of what they call "peer information counselors":

1) term paper assistance, 2) bulletin boards and displays, 3) classroom assistance, 4) online catalog training, 5) role models/mentors, 6) bibliographies and other handouts, 7) campus network maintenance, 8) special outreach program assistance, 9) word processing tutorials, 10) assistance with publicity, 11) reference desk services, and 12) special projects. (p. 8)

In their book, *Reaching a Multicultural Student Community*, Downing et al. provide in-depth discussion and examples of each of the twelve functions.

The overriding constant, however, remains that multicultural students frequently have a more difficult time accessing information services. It is the responsibility of the community college to provide the support mechanisms which will not only allow, but also encourage, library and learning resource personnel to be advocates for all community college students. Library services organized with the student at the center and the emphasis on empowerment and student growth represents the inclusive phase of the infusion model moving toward the transformed phase.

CONCLUSION

Multicultural infusion is a concept whose time has come. It is no longer a matter of sensitivity, or a matter of political correctness, or a matter of social activism. It is a cultural, economic, and workforce imperative. Rather than simply reaching to the needs of multicultural students, the course-infusion model that was presented in Chapter 2 encourages higher education to be proactive in developing multicultural curriculum that is truly transformative.

An ideal multicultural curriculum will move from the exclusive phase which gives mainstream experiences and perspectives to the inclusive phase "which adds alternative perspectives through materials, readings and speakers," and finally to the transformed phase which "reconceptualizes the contact through a shift in paradigm...and presents content through nondominant perspective" (Chapter 2). It will include instructional activities and strategies that use a variety of methods and center on students' experiences and knowledge. The successful multicultural curriculum will assess student knowledge and learning through multiple methods, including alternatives that focus on student growth. Finally, the instructor will no longer be seen as the sole purveyor of knowledge. There will be a "change in power structure of the classroom so that students and instructor learn from each other, encouraging students to find their voice" (Chapter 2).

Community colleges, by the nature of their clientele—the high percentage of minority, female, and older students—are ideally positioned to implement a multiculturally infused curriculum. There is, as explained by English instructor Laurie Temple (personal interview, February 14, 1994), "built-in diversity in the classroom, a diversity that is not present in a homogeneous freshman course of white eighteen-year-olds. The community college classroom, with its small class size and individual attention to students, gives learners the opportunity to see through someone else's point of view without feeling threatened or defensive." The community college, "the people's college," must continue to take a leadership role in advancing education that is genuinely multicultural.

CHAPTER 15

Evaluating the Results of Multicultural Education: Taking the Long Way Home

Jeffrey S. Beaudry, Ph.D.
Assistant Professor
Department of Professional Education
University of Southern Maine

James Earl Davis, Ph.D.
Assistant Professor
Department of Educational Studies
University of Delaware

Editor's Notes:
Jeffrey Beaudry and James Davis remind us that, as faculty members, we have a responsibility to evaluate our courses for the purpose of continual improvement. When we make the commitment to modify our courses to incorporate multicultural content, instructional strategies, assessment processes, and/or interactions, we have an additional responsibility to determine the impact of those changes. Evaluation of multicultural course or program change can inspire further transformations and support continued institutional progress. The authors offer fourteen guidelines for engaging in course and program evaluation that also encourage activism in supporting systemic improvement. They argue that without institutional commitment, even dramatic evidence of the efficacy of incorporating multicultural content and processes will have limited impact.

The guidelines extend generic recommendations for course evaluation by including emphases on faculty self-assessment of cultural understanding, integrating evaluation with content, use of evaluation teams that include multicultural expertise, reporting data by all diversity categories, being sensitive to labeling, and developing a systemic view. In presenting their guidelines, the authors review the literature, including available instrumentation for assessing attitude change. They also critique one of Beaudry's own experiences in evaluating a diversity program. They conclude with the idea that evaluating our efforts to incorporate multicultural education in our courses can result in changes to ourselves and our students. ■

In recent years, stories about the nature and impact of multicultural education have appeared with some regularity in higher education media. Competing voices demand more concerted efforts in support of multicultural content and a more diverse faculty on the one hand, and decry these same efforts as infringements upon academic freedom, on the other. As Morey emphasizes in the final chapter, achieving sustained commitment to the value of multicultural education requires building institutional capacity to plan, implement, and evaluate changes that support diversity. In fact, evaluation of outcomes produced by multicultural transformation can lend some objectivity to the passionate debate. In this era of educational reform, the key values of *education for all* and a *commitment to equity* inspire us to understand the meaning, as well as the impact of multicultural education through evaluation. Despite prevailing constraints of limited resources, emerging standards of accountability for multicultural education are expanding the roles expected of faculty and administrators to include evaluation and assessment.

Multicultural evaluation studies are just beginning to be reported in the literature. One reason may be the relative recency of multicultural change efforts; another stems from the complexities involved. As defined in Chapter 1, multicultural education encompasses gender equity; the complex, lifelong development of cultural, ethnic, national, and personal identity; issues of disability; and the effects of social class. Moreover, multicultural education is conceptualized "as a field that consists of 1) content integration, 2) the knowledge construction process, 3) prejudice reduction, 4) an equity pedagogy, and 5) an empowering school culture and social structure" (Banks, 1994b, p. 4). Goals vary from increased achievement of ethnic students and acquisition of new scholarship (content) to valuing of diversity (affect) to working effecting social change (behavior). The unit of evaluation might be a single transformed course (e.g., Chapter 11, introductory economics), an entire program (e.g., Chapter 12, teacher preparation), or an institution (Chapter 16) and involve any number of subject matter disciplines.

Nevertheless, recognition of the moral imperative has encouraged faculty and administrators in higher education to shift the question from "if" to "when and how" multicultural transformation will occur in each course and on each campus. The reforms in higher education now focus on *education for all*, not for the few. However, this is a time for risk-taking and passion mixed with rigorous evaluation and caution. To be culturally competent means at times to proceed carefully, anticipate and learn from controversy, and respectfully allow for the inclusion of multiple perspectives (Yen, 1992).

The purpose of this chapter is to suggest guidelines for evaluating multicultural course change. We begin with a brief review of research in multicultural education to highlight themes and recommendations for evaluation. We then examine specific applications of course evaluation in higher education, concentrating on the conditions, process, and impact of multicultural education on teaching and learning. A sample case in evaluating organizational change illustrates one experience in practice. We conclude with a consideration of multicultural course evaluation within the broader institutional context. Fourteen guidelines for evaluating multicultural change emerge from and are interspersed with these discussions (see Table 15–1).

REVIEWING THE RESEARCH ON MULTICULTURAL EDUCATION

Persistent inquiry is vital to critically probe the assumptions of multicultural education and to expand definitions, strategies, and questions for future research. The knowledge base for multicultural education is developing rapidly. Two recent exemplars of research-based publications are Carl Grant's book *Research and Multicultural Education* (1992), and the *Handbook of Research on Multicultural Education* (Banks & Banks, 1995). With its coherence, strength, and discipline, multicultural education research validates basic concepts, offers definition and critical review, provides concrete examples of promising practices, and assists in raising performance standards for students and faculty.

TABLE 15–1   Guidelines and Suggestions for Evaluating Cultural Infusion

Course Evaluation

- Review the research literature in multicultural education to identify evaluation strategies and useful outcomes.
- Increase the effectiveness of the program by using diverse strategies, lengthening course sequences, and including experiential and field-based learning.
- Understand the connections among beliefs, needs, and goals through self-assessment and then through needs assessment.
- Multiple data sources and data collection methods strengthen inferences and empower stakeholders.
- Comparisons strengthen evaluation findings.
- Integrate evaluation with course content whenever possible.
- Reciprocal benefits occur for students, faculty and administrators engaging in multicultural team-building activities.

Institutional Culture and Context— Systemic Evaluation

- Establish and monitor a positive campus climate, include a focus on explicit support for cultural diversity.
- Evaluate benefits and costs.
- Identify diverse audiences and customize variations on evaluation reports.
- Support diverse, ethnic scholars.
- Be sensitive to the side effects of labeling students by racial categories.
- Publish enrollment data with breakdowns by cultural/ethnic and gender breakdowns.
- Develop a systemic evaluation perspective to multicultural education.

Guideline #1: Review the Research Literature in Multicultural Education to Identify Useful Outcomes and Evaluation Strategies

Faculty members frequently raise the question of how multicultural education can improve the quality of teaching and learning in a given course. The integration of multicultural education with teaching, learning, and assessment has been discussed in previous chapters. This chapter seeks to extend and deepen the understanding of evaluation of courses and programs. One way to assess the strength of multicultural education is to sample the reviews of literature on this topic (Beaudry, 1992; Banks, 1994b). Two reviews merit particular consideration because they clarify the types of outcomes examined in the literature on multicultural education and employed empirical criteria for their selection of studies. Sleeter and Grant (1987) used a vote-count procedure to rate the outcomes of ten empirically based research articles. They found that

> 90 percent of the studies measured changes in attitudes, particularly negative prejudice toward minority racial and ethnic groups. Measures of multicultural knowledge were examined in 30 percent of the studies, while teachers' behaviors were examined in 20 percent of the studies. Of the measured outcomes, 50 percent showed improvement and 50 percent showed mixed results immediately after coursework. In follow-up measures, changes in knowledge and changes in attitudes were reversed and showed a decline to original, pre-program levels. (Beaudry, 1992, p. 77)

The second review, by Grant and Secada (1989), focused strictly on examining the effects of multicultural education on preservice and inservice teacher education programs. Their selection criteria specified that the research had to have a design that included a comparison group and that the field be limited to preservice and inservice education. The types of outcomes studied were changes in participants' attitudes and knowledge and their adoption of appropriate teaching and learning behaviors. Analyses indicated that 52 percent of the studies on preservice teacher education reported positive outcomes; approximately 42 percent for inservice. "Some of the findings are that length and intensity of the program were positively correlated with increasing multicultural knowledge and changing attitudes, that courses were more effective than workshops, and that two or more courses (especially combined with field experiences) were more effective than just one" (Beaudry, 1992, p. 77).

Beaudry's (1992) review of research questioned the value of quantitative synthesis of the multicultural education research literature. The meta-analysis technique initially considered was abandoned for the reason that it blends results without adequate reflection on the cultural validity of the methods and results. In a symposium on multicultural validity, House (1992) argued that even to think of using meta-analysis was an assimilationist strategy, one that was antithetical to liberationist ideology and critical theory and therefore unsuited to understanding multicultural validity. Certainly measurement has been abused by eugenic theorists to the detriment of women, people of color, the disabled, and low socioeconomic class (Gould, 1981).

Meta-analysis may represent the extreme in reductionist research methods by creating a single index or metric at the expense of richer, contextual understanding and combining disparate findings. Meta-analysis may mask a study's ill-defined research topic, for example, or may not be feasible due to insufficient numbers of research studies or poor statistical reporting (Beaudry, 1992). However, research reviews are a powerful, though taken-for-granted evaluation tool.

Evaluation of multicultural education cannot be restricted to descriptive and qualitative methods as the sole means of constructing and validating our new models and new meanings. Ongoing research reveals continuing disciplined efforts to build a knowledge base in multicultural education. Is meta-analysis a standard for judging the maturity of the multicultural education literature (Walberg, 1985)? The whole issue over meta-analysis remains a highly charged, unanswered question. A relevant example is the fierce debate prompted by Willig's favorable conclusions on the effectiveness of bilingual education (1985) and the critical response by Baker (1987). It is not simply a matter of the preferred and defensible method of inquiry. Rather, evaluation is linked with the politics of deciding what is worthwhile. It is in dialogue and argument that we challenge our knowledge, values and commitment to evaluating multicultural education research literature. In conclusion, knowing the paradigms of multicultural education can contribute directly to course and program design, evaluation, and subsequent theorizing.

Guideline #2: Increase the Effectiveness of Teaching Multicultural Education by Lengthening Courses and Including Experiential and Field-based Learning

There are elements in the design of courses and programs for multicultural education that increase effectiveness (Banks, 1994a; Grant & Secada, 1989). For example, courses taught in conjunction with fieldwork and hands-on experiences have demonstrated greater effectiveness than stand-alone courses (Grant, 1981; Ladson-Billings, 1991). Having multicultural field-based experiences in teacher education is currently a standard supported by the National Council for Accreditation of Teacher Education (NCATE, 1990). Undergraduate courses designed as long-term immersion in Native American tribal cultures revealed tremendous effects (Mahan, 1982; Noordhoff & Kleinfeld, 1991). Even a single course of sufficient length (4 or more credits) and depth is likely to make a difference on teachers' classroom behaviors as indicated by Sleeter's analysis of teachers' behaviors and the credits received in human relations (1985). Based on the evaluation of multicultural education courses, offering options to students in courses may be advantageous. For example, Noordhoff and Kleinfeld (1991) and Ahlquist (1992) indicated that dialogue and reflective writing were not sufficiently motivating, even when mixed with field experiences. Noordhoff and Kleinfeld added videotaping to the experience and reflection and seemed to achieve better results (1991).

These learnings can be transferred to professional programs in health care, law, and engineering. Still, faculty members' skepticism and often their personal biases represent a continuing challenge to integrating equity and ethnic and cultural identity issues into their courses. It is a continuous challenge to sustain the developmental interaction between attitude and action.

Excitement over positive short-term results should be tempered by recent research findings. Again, studies have indicated that short-term workshops and minicourses (Adeeb, 1994) have limited success. This caution also applied to a series of inservice workshops to support implementation of school-wide programs (Sleeter, 1992) aimed at reduction of prejudice in teachers and students. As McGee Banks noted, "To a great extent, we know what to do. What we seem to lack is the ability to act" (1993, p. 43). How can the strenuous and risk-filled task of evaluating results assist in efforts to change attitudes and actions? If we are thinking about how to incorporate multicultural themes in our courses, how do we strengthen the design of teaching and learning and evaluation?

APPLICATIONS OF EVALUATION PRINCIPLES TO MULTICULTURAL INFUSION IN COURSES AND PROGRAMS

In this section specific guidelines for evaluating multicultural education will be discussed. These critical concepts focus on: 1) self-assessment of sensitivity and understanding of cultural diversity by faculty and students, 2) triangulation of data sources and methods, 3) applications of evaluation models that incorporate comparison groups and multiple measures (i.e., use of baseline and follow-up data collection), 4) integrating course content with evaluation, and 5) inclusion of multiple stakeholders on evaluation teams.

Guideline #3: Understand the Connections Among Beliefs, Needs, and Goals Through Self-assessment, Then Through Needs Assessment

Efforts to infuse cultural diversity into higher education focus on two key stakeholders—students and teachers. Faculty members must reflect on their own cultural and cross-cultural beliefs and assumptions before trying to influence their students' beliefs (Banks, 1994b). Faculty can seek out professional development opportunities, consult the literature, and begin to conduct classroom-based inquiry into multicultural education.

As an essential first step to design or to infuse multicultural education in a course, faculty members must first think about and clarify their own personal, ethnic, cultural, and national identity. The critical, implicit need is for faculty members to develop cross-cultural competencies (Banks, 1994b; Larke & McJamerson, 1990). How to get started is a matter of resolve, since resources are readily available through literature, videos, and professional associations like the

National Association of Multicultural Education.

It is also necessary to assess student needs, as this information will provide the rationale for creating reasonable goals. (See Stecher & Davis, 1987). Some questions can be answered through needs assessment: What is it that multicultural education approaches can provide that will change and benefit students? Is your location one of rural isolation or urban center? What are the implications for the course? For the university? Is the university community (i.e., students and parents, faculty, administrators, and staff) predominantly White, of mixed cultural and ethnic background, gender, and social class? Specifically for the course, what are the purposes and goals to be attained? Is the focus to be some combination of attitudes and awareness, behaviors, and knowledge? What types of classroom experiences will be used to demonstrate and model the desired goals? What are the acceptable standards for judging multicultural education outcomes (See Stufflebeam, McCormick, Brinkerhoff, & Nelson, 1985)?

In some colleges and universities, the need for multicultural education may already be established, and faculty can rely on this work to justify changes in courses. For example, there may already be strategies for dealing with language-different students, for faculty with English as a native language and as a second language (see Chapter 7). A college may have developed a cadre of students, faculty, and administrators who would serve as a resource for translation of documents and interviews. If a needs assessment has not been completed, the research literature can provide the initial rationale for making research-based changes.

Guideline #4: Multiple Data Sources and Data Collection Methods Strengthen Inferences and Empower Stakeholders

Use of diverse evaluation strategies strengthens any recommendations and inferences. Triangulation of multiple data sources and data collection methods is a major goal for multicultural evaluation. Stratified sampling is important and in some cases, over-sampling the groups of interest. (See Henry, 1990, *Practical Sampling*). Key factors in survey research are the sample size and sampling strategy. As mentioned above, evaluation can add a significant component to students' understanding of quality if it is integrated with teaching and learning activities. Again, faculty should evaluate change in manageable steps and through well-researched field tests before implementing complex designs with lengthy, comprehensive surveys (Scriven, 1975).

Faculty may choose to measure general attitudes, knowledge, and behaviors solely with quantitative instruments. Survey instruments like the *Cultural Diversity Awareness Inventory*; the *Cross-cultural Adaptability Inventory* (Kelley & Meyers, 1992); the *Bogardus Social Distance Scale*; the *Diversity Awareness Profile* (Grote, 1994), and socio-demographic profiles of participants have been the most frequent choices. Contreras (1988) and Wayson (1988) used another set of instruments including the *Multi-Factor Attitude Inventory*; the *Multicultural Education Survey*; the *Ethnic History and Cultural Awareness Survey*; and the *Multicultural Teaching Scale*. While valuable for evaluation, many of these instruments are new, and little is known about their validity and reliability. That is, few of these instruments have been used and replicated in other studies, leaving big gaps in knowledge about their psychometric properties (e.g., latent factors and expected results or norms). For this reason, it becomes even more critical to obtain information about the surveys directly from authors and from the literature.

Surveys can be modified to suit the specific interests of faculty. For example, a faculty member may wish to use only the items pertaining to the culturally diverse family from the twenty-six items on the *Cultural Diversity Awareness Inventory*. Consisting of twenty-six items, the instrument contains five sections: 1) cultural awareness and acceptance of people who are culturally different, 2) the relationship with culturally different parents and families, 3) perceptions of difficulties in cross-cultural communications, 4) issues related to assessment, and 5) creating a multicultural environment using multicultural methods and materials (Larke & McJamerson, 1990). To increase the usefulness and meaning of these items, the user should provide space after each item for comments and explanation and ask students to write their reflections about each item. The instructor should take the time to assist students in responding to the surveys in order to maximize thoroughness and minimize missing data, and to decrease the threat of not knowing how this information will be used.

A very promising approach provides more linkage of surveys with interviews by using the same or modified items for interview protocols (Morgan, 1993). Frequently evaluators adapt existing instruments or are compelled to create new instruments. As yet there are few well-accepted measures for multicultural education use. The specific development of questions for surveys is one of fascination and inspiration, initially linked to issues of content, construct, and face validity. A search of ERIC produced a growing cache of multicultural evaluation instrumentation. What may be useful now would be further rigorous reviewing of these instruments from a multicultural education perspective to strengthen construct validity. Another useful activity would be to focus on the process of translating instruments from English into other languages. Attending to this process involves forward translation (from English into the second

language), as well as back translation (second language to English). From a multicultural education perspective, the two-way procedure addresses face validity and content validity issues.

Surveys, while efficient, represent a limited choice of data collection methods. Especially in a sensitive area like multicultural education, a need exists to verify results of surveys with observations or by review of documents. It would be useful to determine the "amount of over-reporting and under-reporting of behavior by checking respondents' reports with external records" (Bradburn & Sudman, 1979, p. 164). The existence of cultural differences in perspectives suggests that it would be useful to have respondents rate the topics to understand their perceptions of the topics' importance and how comfortable they feel talking about or responding to various issues. For example, in many models of multicultural education the family and parental involvement in education are central themes. Parents assume very different roles in various cultures, and responses to direct questions may create discomfort in students (Campbell, 1994). One way to arrange an interview or a survey on perceived threatening topics is to create a scenario depicting a problematic situation and ask students to respond to the situation as a member of their cultural or ethnic group. Padilla (1993) gives an excellent example of using the narrative vignette, "Josefina Goes To College," as a stimulus to guide discussions in focus groups of Hispanic undergraduate students. Based on the dialogue prompted by the vignette, researchers identified two themes: the struggle to achieve an education and overcome internal and external barriers and the difficulty of maintaining an ethnic identity (Padilla, 1993).

A significant reason for evaluating courses for multicultural education is to search for and understand the influences of culture, ethnicity, gender, and social class on achievement and success in school. One of the most persistent themes in the research in multicultural education is the preference for anthropological inquiry methods (i.e., interviews, participant-observation) in evaluating cultural diversity in courses (Arvizu & Saravia-Shore, 1990). This trend does not signify a call advocating cultural relativism. Rather the value of anthropological approaches is that field methods like ethnography have provided face-to-face, in-depth understanding of complex issues while preserving the language, values, and customs of ethnic groups, cultures and societies (Fetterman, 1989). Investigating the complex question of whether ethnic or cultural groups define cultural and language differences as barriers to overcome, or as "markers for collective identity that must be maintained" (Ogbu, 1990, p. 428) will necessitate some combination of qualitative and quantitative methods.

The process of asking key stakeholders for their perceptions about cultural diversity then facilitates the crossing of cultural, ethnic, gender, language, and social class boundaries "without feeling threatened" (Ogbu, 1990, p. 429). The issue of being threatened is a real one which must be protected first by procedures in human subjects research, especially confidentiality and participants' informed consent. For example, the use of *race* as a category for discrimination and categorical breakdowns of data today are extremely sensitive issues which result in students receiving mixed messages (Davis, 1992). While requesting racial self-identification has provided a categorical scheme for ensuring equal opportunity, the practice has serious psychological side effects on bicultural students (Belgarde, 1994) and confounds the vision of multicultural education which seeks to deal directly with attitudes and behaviors exhibiting negative prejudice of one group over

another. Belgarde indicated that Native American students were particularly vulnerable to the dual loss of identity and the ceremony and appropriate community events (1994). Evaluation must relate to the academic and social activities of students (Padilla, 1993).

In addition to one-to-one interviews and observations, focus group interviewing of five to eight students represents an alternative, group strategy for inquiring into students' thinking before, during, and/or after a course (Krueger, 1988; Morgan, 1993). Morgan and Krueger (1993) suggest that focus groups be used for evaluation and research and not for building consensus, resolving conflict, or making decisions. Faculty can have another trained interviewer moderate the focus group to allow for dialogue by students whose culture and background may foster reluctance to criticize their teacher. As mentioned above, the prompts for focus groups can be questions or narrative vignettes (Padilla, 1993). The focus group approach may lead to the development and improvement of written survey items and to individual interviews (Morgan & Kreuger, 1993).

The payoff from in-depth data collection strategies may reside in the power of communications and language to convey the complex and sensitive issues relating to cultural diversity. The challenge is to honor the process and participants by devoting the time and resources for thorough data analysis and interpretation. In higher education there may be resources available in graduate students who are interested in multicultural education. In addition to moderating and observing, students can be invaluable as translators. Cummins (1986) argues forcefully that teachers and students should learn in, and in this case be evaluated in their native language and English. Using interviews and face-to-face data collection strategies encourages students to form significant contacts and relationships with faculty (Padilla, 1993). In this way, the data collection becomes a part of the program intervention.

Guideline #5: Comparisons Strengthen Evaluation Findings

The strength of evaluation findings for a group of students in a course can be enhanced significantly by establishing a comparison with other groups or by comparing changes over time, as in a pre- and post-test evaluation design. Or, data from interviews and surveys can be compared with data from other groups, resulting in a quasi-experimental design (Cook & Campbell, 1979). Employing a comparison group constitutes one of the most worthwhile techniques for strengthening the evaluation design. Analysis of the composition of the groups by gender, ethnicity (particularly language use), and level of education is vital for comparison. For example, attitudes of business managers were compared with business-major students after they were given a short diversity education course. No significant improvement "in attitudes towards diversity on the basis of age, gender, race/ethnicity was found for business managers, while gender accounted for the only significant difference in business-major students, with females improving their attitudes" (Samiian, p. viii, 1994).

An even stronger evaluation model takes advantage of multiple measures and repeated data collection. The repeated measures design for small groups and the longitudinal or time series design are extensions of pre-test and post-test, with additional measures at selected intervals (Cook & Campbell, 1979). As earlier mentioned, interviews conducted at the beginning and end of courses can be an important starting point for course evaluation, as repeated interviews contribute to in-depth understanding and a validating of students' perceptions. Follow-up measures and observations that take place six months or a year or two years after the educational experiences add even more weight to arguments for supporting multicultural education. Follow-up measures of students, or impact evaluation, may consist of surveys or observations of classroom behaviors, assessment of work-place climate, and attitudes. Universities can employ institutional research departments to facilitate the identification of comparison groups, sampling strategies for evaluation, survey design, and even data collection and analysis.

Guideline #6: Integrate Evaluation with Course Content Whenever Possible

In addition to developing multiple assessment measures, evaluation strategies can be extremely beneficial if they are integrated with teaching activities. A suggestion for integrating teaching and evaluation is to involve students in developing and understanding the criteria for assessing quality. That is, plan the time to seek out student perceptions of activities by debriefing after midterm tests, simulations, and selected lectures. After a test, instructors might allow students to see their test, talk through the answers and questions, and promote a dialogue in which instructors justify their beliefs and assumptions with the students as they construct their understanding of the subject matter. The potential threat to instructors' authority can be outweighed by the critical awareness of the connection between evaluation and pedagogy, especially the pervasive image that tests contain secret, privileged information. It is vital for faculty to take the risk as an evaluator to be forced to justify their beliefs to various audiences (students first!) concerning the connections between subject matter and evaluation. This step toward equalizing power relations supports faculty efforts to transform the instructional component of a course (see Chapter 2).

Use of cooperative learning strategies for inclusive instruction can also support evaluation (Chapter 5). Cooperative groups provide a venue for applying open-ended assessment strategies advocated by cognitive-based instruction (Mercer, 1989). For example, in mathematics the evaluative questions could focus on four dimensions of classroom activities: 1) content or conceptual understanding, 2) procedural knowledge, 3) strategies to solve problems, and 4) communications. For each of these criteria a set of scales would be constructed representing substantive requirements indicating varying degrees of success (Stenmark, 1989, p. 17).

Another principle of multicultural education is to use simulations and experiential learning for instruction, assessment, and course evaluation. For example, in-class theater can bring experience directly into the classroom. Students can direct, act in, and re-write dialogue. If students read Sartre's *No Exit* or Ntozake Shange's *For Colored Girls Who Have Considered Suicide When the Rainbow Is Enuf*, they can dramatize different parts, re-write dialogue individually or problem-solve as a group, and reflect on their experience. Evaluating these activities can occur through an observation instrument developed over the time span of two or three courses through focus group debriefing interviews.

Guideline #7: Students, Faculty, and Administrators May Benefit from Team-building

Depending on the characteristics of the students, instructor, and course content, a team of individuals with relevant expertise might provide a more valid and comprehensive evaluation than any single individual can offer. For example, evaluating the impact of

multicultural change intended by a course on second language development taken by students with diverse cultural backgrounds may benefit from someone with expertise in the students' languages and culture as well as persons with expertise in the course content and in evaluation. The team approach to evaluating multicultural education has been used by researchers like Slaughter (1991) who involved "language different stakeholders in cross-cultural evaluation teams" (Beaudry, 1992, p. 82). It is also suggested that a support team of faculty be available for translation of instructional materials, interview transcripts, examinations, and surveys. The team members might be the instructor/evaluator and representative students or colleagues.

A VIGNETTE: LANGUAGES, COMMUNICATIONS, AND CULTURAL/ETHNIC IDENTIFICATION IN A MULTICULTURAL EDUCATION COURSE

As a professor at a university in New York City, the first author had the opportunity to teach and evaluate a course offered to participants in the Teacher Opportunity Corps, a program to recruit minorities into teaching. I was challenged by the issues of language competencies and cultural definitions of key concepts. The program provided academic as well as social support through campus-based activities. The academic program consisted of two courses, one entitled *Multicultural Education* and the second *Teaching the At-risk Child*. The implied relationship of these concepts led me to question the assumptions and beliefs of these courses as they were taught by the instructors and interpreted by the participants. The course instructor for *Teaching the At-risk Child* was an African American woman. I am a White, Euro-American male and taught the course on multicultural education. I am multilingual, speaking German and Arabic and have lived in Latin America, Europe, and in Egypt where I worked three years as an instructional technology consultant.

I outlined a two-year study for evaluating this effort. The first step to evaluating the course was to develop a database of demographic background information on all students. The evaluation design focused on three questions: 1) As a result of the course, what was the students' understanding of the terms *multicultural education* and *at-risk* student? 2) Did improvements occur in students' self-esteem and perception of education? 3) Did improvements occur in students' attitudes about cultural diversity, as measured by the *Cultural Diversity Awareness Inventory*? The primary data sources were the students and the faculty.

The first part of the evaluation was to be based on individual student interviews at the end of the course. All 21 students were interviewed by experienced graduate research assistants during the final three weeks of the semester. The interviews were taped, transcribed, and analyzed with The *Ethnograph*, a computer-based text-analysis program. Questions on the interview protocol focused on their definitions of the key terms—multicultural education and at-risk students. How had their field experiences assisted them in understanding these terms? If the students spoke another language, was there a clear translation of these terms? Most of the bilingual students were Spanish-speaking. Did they have a term like at-risk in their vocabulary? What was their experience in school; did they have teachers of the same cultural or ethnic background as role models? Did they think that matching students based on cultural or ethnic background made a difference? The analysis of the interviews occurred after the course was completed. Participation in the interviews was mandatory and accounted

for 10 percent of their final grade. Interviews were conducted with each cohort of students in the course.

While the content of the students' interviews was not part of their course grade, the process of interviewing produced some very significant findings and side effects. Students were curious as to why their opinion mattered, as though it was part of their grade. This concern prompted discussion about the need for evaluating participants' perceptions. Even though most students had grown up in New York City, they had very few, if any role model teachers of the same ethnic or cultural background. They expressed highly divergent opinions about intentionally matching students and teachers based on ethnicity and culture. Some students felt threatened by the questions dealing with matching students based on ethnicity and culture. Finally, when asked to translate the term "at-risk," bilingual Spanish-speaking students seemed to be unfamiliar with a Spanish term that would have a similar meaning. The students' overwhelming response was that the term did not have any straightforward translation. Checking with Spanish-speaking colleagues confirmed that there was difficulty in defining and translating this term.

Administering and evaluating the surveys was more efficient but also incurred difficulties. As part of the evaluation of the Teacher Opportunity Corps program, all students were asked to complete the Coopersmith Self-esteem Inventory and Schutz's Val-Ed (FIRO) and FIRO-B. The results of these surveys indicated no changes in students' self-esteem or perceptions of education based on pre- and post-course measures. In some cases, students became resentful of the continuous barrage of surveys and forms to complete. Students suggested that more time be spent discussing the purposes, the language of the surveys, and assumptions in order to increase the usefulness of the results. In essence, the survey method as an evaluation tool was a topic of intense interest, and the discussion revolved around the measurement issues of face validity and construct validity. An indicator of students' uncertainty and ambivalence to the surveys was the inconsistency of some respondents as shown by inflated lie scale scores on the self-esteem inventory.

Results from the *Cultural Diversity Awareness Inventory* were designed to be a part of the course, and concepts were directly related to course-teaching activities. Pre- and post-course surveys of each group indicated little change. However, comparing different cohorts showed significant differences in areas of parents and families and in the effects of cross-cultural communications. Even more compelling was the tremendous difference in survey results when comparisons were made between the predominantly White, female sample reported by Larke and McJamerson (1990) and our very culturally and ethnically mixed urban samples. This finding was especially significant because it suggested that we pursue further study of the linkage between students' background and experience and type of community—urban, suburban, rural—with variables related to changes in attitudes.

As a whole, the results clearly attest to the need for the faculty/evaluator and students to interact as partners in the evaluation from the course's inception. What could I have done differently? As junior faculty we could have worked more closely together, but the constraints of teaching, research, and raising families seemed to conspire against our collaboration. I could have used focus group interviews to accommodate cultural learning patterns related to the benefits of group learning for African Americans (Shade, 1982) and Latinos (Rakow & Bermudez, 1993). The qualitative evaluation design could have been improved by sampling. By

the same token, students could have interviewed each other, and we could have used these analyses for reflection and improvement. Empowering students to think reflectively was an evaluation objective.

A persistent question in multicultural education concerns the effects of matching teachers and students by ethnicity and culture. On the one hand we should seek to integrate classrooms and experience. Yet, matching students and teachers is perceived as beneficial for social as well as academic integration (Beaudry, 1990). This is an issue for teachers as well as evaluators (Delgado-Gaitan, 1993). While it is not necessary to have multilingual competency, knowledge of cultural diversity can provide the foundation for trust and understanding that is necessary for evaluation and research.

EVALUATING MULTICULTURAL CHANGE WITHIN THE INSTITUTIONAL CONTEXT

What are some of the persistent themes in this literature? Evaluating multicultural education should be a developmental process, based on the construction of knowledge between and among faculty, students, and administrators. In designing the evaluation of multicultural education, it is suggested that faculty begin with the breadth-first approach to gain understanding of multicultural literature and clarify personal cultural and cross-cultural values. After this step, faculty should take on in-depth evaluation of courses to explore the value of integrative, interdisciplinary, and experiential teaching and learning experiences.

But previous research findings indicate that if positive changes in teacher attitudes and practices are not accompanied by organizational learning, the innovations dissipate (Chapter 16; Beaudry, 1992; Sleeter, 1992). A few faculty can achieve astonishing results and not be accepted or supported by their college or university. Even where multicultural scholarship is well established there can be negative reactions to campus changes supportive of diversity. A similar, disturbing trend was also observed by Warshaw, Olson, and Beaudry (1991). In their study of bilingual programs in elementary schools, the more complete and pervasive the program, the more polarized the participants, especially the monolingual teachers. Administrators often were the limiting factor in the implementation of programs supporting cultural diversity. With faculty members committed to revising courses, what can colleges and universities do to facilitate the improvement of multicultural education through evaluation? The following discussion outlines issues and evaluation strategies for administrators and faculty at the college and institution level. Integrated guidelines focus on obtaining central administrative support and commitment to resources; considering the audiences for evaluation reporting; supporting ethnic scholars; considering the impact of labeling; reporting enrollment data by all categories of diversity; and developing a systemic view.

Guideline #8: Establish a Positive Campus Climate by Getting the University Administration to Be Explicit About Their Support of Multicultural Education

First, the values of multicultural education must be accepted by department heads, deans, and presidents. A great deal of pressure is removed from individual faculty if multicultural education is justified through needs assessment and strategic planning by the university administrators. In this manner, the institution acknowledges that multicultural values are important and relevant, and university-wide needs assessment and planning can produce standards to evaluate desired outcomes.

Accomplishing a thorough needs assessment at the institutional level will facilitate other actions taken by encouraging more faculty to change courses. (Needs assessment data also provide excellent background for grant-writing.) Those interested in evaluation will be able to more clearly assess whether their course goals are unrealistically high or unnecessarily low. As a result, faculty, administrators, and evaluators can risk raising the standards of judgment regarding multicultural education results.

A promising example of bringing needs assessment together with cultural diversity can be found in the collection of possible strategies for change in the *Resource Guide for Assessing Campus Climate* (California Postsecondary Education Commission, 1992). The measurement strategies and instruments are presented, and strengths and weaknesses for evaluation are considered. The California Postsecondary Education Commission completed a three-year study "on the feasibility of developing an educational equity assessment system designed to obtain information on the perceptions of institutional participants about their campus climate" (1992, p. I). Needs assessment is a very essential and powerful evaluation tool that can have important effects on multicultural education.

Related to institutional leadership is the more specific concern of encouraging faculty research and evaluation on multicultural course and program change. One strategy involves the targeting of funding opportunities and special recognition for such endeavors. An additional consideration is university requirements governing human subjects. It is critical to ensure that evaluation of courses, also a research endeavor, is allowed and facilitated by university and faculty regulations. Evaluating courses could be considered action research, so that rules and restrictions may apply.

Guideline #9: Encourage Institutional Commitment to Benefits and Costs of Multicultural Education

Changes to incorporate multicultural education require long-term support in terms of both time and money as well as a formidable political will. While there are few data about resource support of multicultural education, a leading institution for innovation and sound education, Alverno College, "spends about 3 percent of its operating budget to research and improve its programs, a relatively large amount for an institution of higher education" (Ann Bradley in the May 11, 1994 issue of *Education Week*) What level of resources and funding are required to support research and implementation of multicultural education? Infusion means resource support, a very clear, measurable indicator of institutional commitment.

Guideline #10: Clarify the Audiences for Evaluation Reports

The purpose for evaluation and the audience that will receive the report are highly connected. Typically, faculty members choose to evaluate the impact of their efforts to integrate multicultural content and strategies in a course in order to satisfy their professional curiosity about the effects of multicultural change in general and to derive information for self-improvement. In such cases, the audience should be the faculty member or the faculty member and students.

However, additional audiences can benefit from course evaluation. An accumulation of evaluations can further the knowledge base for professionals in higher education and the specific content fields who are seeking to engage in multicultural course change (see Morris, Fitz-Gibbon & Freeman, 1987). In addition, evaluations of course and program modifications to support diversity can enhance the institution's self-study for accreditation agencies in the various disciplines. Finally, university administrators might find the reports useful for data-driven decisions and risk-taking.

Guideline #11: Support Ethnic Scholars

We suggested earlier that evaluation teams might benefit from the expertise of ethnic scholars. However, the recruitment of minority scholars must occur as a process of building evaluation capacity, and not as coercing available minority faculty who may have other interests and little time to spare (Padilla, 1994). Padilla argues that unless the minority scholar has teaching or research interests in the evaluation project, the extra work in the capacity of translator or emergency counselor may be likened to the imposition of a tax due to cultural background. Administrators who are not sensitive to this issue "fail to understand that ethnic issues cannot be turned on and off like a faucet" (Padilla, 1994, p. 26). The lesson is twofold: we must understand that faculty have their own interests, and we must request faculty consent and be ready to accept "no" as an answer.

Guideline #12: Be Sensitive to the Side Effects of Labeling and Affirmative Action

How have labels been incorporated in multicultural research and evaluation? This question has relevance in terms of the accuracy of our interpretations of data and consequent policy decisions. More specific requests for students to self-identify by selecting census categories can communicate a disregard for complex issues of cultural and ethnic identification (including assimilation, bi-culturalism, and bi- or multi-racialism).

Affirmative Action is a program which is iconoclastic and controversial. Disaggregation of data according to census categories is a process with sociological as well as psychological consequences for individuals depending on their ethnic or cultural identity. What are the implications of disaggregating data and the act of labeling (Davis, 1992; Belgarde, 1994)? In one case, careful scrutiny of the admissions records for Asian Americans shifted the discourse from the stereotyped view of Asian Americans being overrepresented in graduate school to an informed evaluation based on records. In fact, Asian Americans were underrepresented in graduate schools. Through litigation the participants redefined the problem (Takaki, 1992, p. 9). Technical issues may drive continuing quantifying and categorizing of groups for the sake of program support, but there may be a price to pay.

Guideline #13: Publish Enrollment Data with Breakdowns by Gender, Culture, Ethnicity, and Social Class in All Reports

At the risk of belaboring the point, it is important to include gender and social class as well as culture and ethnicity in multicultural evaluation. In an evaluation of activities by the Holmes consortium of universities, Fuller (1992) realized too late that all of the institutional evaluation emphasis was on ethnicity and culture and not on gender or social class.

What is the composition of the classroom by gender, by cultural or ethnic background, by age and experience? It may be that teacher preparation courses have a predominance of White female students. However, upper division organic chemistry, physics, and calculus courses may reflect a predominance of White male students. It is useful to have breakdowns of course enrollments by culture and ethnicity as well. What is the match between students and teachers based on culture, ethnicity, language, gender, and social class? How can this knowledge be respectfully acknowledged and become a part of the classroom or part of change efforts?

Guideline #14: Develop a Systemic Perspective of Multicultural Education

The idea of systemic improvement, not systematic change, has been documented (e.g., Fullan, 1991). Hagans, Crohn, Walkush, and Nelson (1992) developed five analytic dimensions and questions useful for evaluating systemic im-provement related to multicultural change: 1) infusion—is the improvement accepted within components of the existing system? 2) pervasive—does the improvement spread throughout the entire system? 3) potent—does the improvement have the power and robustness to make visible desired processes and outcomes? 4) coherence—is there increased close coupling and stronger, more diverse relationships between and among components? and 5) sustainable—do the components become a part of and improve the culture and climate of the system?

Adding the following two dimensions and questions to the evaluation of institutional progress with respect to other goals will help ensure changes that are also responsive to diversity: 6) multicultural—does the proposed improvement focus on the social agenda addressing gender, culture, ethnicity, and social class; is it explicit in accepting inclusion and respectful of diversity? 7) reflective and transformative—how can we evaluate and hold the system accountable? A systemic perspective is important for evaluating results of multicultural infusion because long-term change can be expected only to the extent that the values are solidly imbedded in the complex, varied components that comprise a higher education organization.

CONCLUDING COMMENTS

Banks proposes that individuals should analyze their own cross-cultural behavior

(1994b). Applying this dictum to evaluating courses for multicultural change, we suggest that instructors consult the resources mentioned in previous discussions, consider questions that connect with their own interests, and seek to integrate teaching and learning, cultural knowledge and content, and evaluation.

There is the suspicion that interest and commitment to multicultural education is not sufficient to overcome other competing needs (Sleeter, 1992). Apparently, the need has been broadly accepted but not manifested in action. This discrepancy between talk and action may be the most recurring theme of evaluation applied to multicultural change. Why is this the case? As part of implementing and evaluating multicultural course change, all faculty must seek to understand their own cultural, gender, and social class biases. Further, we must directly examine our own constructions of these terms as evidenced in both our ideas and actions. If we collectively force consistency between our constructs and behaviors in favor of multicultural change, then our courses and their evaluations may increasingly reflect actual implementation of multicultural values.

It is critical to understand that multicultural evaluation integrates the content of the course being evaluated with the people (faculty, students, evaluator) and processes of evaluation. The list of guidelines and recommendations presented in this chapter thus constitute a mixture of methodology and substantive ideas. Banks (1994b) pulls together multicultural teaching, learning, and evaluation by noting that faculty must seek to 1) diversify their teaching strategies to include cooperative learning and individual learning, 2) implement gender equity in their teaching, 3) provide students with opportunities to develop and understand their own evaluation capacity, and 4) integrate evaluation with teaching. As for Banks' tenants regarding multicultural education, our guidelines for evaluating multicultural course change apply across disciplines.

It is critical for faculty in all disciplines, but especially mathematics and science, to be challenged to implement multicultural education since these areas reflect the most serious underrepresentation of ethnic and cultural minorities and women. Faculty in these disciplines may have to ascertain how their courses can positively influence and attract students rather than acting as a filter. How can their courses become more involved in language-based learning activities? Faculty need to reflect on the connection between their own pedagogical and evaluation assumptions and their cross-cultural experiences. The goal is for students to be included in the teaching and learning process. The goal of evaluating courses is for faculty to facilitate students' understanding of quality.

Implemented as described, evaluating our courses for multicultural change can result in changes to ourselves and our students. In our role as course evaluators, faculty may become participants in the process of change and choose to conduct liberating inquiry (Grant & Sleeter, 1986), research as praxis (Delgado-Gaitan, 1993; Lather, 1986), and as emergent alternative discourse (King, 1994). The meaning of multicultural education is defined and negotiated with the participation of key stakeholders who must strive to develop their own multicultural evaluation competence. Evaluating and critiquing the goals, activities, and outcomes of a course for multicultural change is a significant step toward transformative education.

CHAPTER 16

Organizational Change and Implementation Strategies for Multicultural Infusion

Ann Intili Morey, *Dean, College of Education*
San Diego State University

Editor's Notes:
The preceding chapters have focused on specific components of the course-change model and examples of multicultural course change in specific disciplines and higher education settings. Ann Morey's concluding chapter presents a framework for systemic, institutional change. It highlights some key concepts about organizational change and relates these concepts to colleges and universities. Based on her experience and research, Morey presents a model for systemic change and offers practical advice for faculty and administrators who are interested in implementing, supporting, and maintaining change.

The most critical factor in bringing about systemic change to respond to the increasingly diverse student bodies and society is a knowledgeable and committed faculty. Faculty expertise is central to the infusion of multicultural content and strategies into courses, and thus faculty development opportunities to enhance expertise are essential to making significant progress.

Morey details seven components of a faculty development program to infuse multiculturalism into the curriculum. In support of these components, she describes a variety of activities and strategies that can be employed in faculty development efforts. Lastly, she outlines elements which facilitate systemic change. ∎

THE CASE OF A COLLEGE AT WESTERN UNIVERSITY

The 1995 headline read: "Western University's Entering Freshmen Forty Percent Ethnic." What a dramatic change for this 31,000 student, comprehensive university. Just 15 years earlier, students of color comprised only 12 percent of its student body. At the President's cabinet meeting that headline morning, there was increased urgency to their ongoing conversation about how prepared WU was for this change. Later, the provost initiated the same conversation with the deans. As we once again talked about needed changes, I drifted off into my thoughts about my experiences as dean of a large college. It had been quite a journey and it seemed to start so long ago. In fact the multicultural transformation of the College had its awkward beginnings before I arrived. In 1982, the prior dean appointed a Committee on Cultural Diversity to "examine the College's response to diversity." A year later, the Committee forwarded a series of recommendations to the Dean which subsequently was approved by the full faculty.

Two years later, not much had happened. A student recruitment effort and a few special lectures had occurred, but the Committee deemed unsatisfactory curriculum reform and efforts to recruit ethnic faculty. Some possible reasons put forward for the results were: 1) no specific procedures were adopted for curricular documentation, and no one was designated as having the "clout" to ensure it; 2) many faculty may have adopted the policy because it seemed like the correct thing to do; 3) the task may have seemed formidable to many faculty members who lack expertise and knowledge in multicultural education; 4) few special efforts were made to recruit minority faculty.

When I arrived in 1985, as a naive first-time dean, my own reflection was that adoption of policies by the faculty are ineffective unless accompanied by action plans, incentives, accountability mechanisms, and designation of internal persons who are passionate and committed to assume specific responsibilities. I was unsure about how to bring this about.

I discussed with the department chairs the possibility of requiring a course in multiculturalism to signal students that this was a value in the college. Despite their lukewarm reception, I asked them to get faculty approval for the course. Two years later, the matter was still "under discussion" in some departments. In an effort to increase faculty awareness and expertise, I supported guest speakers on diversity, gave mini-grants to faculty, held a few workshops, and initiated efforts to attract more ethnic faculty and students. The results were discouraging.

During Spring 1987, I finally realized that no matter how eloquent, creative, and

committed I might be, a shift in strategy was essential. I began to ask questions, listen and read. At a retreat at my home, I asked the chairs to design a program for increasing faculty attention to diversity as well as a "strategic planning process" that would identify broad directions of travel. The chairs designed a planning process involving three workshops and outlined other strategies. The campus president opened the first workshop and his remarks focused heavily on diversity (I wrote them). As part of this strategic planning process, the faculty chose "addressing diversity" as one of three strategic choices. Throughout the Fall, faculty and administrators had meetings to design and implement a comprehensive plan for each strategic choice. With regard to diversity, my strategy was to provide an enabling environment.

The 1988–89 academic year saw many activities in the College: guest speakers, faculty workshops on different paradigms, and department level discussions. Student and faculty recruitment efforts were initiated at the College and departmental levels with improved results. I depleted most of my discretionary funds and successfully sought assistance from the president.

I then met with the chairs to discuss the current faculty "environment" regarding diversity and "next steps." As a result, the chairs decided to invite a select group of 35 faculty to meet during the summer to refine the existing plan in light of the new "presidential" funding support. (Faculty were selected on the basis of their being "doers" and having demonstrated interest in diversity.) The faculty developed a statement of purpose, a set of operating principles, and a list of outcomes for what has come to be called the Multicultural Infusion Initiative (MII). The guidelines for this initiative acknowledged the need to accommodate individual faculty differences in levels of multicultural sophistication and the important role of collaboration. They also recognized that consensus probably could not be reached and tension might occur. They sent a letter to their peers that summer inviting them to join the initiative. They noted that risk-taking, self-reflection and personal investment would be required.

From Fall 1990 to the present, the MII has been the major initiative in the College. Its primary focus is the infusion of multicultural curriculum and instructional strategies throughout the College's programs. As such, the emphasis has been on faculty development and curricular infusion. Other aspects of structural/systemic change have included recruiting faculty and students of color, increasing the knowledge base about diversity, and integrating the College's efforts with those of other agencies.

Two groups have provided leadership and administrative support: 1) the College chairs and deans and 2) a Coordinators Group, consisting of the MII coordinators, an Associate Dean and a small staff. Among many other activities, the Coordinators Group has conducted yearly surveys to assess faculty needs and stimulate programs and activities accordingly. Faculty development opportunities and recognition have occurred at college, departmental, and individual levels.

The College has made significant progress toward its goals. The majority of courses have been infused, ethnic faculty and student representation has changed dramatically, linkages with our communities have strengthened, and faculty scholarship reflects our new emphasis.

The provost suddenly broke my reverie: "Jan, your college has made the most progress, how did you go about it?" I thought and then replied: "Successive approximations."

The above case is based on my work with two universities. It illustrates that the type of course and curriculum changes envisioned in this book require a significant commitment to change on the part of faculty, administrators, and their institutions. In fact, many of the colleges and universities which have tried to implement these changes have concluded that comprehensive efforts to address diversity involve systemic/structural change of the academic organizations themselves. Knowledge of the processes of organizational change and faculty development are essential to making progress in this regard. An extensive literature exists on these topics, and key resources are available in both the higher education and behavior science literature. While it is beyond the scope of this chapter to even summarize this literature, some concepts critical to practice are highlighted below. Further, based upon the literature and on our expereinces in working with over twenty-five universities, the chapter also provides some practical guidance for faculty and administrators seeking to make the curriculum more inclusive of a broader truth and more reflective of our increasingly diverse society and its connection to an emergent global community. The chapter concludes with an analysis of factors influencing systemic change in this regard.

ORGANIZATIONAL DIMENSIONS OF CHANGE

The Nature of Change

Change seems to be occurring at an ever-accelerating rate. The evidence is abundant in each of our own life experiences. The rapid expansion of knowledge and the new communication technologies alone have transformed the ways in which we relate to our world. It also has had a profound effect on the way we think about change itself, so much so that scholars have begun to conceptualize a paradigm shift about it: a shift away from rational, linear models of change to ones that are nonlinear and characterized by understanding dynamic complexity and relationships and the concept of learning communities (Beer, Eisenstat, & Spector, 1990; Lincoln, 1985; Pascale, 1990; Senge, 1990).

The rational and empirical approach has dominated the educational change literature for some time. This approach stresses rational planning, management information systems and development programs with strategic planning being its most recent manifestation. Goodman (1982) described a shift from this old organizational change paradigm based on formal plans for effective change and on specific short-term interventions toward a new paradigm which is characterized by self-critical analysis of the change process and attempts to incorporate complex influences including sociopolitical and psychocultural factors. Other new models in the 1980's and 1990's are more entrepreneurial, in that change is seen as an uncertain and ambiguous process. Further, the focus is on the client or user from whom relevant information is sought. Peters and Austin (1985) noted that some of the characteristics of change include teamwork, recognizing past failures, challenging organizational rules, and seeking innovative ideas from clients.

The emergent, postmodern paradigm for change is not built on rationalist, linear, policy, and implementation models. Change is thought to be messy and nonlinear. It occurs under conditions of dynamic complexity (Senge, 1990). Most reforms are so complex that it is impossible to write a detailed blueprint. Moreover, the nature of change is such that opportunities and problems reveal themselves as one goes along this journey. One simply cannot foresee all that is needed or will happen (Fullan, 1993).

Postmodern theories emphasize rapid currents of change marked by decentraliza-tion, multiple voices, and system redesign (Maxcy, 1994). Senge (1990) characterized the emergent successful corporation as a "learning organization." He believed that "the real leverage in most management situations lies in understanding dynamic complexity, not detailed complexity" (p. 72). The essence for leaders lies in "seeing relationships rather than linear cause-effect chains" and in "seeing processes for change rather than snapshots" (p. 73). Fullan (1993) echoed the concept that the emergent paradigm is based on a generative concept of a learning community where "seemingly incompatible pairs like continuity and change, personal mastery and collective action, vision and openness, failure and success, and pressure and support, not only can but also must go together in successful change processes" (p. 6). In a nonlinear process, seeing relationships becomes important.

Chaos theory is helpful here because in the seeming disorder of things, patterns emerge which provide new insights and meanings. Stacey (1992) put it this way: "…successful human organizations cannot be the realization of some shared intention formed well ahead of action. Instead, success has to be the discovery of patterns that emerge through actions we take in response to the changing agendas of issues we identify" (p. 124).

The change process must be viewed within the culture of an organization. In discussing organizations, Chaffee and Tierney (1988) talked about the strong forces that emanate from within an organization:

This internal dynamic has its roots in the history of the organization and derives its force from the values, traditions, processes and goals held by those most intimately involved in the organization's workings. The most fundamental construct of an organization, as a society, is its culture. An organization's culture is reflected in what is done, how it is done, and who is involved in doing it. It concerns decisions, actions, and communication both on an instrumental and a symbolic level. (p. 7)

Different schemes have been developed to describe such cultures. Cultures which are task-oriented and stress team-based activities are more easy to engage in change than organizations that are based more on individual needs and expectations (Handy, 1978).

Using the perspective of organizational culture studies, Bergquist (1993) analyzed collegiate institutions in order to clarify their specific cultural dimensions. He described four different yet interrelated cultures that he has found in American higher education. Two have historical roots in the origins of higher education: *collegial* and *managerial*; and the other two, *developmental* and *negotiating*, have emerged more recently. Bergquist's theory is that "any efforts to bring about change and increase stability in a chaotic collegiate setting must be based on an understanding of these 4 cultures and that most of the efforts must be multidimensional in nature…" (p. xiv). Thus, change efforts must involve different strategies that are appropriate for each culture.

Successful change must be implemented in ways that are congruent with the organization's dominate culture (Schofield, 1991). Moreover, since colleges on a campus have different cultures reflecting the different disciplines and professional fields they house, change strategies should allow for sufficient flexibility to accommodate these subcultures. Moreover, Benjamin, Carroll, Jacobi, Krop, and Shires (1993) asserted that successful change programs must be congruent with the campus' governance structure. They believed that educational reform has failed because of externally developed

and imposed solutions that are frequently "rational constructs developed by policy analysts. Such constructs invariably ignore or oversimplify the existing formal and informal forces that impose determinative constraints on the current governance structures" (p. 36).

Resistance to Change

The resistance to change that the former and current deans experienced at Western University is a commonplace occurrence. Both deans initially underestimated this dynamic. When the faculty approved the plan of the first dean's committee, the dean thought that change would follow through the implementation procedures in the document. The second dean's analysis of why her predecessor's efforts failed reflected her lack of understanding about the complexity of change, its nonlinear nature and the important factor of resistance to change.

Resistance to change is often a natural and valid response. Such resistance to an organizational change effort may have historical roots and relate to the failure of past attempts as well as the experience and background of personnel. It can also be a healthy response to chaos, turbulence, and stress. Efforts to promote stability will in such cases paradoxically create a greater tolerance for changes (Boyd, 1992).

Most, if not all change, involves loss, struggle, anxiety, and conflict. As Schon has noted, when experiencing change, people pass through "zones of uncertainty" (quoted by Fullan, 1982, p. 25). When ignored, resistance tends to grow and become entrenched, often driving conflict underground and toward a level of subtlety that is difficult to erase (Bolman & Deal, 1991; Gutknecht & Miller, 1990).

Several characteristics of higher education further inhibit change. Tenure and academic freedom act as a conservative force because tenured faculty are not concerned about job security, and they believe that academic freedom insulates them from anyone but themselves ultimately determining the content of their courses. Further, faculty beliefs and assumptions about teaching and learning can be stumbling blocks. In this regard Weimer observed: "The equating of content mastery with instructional effectiveness inhibits instructional improvement because it makes teaching an activity without form or substance in its own right" (1990, p. 5).

The effective management of change also must take into consideration the nature of higher education as an institution. Consensual approaches to decision making in higher education can often make change and innovation a prolonged process. Moreover, those institutions which are focused on themselves and their own activities, such as established research universities, are less likely to espouse change. In contrast, those that are more externally oriented and look outward to the communities they serve, such as community colleges and some public comprehensive universities, are more able to be responsive to social and political factors of the larger society (Peters & Austin, 1985; Schofield, 1991).

Resistance to change by employees can be seen as a response to trying to maintain an implicit system goal and stability. Until this goal is recognized, the change effort is "doomed to failure." Senge (1990) offered the following insight and advice:

> Whenever there is "resistance to change," you can count on there being one or more "hidden" balancing processes. Resistance to change is neither capricious nor mysterious. It almost always arises from threats to traditional norms...rather than pushing harder to overcome resistance, artful leaders discern the source of resistance. They focus directly on the implicit norms and

power relationships within which the norms are embedded. (p. 88)

Thus, familiarity with the change process fosters the ability to focus on the powerful counter-response of resistance to change and the necessity of working with this force rather than against or in spite of it. Coping successfully with resistance will enhance empowerment of employees. Such empowerment also contributes to new definitions of leadership that encourage sharing of authority and promotion of the change process in individuals.

Ownership of the innovation is essential to success. The Dean's agenda did not take hold until she was willing to risk that the faculty would be committed to change to the extent that it would move forward. Cohen and March (1974) noted the importance of involving high-status professionals and sometimes even handing over the proposed innovation to them.

The emergent paradigm requires the formation of learning communities if an organization is going to be successful in the years ahead. How can we achieve this when our institutions are basically conservative? If change is not part of the organizational culture, then efforts to impose change will probably fail in the long run. As Fullan (1993) asserted: "You cannot have an educational environment in which change is continuously expected alongside a conservative system and expect anything but constant aggravation" (p. 3).

The uncertainty and ambiguity that surround the process can make some people very uncomfortable and uneasy about engaging in such an endeavor. The WU dean knew that the faculty took a significant step when they acknowledged the need for risk taking. Fullan (1993) said it this way:

> Under conditions of uncertainty, learning, anxiety, difficulties, and fear of the unknown are *intrinsic* to all change

processes, especially at the early stages. One can see why a risk-taking mentality and climate are so critical. People will not venture into uncertainty unless they or others appreciate that difficulties are a natural part of any change scenario. And if people do not venture into uncertainty, no significant change will occur.... (p. 25)

Leadership

Leadership is central to change initiatives; without it most change fails. The emerging change models require a different type of leader: individuals who do not emphasize control through systems and rationalist problem-solving, stability, and efficiency (e.g., Chaffee & Tierney, 1988; Kouzes & Posner, 1990). Beckhard and Pitchard's study on leadership highlighted a necessary shift from a result-oriented mode to what they label a "learning mode, probably the most important single process involved in effective change" (1992, p. 4).

Educational change theorists in general emphasize the need for a new brand of leadership. Leaders must be able to critique their own positions of power, be skilled at facilitating change, and comfortable with ambiguity and openness. Such leaders need to be aware of entrenched assumptions and beliefs regarding organizational change and how their own socialization into positions of power probably reflects and reinforces these outmoded attitudes (Fullan, 1993). Mauriel (1989) stressed the importance of visionary and inspirational skills; Quantz (1991) asserted that leaders should be skilled at and comfortable with the delegation of power, decentralization of tasks and democratic practices. Rhoades (1990) called for a different type of leadership—personal, catalytic, encouraging—which will enlist, entrust and empower faculty with their mission.

Fombrun (1992) encourages transformational leaders who "identify themselves as agents of change and act accordingly; they empower employees, insist on core values, foster learning, and welcome ambiguity" (p. 166). They value outsider opinions, obser-vations, and diversity. Tierney (1989) viewed leadership as a "specific form of empowerment which is intimately connected to the culture of an organization" (p. 164). Further, he noted that "Rather than to conceive of leadership as something that resides in an individual, the critical theorist views leadership as a reciprocal relationship amongst individuals" (p. 164).

Leadership is increasingly viewed as a shared responsibility which encourages others to assume qualities of leadership in their daily activities. The WU dean made a decision to change her leadership style and become more team-oriented, focused on empowering others, and committed to creating a facilitating environment. She began to develop the chairs as a collaborative group to foster and help design the change process. She realized that a team-centered managerial approach "enhances the capacity of organizations to master new knowledge and to use it effectively to improve innovation, problem solving, and productivity" (Bensimon & Neumann, 1993, p. ix). The ideal leader in this regard is "someone who knows how to find and bring together diverse minds...an orchestrator of multiple complex tasks..." (p. 1). Bensimon and Neumann went on to state: "Good team building focuses on the enactment of processes for engendering connected, collaborative, interactive, and inclusive group work" (p. 106).

It took the dean several years to fully understand that you simply cannot announce a new direction of travel—a vision of a curriculum that is infused with multicultural content and instructional strategies—and expect others to follow, even if it is the right direction. Surely, she should provide leadership in defining an emergent vision, but her leadership had to empower others, promote ownership, and allow the idea to be theirs.

Vision

Change efforts are most successful when they are guided by a vision of the future, by what is possible (Birnbaum, 1992; Fullan, 1993). Congruent with the notion that change is nonlinear, vision is not something set, communicated, and orchestrated by leadership alone. A beginning vision developed or espoused by leadership is a starting point and as others join in the exploration of the possible futures for an institution, a shared and clearer vision will emerge. This vision will most likely stem from the consideration by organizational members and leaders of challenges, issues, and alternatives. It also will be given initial shape by members becoming more aware and reflective about such matters and forming their own meanings. This beginning vision can be a statement of challenges and intentions rather than a crystal clear vision for the organization. Thus, to some extent we agree with Stacey (1992) who stated: "The dynamic systems perspective thus leads managers to think in terms, not of the prior intention represented by objectives and visions, but of continuously developing agendas of issues, aspirations, challenges and individual intentions" (p. 124). Once a vision emerges, there is still much wisdom in Bennis' view that leaders should be able to draw people to a compelling vision of what is possible and to shape the work environment to bring about the vision (1989).

IMPLEMENTATION OF CHANGE

Knowledge and understanding of the change process is essential to any effort to implement change. The previous section sought to highlight some key concepts in the change process and to provide a context for the following discussion on the implementation of change. The intention of this section is to provide some practical guidance for administrators and faculty seeking to infuse college courses and curricula with content and instructional strategies responsive to our diverse society.

For change to occur, a readiness for change must be apparent. Such readiness is predicated on an awareness of the need for change and a beginning willingness to tackle it. With regard to multiculturalism, this awareness can be furthered by institutional communications and actions which foster increased understanding of diversity and its implications for higher education. Both administrative and faculty leaders must draw attention to the need for change and stimulate debate and analysis. Outside forces such as community pressure, accrediting agency requirements, and legislative mandates can also play a role. Some of these factors were underscored in a study of fifty-two college deans about conditions necessary for change. The most frequent response was readiness for change, especially having an appropriate institutional climate, faculty recognition of need, and administrative support and commitment (Morey & Allen, 1993).

An important aspect is laying the foundation to become a learning community. A community of scholars is a much-used phrase, and invisible colleges now link scholars in the same disciplines across universities and increasingly across international boundaries. Yet, becoming a learning community for teaching is not a well-established concept, although significant steps in this direction are underway. Forming a new learning culture, one where teaching and scholarship and their relationship are valued, will take concerted and sustained effort over a long period of time. Further, the concept that change is now an integral part of life and that we must continually learn in order to be effective is a fundamental reason for becoming a learning organization. Leadership, and involvement of informal and senior faculty leaders, will hasten the formation of such a culture.

Identification of the constraints and obstacles to change is essential to developing and implementing a successful change process. Among the frequently cited constraints and obstacles are: lack of faculty and/or administrative awareness and commitment, faculty resistance to change, lack of faculty involvement, lack of adequate resources, faculty constraints such as time and workload, insufficient attention to the needs and general support of faculty, lack of knowledge and understanding related to the area of change, poor conceptualization and design of innovation/change, lack of incentives and rewards, unclear connection to institutional mission and goals, and poor communication.

Of particular importance in academic settings is overcoming faculty resistance to change. It is important to acknowledge that resistance is natural and should be responded to. Some reasons for faculty resistance will be rooted in faculty culture, others in their experience and still others in the anxiety, ambiguity, conflict, and risk-taking associated with change. Motivating faculty and removing obstacles are critical to this process. Intrinsic motivation can be developed through increased faculty awareness of the need for change and the belief that such a change will increase the meaningfulness of their work to themselves, others, and society at large. Thus, faculty must work out their own meanings of the reasons for change, the process, and its outcomes. Activities that promote clarification through discussion and debate can be helpful. Conflict will be inevitable and should be wel-

comed. It allows for people to express their concerns and different views about the reasons for change and the desired outcomes. As people believe in the purposes of change, they can find meaning in its direction and become change agents themselves.

Faculty involvement and ownership, then, reduces their resistance to change. Respected scholars in the field of instructional improvement stress the importance of faculty-initiated activities. They maintain that externally imposed requirements are counter to the academic culture, the realities of tenure, and are usually met with resistance. They place emphasis on individual faculty initiative, and while this is undoubtedly true for the improvement of a faculty member's teaching, a somewhat different scenario exists in the case of course infusion when it is part of a larger, systemic change effort. Here, the general environment, purposes and goals, strategies and resources are developed by faculty and administrative groups as well as individual faculty members.

Extrinsic incentives and rewards are also important. Released time, travel, merit pay, grants, and recognition of accomplishments encourage and allow faculty to engage in development efforts. Equally important is the provision of other resources, such as monetary support, resource materials, knowledgeable personnel, and student assistants. Successful strategies that we have employed to overcome faculty resistance during the change process include: recognizing and celebrating faculty expertise, trying to serve a range of interests and levels, providing resources to acquire new competencies and to experiment with change, collaboration, believing in faculty, providing a safe environment for risk-taking, welcoming diverse views, and exploring what underlies attitudes that appear destructive and providing support as possible (Morey & Kitano, 1993).

Faculty should be invited to design and participate in activities on a voluntary basis and supported for their efforts. Our advice is to try not to turn a faculty request down, especially if it represents the initial involvement of a faculty member. Further, individuals and academic units have different starting points and this fact must be respected and accommodated. WU's dean funded a project proposed by a faculty member on assimilation as the best solution to dealing with diversity. The project did not change the faculty member's perspectives, yet it did bring him into the process by focusing him more on his and the university's responsibilities to diverse students.

Change does take time, and it is difficult at the start of the process to predict its duration and its differential impact on individuals and academic units. The change process can be very slow, and impatient faculty and administrators will be frustrated if they do not fully appreciate this fact. They should focus on successes along the way and encourage those who are engaged in the process. The success and enthusiasm of some individuals can have an impact on bringing others into the change process. Factors affecting time include resources, disagreement with values implicit or explicit in the change process, and failure to overcome resistance.

Change is messy and nonlinear, and the design of the process must accommodate this reality. When the WU dean responded, "Successive approximations" to the provost's question about how her college had accomplished so much, she was reflecting a deepened understanding of the nonlinear nature of change and the ambiguities and opportunities that occur. Thus, the initial design of the process should have built-in flexibility which permits initiative and change in the process itself along the way. Certainly continual assessment contributes to this effort.

In developing a structure for change, leadership at all levels is important. Leaders must articulate the importance of addressing diversity, empower faculty, create enabling and learning environments, and along with others assist in developing a compelling and dynamic vision for the institution. Without the president's commitment and involvement, change efforts toward that vision will probably fail; this is true whether the effort is at a university-wide or college-specific level. Senior staff, vice presidents, and deans all have critical roles to play. Not to be overlooked is the importance of the department as an organizing unit for change. Leadership and incentives at this level are critical to the participation of department faculty and to assuring that the development activities have relevance to department-based faculty. All these individuals should have as one of their main tasks the creation of an environment which facilitates faculty work and creativity. As faculty and administrators work together, effective, frequent, and consistent communication becomes a key variable in the continual development of ideas and in the assessment of successes, failures, and next steps.

Deciding on a Framework for Change

When the WU dean came to Western University, she had some ideas about how to bring about change. She was an energetic person whose style tended to draw people to join her agendas. She really did not have a clear understanding of the change process in higher education. But, after two years she realized that she had to alter her approach to stimulating change if she was to be successful. She thought about organizational culture and ways to address faculty resistance including developing ownership and providing incentives. Through her conversations, readings, and self-reflection, she came to understand that nothing less than fundamental systemic/structural change of the college itself was necessary.

Morey (1988) developed, implemented and evaluated a framework for systemic change at the college level which also has institution level applications (see Figure 16–1). This framework entails the fostering of an enabling environment for change and involves several components: 1) increasing faculty expertise in multicultural education, including hiring faculty with this area of expertise; 2) increasing the knowledge base on multiculturalism through faculty research and other scholarship; 3) infusing the curriculum with content appropriate for improving teaching and learning in a multicultural context; 4) integrating efforts with those of other colleges and the community; and 5) increasing the ethnic diversity of students.

Systemic change alters the way a college or university behaves. Its multifaceted nature impacts decision making practices, reward systems, student and faculty recruitment, information systems, and even work structures. It can entail new forms of scholarship—new topics that cannot be marginalized by the dominant research paradigm. Systemic change calls on current administrators, faculty, and students to shift, assess their values, have an openness to new ideas and act in different ways. It should change mission statements and have an impact on retention, promotion and tenure decisions through valuing multiculturalism in research and teaching.

Components of the Faculty Development Program

The most critical factor in bringing about structural change and making progress toward the goal of an infused or transformed curriculum is a committed and knowledge-

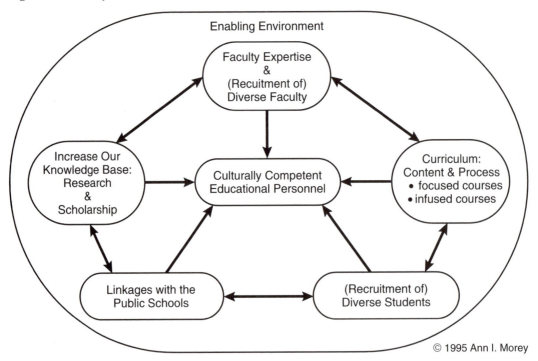

© 1995 Ann I. Morey

FIGURE 16–1

able faculty. Enhancing faculty expertise is central to the infusion of multicultural content and instructional strategies into courses, and thus faculty development opportunities are essential to making significant progress. A growing literature exists on faculty development and vitality. Menges and Mathis (1988) provided an annotated list of key resources on this topic. Centra (1985) identified four factors or groups of faculty development practices. These were: 1) high faculty involvement, such as workshops and seminars, informal peer assessment of courses, and faculty "mentors"; 2) instructional assistance practices in which specialists assist faculty in instructional development, student assessment and the use of technology; 3) traditional practices, such as visiting scholars, sabbaticals, travel grants, and temporary teaching load reductions; and 4) assessment practices which emphasize various assessment techniques to improve instruction.

Bergquist and Phillips (1975) authored a handbook series that remains a practical guide to faculty development as well as what they believed are the related areas of personal, instructional, and organizational development. This observation, affirmed by other research, is consistent with the idea of systemic/structural change in that personal development, particularly in affective areas, is necessary for many faculty to be able to move forward with multicultural infusion. In addition, the organizational development of colleges and universities is essential to providing an enabling environment and entails leadership, resources and other support, decision making processes, and review of policies and practices.

The extensive work of Weimer (1990, 1993) on improving college teaching provides useful information and insights about faculty and instructional development. Weimer (1993) observed that instructors need to debunk two myths about teaching if they are to understand and improve their teaching skills. These myths are that "Nobody Knows What Makes Teaching Effective" and "Good Teachers Are Born, Not Made" (pp. 5, 7).

Within this context, some major components of the faculty development program aimed at infusing multicultural content and strategies into courses and curricula are outlined below. Some of the components could occur simultaneously and in a different order than presented.

1. *Awareness and understanding level: period of self-reflection.* Individuals will have different levels of awareness about the increasing diversity of students and the larger society. Initial activities might focus on defining what is meant by diversity as well as providing demographic and foundational information on gender, ethnicity, language, race, religion, disability, and sexual orientation in American society. The process should encourage opportunities for introspection and self-evaluation so that faculty can examine their current attitudes, knowledge, and understanding about multiculturalism.

Often faculty of European descent are unaware of their own values and beliefs, are unable to describe their own culture, and do not see how their cultural perspectives influence their teaching and impact students. Many of these faculty perceive and may appreciate the ethnicity and culture of students of color and other nontraditional students, and at the same time do not perceive their own cultural lenses. Thus, activities should foster awareness of one's own culture, socialization, experiences, and assumptions. Examination of one's own culture should enhance awareness of the assumptions underlying one's teaching and even expand to obtaining information and insights on how students from diverse backgrounds experience the classroom. If done in a group, an environment where discussion can occur in a nonjudgmental and safe manner is essential for faculty self-examination and for the early establishment of an accepting climate for professional exploration and growth. This initial period in the development process might also include an analysis of one's teaching in a general sense. An important part of this process is examination of their willingness to engage in professional development toward the end of better serving the needs of all students.

2. *Acquiring institutional change knowledge.* Faculty and administrators need to have knowledge and understanding of the change process. A review of the literature, consultations with experts, and self-reflection are important to developing a working knowledge. Group discussions should encourage analysis and debate about different conceptions of the change process as well as an assessment of what concepts seem most appropriate for the particular institution.

3. *Establishment of an organizational structure to design and implement change.* There is no one best organizational structure to bring about change, but multiple effective arrangements based on many of the concepts discussed in this chapter, leadership at all levels, overcoming resistance to change and faculty ownership are important factors. With this caveat, we would like to suggest a starting point for discussion. One possible structure might involve each level of the institution having a role. Central leadership should include the president, provost, deans, and faculty senate leaders. Perhaps a campus-wide advisory committee might be formed as well as some at the college level. These groups would provide high visibility for the undertaking and be important to priority setting. A university-wide office to coordinate and provide leadership to the multicultural infusion effort would be essential. This office would provide consultation and planning, make planning and

priority recommendations congruent with the qualities associated with successful faculty development efforts, sponsor events and activities designed to facilitate symbiotic relationships, and address faculty needs that cut across colleges. Further, the office would foster collaboration, identify and develop resource people and materials, increase communication, and provide faculty incentives. In describing one such organizational arrangement at a large university, Mikitka, Morey and Kitano (1993) observed:

> Coordinating the program required continuous consultation and discovery. It involved creating and maintaining a network of individuals and organizations, designing and acquiring a multitude of materials, and reading broadly in the areas of faculty development and higher education.... In particular, a distinct identity, high visibility, leadership roles for both faculty and administrators, increased collegiality and tangible results were our program administration goals.... We expected some resistance from both administrative and faculty domains and were challenged to incorporate strategies that would minimize conflicts of interest. To foster collegiality within and across departments, colleges, and the university, our framework supported both generic and discipline-specific activities.... Strategies used in implementing this program involved the powerful concept of collaboration in the approach to balancing the multiple responsibilities of faculty, shared interchange, creating a sense of identity, and the complex requirements of individuals with diverse faculty roles. (pp. 151–153)

Leadership and coordination should also occur at the college level. College-wide events and activities would address the diverse faculty needs at the college level. Planning and coordination of these events would emanate from a qualified faculty person attached to the dean's office. This individual would work with department-level faculty coordinators to plan events designed to develop faculty expertise, facilitate interdepartmental discussion, and encourage participation of individuals at different levels of sophistication with regard to multicultural knowledge. Similarly, department initiatives would reflect the unit's self-identified needs and perhaps be guided by a department-developed plan. In addition, provision could be made for faculty-initiated research and curriculum development projects. All levels of the institution, from the president's office to departments would be expected to contribute resources to the effort.

Further, faculty and administrative leaders should have as one of their main tasks the creation of an environment which facilitates faculty work and creativity. As faculty and administrators work together, effective, frequent, and consistent communication becomes a key variable in the continual development of ideas and in the assessment of successes, failures, and next steps.

4. *Foundational studies and needs assessment.* Recognizing that individuals have different starting points, infusion activities should provide faculty with a basic foundation regarding multiculturalism and exposure to different cultural contexts. Such studies might include basic concepts, definitions and paradigms, and an introduction to the research literature on these topics. They might include:

- Examining frameworks for understanding multicultural education.
- Expanding faculty knowledge of the academic needs and cultural strengths of diverse learners.
- Learning specific cultural content and strategies which can be integrated into core classes in the discipline.

- Identifying multicultural resources which can be used in the classroom.
- Understanding cultural diversity, characteristics and value systems, conflict, pluralism and assimilation, and relationships between cultural diversity, educational equity, academic achievement, and socioeconomic status.
- Increasing knowledge about theories, concepts, and strategies for effectively discussing prejudice and discrimination as they relate to racism, sexism, and classism.
- Expanding knowledge of conflict resolution.
- Developing strategies for change.
- Examining frameworks for multicultural course infusion.

Of particular importance is the introduction of different frameworks and their rationale for course infusion. The Multicultural Education Infusion Center at San Diego State University has found the framework presented by Kitano in Chapter 2 to be especially useful to the 23 universities affiliated with the Center. Faculty will also want information on what an infused or transformed course might look like in their specific discipline.

The process of self-reflection and acquiring foundational knowledge and understanding will allow individual faculty to respond to a needs assessment. A formalized needs assessment conducted by a campus unit will provide information vital to planning and implementing appropriate development activities. Such a needs assessment might include inquiry about one's knowledge and skills related to 1) the cultural, learning, and language characteristics of specific groups; 2) impact of culture on the learning process; 3) paradigms and approaches to multicultural education; 4) multicultural content and strategies in general and in specific to a discipline; 5) research-based instructional strategies for diverse learners; 6) resource materials; 7) organizational change and systemic factors related to diversity; 8) obstacles that impede multicultural infusion and motivational factors; and 9) effective learning styles of the faculty member.

The needs assessment will inform the content and learning strategies to be employed in the development process. A faculty attitude survey can also provide information useful to the design of development programs. Several instruments are available for this purpose. Another perspective can be obtained from students. At one institution associated with the Multicultural Education Infusion Center, faculty indicated that they did not have a need to further infuse their courses, but a student survey indicated otherwise.

5. *Establishment of assumptions and guidelines.* The establishment of assumptions and guidelines is important to gaining support and ownership of the process and for acknowledging diversity among the participants. Examples of assumptions and guidelines that have been used by some campuses include:

- The campus is committed to serving the needs of the diverse learner and having an inclusive curriculum and recognizes that the further development of faculty expertise in multicultural education is an essential prerequisite to achieving this goal.
- The development effort recognizes the considerable strengths that individuals bring to this endeavor and seeks to draw upon these strengths and foster their continued enhancement.
- Individuals and academic units have different starting points, needs, exper-

tise, contexts, and opportunities and thus the change process will be responsive, flexible, and employ a variety of strategies and processes.

- Collaboration, cooperation, and collegiality are necessary to meet the goals regarding faculty development and multicultural infusion.
- Multicultural content is not an "add-on" to the curriculum, but in fact must be integrated into the core of the entire curriculum.
- The campus espouses a set of values regarding human diversity and human dignity. These values do not require consensus, but do require risk-taking, personal reflection, and personal investment.
- Conflict, resistance to change, and problems are considered positively and as part of the change process.
- Change is nonlinear and complex.

6. *Acquiring content knowledge and instructional strategies.* This component concentrates on assisting faculty to expand their knowledge and skills in their disciplines and is at the heart of the effort to increase faculty expertise and application of these learnings. There is a growing literature on multicultural course infusion and beginning electronic and other networks to assist faculty. Identification and access to these and other materials and resources is most useful. Further, both individual and group activities should be based on learning styles preferred by faculty in specific disciplines, and a variety of formats can be used. The extensive literature on adult learning can be helpful in this regard (e.g., Rynes & Rosen, 1994; Stolovitch & Lane, 1989; Tucker-Ladd, Merchant & Thurston, 1992).

7. *Assessment and revision.* The change process should include ongoing assessment and revision. The assessment should provide information about faculty participation, the level of course infusion, faculty and administrator assessment of what is beneficial and what is not, effectiveness of program structure, general progress toward systemic change, and so forth. It is especially important to assess and understand faculty resistance to change and to seek input on ways to encourage participation. The assessment information should be widely reviewed and discussed, and revisions and new initiatives undertaken as appropriate.

Another aspect of assessment is providing faculty individual feedback about their course content and teaching effectiveness. Formative evaluation provides feedback that is diagnostic, descriptive, and useful for course improvement. Such evaluations are best conducted at the request of a faculty member and under no circumstances should be used as part of the personnel process. Weimer (1990) recommends that faculty engaging in this process seek input from multiple sources and receive a blend of both positive and negative feedback. She encourages faculty dialog about the results as part of the ongoing improvement process.

Development Activities and Strategies

There are a variety of activities and strategies that can be employed in faculty development efforts. The following discussion is a sampling of some successful development activities.

1. *Self-reflections and self-evaluations.* As noted earlier, self-reflection and self-evaluation can clarify one's thinking, values and behaviors. The process can identify satisfying experiences and strengths as well as heighten one's awareness and readiness for growth experiences. There are many ways

in which reflection can occur. Journaling can be an important tool to promote reflection and analysis that can lead to professional enhancement. Certainly, journaling can record one's reactions to speakers, readings, and discussion groups on the topic of multiculturalism. Further, reflecting on one's teaching and interactions with students and colleagues can stimulate new insights and ideas. Over time, written self-reflections can provide a record of one's professional journey through the process of course transformation.

Faculty-initiated evaluations of their teaching and syllabi can result in useful information that can lead to further course revisions. Input from students and colleagues can "clarify, elaborate, and correct faculty members' understanding of how they teach" (Weimer, 1990, p. 53). As noted earlier, such feedback should be formative in nature and provide information in a non-evaluative format. It can include suggestions for alternatives to increase the effectiveness of a faculty member's work. Weimer provided an overview of types of formative feedback instruments.

2. *Experiential activities.* Experiential activities afford an opportunity for a different type of learning and can underscore the point that knowledge is constructed in the context of a culture. Direct experiences, such as cultural plunges and conversations with ethnic students and faculty, support recognition of the need for change and encourage values and attitudes supportive of change. Other experiential activities that have been successfully used in workshop formats with faculty include simulations, role playing, and games, such as Star Power (Junn, 1994). Still others are foreign travel, visitations to classes, and demonstrations of exemplary practices. Not to be overlooked are activities with recognized high school teachers who often are more experienced in multicultural infusion than are university faculty.

One strategy that we have used successfully with faculty is cultural plunges, such as visiting an African American church, a community center and the like. These plunges must be carefully organized, preceded by a period of planning and a means of reflection before, immediately after, and several days after the event. It is important that such plunges be preceded by a period of preparation and that journaling occur before, immediately after, and a few days after the event. Opportunities to discuss these experiences, especially in a group format, can be a powerful tool for learning, especially attitude clarification and change.

Cracker-barrel sessions around various topics and individuals can be designed to heighten faculty awareness and understanding. For example, an event called "Student Voices" brought together students from various ethnic groups with faculty members in roundtable discussions. Using the cracker-barrel format, groups of students remained at each of the appointed tables and faculty members rotated to different tables at set times. Faculty members listened to student perceptions of life in a diverse society, what their experiences in classes were, what constituted good and poor teaching, and ideas they had to improve their college experience. Another cracker-barrel event involved faculty members describing their experiences in transforming their courses and/or presenting examples of infused courses and curriculum in specific disciplines. Cracker-barrels and other experiential strategies are also useful classroom teaching tools.

3. *Readings*. Reading is an integral part of academic life and constitutes an important tool for increasing awareness and expertise in multiculturalism. As demonstrated by the other chapters in this book, a growing literature exists both on the general topic and pertaining to specific disciplines. Reading literature provides another opportunity for reflection on different cultures and lifestyles. When readings are accompanied by discussion groups, the impact can be greatly enhanced and a sense of common purpose and increased colleagueship developed. For example, at Western University two professors selected books and short stories by ethnic writers and invited interested faculty across academic units to join in brown-bag discussions. Readings included Soto's *Baseball in April*, Cisneros's *Woman Hollering Creek*, and Morrison's *The Bluest Eye*. Similarly, as part of formal workshops at San Diego State's Multicultural Education Infusion Center, participants were asked to read short stories, such as Sasaki's *The Loom* and Candelaria's *The Day the Cisco Kid Shot John Wayne*, and then discussed the stories in small groups. Each group, in this case, was led by a facilitator who had analyzed the readings in advance.

In both these examples, the readings were selected by faculty members who had some familiarity with the literature. Most faculty, however, do not have the time to identify and obtain relevant readings. A well conceived development plan would alert faculty to journals and other literature in each discipline as well as readings that would be applicable across the disciplines. Collections of readings compiled locally or nationally are especially helpful.

4. *Working with others: Collaborations, coaches, and consultants.* Collaboration is a powerful tool for bringing about change. While the notion of colleague involvement in the instructional process is not well established in higher education, a collaborative environment enhances a learning community and reinforces the idea of continuous quality improvement. It can be cost effective and often acknowledges the different but valuable contributions of specific individuals. Faculty members working together provide motivation and support, stimulate

creativity, and allow for discussion and analysis of ideas, strategies, and products. For example, faculty teaching in the same program and/or teaching similar courses can work together to infuse their courses. Such groups have been most successful when, as part of their process, they generate clear goals and expectations and create a trusting environment which allows for risk-taking and sharing work in a nonjudgmental, supportive, yet honest, atmosphere. Such collaboration can be encouraged by giving priority to collaborative mini-grants funded by the institution and by making efforts to bring faculty together who share common interests and needs.

Often there is considerable expertise within a faculty that can be useful at various stages of the infusion process. Colleagues in various disciplines can share their knowledge and understanding through a variety of formats: as speakers, consultants, mentors, peer coaches, team teachers, and reviewers of course materials, and so forth. Depending on the task at hand, facilitators/coaches (be they colleagues, graduate students or other individuals) can be most helpful. Coaches are funded by a department, college and/or university to be available to faculty, individually or in groups. They can be instructional development specialists and other professionals in a faculty support unit on campus.

5. *Workshops, dialogs, and retreats.* Workshops are the most frequent strategy used in faculty development efforts. They can be effective tools for increasing faculty awareness and expertise as well as providing motivation and promoting commitment to the goals of multicultural education. Workshops can also encourage participation of faculty representing a wide range of understanding and knowledge (Weimer, 1990).

Effective workshops and seminars are designed to involve the participants actively. They should include follow-up activities; otherwise their impact will usually be short-lived. Outside experts are useful as speakers and facilitators, and sometimes their influence can be amplified by asking them to do a series of activities with faculty over time. Their acquaintance with the faculty increases their effectiveness and provides an environment for faculty to engage in more probing and candid ways. The expertise of local faculty should not be overlooked. Their ability to work as colleagues, particularly over a long period of time, can have positive results. Videotaping key speakers contributes to a library of resource materials to be used in faculty development activities and classes.

Dialogs—be they part of workshops or separate discussion groups—allow for the exchange and exploration of ideas and thus can contribute to clarifying, challenging, and expanding an individual's knowledge and understanding (Weimer, 1990). Such discussions should be focused and hopefully occur on more than one occasion. They can result in the formation of new cross-departmental and cross-college linkages, and relatedly, have the potential of developing new collaborations.

Retreats signal that important work is to be done, and when planned correctly allow time for individuals to reflect and share ideas and concerns in an informal atmosphere. Effective retreats employ a variety of formats and engage faculty in the planning process for them.

Thoughtful combinations of these and other formats can encourage participation and growth. For example, we have employed a "cohort" approach to some aspects of course-infusion activities. One cohort of ten faculty in Education agreed to spend a week between semesters in a workshop to increase their knowledge about language acquisition. During the workshop they learned about second-language acquisition in children, kept journals of their reactions and ideas, and developed some beginning materials to use in their courses. As part of the workshop, they designed their spring semester follow-up activities. These included presentations by local experts as well as members of the cohort group; discussions around key issues; sharing of books, curriculum materials, and other resources; and visitations to each other's classes. By the following fall semester, they were a "bonded" group and undertook a revision of their entire curriculum which would not have happened otherwise. The following intersession, a second cohort of fifteen faculty was formed. They designed their program with the advice of the first group. Other applications include the use of videos and case studies to inform and stimulate discussions.

6. *Technology.* The applications of technology to teaching and learning are expanding at an ever-increasing rate. As Halpern noted: "…the potential in these new forms of media lies not just in their speed, but in their ability to completely alter the way we think, learn, remember, and communicate information" (1994, p. 189). For example, e-mail has allowed easy communication among colleagues and, in some cases, among faculty and students. Access across the Internet to people in other countries, information resources, and an incredible array of services have the potential to revolutionize education. No sooner have we begun to explore the Internet and contemplate its uses than other networking capabilities are emerging with applications like networkable multimedia, personalized publications, and virtual reality (Blurton, 1994). Semrau and Boyer (1994) see interactive video as a way to enhance learning and particularly stress its uses for cooperative learning, cultural literacy, and critical thinking. Like other observers, they caution that thus far most software is geared toward White males, and appropriate software for diverse cultural groups and women is sorely lack-

ing. Thus, infusion efforts should examine, promote, and cause to be developed applications that are congruent and further the goals of multiculturalism.

Technology will also accelerate and enhance collaboration. Telecommunications will bring the world to a campus and allow for campuses to jointly develop programs and "purchase" others. In terms of multiculturalism, it has the potential of utilizing the best expertise as it is being developed.

No discussion of technology would be complete without noting its real potential to further inequities in our society. Who will provide the computers and access to technology highways? What responsibility will institutions take to assure that the programs and services produced and obtained will be inclusive of the diversity of our society and reflect the broadened truth of our knowledge bases?

7. *Research.* Faculty-initiated research offers another powerful tool for learning and involvement. This research not only can relate to the content area but also extend to classroom effectiveness. It potentially can make a long-lasting contribution to a broadened knowledge base about multicultural education. Institutional encouragement and support is important, including the provision of technical assistance in the development of evaluation and research materials, models and processes, and in implementation and analysis.

8. *Linkages.* Linking the change program to professional associations, other colleges and universities, and accrediting agencies assists faculty to view the change within their discipline and as part of a broader effort. State and regional discipline groups can be very useful in this regard. Also, e-mail networks permit the exchange of differing ideas and identification of resource materials among both established and new colleagues.

CONCLUDING THOUGHTS

Our experience has suggested that systemic change can be an exciting and invigorating journey. To be sure, there are many bumps in the road and unproductive detours. But as systemic change occurs, we continue to grow and our satisfactions come from knowing we are contributing to respecting and valuing human diversity and building a more democratic society. Based on our experience and research, the elements which facilitate systemic change appear to be:

1. The establishment of a shared vision of what is possible
2. The creation of an enabling environment, including an agreed-upon model and strategy for change. Such an environment might be facilitated by:
- A highly participatory planning and decision making process at all stages
- Leadership at all levels, especially faculty leaders at department levels and consistent and strong leadership from organizational unit heads and visible support from the university president
- Periodic needs assessment and evaluation which fosters a sense of involvement and responsiveness to needs and suggestions
- Incentives and rewards: small grants, released time from teaching, and other forms of recognition of faculty accomplishments
- Collaboration
- A well-planned and implemented faculty development program

- Accommodations for individual- and department-specific needs
- Provision of an open forum for discussion of issues related to multicultural paradigms and goals
- Resources
3. The establishment of guidelines
- Allowing different voices to be heard and accepting diverse views
- Accepting that people have different starting points
- Understanding that we do not know many of the answers to important questions (Morey & Kitano, 1993, p. 18)

Well, the WU dean mused, this is going along very well. Then it occurred to her that the culture of the college had shifted—that while not an explicit goal they had become a learning community and they had increased their capacity for change. Perhaps it was time to make the goal of a learning community explicit and to work continuously at its maintenance and enhancement.

As we move into a new age where change will be a normal part of life, the ability to have the capacity to change, to integrate it into one's work, and to understand that change is complex, nonlinear, and sometimes unpredictable is essential for our success and happiness. It is critical for our contributions to prepare all students to participate fully and productively in our emergent, multicultural, global, and dynamic world.

References

1 in 7 don't speak English at home. (1993, April). *Los Angeles Times*, p. A15.

Abruscato, J. (1993). Early results and tentative implications from the Vermont Portfolio Project. *Phi Delta Kappan, 74*, 474–477.

Adams, J. Q., & Welsch, J. R. (Eds.). (1993). *Multicultural education: Strategies for implementation in colleges and universities, Vol. 3*. Springfield, IL: Illinois State Board of Education.

Adams, K. L. & Ware, N. C. (1989). Sexism and the English language. In J. Freeman, (Ed.), Women: A feminist perspective. (4th ed., pp. 470–484) Mountain View, CA: Mayfield Publishing Company.

Adamson, H. D. (1993). *Academic competence: Theory and classroom practice: Preparing ESL students for content courses*. New York: Longman.

Adeeb, P. (1994). *A quasi-experimental design to study the effect of multicultural coursework and culturally diverse field placements on preservice teachers' attitudes towards diversity*. Unpublished doctoral dissertation, University of North Florida, Jacksonville.

Adelman, C. (1991). *Women at thirtysomething: Paradoxes of attainment*. Washington, D.C.: U.S. Department of Education.

Ahlquist, R. (1992). Manifestations of inequality: Overcoming resistance in a multicultural education foundations course. In Grant, C. (Ed.), *Research and multicultural education: From the margins to the mainstream* (pp. 89–105). London: The Falmer Press.

Aliaga, M. (1993). How I teach mathematics to minorities. In D. Schoem, L. Frankel, X. Zúñiga, & E. A. Lewis (Eds.), *Multicultural teaching in the university* (pp. 172–179). Westport, CT: Praeger.

Allen, B. P., & Niss, J. F. (1990). A chill in the college classroom? *Phi Delta Kappan, 71*, 607–609.

Allen, P. G. (1986) *The sacred hoop: Recovering the feminine in American indian traditions*. Boston: Beacon Press.

Allport, G. (1958). *The nature of prejudice*. Garden City, NY: Anchor Doubleday Books.

Altman, H. B., & Cashin, W. E. (1992). *Writing a syllabus*. Idea Paper No. 27. Manhattan, KS: Kansas State University Center for Faculty Evaluation and Development.

Altman, L. K. (1992a, January 28). Drug-resistant TB makes U.S. rethink Elimination Program. *The New York Times*, p. C3.

Altman, L. K. (1992b, October 15). Stymied by resurgence of TB, doctors reconsider a decades-old vaccine. *The New York Times*, p. B4.

American Association of Colleges for Teacher Education (AACTE). (1987, 1990). *RATE I–IV. Teaching teachers. Facts and figures*. Washington, DC: American Association of Colleges for Teacher Education.

American Association of University Women. (1993). Creating a gender-fair multicultural curriculum. *Outlook, 86*(40), 33–38.

American Psychological Association Task Force on Psychology in Education and the Mid-continent Regional Educational Laboratory. (August 1992). *Learner-centered psychological principles: Guidelines for school redesign and reform*. Washington, D.C.: American Psychological Association.

Amott, T. L., & Matthei, J. (1991). *Race, gender, and work: A multicultural history of women in the U.S.* Boston: South End Press.

Amsden, A. H. (1980). *The economics of women and work*. New York: St. Martin's.

Andersen, M., & Collins, P. H. (Eds.). (1992). *Race, class, and gender: An anthology* (pp. 88–95). Belmont, CA: Wadsworth Publishing Company.

Anderson J. A. (1988). Cognitive styles and multicultural populations. *Journal of Teacher Education, 39*, 2–9.

Anderson, J. A., & Adams, M. (1992). Acknowledging the learning styles of diverse populations: Implications for instructional design. In L. L. B. Border & N. V. N. Chism (Eds.), *Teaching for diversity* (pp. 19–33). New Directions for Teaching and Learning, no. 49. San Francisco: Jossey-Bass.

Andrews, M. M. (1992, January-February). Cultural perspectives on nursing in the 21st century. *Journal of Professional Nursing, 8*(1), 7–15.

Andrews, M. M., & Boyle, J. S. (1995). Andrews/Boyle transcultural nursing assessment guide. *Transcultural concepts in nursing care.* (2nd ed., pp. 439–444). Philadelphia: J. B. Lippincott Company.

Angelo, T. A., & Cross, K. P. (1993). *Classroom assessment techniques: A handbook for college teachers* (2nd ed.). San Francisco: Jossey-Bass.

Anzaldua, G. (1987). *Borderlands/La Frontera: The New Mestiza.* San Francisco: Aunt Lute Foundation.

Anzaldua, G. (Ed.). (1990). *Making face, making soul = Haciendo caras: Creative and critical perspectives by women of color.* San Francisco: Aunt Lute Foundation Books.

Aragon, J. (1973). An impediment to cultural pluralism: Culturally deficient teachers trying to teach culturally different students. In M. D. Stent, W. R. Hazard & H. N. Rivlin (Eds.), *Cultural pluralism in education: A mandate for change* (pp. 77–84). New York: Appleton Century-Crofts.

Aronowitz, S. (1992). *The politics of identity: Class, culture, and social movements.* New York: Routledge.

Arvizu, S., & Saravia-Shore, M. (1990). Cross-cultural literacy. *Education and Urban Society, 22*(4), 364–376.

Asante, M. K. (1987). *The Afrocentric idea.* Philadelphia: Temple University Press.

Asante, M. K. (1991/92). Afrocentric curriculum. *Educational Leadership, 49*, 28–31.

Association of American Colleges (1985). *Integrity in the college curriculum: A report to the academic community.* Washington, DC: AAC.

Association of American Colleges (1989). *Engaging cultural legacies: Shaping core curricula in the humanities.* A proposal to the National Endowment for the Humanities, Washington, DC.

Association of American Colleges (1991). *The challenge of connecting learning.* Liberal Learning and the Arts and Sciences Major, volume 1. Washington, DC: AAC.

Astin, A. (1993). What matters in college? Implications for cooperative learning of a new national study. *Cooperative Learning and College Teaching, 3*(3), 2–8.

Attneave, C. (1982). American Indians and Alaska Native families: Emigrants in their own homeland. In M. McGoldrick, J. K. Pearce, & J. Giordano (Eds.), *Ethnicity and family therapy* (pp. 55–83). NY: Guilford Press.

Atwater, M. M. (1993). Multicultural science education. *The Science Teacher 60*, 32–37.

Atwater, M. M., & Riley, J. P. (1993). Multicultural science education: Perspectives, definitions, and research agenda. *Science Education, 77*, 661–668.

Au, K. H., & Kawakami, A. J. (1994). Cultural congruence in instruction. In E. R. Hollins, J. E. King, & W. C. Hayman (Eds.), *Teaching diverse populations: Formulating a knowledge base* (pp. 5–23). Albany: University of New York Press.

Auerbach, J., et al. (1985). On Gilligan's In a different voice. *Feminist studies 11*(1), 149–161.

Auletta, G., & Jones, T. (1990). Reconstituting the inner circle. *American Behavioal Scientist, 34*(2), 137–152.

Axtell, J. (1981). *The European and the Indian: Essays in the ethnohistory of Colonial North America.* New York: Oxford University Press.

Ayers, W. (1993). *To teach: The journey of a teacher.* New York: Teachers College Press, Columbia University.

Bacchi, C. L. (1990). *Same difference: Feminism and sexual difference.* Sydney: Allen and Unwin.

Baker, G. (1973). Multicultural training for teacher education. *Journal of Teacher Education, 24,* 306–308.

Baker, G. C. (1974). Instructional priorities in a culturally pluralistic school. *Educational Leadership, 32,* 176–182.

Baker, K. (1987). Comment on Willig's "A meta-analysis of selected studies in the effectiveness of bilingual education." *Review of Educational Research, 57,* 351–362.

Baldwin, James. (1955, 1984). *Notes of a native son.* Boston: Beacon.

Baldwin, James. (1961). *Nobody knows my name.* New York: Dell.

Ballard, B., & Clanchy, J. (1991). Assessment by misconception: Cultural influences and intellectual traditions. In L. Hamp-Lyons (Ed.), *Assessing second language writing in academic contexts* (pp. 19–35). Norwood, NJ: Ablex.

Banks, C. M. (1993). Restructuring schools for equity: What have we learned in two decades? *Phi Delta Kappan, 75*(1), 42–59.

Banks, J. A. (1988). *Multiethnic education: Theory and practice* (2nd ed.). Boston: Allyn and Bacon.

Banks, J. A. (1991). *Teaching strategies for ethnic studies.* Boston: Allyn and Bacon.

Banks, J. A. (1991/92). Multicultural education: For freedom's sake. *Educational Leadership,* 49(4), 32–36.

Banks, J. A. (1993). Approaches to multicultural curriculum reform. In J. A. Banks & C. A. M. Banks (Eds.), *Multicultural education: Issues and perspectives* (pp. 195–214). Boston: Allyn and Bacon.

Banks, J. A. (1993). Multicultural education: Development, dimensions, and challenges. *Phi Delta Kappan, 75*(1), 22–28.

Banks, J. A. (1993). Multicultural education: Historical development, dimensions, and practice. In L. Darling-Hammond (Ed.), *Review of research in education, Vol. 19* (pp. 3–49). Washington, DC: American Educational Research Association.

Banks, J. A. (1994a). *An introduction to multicultural education.* Boston: Allyn and Bacon.

Banks, J. A. (1994b). Multicultural education for all Americans. *Catalyst,* 1, 4–5, 8.

Banks, J. A. (1994c). *Multiethnic education: Theory and practice* (3rd ed.). Boston: Allyn and Bacon.

Banks, J. A. (1995). Multicultural education: Its effects on students' racial and gender role attitudes. In J. A. Banks & C. A. M. Banks (Eds.), *Handbook of research on multicultural education* (pp. 617–627). New York: Macmillan.

Banks, J. A., & Banks, C. M. (Eds.). (1993). *Multicultural education.* (2nd ed.). Boston: Allyn and Bacon.

Banks, J., & Banks, C.M. (1995). *Handbook of research on multicultural education.* New York: Macmillan.

Banks, J. A., Cortes, C. E., Garcia, R. L., Gay, G., & Ochoa, A. S. (1992). Curriculum guidelines for multicultural education. *Social Education, 56,* 274–294.

Banta, T. W. (1992). Student achievement and the assessment of institutional effectiveness. In B. R. Clark & G. R. Neave (Eds.), *The encyclopedia of higher education, Vol. 3* (pp. 1686–1697). Oxford: Pergamon Press.

Barba, R. H. (1993, April). *Multicultural infusion: A strategy for science teacher preparation.* Paper presented at the Annual Meeting of the National Association for Research in Science Teaching.

Bartlett, R. L. (1985). *An introductory lecture in macroeconomics: Integrating the new Scholarship on women.* New York: American Economic Association.

Bartlett, R. L. (Ed.). (In progress). *Integrating race and gender into Economics 101.*

Bartlett, R. L., & Feiner, S. F. (1992). Balancing the economics curriculum: Content, method and pedagogy. *American Economic Review,* 82(2), 559–564.

Bartlett, R. L., & Miller, T. I. (1981). Evaluating the Federal Open Market Committee Simulation: A complimentary teaching technique. *Simulations and Games,* 12(1), 29–49.

Beaudry, J. (1990, April). Pluralistic pedagogy: evaluation of a program to recruit minorities into the teaching profession. Paper presented at the meeting of the American Educational Research Association, Boston, MA.

Beaudry, J. (1992). Synthesizing research in multicultural teacher education: Findings and issues for evaluation of cultural diversity. In Anna Madison (Ed.), *New Directions for Program Evaluation, 53*, 69–83.

Beck, E. T. (1988). The politics of Jewish invisibility. *NWSA journal*, 1(1), 93–102.

Beck, E. T. (1988; reprinted 1992). From "kike" to "JAP": How misogyny, anti-semitism, and racism construct the "Jewish American princess." In Andersen & Collins, (Eds.), *Race, class, and gender* (pp. 88–95). Belmont: Wadsworth.

Beckhard, R., & Pritchard, W. (1992). *Changing the essence*. San Francisco, CA: Jossey-Bass.

Beer, M., Eisenstat, R., & Spector, B. (1990). Why change programs don't produce change. *Harvard Business Review*, 68(6), 158–166.

Belgarde, M. J. (1994, April). *Acculturation at an elite university: Persisting as a Native American undergraduate at Stanford*. Paper presented at the meeting of the American Educational Research Association, New Orleans, LA.

Bell, C. S. (1975). The next revolution. In Laurily K. Epstein (Ed.), *Women in the Profession*. Lexington, MA: Lexington Books.

Bell, C. S. (1984). Economics, sex, and gender. *The Social Science Quarterly*, 55(3), 615–631.

Bem, Sandra Lipsitz. (1991). *The lenses of gender: Transforming the debate on sexual inequality*. New Haven: Yale University Press.

Beneria, L., & Roldan, M. (1987). *The crossroads of class and gender: Industrial homework, subcontracting, and household dynamics in Mexico City*. Chicago: University of Chicago Press.

Beneria, L., & Stimpson, C. R. (1987). *Women, households, and the economy*. New Brunswick: Rutgers University Press.

Benjamin, R., Carroll, S., Jacobi, M., Krop, C., & Shires, M. (1993). *The redesign of governance in higher education*. Santa Monica, CA: Rand.

Bennett, C. (1988). Assessing teachers' abilities for educating multicultural students: The need for conceptual models in teacher education. In C. A. Heid (Ed.), *Multicultural education: Knowledge and perceptions* (pp. 23–35). Bloomington, IN: Indiana University Center for Urban and Multicultural Education.

Bennett, C. I. (1990). *Comprehensive multicultural education*. Needham Heights, MA: Allyn and Bacon.

Bennis, W. G. (1989). *On becoming a leader*. New York: Harper & Row.

Bensimon, E. M., & Neumann, A. (1993). *Redesigning collegiate leadership*. Baltimore: The Johns Hopkins University Press.

Benson, M. (1989). The academic listening task: A case study. *TESOL Quarterly*, 23(3), 421–445.

Bergmann, B. R. (1983). Feminism and economics. *Academe*, 69(5), 22–25.

Bergmann, B. R. (1986). *The economic emergence of women*. New York: Basic Books.

Bergmann, B. R. (1987). Women's roles in the economy: Teaching the issues. *Journal of Economic Education*, 18(4) 393–407.

Bergquist, W. H. (1993). *The postmodern organization: Mastering the art of irreversible change*. San Francisco: Jossey-Bass.

Bergquist, W. H., & Phillips, S. R. (1975–1981). *A handbook for faculty development* (Vols 1–3). Washington, DC: Council of Independent Colleges.

Birnbaum, R. (1992). *How academic leadership works*. San Francisco: Jossey-Bass.

Blau, F. D., & Ferber, M. A. (1986). *The economics of women, men, and work*. Englewood Cliffs, NJ: Prentice-Hall.

Blaxall, M., & Reagan, B. (1976). *Women and the workplace: The Implications of occupational segregation*. Chicago: The University of Chicago Press.

Blier, R. (1984). *Science and gender: A critique of biology and its theories on women*. New York: Pergamon.

Blier, R. (1986). *Feminist approaches to science*. New York: Pergamon.

Blinder, A. S. (1990). Learning by asking those who are doing. *Eastern Economic Journal*, 16(4), 297–306.

Bloom, B. R., & Murray, C. J. L. (1992). Tuberculosis: Commentary on a reemergent killer. *Science, 257*, 1055–1064.

Bloom, B. S. (1956). *Taxonomy of educational objectives: The classification of educational goals. Handbook I: Cognitive domain*. New York: Mckay.

Bloome, D., & Green, J. (1984). Directions in the sociolinguistic study of reading. In P. D. Pearson (Ed.), *Handbook of reading research* (pp. 395–421). New York: Longman.

Blurton, C. (1994). Using the Internet for teaching, learning, and research. In D. F. Halpern

(Ed.), *Changing college classrooms: New teaching and learning strategies for an increasingly complex world* (pp. 191–212). San Francisco: Jossey-Bass.

Bock, G., & J., S. (Eds.). (1992). *Beyond equality and difference; Citizenship, feminist politics, female subjectivity.* London: Routledge.

Bolman, L. G., & Deal, T. E. (1991). *Reframing organizations: Artistry, choice, and leadership.* San Francisco: Jossey-Bass.

Boone, J., Kaiser, R., & Litowitz, D. (1988). *Race and age differences in instruction and testing.* Memphis, TN: Memphis State University, Center for the Study of Higher Education. (ERIC Document Reproduction Service No. ED 304 027)

Border, L. L. B., & Van Note Chism, N. (Eds.). (1992). *Teaching for diversity.* San Francisco: Jossey-Bass.

Bormuth, J. R. (1968). The cloze readability procedure. *Elementary English, 45,* 429–436.

Boulding, K. E. (1970). Increasing the supply of Black economists: Is economics culture bound? *American Economic Review, LX*(2), 406–411.

Bourdieu, P., & Passeron, J. C. (1990). *Reproduction in education, society and culture* (2nd ed.). London: Sage Publications.

Bowser, B., Auletta G., & Jones T. (1993). *Confronting diversity issues on campus.* Newbury Park: Sage Publications.

Boyd, C. (1992). *Individual commitment and organizational change: A guide for human resource and organization development specialists.* New York: Quorum Books.

Boyer, E. L., & Levine, A. (1981). *A quest for common learning.* Washington, DC: Carnegie Foundation for the Advancement of Teaching.

Boyer, J. B. (1990). Teacher education that enhances equity. In H. P. Baptiste, Jr., H. C. Waxman, J. Walker de Felix, & J. E. Anderson (Eds.), *Leadership, equity, and school effectiveness* (pp. 244–258). Newbury Park, CA: Sage.

Bradburn, N., & Sudman, S. (1979). *Improving interview method and questionnaire design.* San Francisco: Jossey-Bass.

Bradley, A. (1994, May). Practice what you teach. *Education Week, 13*(33), 26–28.

Brandt, R. (Ed.). (1993). Inventing new systems. *Educational Leadership, 51*(1).

Brauer, A. (1994). Masters degree portfolio. Seattle: University of Washington.

Braverman, H. (1975). *Labor and monopoly capital: The degradation of work in the twentieth century.* New York: Monthly Review Press.

Brighton Women in Science Group. (1980) *Alice through the microscope: The power of science over women's lives.* London: Virago.

Brinton, D., & Mano, S. (1994). "You have a chance also": Case studies of ESL students at the university. In F. Peitzman & G. Gadda (Eds.), *With different eyes: Insights into teaching language minority students across the disciplines* (pp. 1–21). New York: Longman.

Bronfenbrenner, M. W., Sichel, W., & Gardiner, W. (1990). *Economics.* Boston: Houghton Mifflin.

Bronstein, P., & Quina, K. (Eds) (1988). *Teaching a psychology of people: Resources for gender and sociocultural awareness* (pp. 3–11) Maryland: St. Mary's Press.

Brown, C. E. (1992). Restructuring for a new America. In M. E. Dilworth (Ed.), *Diversity in teacher education: New expectations* (pp. 1–22). San Francisco: Jossey-Bass.

Brown, C., & Pechman, J. A. (1987). *Gender in the workplace.* Washington DC: The Brookings Institution.

Brown, F. G. (1981). *Measuring classroom achievement.* New York: Holt, Rinehart, & Winston.

Brown, W., & Ling, A. (Eds.). (1991). *Imagining America: Stories from the promised land.* New York: Persea Books.

Brown, W., & Ling, A. (Eds.). (1993). *Visions of America: Personal narratives from the promised land.* New York: Persea Books.

Browne, S., et al. (Eds.). (1985). *With the power of each breath: A disabled woman's anthology.* Pittsburgh: Cleis Press.

Buchen, I. H. (1992). The impact of cultural diversity on faculty and students. *Equity & Excellence, 25,* 228–232.

Burlbaw, L. M. (Spring, 1994). Walking in the right direction: Realistic multicultural education infusion. *MEI Center Connection, 2*(2), 6–7. (The newsletter of the Multicultural

Education Infusion Center, College of Education, San Diego State University.)

Butler, J. (1989). *Gender trouble: Feminism and the subversion of identity.* New York: Routledge.

Butler, J. E., & Walter, J. C. (Eds.). (1991). *Transforming the curriculum: ethnic studies and women's studies.* Albany: State University of New York Press.

Cahan, A. (1896; rpt. 1970). Yekl: A tale of the ghetto. In *Yekl and The Imported Bridegroom and other stories of the New York ghetto* (pp. 1–89). New York: Dover.

Cain, G. G. (1966). *Married women in the labor force: An economic analysis.* Chicago: The University of Chicago Press.

California Postsecondary Education Commission. (1992). *Resource Guide for Assessing Campus Climate.* (Report 92-24). Sacramento: Author.

Campbell, D. (1984). Can we be scientific in applied social science? In R. Connor, D. Altman, & H. Preskill (Eds.), *Evaluation Studies Review Annual* (pp. 117–127). Beverly Hills, CA: Sage.

Candelaria, N. (1993). The day the Cisco Kid shot John Wayne. In H. Augenbraum & I. Stavans (Eds.), *Growing up Latino: Memoirs and stories* (pp. 115–130). Boston: Houghton Mifflin.

Cannon, L. W. et al. (1991). Race and class bias in qualitative research on women. In J. Lorber & S. Farrell (Eds.), *The social construction of gender* (pp. 237–248). Newbury Park, CA: Sage Publications.

Carnegie Foundation for the Advancement of Teaching (1992, January/February) Signs of a changing curriculum. *Change, 24,*   49–52.

Carpio, B. A., & Majumdar, B. (Winter, 1993). Experiential learning: An approach to transcultural education for nursing. *Journal of Transcultural Nursing: Transcultural Nursing Society,* 4(2), 9.

Carrell, P. L. (1983). Three components of background knowledge in reading comprehension. *Language Learning, 33,* 183–207.

Carrell, P. L., & Eisterhold, J. C. (1983). Schema theory and ESL reading pedagogy. *TESOL Quarterly,* 17(4), 553–573.

Carter, D. J., & Wilson, R. (1991). *Tenth annual status report: Minorities in higher education.* Washington, DC: American Council on

Education, Office of Minorities in Higher Education.

Carter, D. J., & Wilson, R. (1994). *Minorities in higher education. 1993 twelfth annual status report.* Washington, DC: American Council on Education.

Carter, D. J., & Wilson, R. (1995). *Minorities in higher education. 1994 thirteenth annual status report.* Washington, DC: American Council on Education.

Case, C., & Lau, G. (1991). Teaching strategies for the multicultural/ multilingual classroom. In C. Johnson (Ed.), *Strategies for success in anatomy & physiology and life sciences.* Issue 6, 1–3. Redwood City, CA: Benjamin/Cummings.

Castenell, L. A., Jr., & Pinar, W. F. (Eds.). (1993). *Understanding curriculum as racial text: representations of identity and difference in education.* Albany, NY: State University of New York Press.

Centra, J. A. (1985). Maintaining Faculty Vitality Through Faculty Development. In S. M. Clark & D. R. Lewis (Eds.), *Faculty Vitality and Institutional Productivity* (139–156). New York: Teachers College Press.

Ch'maj, B. E. M. (Ed.). (1993). *Multicultural America: A resource for teachers of Humanities and American Studies: Syllabi, essays, projects, bibliographies.* Lanham, Maryland: University Press of America.

Chaffee, E. E., & Tierney, W. G. (1988). *Collegiate culture and leadership strategies.* New York: Macmillan.

Chan, S. (1992). Families with Asian roots. In E. W. Lynch & M. J. Hanson (Eds.), *Developing cross-cultural competence: A guide to working with young children and their families* (pp. 181–257). Baltimore, MD: Paul H. Brookes.

Changing America: The New Face of Science and Engineering. (1989). The Final Report on Women, Minorities, and the Handicapped in Science and Technology. Washington, DC: National Science Foundation.

Chaudron, C., & Richards, J. C. (1986). The effects of discourse markers on the comprehension of lectures. *Applied Linguistics, 7,* 113–127.

Cheng, L. (1993). Faculty challenges in the education of foreign-born students. In L. W. Clark (Ed.), *Faculty and student challenges in facing cultural and linguistic diversity* (pp. 173–185). Springfield, IL: Charles C. Thomas.

Cheng, L. L. (1987). *Assessing Asian language performance*. Rockville, MD: Aspen Publishers.

Chesler, M. A., & Crowfoot, J. E. (1990). Racism on campus. In W. W. May (Ed.), *Ethics and higher education* (pp. 195–230). New York: American Council on Education, Macmillan Publishing Co.

Chiang, C., & Dunkel, P. (1992). The effect of speech modification, prior knowledge, and listening proficiency on ESL lecture learning. *TESOL Quarterly, 26*(2), 345–374.

Chodorow, N. (1978). *The reproduction of mothering: Psychoanalysis and the sociology of gender*. Berkeley: University of California Press.

Christensen, R. C., & Hansen, A. J. (1987). *Teaching and the Case Method*. Boston: Harvard Business School.

Christison, M. A., & Krahnke, K. J. (1986). Student perceptions of academic language study. *TESOL Quarterly, 20*(1), 61–81.

Chronicle of Higher Education (August 25, 1993). Almanac Issue, 40(1).

Cisneros, S. (1991). *Woman Hollering Creek, and other stories*. New York: Random House.

Claxton, C. S., & Murrell, P. H. (1987). *Learning styles: Implications for improving educational practices*. ASHE-ERIC Higher Education Report No. 4. Washington, DC: Association for the Study of Higher Education.

Cliff, M. (1983). If I could write this in fire I would write this in fire. In B. Smith (Ed.), *Home girls: A Black feminist anthology* (pp. 15–30). New York: Kitchen Table: Women of Color Press.

Cohen, E. (1986). *Designing groupwork*. New York: Teachers College Press.

Cohen, M. D., & March, J. G. (1974). *Leadership and ambiguity: The American college president*. New York: McGraw-Hill.

Cohn, C. (1990). "'Clean bombs' & clean language." In J. Elshtain & S. Tobias (Eds.), *Women, militarism, and war: Essays in history, politics, and social theory* (pp. 33–35). Savage, MD: Rowan and Littlefield.

Cole, M., & Bruner, J. (1971). Cultural differences and inferences about psychological processes. *American Psychologist, 26*(10), 867–875.

Collier, V. P. (1987). Age and rate of acquisition of second language for academic purposes. *TESOL Quarterly, 21*, 617–641.

Collier, V. P. (1989). How long? A synthesis of research on academic achievement in a second language. *TESOL Quarterly, 23*(3), 509–531.

Collier, V. P., & Thomas, W. P. (1988, April). *Acquisition of cognitive-academic second language proficiency: A six-year study*. Paper presented at the annual meeting of the American Educational Research Association, New Orleans.

Collins, P. H. (1990). *Black feminist thought: Knowledge, consciousness, and the politics of empowerment*. Boston: Unwin Hyman.

Commission on Civil Rights (1992). *Civil rights issues facing Asian Americans in the 1990s*. Washington, DC.

Committee for Economic Development. (1987). *Children in need: Investment strategies for the educationally disadvantaged*. New York: Author.

Conaway, M. S. (1982). Listening: Learning tool and retention agent. In A. S. Algier & K. W. Algier (Eds.), *Improving reading and study skills*. San Francisco: Josey-Bass.

Conciatore, J. (1990). From flunking to mastering calculus. *Black Issues in Higher Education, 6*, 5–6.

Conrad, C. (1992). Evaluating undergraduate courses on women in the economy. *American Economic Review, 82*(2), 565–569.

Contreras, A. (1988, April) "Multicultural attitudes and knowledge of education students at Indiana University." Paper presented at the annual meeting of the American Educational Research Association. New Orleans.

Cook, T., & Campbell, D. (1979). *Quasi-experimentation: Design and analysis issues for field settings*. Chicago: Rand McNally.

Cooper, J. (Ed.). (1993). Last FIPSE-sponsored newsletter highlights contributors to October cooperative learning conference. *Cooperative Learning and College Teaching, 3*(3), 1–2.

Cooper, J. A., Jones, W. A., & Weber, H. L. (1973). Specifying teacher competencies. *Journal of Teacher Education, 24*, 17–23.

Cott, N. (1986). Feminist theory and feminist movements: The past before us. In J. Mitchell and A. Oakley (Eds.), *What is feminism?* (pp. 49–62). New York: Pantheon Books.

Crenshaw, K. (1992). Whose story is it, anyway? Feminist and antiracist appropriations of Anita Hill. In T. Morrison (Ed.), *Race-ing justice, en-gendering power: Essays on Anita Hill, Clarence Thomas and the construction of social reality* (pp. 402–440). New York: Pantheon Books.

Crow, G. K. (1988). *Toward a theory of therapeutic syncretism: The Southeast Asian experience: A study of the Cambodians' use of traditional and cosmopolitan health systems.* Unpublished doctoral dissertation, University of Utah, Salt Lake City, Utah.

Cuban, L. (1973). Ethnic content and "white" instruction. In J. A. Banks (Ed.), *Teaching ethnic studies: Concepts and strategies* (pp. 103–113). Washington, DC: National Council for the Social Studies.

Cummins, J. (1981a). Age on arrival and immigrant second language learning in Canada: A reassessment. *Applied Linguistics, 2,* 131–149.

Cummins, J. (1981b). The role of primary language development in promoting educational success for language minority students. In California Office of Bilingual Bicultural Education, *Schooling and language minority students: A theoretical framework.* Sacramento, CA: CA Dept. of Education.

Cummins, J. (1986). Empowering minority students: A framework for intervention. *Harvard Educational Review, 56*(1), 18–36.

Darder, A. (1991). *Culture and power in the classroom.* New York: Bergin & Garvey.

Davis, J. (1992). Race as a variable for evaluation. *New Directions in Program Evaluation, 53,* 55–67.

De Lauretis, Teresa. (1987). *Technologies of gender.* Bloomington and Indianapolis: Indiana University Press.

Delgado-Gaitan, C. (1993). Researching change and changing the researcher. *Harvard Educational Review, 63*(4), 389–411.

Delgado-Gaitan, C., & Trueba, H. (1991). *Crossing cultural borders: Education for immigrant families in America.* New York: Falmer.

Department of Commerce. (1992). *Statistical abstracts of the United States 1992.* Washington, DC: U.S. Department of Commerce, Bureau of the Census.

Department of Education. (1993a). *Digest of education statistics 1992.* Washington, DC: U.S. Department of Education Office of Educational Research and Improvement.

Department of Education. (1993b). *The Pocket Condition of Education 1993.* Washington, DC: U.S. Department of Education Office of Educational Research and Improvement.

Deyhle, D. (1986). Success and failure: A micro-ethnographic comparison of Navajo and Anglo students' perceptions of testing. *Curriculum Inquiry, 16*(4), 365–389.

Diaz, C. (Ed.). (1992). *Multicultural education for the 21st century.* Washington, DC: NEA Professional Library.

Dill, B. T. (1988, reprinted 1992). Our mothers' grief: Racial ethnic women and the maintenance of families. In M. L. Andersen & P. H. Collins (Eds.), *Race, class, and gender* (pp. 215–238). Belmont, CA: Wadsworth.

Dill, D. D. (Ed.). (1990). *What teachers need to know: The knowledge, skills, and values essential to good teaching.* San Francisco: Jossey-Bass.

Dixon, V. (1970). The diunital approach to "Black Economics." *American Economic Review , LX*(2), 424–429.

Dixon, V. (1977). African-oriented and Euro-American-oriented world views: Research methodology and economics. *The Review of Black Political Economy, 7*(2), 119–156.

Dolan, E. G., & Lindsay, D. E. (1987). *Basic economics.* Chicago: Dryden Press.

Donato, M. (1994, April 28). Stronger penalties in place for hate crimes. *Chicago Tribune*, Section 2, p. 9.

Dornic, S. (1979). Information processing in bilinguals: Some selected issues. *Psychological Research, 40*(4), 329–348.

Downing, K. E., Mac Adam, B., & Nichols, D. P. (1993). *Reaching a multicultural student community.* Westport, CT: Greenwood Press.

Du Bois, W. E. B. (1903, this ed. 1989). *The souls of black folk.* New York: Viking Penguin.

Du Bois, W. E. B. (1973). *The education of Black people: Ten critiques, 1906–1960.* Edited by H. Aptheker. New York: Monthly Review Press.

Duberman, M. (1993). "A matter of difference." *The Nation, 5*, 22.

Dunbar, L. W. (1984). *Minority report: What has happened to Blacks, Hispanics, American Indians, and other minorities in the eighties?* New York: Pantheon.

Dunn, R., Bruno, J., Sklar, R., & Beaudry, J. (1990). The effects of matching and mismatching minority developmental college students' hemispheric preferences on mathematics test scores. *Journal of Educational Research, 83*, 283–288.

Dunn, R., Gemake, J., Jalali, F., & Zenhausern, R. (1990). Cross-cultural differences in learning styles of elementary-age students from four ethnic backgrounds. *Journal of Multicultural Counseling and Development, 18*, 68–91.

Dyson, M. E. (1993). *Reflecting Black: African-American cultural criticism.* Minneapolis: University of Minnesota Press.

Edmondson, K. M., & Novak, J. D. (1993). The interplay of scientific epistemological views, learning strategies, and attitudes of college students. *Journal of Research in Science Teaching, 30*, 547–559.

Edwards, R. C., Reich, M., & Gordon, D. M. (1975). *Labor market segmentation.* Lexington, MA: D. C. Heath.

Ehrenreich, B. (1991, April 8). Teach diversity—with a smile. *Time, 137*(14), 84.

Ehrenreich, B., & Ehrenreich, J. (1979). The professional-managerial class. In P. Walker (Ed.), *Between Labor and Capital* (pp. 5–45). Boston: South End Press.

Elliott, J. E. (1993). Lesbian and gay concerns in career development. In L. Diamant (Ed.), *Homosexual issues in the workplace* (pp. 25–43). Washington, DC: Taylor & Francis.

Ellsworth, E (1989). Why doesn't this feel empowering? Working through the repressive myths of critical pedagogy. *Harvard Educational Review, 59*(3), 297–324.

English, K. M. (1993). *The role of support services in the integration and retention of college students who are hearing impaired.* Unpublished doctoral dissertation, The Claremont Graduate School and San Diego State University.

Enloe, C. H. (1990). *Bananas, beaches, and bases: Making feminist sense of international politics.* Berkeley: University of California Press.

Epstein, S. (1987, May-August). Gay politics, ethnic identity: The limits of social constructionism. *Socialist review, 17*(3–4) 9–54.

Ewell, P. T. (1991). To capture the ineffable: New forms of assessment in higher education. In G. Grant (Ed.), *Review of research in education, Vol. 17* (pp. 75–125). Washington, DC: American Educational Research Association.

Faludi, S. (1991). *Backlash: The undeclared war against American women.* New York: Crown.

Faragher, J. M. et al. (1994). *Out of Many.* [Brochure]. Englewood Cliffs, NJ: Prentice Hall.

Fassinger, R. W. (1993). Lesbian and gay issues in education. In L. Diamant (Ed.), *Homosexual issues in the workplace* (pp. 119–142). Washington, DC: Taylor & Francis.

Fausto-Sterling, A. (1992a). *Myths of gender: Biological theories about women and men.* 2nd edition. New York: Basic Books.

Fausto-Sterling, A. (1992b). Race, gender, and science. *Transformations, 2*(2), 4–12.

Federal Glass Ceiling Commission. (March 1995). *Good for business: Making full use of the nation's human capital. The environmental scan.* Washington, DC: U.S. Department of Labor.

Feiner, S. F. (1993). Women and minorities in introductory economics textbooks: A look at the last 15 years. *The Journal of Economic Education, 24*(2), 145–162.

Feiner, S. F. (1994). *Race and gender in the American economy: Views from across the spectrum.* New York: Prentice-Hall.

Feiner, S. F., & Morgan, B. A. (1987). Women and minorities in introductory economics textbooks: 1974–1984. *The Journal of Economic Education, 18*(4), 376–392.

Feiner, S. F., & Roberts, B. B. (1990). Hidden by the invisible hand: Neoclassical economic theory and the textbook treatment of race and gender. *Gender and Society, 4*(2), 159–181.

Ferguson, A. et al. (1981). On "Compulsory heterosexuality and lesbian existence." *Signs: Journal of women in culture and society, 5*(4), 631–660.

Fetterman, D. (1989). *Ethnography: Step by step.* Newbury Park, CA: Sage.

Feuer, M. J., & Fulton, K. (1993). The many faces of performance assessment. *Phi Delta Kappan, 74,* 478.

Fischbach, R. M., & Johnson, S. D. (1992). *Teaching problem solving and technical mathematics through cognitive apprenticeship at the community college level.* University of California, Berkeley: National Center for Research in Vocational Education.

Fisher, D. (Ed.). (1980). *The third woman: Minority women writers of the United States.* Boston: Houghton Mifflin.

Fisher, K. M., Lipson, J. I., Hildebrand, A. C., Miguel, L., Schoenberg, N., & Porter, N. (1986). Student misconceptions and teacher assumptions in college biology. *Journal of College Science Teaching, 15,* 276–280.

Fisk-Skinner, E., & Gaither, T. (1992). Nontraditional students: Ethnic minorities. *The encyclopedia of higher education* (Vol. 3, pp. 1658–1666). New York: Pergamon Press.

Florio-Ruane, S. (1989). Social organization of classes and schools. In M. C. Reynolds (Ed.), *Knowledge base for the beginning teacher* (pp. 163–172). Published for the American Association of Colleges for Teacher Education. New York: Pergamon Press.

Fombrun, C. J. (1992). *Turning points: Creating strategic change in corporations.* New York: McGraw-Hill.

Frankenberg, R. (1993). *White women, race matters: The social construction of whiteness.* Minneapolis: Universitiy of Minnesota Press.

Franklin, M. E. (1992). Culturally sensitive instructional practices for African-American learners with disabilities. *Exceptional Children, 59,* 115–122.

Freire, P. (1970). *Pedagogy of the Oppressed.* New York: Seabury Press.

Freire, P. (1985). *The politics of education.* South Hadley, Mass.: Bergin and Garvey.

Fried, J. (1993). Bridging emotion and intellect: classroom diversity in process *College Teaching* 41(4), 123–128.

Fuchs, V. R. (1988). *Women's quest for economic equality.* Cambridge, MA: Harvard University Press.

Fullan, M. (1982). *The meaning of educational change.* New York: Teachers College Press.

Fullan, M. (1991). *The new meaning of educational change.* New York: Teachers College Press.

Fullan, M. (1993). *Change forces: Probing the depths of educational reform.* New York: Falmer Press.

Fuller, M. (1992). Teacher education programs and increasing minority school populations: An educational mismatch? In Grant, C. (Ed.), *Research and multicultural education: From the margins to the mainstream* (pp. 184–200). London: The Falmer Press.

Fullilove, R., & Treisman, U. (1990). Mathematics achievement among African American undergraduates at the University of California, Berkeley: An evaluation of the Mathematics Workshop Program. *Journal of Negro Education, 59,* 463–478.

Gaff, J. G. (1991). *New life for the college curriculum: Assessing achievements and furthering progress in the reform of general education.* San Francisco: Jossey-Bass.

Gaff, J. G. (January/February 1992). Beyond politics: The educational issues inherent in multicultural education. *Change,* 24(1), 31–35.

García, E. (1994). *Understanding and meeting the challenge of student cultural diversity.* Boston: Houghton Mifflin.

García, R. (1991). *Teaching in a pluralistic society: concepts, models, strategies* (2nd ed.). New York: Harper Collins.

Gardner, H. (1987). Beyond the IQ: Education and human development. *Harvard Educational Review, 57,* 187–193.

Gardner, J. W. (1981). *Self-renewal: The individual and the innovative society.* Revised Edition. New York: W. W. Norton and Company.

Gardner, J. W. (1984). *Excellence. Can we be equal and excellent too?* Revised Edition. New York: W. W. Norton and Company.

Garibaldi, A. M. (1992). Preparing teachers for culturally diverse classrooms. In M. E. Dilworth (Ed.), *Diversity in teacher education: New expectations* (pp. 23–39). San Francisco: Jossey-Bass.

Gates, H. L., Jr. (1992). TV's Black world turns—But stays unreal. In M. L. Andersen & P. H. Collins (Eds.), *Race, class, and gender* (pp. 310–317). Belmont, CA: Wadsworth Publishing Company.

Gaudiani, C. (1991). In pursuit of global civic virtues: Multiculturalism in the curriculum. *Liberal Education, 77*(3), 12–15.

Gawelek, M. A. (1993). *The social construction of faculty-student power relations*. A Presentation for the College of Arts and Letters Faculty Development Seminar, San Diego State University, San Diego, CA, November 5, 1993.

Gay, G. (1977). Curriculum for multicultural teacher education. In F. H. Klassen & D. M. Gollnick (Eds.), *Pluralism and the American teacher: Issues and case studies* (pp. 31–62). Washington, DC: American Association of Colleges for Teacher Education.

Gay, G. (1986). Multicultural teacher education. In J. A. Banks & J. Lynch (Eds.), *Multicultural education in western societies* (pp. 154–177). New York: Holt, Rinehart and Winston.

Gay, G. (1990). Teacher preparation for equity. In H. P. Baptiste, Jr., H. C. Waxman, J. Walker de Felix, & J. E. Anderson (Eds.), *Leadership, equity, and school effectiveness* (pp. 224–243). Newbury Park, CA: Sage.

Gay. G. (1993a). Building cultural bridges: A bold proposal for teacher education. *Education and Urban Society, 25*, 285–299.

Gay, G. (1993b). Ethnic minorities and educational equality. In J. A. Banks & C. A. M. Banks (Eds.), *Multicultural education: Issues and perspectives* (pp. 171–194). Second Edition. Boston: Allyn and Bacon.

Gay, G. (1994). *At the essence of learning: Multicultural education*. West Lafayette, IN: Kappa Delta Pi.

Gay, L. R. (1985). *Educational evaluation and measurement* (2nd ed.). New York: Macmillan.

Gentemann, K. M., & Whitehead, T. L. (1983). The cultural broker concept in bilingual education. *Journal of Negro Education, 54*, 118–129.

George, P. S., & Alexander, W. M. (1993). *The exemplary middle school*. Second Edition. New York: Harcourt Brace Jovanovich.

Gilligan, C. (1982). *In a different voice*. Cambridge, MA: Harvard University Press.

Gilmore, D. (1990). *Manhood in the making: Cultural concepts of masculinity*. New Haven: Yale University Press.

Giroux, H. (1981). Hegemony, resistence, and the paradox of educational reform. In H. Giroux, A. Penna, & W. Pinar (Eds.), *Curriculum and Instruction*. Berkeley, CA: McCutchan.

Giroux, H. A. (1988). *Teachers as intellectuals*. Granby, MA: Bergin & Garvey.

Giroux, H. A. (1993). *Border crossings: Cultural workers and the politics of education*. New York: Routledge.

Glatthorn, A. A. (1987). "The hidden curriculum." *Curriculum Leadership* (pp. 20–22). Scott Foresman Publishing.

Gluck, S. B. & Patai, D. (Eds.). (1991). *Women's words: The feminist practice of oral history*. New York: Routledge, Chapman, and Hall.

Goldin, C. (1990). *Understanding the gender gap: An economic history of American women*. New York: Oxford University Press.

Gollnick, D. (1976). *Multicultural education and ethnic studies in the United States: An analysis and annotated bilbiliography of selected ERIC documents*. Washington, DC: AACTE

Gollnick, D. (1992). Multicultural education: Policies and practices in teacher education. In Grant, C. (Ed.), *Research and multicultural education: From the margins to the mainstream* (pp. 218–239). London: The Falmer Press.

Gollnick, D. (1995). National and state initiatives for multicultural education. In J. A. Banks & C. A. M. Banks (Eds.). *Handbook of research on multicultural education* (pp. 44–64). New York: Macmillan.

Gollnick, D. M., & Chinn, P. C. (1990). *Multicultural education in a pluralistic society* (3rd ed.). New York: Merrill.

Gonsiorek, J. C., & Weinrich, J. D. (1991). The definition and scope of sexual orientation. In J. C. Gonsiorek & J. D. Weinrich (Eds.), *Homosexuality: Research implications for public policy* (pp. 1–12). Newbury Park, CA: Sage.

Good, T. L., & Brophy, J. E. (1987). *Looking in classrooms*. New York: Harper & Row.

Gooding-Williams, R. (1993). *Reading Rodney King/Reading urban uprising*. New York and London: Routledge.

Goodman, P. S. (1982). *Change in organizations*. San Francisco: Jossey-Bass.

Gordon, E. W., Miller, F., & Rollock, D. (1990). Coping with communicentric bias in knowledge production in the social sciences. *Educational Researcher, 19*, 14–19.

Gould, S. (1981). *The mismeasure of man.* New York: W. W. Norton & Company.

Grady, E. (1992). *The portfolio approach to assessment.* Bloomington, IN: Phi Delta Kappa Educational Foundation.

Grant, C. (1981). Education that is multicultural and teacher preparation: An examination from the perspective of preservice students. *Journal of Educational Research, 75,* 95–99.

Grant, C. (1992). *Research and multicultural education: From the margins to the mainstream.* London: The Falmer Press.

Grant, C. (1994, April). More policy, less research. In M. Dilworth (Chair), *Culturally responsive research: Preaching to the choir.* Symposium conducted at the meeting of the American Educational Research Association, New Orleans, LA.

Grant, C., & Grant, G. (1985). Staff development and education that is multicultural: A study of an in-service institute for teachers and principals. *British Journal of Inservice Education, 2,* 6–18.

Grant, C., & Koskela, R. (1985). Education that is multicultural and the relationship between preservice campus learning and field experiences. *Journal of Educational Research, 79,* 197–203.

Grant, C., & Secada, W. (1989). Preparing teachers for diversity. In R. Houston (Ed.), *Handbook of Research in Teacher Education* (pp. 403–422). New York: Macmillan.

Grant, C., & Sleeter, C. (1986). Race, class, and gender in education research: An argument for integrative analysis. *Review of Educational Research, 56,* 195–211.

Grant, C., & Sleeter, C. (1989). *Turning on learning: Five approaches for multicultural teaching for race, class, gender, and disability.* Columbus, OH: Merrill Publishing.

Grant, C. A., & Tate, W. F. (1995). Multicultural education through the lens of the multicultural education research literature. In J. A. Banks & C. A. McGee Banks (Eds.), *Handbook of research on multicultural education* (pp. 145–166). New York: Macmillan.

Green, M. F. (Ed.). (1989). *Minorities on campus: A handbook for enhancing diversity.* Washington, DC: American Council on Education.

Greenblat, C. S. (1988). *Designing games and simulations: An illustrated handbook.* Newbury Park, CA: Sage.

Greene, M. (1994, April). *Beginnings, identities, and possibilities: The uses of social imagination.* Paper presented at the meeting of the American Educational Research Association, New Orleans, LA.

Greenwood, D. (1984). The economic significance of "women's place" in society: A new-institutionalist view. *Journal of Economic Issues, XVIII* (3) (pp. 663–680).

Greve, F. (October 24, 1994). Blacks fired at twice the rate. *The San Diego Union Tribune,* A-1, A-11.

Grossberg, L., Nelson, C. & Treichler, P. (Eds.). (1992). *Cultural studies.* New York and London: Routledge.

Grote, K. (1994). Diversity Awareness Profile. (Available from Karen Grote, *Diversity Awareness Profile,* Pfeiffer & Company, San Diego, CA).

Gutknecht, D. B., & Miller, J. R. (1990). *The organizational and human resources sourcebook* (Second Ed.). Lanham, MD: University Press of America.

Hackman, J. D. (1992). What is going on in higher education? Is it time for a change? *The Review of Higher Education, 16*(1), 1–17.

Hadas, M. (1962). *Old wine, new bottles.* New York: Pocket Books.

Haertel, G., & Walberg, H. (1988). Assessing social-psychological classroom environments. In K. Conrad, & C. Roberts-Gray (Eds.), *Evaluating program environments* (pp. 45–62). San Francisco: Jossey-Bass.

Hagans, R., Crohn, L., Walkush, L., & Nelson, S. (1991). *The state's role on effecting systemic change: A northwest depiction.* (Available from Northwest Regional Educational Laboratory, 101 S.W. Main, Portland, OR.)

Hagey, R. (1984). The phenomenon, the explanations, and the responses: Metaphors surrounding diabetes in urban Canadian Indians. *Social Science Medicine, 18*(3), 265–272.

Hale-Benson, J. (1986). *Black children: Their roots, culture and learning styles.* Baltimore, MD: Johns Hopkins University Press.

Hall, R. M., & Sandler, B. R. (1982). *The classroom climate: A chilly one for women?* (Report from the Project on the Status and Education of WOMEN). Washington, DC: Association of American Colleges.

Halpern, D. F. and Associates. (1994). *Changing college classrooms.* San Francisco: Jossey-Bass.

Handy, C. (1978). *Understanding organizations.* New York: Penguin Books.

Hanson, M. J., & Lynch, E. W. (1995). *Early intervention* (2nd ed.). Austin, TX: PRO-ED.

Haraway, D. (1989). *Primate visions: Gender, race, and nature in the world of modern science.* New York: Routledge, Chapman, and Hall.

Haraway, D. (1991). *Simians, cyborgs, and women: The reinvention of nature.* New York: Routledge.

Harding, S. (1986). *The science question in feminism.* Ithaca, NY: Cornell University Press.

Harding, S. (1987a). *Feminism and methodology.* Bloomington, IN: Indiana University Press.

Harding, S. (1987b). Introduction: Is there a feminist method? S. Harding (Ed.), *Feminism and methodology* (pp. 1–14). Bloomington, IN: Indiana University Press.

Harding, S. (1987c). The curious coincidence of feminine and African moralities and world views: Problems for feminist theory. In E. Kittay & D. Meyers (Eds.), *Women and moral theory* (pp. 296–315). Totowa, NJ: Roman and Littlefield.

Harding, S. (1991). *Whose science? Whose knowledge? Thinking from women's lives.* Ithaca: Cornell University Press.

Harding, S. (Ed.). (1993). *The "racial" economy of science: Toward a democratic future.* Bloomington, IN: Indiana University Press.

Harding, S., & O'Barr, J. (1987). *Sex and scientific inquiry.* Chicago: The University of Chicago Press.

Hardy, S. B. (1981). *The woman that never evolved.* Cambridge, MA: Harvard University Press.

Harris, A., & Wideman, D. (1988). The construction of gender and disability in early attachment. In M. Fine & A. Asch (Eds.), *Women with Disabilities: Essays in psychology, culture, and politics* (pp. 115–138). Philadelphia: Temple University Press.

Harrison, P. J. (1992, December 7). Personal communication.

Hartsock, N. C. M. (1983). *Money, sex, and power: Toward a feminist historical materialism.* Boston: Northeastern University Press.

Harvey, W. B. (1991). Faculty responsibility and tolerance. *Thought & Action, VII*(2), 115–136.

Hatch, E. (1983). Simplified input and second language acquisition. In R. Anderson (Ed.), *Pidginization and creolization as language acquisition* (pp. 64–86). Rowley, MA: Newbury House.

Haukoos, G. D., & Satterfield, R. (1986). Learning styles of minority students (Native Americans) and their application in developing a culturally sensitive science classroom. *Community/Junior College Quarterly, 10,* 193–201.

Hearn, J., & Morgan, D. (Eds.). (1991). *Men, masculinities and social theory.* Boston: Unwin Hyman.

Henry, G. (1990). *Practical sampling.* Newbury Park, CA: Sage Publications.

Hernandez, H. (1992). The language minority student and multicultural education. In C. Grant (Ed.) *Research and multicultural education: From the margins to the mainstream* (pp. 218–239). London: The Falmer Press.

Higginbotham, E. B. (1992). African-American women's history and the metalanguage of race. *Signs: Journal of women in culture and society, 17*(2), 251–274.

Hilliard, A. G., III. (1989). Teachers and cultural styles in a pluralistic society. *NEA Today–Special Edition, 7*(6), 65–69.

Hilliard, A. G., III. (1991/92). Why we must pluralize the curriculum. *Educational Leadership, 49*(4), 12–15.

Hitchens, C. (1994, November 28). "Minority Report." *The Nation, 259*(18), 240.

Hodgkinson, H. (1991). Reform versus reality. *Phi Delta Kappan, 73*(1), 9–16.

Hodson, D. (1993). In search of a rationale for multicultural science education. *Science Education, 77,* 685–711.

Hoffman, S. L., Nussenzweig, V., Sadoff, J. C., & Nussenzweig, R. S. (1991). Progress toward malaria preerythrocytic vaccines. *Science, 252,* 520–521.

Holden, C. (1993). Foreign nationals change the face of U.S. science. *Science, 261,* 1769–1771.

Hollins, E. R., King, J. E., & Hayman, W. C. (Eds.). (1994). *Teaching diverse populations: Formulating a knowledge base.* Albany: State University of New York Press.

hooks, b. (1984). *Ain't I a woman: Black women and feminism.* Boston: South End Press.

hooks, b. (1990). Postmodern blackness. *Yearning: Race, gender, and cultural politics* (pp. 23–31). Boston: South End.

hooks, b. (1992). The oppositional gaze: Black female spectators. *Black looks: Race and representation.* Boston: South End Press.

Hoots, R. A. (1992). An outsider's insights on neglected issues in science education: An interview with Sheila Tobias. *Journal of College Science Teaching, 18,* 300–304.

Horn, R. E., & Cleaves, A. (Eds.). (1980). *The guide to simulations/games for education and training.* Beverly Hills, CA: Sage Publications.

House, E. (1991). Evaluation and social justice. In M. McLaughlin & D. Phillips (Eds.), *Ninetieth Yearbook of the National Society for the Study of Education* (233–247). Chicago: The University of Chicago Press.

House, E. (1992, November). *Issues concerning multicultural validity.* Paper presented at the American Evaluation Association, Seattle, WA.

Hubbard, R. (1990). *The politics of women's biology.* New Brunswick, NJ: Rutgers University Press.

Hunter, W. A. (Ed). (1977). *Multicultural education through competency-based teacher education.* Washington, DC: American Association for Colleges of Teacher Education.

Intercollegiate Center for Nursing Education. (1995, April). A working draft copy of a statement of diversity.

Intersegmental Coordinating Council. (1991). *Toward a more diverse faculty for California's schools, colleges, and universities.* Sacramento, CA: Intersegmental Coordinating Council.

Irvin, J. L. (Ed.). (1992). *Transforming middle level education: Perspectives and possibilities.* Boston: Allyn and Bacon.

Irvine, J. J., & York, D. E. (1995). Learning styles and culturally diverse students: A literature review. In J. A. Banks & C. A. McGee Banks (Eds.). *Handbook of research on multicultural education* (pp. 484–497). New York: Macmillan.

Jackson, B. W., & Holvino, E. (1988). Developing multicultural organizations. *Journal of Religion and the Applied Behavioral Sciences, 9*(2), 14–19.

Jackson, P. W. (1968). *Life in classrooms.* New York: Holt, Rinehart, & Winston.

Jenkins, M. M. (1992). Guidelines for cross-cultural communication between students and faculty. In G. S. Auletta, & T. Jones (Leaders). *Teaching and learning in a changing university: Strategies for the multicultural classroom.* California State University, Hayward: Center for the Study of Intercultural Relations. Handouts for the CSU Teaching and Learning Exchange, March 1, 1992.

Joe, J. R. (1995, April 28–29). Traditional medicine; Historical framework. [speech]. In *Healing: Today, Yesterday, and Tomorrow–Bridge Between Traditional and Western Medicine: The 5th Annual Indian Nursing Education Conference.* Buffalo, New York.

Joe, J. R., & Malach, R. S. (1992). Families with Native American roots. In E. W. Lynch & M. J. Hanson (Eds.), *Developing cross-cultural competence* (pp. 89–119). Baltimore: Paul H. Brookes.

Johnson, D. W., & Johnson, R. (1989). *Cooperation and competition: Theory and research.* Edina, MN: Interaction Book Company.

Johnson, D., & Johnson, R. (1991). *Learning together and alone: Cooperative, competitive, and individualistic.* Englewood Cliffs, NJ: Prentice-Hall.

Johnson, D. W., Johnson, R. T., & Smith, K. A. (1991a). *Active learning: cooperation in the college classroom.* Edina, MN: Interaction Book Co.

Johnson, D. W., Johnson, R. T., & Smith, K. A., (1991b). *Cooperative learning: Increasing college faculty instructional productivity.* Washington, DC, George Washington University, ASHE-ERIC, Higher Education Report, no. 4.

Jongsma, E. (1971). *The cloze procedure as a teaching technique.* Newark, DE: International Reading Association.

Junn, E. N. (1994). Experiential approaches to enhancing cultural awareness. In D. F. Halpern & Associates, *Changing college classrooms* (pp. 128–164). San Francisco: Jossey-Bass.

Kafka, P. (1991). A multicultural introduction to literature. In J. M Cahalan & D. B. Downing (Eds.), *Practicing theory in introductory college literature courses* (pp. 179–188). Urbana, Illinois: National Council of Teachers of English.

Kayes, P. E. (1992, July). Access, equity, and cultural diversity: Rediscovering the community college mission. In J. Q. Adams & Jamie R. Welsch (Eds.), *Multicultural education: Strategies for implementation in colleges and universities, Vol. 2* (pp. 85–92). Macomb, IL: Western Illinois University.

Keller, E. F. (1983). *A feeling for the organism: The life and work of Barbara McClintock.* San Francisco: W. H. Freeman.

Keller, E. F. (1985). *Reflections on gender and science.* New Haven: Yale University Press.

Kelley, C., & Meyers, J. (1992). *The cross-cultural adaptability inventory.* (Available from Colleen Kelley Human Relations, La Jolla, CA 92037).

Kellogg, S. (1994, January 21). Biology + music = Cultural diversity. *Innovation Abstracts, XVI*(1). Publisher: The National Institute for Staff and Organizational Development, College of Education, The University of Texas at Austin.

Kelly, G. J., Carlsen, W. S. & Cunningham, C. M. (1993). Science education in sociocultural context: Perspectives from the sociology of science. *Science Education, 77*, 207–220.

Keltner, B. R. (1993, Oct-Dec). Native American children and adolescents: Cultural distinctiveness and mental health needs. *Journal of Child and Adolescent Psychiatric and Mental Health Nursing, 6*(4), 19–23.

Kent, D. (1988). In search of a heroine: Images of women with disabilities in fiction and drama. In M. Fine and A. Asch (Eds.), *Women with Disabilities: Essays in Psychology, Culture, and Politics* (pp. 90–110). Philadelphia: Temple University Press.

Kerber, K. A. & Folgiani, A. A. (1993, January). Tech prep: Preparation for work force diversity. In J. Q. Adams & Jamie R. Welsch (Eds.), *Multicultural education: Strategies for implementation in colleges and universities, Vol. 3* (pp. 93–100). Macomb, IL: Western Illinois University.

Kessler, C., & Quinn, M. E. (1987). ESL and science learning. In J. Crandall (Ed.), *ESL through content-area instruction* (pp. 55–87). Englewood Cliffs, NJ: Prentice-Hall.

Kim, S., McLeod, J., & Shantzis, C. (1992). Cultural competence for evaluators working with Asian-American communities: Some practical considerations. In M. Orlandi (Ed.), *Cultural Competence for Evaluators: A Guide for Alcohol and Other Drug Abuse Prevention Practitioners Working with Ethnic/Racial Communities* (pp. 203–260). Rockville, MD: U.S. Dept. of Health and Human Services.

King, J. (1994, April). *Perceiving reality in a new way: Rethinking the black/white duality of our time.* Paper presented at the meeting of the American Educational Research Association, New Orleans, LA.

Kingston, M. H. (1975). *The woman warrior: Memoirs of a girlhood among ghosts.* New York: Vintage.

Kinsella, K., & Sherak, K. (1993, March). *Making group work really work: More than meets the eye.* Atlanta, GA: Presentation at the annual international convention of the Teachers of English to Speakers of Other Languages.

Kitano, H. (1973). Highlights of Institute on Language and Culture: Asian component. In L. A. Bransford, L. M. Baca, & K. Lane (Eds.), *Cultural diversity and the exceptional child* (pp. 14–15). Reston, VA: The Council for Exceptional Children.

Klepfisz, I. (1990). *Dreams of an Insomniac: Jewish Feminist Essays, Speeches and Diatribes.* Portland: Eighth Mountain Press.

Knoki-Wilson, U. (1995, April 28–29). Women's health issues: Blending traditional and western medicine. In *Healing: Today, Yesterday, and Tomorrow–Bridge Between Traditional and Western Medicine: The 5th Annual Indian Nursing Education Conference.* Buffalo, New York.

Knowles, M. S. (1970). *The modern practice of adult education.* New York: Association Press.

Knowles, M. S. (1973). *The adult learner: A neglected species.* Houston: Gulf.

Kolb, D. A. (1981). Learning styles and disciplinary differences. In A. W. Chickering & Associates (Eds.), *The modern American college* (pp. 232–255). San Francisco: Jossey-Bass.

Kouzes, J. M., & Posner, B. Z. (1990). *The leadership challenge: How to get extraordinary things done in organizations.* San Francisco: Jossey-Bass.

Krashen, S. (1985). *The input hypothesis.* New York: Longman.

Krueger, R. (1988). *Focus groups.* Newbury Park, CA: Sage Publications.

Krupat, A. (1992). *Ethnocriticism: Ethnography, history, literature.* Berkeley: University of California Press.

Ladner, J. (1972). *Tomorrow's tomorrow: The Black woman.* Garden City, NY: Doubleday.

Ladner, J. (1973). *The death of white sociology.* New York: Random House.

Ladson-Billings, G. (1991). Beyond multicultural illiteracy. *Journal of Negro Education, 60,* 147–157.

Ladson-Billings, G. (1994a). *The dreamkeepers: Successful teachers of African-American children.* San Francisco: Jossey-Bass

Ladson-Billings, G. (1994b). Who will teach our children: Preparing teachers to successfully teach African American students. In E. R. Hollins, J. E. King, & W. C. Hayman (Eds.), *Teaching diverse populations: Formulating a knowledge base* (pp. 129–142). Albany: University of New York Press.

Ladson-Billings, G. (1994c, April). *Your blues ain't like mine: Keeping issues of race and racism on the multicultural agenda.* Paper presented at the meeting of the American Educational Research Association, New Orleans, LA.

LaFleur, R. Course syllabus to Principles of Sociology, Spring 1994. Also presentation at Staff Development Day activity, Eastern Iowa Community College District, October, 1993.

Landis, R. B. (Ed.). (1985). *Handbook on improving the retention and graduation of minorities in engineering.* New York: National Action Council for Minorities in Engineering, Inc.

Larke, P., & McJamerson, E. (1990, April). *Cultural diversity awareness inventory of preservice teachers.* Paper presented at the meeting

of the American Educational Research Association, Boston, MA.

Lather, P. (1986). Research as praxis. *Harvard Educational Review, 56,* 257–277.

Laurence, L., & Moore, R. (Forthcoming). Gender and race and the decision to go to college. In R. L. Bartlett (Ed.), *Integrating race and gender into Economics 101.*

Lauter, P. (1991). *Canons and contexts.* New York: Oxford University Press.

Lauter, P. (General Ed.). (1994). *The Heath Anthology of American Literature.* (2nd ed.). Lexington, MA: D.C. Heath & Co.

LeCompte, M. (1987). Learning to work: The hidden curriculum of the classroom. *Anthropology and Education Quarterly, 9,* 23–27.

Leininger, M. M. (1990, Summer). Issues, questions, and concerns related to the nursing diagnosis cultural movement from a transcultural nursing perspective. *Journal of Transcultural Nursing, 2*(1), 23–32.

Leininger, M. M. (1991). Leininger's acculturation health care assessment tool for cultural patterns in traditional and nontraditional lifeways. *Journal of Transcultural Nursing, 2*(2), 40.

Leogrande, C. (1994, April). *Using children's literature to increase the cultural sensitivity of preservice teachers.* Paper presented at the meeting of the American Educational Research Association, New Orleans, LA.

Levine, A., & Cureton, J. (1992). The quiet revolution: Eleven facts about multiculturalism and the curriculum. *Change, 24,* 24–30.

Lewis, M., & Peterson, J. (Forthcoming). The labor supply decision: Differences between gender and races. In R. L. Bartlett (Ed.*),* *Integrating race and gender into Economics 101.*

Lewis, R. B. (1993). *Special education technology: Classroom applications.* Pacific Grove, CA: Brooks/Cole.

Lewis, R. B., & Doorlag, D. H. (1991). *Teaching special students in the mainstream* (3rd ed.). New York: Merrill.

Lewontin, R. C., Rose, S., & Kamin, L. J. (1984). *Not in our genes: Biology, ideology and human nature.* New York: Pantheon.

Liberal Education, 77(3). (1991). Special issue: Engaging cultural legacies.

Lincoln, Y. S. (1985). *Organizational theory and inquiry*. London: Sage Publishers.

Lipson, A., & Tobias, S. (1991). Why do (some of our best) college students leave science? *Journal of College Science Teaching, 21*, 92–95.

Lloyd, C. B., Andrews, E. S., & Gilroy, C. L. (1979). *Women in the labor market*. New York: Columbia University Press.

Lloyd, C. B., & Niemi, B. T. (1979). *The economics of sex differentials*. New York: Columbia University Press.

Long, M., & Porter, P. (1985). Group work, interlanguage talk, and second language acquisition. *TESOL Quarterly, 19*(3), 207–228.

Lorde, A. (1982). *Zami: A new spelling of my name*. Trumansberg, NY: The Crossing Press.

Lorde, A. (1984). *Sister outsider: essays and speeches*. Trumansberg, NY: The Crossing Press.

Lugones, M. C. (1992). Sisterhood and friendship as feminist models. In C. Kramarae & D. Spender (Eds.), *The knowledge explosion* (pp. 406–412). New York: Teachers College Press.

Luke, C., & Gore, J. (Eds.). (1992). *Feminism and critical pedagogy*. New York: Routledge.

Lynch, E. W. (1992). Developing cross-cultural competence. In E. W. Lynch & M. J. Hanson (Eds.), *Developing cross-cultural competence* (pp. 35–59). Baltimore: Paul H. Brookes.

Lynch, E. W., & Hanson, M. J. (Eds.). (1992). *Developing cross-cultural competence*. Baltimore, MD: Paul H. Brookes.

Lyons, N. (1989). Teaching by the Case Method. *On Teaching and Learning 3*, 28–35.

MacPhee, D., Kreutzer, J. C., & Fritz, J. J. (1994). Infusing a diversity perspective into human development courses. *Child Development, 65*, 699–715.

Maddock, M. (1986). Developing better science education programs: Culture, alienation, and attitudes. In J. J. Gallagher & G. Dawson (Eds.), *Science education & cultural environments in the Americas* (pp. 40–47). Washington, DC: National Science Teachers Association.

Mahan, J. (1982). Native Americans as teacher trainers: Anatomy and outcomes of a cultural immersion project. *Journal of Equity and Leadership, 2*, 100–110.

Maher, F., & Tetreault, M. K. T. (1992). Inside feminist classrooms: An ethnographic approach. In L. L. B. Border & N. V. N. Chism (Eds.), *Teaching for diversity* (pp. 57–74). *New Directions for Teaching and Learning* No. 49. San Francisco: Jossey-Bass.

Mairs, N. (1986). *Plaintext*. Tucson: University of Arizona Press.

Malveaux, J. M., & Simms, M. C. (1986). *Slipping through the cracks: The status of Black women*. New Brunswick, NJ: Transaction Books.

Marchesani, L. S., & Adams, M. (1992). In M. Adams (Ed.), *Promoting diversity in college classrooms: Innovative responses for the curriculum, faculty, and institutions* (pp. 9–19). New Directions for Teaching and Learning, no. 52. San Francisco: Jossey-Bass.

Marshall, E. (1990). Malaria research—What next? *Science, 247*, 399–402.

Marshall, E. (1991). Malaria parasite gaining ground against science. *Science, 254*, 190.

Marshall, E. (1994). New law brings affirmative action to clinical research. *Science, 263*, 602.

Marshall, P. (1983). *Reena and Other Stories*. New York: The Feminist Press.

Mason, C. L., & Barba, R. H. (1992). Equal opportunity science. *The Science Teacher, 59*, 22–26.

Matthaei, J. A. (1982). *An economic history of women in America: Women's work, the sexual division of labor, and the development of capitalism*. New York: Shocken Books.

Mauriel, J. J. (1989). *Strategic leadership for schools: Creating and sustaining productive change*. San Francisco: Jossey-Bass.

Maxcy, S. J. (1994). *Postmodern school leadership: Meeting the crisis in educational administration*. London: Praeger.

McCaffrey, J. (1991). Emerging Scholars at UT Austin. *UME Trends, 3*, 4.

McClary, Susan. (1991). *Feminine Endings: Music, gender, and sexuality*. Minneapolis: University of Minnesota Press.

McCloskey, D. N. (1983). The rhetoric of economics. *The Journal of Economic Literature, 21*(2), 481–517.

McCloskey, D. N. (1985). *Some consequences of a feminine economics*. American Economic Association Meetings, New York, December.

McConnele, C. R., & Brue, S. L. (1990). *Economics: Principles, problems, and policies*. New York: McGraw-Hill.

McGroarty, M. (1989). The benefits of cooperative learning arrangements in second language instruction. *NABE Journal,* 13(2), 127–143.

McIntosh, P. (1983). *Interactive phases of the curriculum re-vision: A feminist perspective.* Working Paper No. 124. Wellesley, MA: Wellesley College Center for Research on Women.

McIntosh, P. (1988, reprinted 1992). White privilege and male privilege: A personal account of coming to see correspondences through work in women's studies. In M. Andersen & P. H. Collins (Eds.), *Race, class and gender* (pp. 70–81). Belmont, CA: Wadsworth Publishing Co.

McLoughlin, J. A., & Lewis, R. B. (1994). *Assessing special students* (4th ed.). New York: Macmillan.

McLuhan, T. C. (1971). *Touch the earth a self-portrait of Indian existence.* (p. 113). New York: Promontory Press.

Mehan, H., Lintz, A., Okamoto, D., & Wills, J. S. (1995). Ethnographic studies of multicultural education in classrooms and schools. In J. A. Banks & C. A. McGee Banks (Eds.), *Handbook of research on multicultural education* (pp. 129–144). New York: Macmillan.

Menges, R. J., & Mathis, B. C. (1988). *Key resources on teaching, learning, curriculum, and faculty development.* San Francisco: Jossey-Bass.

Mercer, J. (1989). Alternative paradigms for assessment in a pluralistic society. In J. Banks & C. Banks (Eds.), *Multicultural education: Issues and perspectives* (pp. 289–304). Boston: Allyn & Bacon.

Merson, M. H. (1993). Slowing the spread of HIV: Agenda for the 1990s. *Science, 260,* 1266–1268.

Messick, S. (1994). The interplay of evidence and consequences in the validation of performance assessment. *Educational Researcher,* 22(3), 13–23.

Meyer, D. K. (1993). Recognizing and changing students' misconceptions. *College Teaching,* 41, 104–108.

Middlecamp, C. H. (1995). Culturally inclusive chemistry. In S. V. Rosser (Ed.), *Teaching the majority* (pp. 79–97). New York: Teachers College Press.

Mikitka, K., Morey, A. I., & Kitano, M. K. (1993). Celebrating the teacher scholar: A theme year. *The Journal on excellence in College Teaching, 4,* 145–164.

Milem, J. (1992). *The Impact of College on Student's Racial Attitudes and Levels of Racial Awareness and Acceptance.* Dissertation. Department of Education, UCLA.

Milkman, R. (1986). Women's history and the Sears case. *Feminist Studies,* 12(2), 375–400.

Miller, D. (1991). *Handbook of research design and social measurement.* Beverly Hills, CA: Sage.

Miller, R. (1991). *Economics today.* New York: HarperCollins.

Minnich, E. K. (1990). *Transforming Knowledge.* Philadelphia: Temple University Press.

Minow, M. (1990). Adjudicating differences: Conflicts among feminist lawyers. In M. Hirsch & E. F. Keller, (Eds.), *Conflicts in Feminism* (pp. 149–163). New York and London: Routledge.

Mohanty, C. T. (1991). Under Western eyes: Feminist scholarship and colonial discourses. In C. T. Mohanty et al. (Eds.), *Third world women and the politics of feminism* (pp. 50–80). Bloomington: Indiana University Press.

Momaday, N. S. (1976). *The Names: A Memoir.* New York: Harper & Row.

Moore, R. B. (1992). Racist stereotyping in the English language. In M. L. Andersen & P. H. Collins, (Eds.), *Race, Class, and Gender* (pp. 317–329). Belmont, CA: Wadsworth Publishing Co.

Moraga, C. & Anzaldua, G. (Eds.). (1981). *This Bridge Called My Back: Writings by Radical Women of Color.* Watertown, MA: Persephone Press.

More, A. J. (1987). Native Indian learning styles: A review for researchers and teachers. *Journal of American Indian Education,* 27, 17–29.

Morey, A. I. (1988). *Addressing diversity: A framework for structural change of a college of education.* San Diego, CA: College of Education, San Diego State University.

Morey, A. I., & Allen, B. (1993). *Report of the 1993 Deans of Education Roundtable.* San Diego, CA: Multicultural Education Infusion Center, San Diego State University.

Morey, A. I., & Kitano, M. (1993, August). *Promoting structural change in teacher education for a diverse society.* Paper presented at the 15th Annual EAIR Forum, Turku, Finland.

Morgan, D. (1993). *Successful focus groups: Advancing the state of the art*. Newbury Park, CA: Sage.

Morgan, D., & Krueger, R. (1993). When to use focus groups and why. In D. Morgan (Ed.), *Successful focus groups: Advancing the state of the art* (pp. 3–19). Newbury Park, CA: Sage.

Morris, L., Fitz-Gibbon, C., & Freeman, M. (1987). *How to Communicate Evaluation Findings*. Newbury Park, CA: Sage.

Morrison, T. (1992). *Playing in the dark: whiteness and the literary imagination*. Cambridge, MA: Harvard University Press.

Morrison, T. (Ed.) (1992). *Race-ing justice, en-gendering power: Essays on Anita Hill, Clarence Thomas, and the construction of social reality*. New York: Pantheon Books.

Morrison, T. (1993). *The Bluest Eye*. New York: Random House.

Mosely, F., Gunn, C., & Georges, C. (1991). Emphasizing controversy in the economics curriculum. *The Journal of Economic Education*, 22(3), 235–240.

Moynihan, D. P. (1965). *The Negro family: The case for national action*. Washington, DC: GPO.

Nagata, D. K. (1989). Japanese American children and adolescents. In J. T. Gibbs & L. N. Huang (Eds.), *Children of color* (pp. 67–113). San Francisco: Jossey-Bass.

National Center for Educational Statistics. (1989). *Digest of education statistics*. U.S. Department of Education, Office of Educational Research and Improvement.

National Education Association. (1992). *Status of the American school teacher, 1990–1991*. Washington, DC: National Education Association, Research Division.

National Education Association. (1992). *The NEA 1992 almanac of higher education*. Washington, DC: National Education Association.

National Science Teachers Association. (July 1991). Position Statement on Multicultural Science Education.

NCATE (1990). *NCATE standards for the accreditation of teacher education*. Washington, DC: National Council for the Accreditation of Teacher Education.

NCSS Task Force on Ethnic Studies Curriculum Guidelines. (September 1992). Curriculum guidelines for multicultural education. *Social Education*, 274–294.

Nielson, J. M. (Ed.). (1990). *Feminist research methods: Exemplary readings in the social sciences*. Boulder, CO: Westview Press.

Noley, G. (1991). Fear, higher education, and change. *Thought and Action*, VII(2), 105–114.

Noordhoff, K., & Kleinfeld, J. (1991, April). *Preparing teachers for multicultural classrooms: A case study in rural Alaska*. Paper presented at the meeting of the American Educational Research Association, Chicago, IL.

Odulani, J. A. (1994, February 11). Paper presentation at the National Association for Multicultural Education Annual Conference.

Ogbu, J. (1990). Understanding diversity: Summary comments. *Education and Urban Society*, 22(4), 425–429.

Ognibene, E. R. (1989). Integrating the curriculum: From impossible to possible. *College Teaching*, 37(3), 105–110.

Oleska, M. (1993, March). *Communicating across cultures*. Presentation at the 12th Annual Early Childhood Conference of the National Association for the Education of Young Children—Southeast Alaska, Juneau, AL.

Oliver, J., & Brown, L.B. (1988). The development and implementation of a minority recruitment plan: Process, strategy and results. *Journal of Social Work Education*, 24, 175–185.

Olsen, T. (1978). *Silences*. New York: Delacorte Press/ Seymour Lawrence.

Olson, J. K., & Olson, M. (1991). Including the unincluded in mathematics. In J. Q. Adams (Ed.), *Multicultural education: A rationale for development and implementation* (pp. 41–45). Springfield, Illinois: Western Illinois University.

Omi, M., and Winant, H. (1986). *Racial formation in the United States: From the 1960's to the 1980's*. New York: Routledge and Kegan Paul.

Omi, M. & Winant, H. (1993). On the theoretical status of the concept of race. In C. McCarthy & W. Crichlow (Eds.), *Race, identity, and representation in education* (pp. 3–10). New York: Routledge.

Orque, M. S., Block, B., & Monrroy, K. S. A. (1983). *Block's ethnic-cultural assessment guide: Ethnic nursing care: a multicultural approach.* St. Louis: Mosby.

Ostler, S. E. (1980). Survey of academic needs for advanced ESL. *TESOL Quarterly, 14*(3), 489–502.

Padilla, A. (1994). Ethnic minority scholards, research, and mentoring: Current and future issues. *Educational Researcher, 23*(4), 24–26.

Padilla, R. (1993). Using dialogical research methods in group interviews. In D. Morgan (Ed.), *Successful focus groups: Advancing the state of the art* (pp. 153–166). Newbury Park, CA: Sage.

Palca, J. (1991). The sobering geography of AIDS. *Science, 252,* 372–373.

Palmatier, R. A., & Bennett, J. M. (1974). Note taking habits of college students. *Journal of Reading, 18,* 215–218.

Palmer, P. (1983). *To know as we are known.* San Francisco: Harper and Row.

Pareek, U. & Rao, T. V. (1980). Cross-cultural surveys and interviewing. In H. C. Triandis & J. W. Berry (Eds.), *Handbook of cross-cultural psychology: Methodology: Vol. 2* (pp. 125–179). Boston: Allyn and Bacon.

Pascale, P. (1990). *Managing on the edge.* New York: Touchstone.

Pepper, F. C. (1976). Teaching the American Indian child in mainstream settings. In R. L. Jones (Ed.), *Mainstreaming and the minority child* (pp. 133–158). Reston, VA: The Council for Exceptional Children.

Persell, R. (1994). Reworking the science curriculum: A case study in the interdependence between introductory biology and multiculturalism. *Journal of Science Education and Technology, 3,* 249–258.

Peters, T., & Austin, N. (1985). *A passion for excellence.* New York: Random House.

Pewewardy, C. D. (1994). Culturally responsible pedagogy in action: An American Indian magnet school. In E. R. Hollins, J. E. King, & W. C. Hayman (Eds.), *Teaching diverse populations: Formulating a knowledge base* (pp. 77–92). Albany: University of New York Press.

Phelan, P., Davidson, A. L., & Yu, H. C. (1993). Students' multiple worlds: Navigating the borders of family, peer, and school cultures. In P. Phelan & A. L. Davidson (Eds.), *Renegotiating cultural diversity in American schools*

(pp. 52–88). New York: Teachers College, Columbia University.

Philipp, R. A. (1994). Alternative algorithm assignment. From Syllabus for TE 910A: Teaching Mathematics in the Elementary School. School of Teacher Education, San Diego State University.

Piercy, M. (1976). *Woman on the edge of time.* New York: Alfred A. Knopf.

Piercy, M. (1991). *He, she, and it.* New York: Fawcett Crest.

Pratt, M. B. (1991). *Rebellion: Essays 1980–1991.* Ithaca: Firebrand Books.

Quantz, R. A. (1991). Preparing school administrators for democratic authority: A critical approach to graduate education. *Urban Review, 23*(1), 3–19.

Rakow, S., & Bermudez, A. (1993). Science is "Cienzia": Meeting the needs of Hispanic American students. *Science Education, 77*(6), 669–683.

Ramsden, P. (1992). *Learning to teach in higher education.* New York: Routledge.

Reagon, B. J., and Sweet Honey in the Rock. (1993). *We who believe in freedom: Sweet honey in the rock. . . . Still on the journey.* New York: Anchor Books, 1993.

Reyhner, J. (Ed.). (1992). *Teaching American Indian students.* Norman, OK: University of Oklahoma Press.

Reynolds, M. C. (Ed.). (1989). *Knowledge base for the beginning teacher.* New York: Pergamon Press.

Rhoades, G. (1990). Change in an unanchored enterprise: Colleges of education. *Review of Higher Education, 13*(2), 187–214.

Rhode, D. L. (Ed.). (1990). *Theoretical perspectives on sexual difference.* New Haven: Yale University Press.

Rich, A. (1980). Compulsory heterosexuality and lesbian existence. *Signs 5*(4), 631–660.

Rich, A. (1986). Split at the root: An essay on Jewish identity. *Blood, bread, and poetry: Selected prose 1979–1985.* New York: W. W. Norton.

Richardson, R. C. (1989). *Institutional climate and minority achievement.* Denver: Education Commission of the States. (ERIC Document Reproduction Service No. ED 322 244)

Rivlin, A. (1990). Correspondence of July 20, 1990 from Rivlin to Feiner.

Roach, D. W. (1992, July). Multicultural music: Philosophy and learning strategies. In J. Q. Adams & Jamie R. Welsch (Eds.), *Multicultural Education: Strategies for implementation in colleges and universities, Vol. 2* (pp. 39–42). Macomb, IL: Western Illinois University.

Robbins, R. L. (Ed.). (1993). *The NEA 1993 Almanac of Higher Education.* Washington, DC: National Education Association.

Rodriguez, A. M. (1991). *Multicultural education: Some considerations for a university setting.* Hayward, CA: California State University, Hayward. (ERIC Document Reproduction Service No. ED 337 094)

Rodriguez, R. (1992). *Days of obligation: An argument with my Mexican father.* New York: Viking.

Roediger, D. R. (1991). *The wages of whiteness: Race and the making of the American working class.* New York: Verso.

Rollins, J. (1985). *Between women: Domestics and their employers.* Philadelphia.

Romero, M. (1992). *Maid in the U.S.A.* New York: Routledge.

Rosenfelt, D. (1994). "Definitive" issues: women's studies, multicultural education and curriculum transformation in policy and practice in the United States. *Women's studies quarterly, 22*(3 and 4), 26–41.

Rosenthal, E. (1991, February 12). Outwitted by malaria, desperate doctors seek new remedies. *The New York Times,* pp. C1 and C8.

Rosenthal, E. (1992, October 13). TB, easily transmitted, adds a peril to medicine. *The New York Times,* pp. 1 and B2.

Rosenthal, J. W. (1992/93). The limited English proficient student in the college science classroom. *Journal of College Science Teaching, 22,* 182–186.

Rosenthal, J. W. (1993a). Theory and practice: Science for undergraduates of limited English proficiency. *Journal of Science Education and Technology 2,* 435–443.

Rosenthal, J. W. (1993b, November 3). Science students who are still learning English. *The Chronicle of Higher Education,* pp. B1–B2.

Rosenthal, J. W. (in press). *Teaching science to language minority students.* Clevedon, England: Multilingal Matters Ltd.

Rosser, S. V. (1990). *Female-friendly science.* Elmsford, NY: Pergamon Press.

Rosser, S.V. (1993). Female friendly science: including women in curricular content and pedagogy in science. *Journal of general education, 42*(3), 191–220.

Rothenberg, P. S. (1992). *Race, class, & gender in the United States: An integrated study.* (2nd ed.). New York: St. Martin's Press.

Ruddick, S. (1989). *Maternal thinking: Toward a politics of peace.* Boston: Beacon Press.

Ruffin, R. J., & Gregory, P. R. (1990). *Principles of economics.* Glenview, IL: Scott, Foresman.

Rumelhart, D. E. (1980). Schemata: The building blocks of cognition. In R. J. Spiro, B. C. Bruce, & W. F. Brewer (Eds.), *Theoretical issues in reading comprehension* (pp. 33–58). Hillsdale, NJ: Erlbaum.

Rynes, S., & Rosen, B. (1994, October). What makes diversity programs work? *HRM Magazine,* 67–73.

Sadker, M., & Sadker, D. (1992). Ensuring equitable participation in college classes. In L. L. B. Border & N. V. N. Chism (Eds.), *Teaching for diversity* (pp. 49–56). *New Directions for Teaching and Learning* No. 49. San Francisco: Jossey-Bass.

Sadker, M., & Sadker, D. (1994). *Failing at fairness: How our schools cheat girls.* New York: Touchstone.

Said, E. (1978) *Orientalism.* New York: Vintage Books.

Samiian, B. (1994). *A study of attitudes toward diversity: Comparing business managers and business-major students.* Unpublished doctoral dissertation, University of North Florida, Jacksonville.

Samovar, L. A., Porter, R. E., & Jain, N. C. (1981). *Understanding intercultural communication.* Belmont, CA: Wadsworth.

Santa Cruz, R. (1993). Personal communication.

Sarris, G. (1993). Keeping slug woman alive: the challenge of reading in a reservation classroom. In J. Boyarin (Ed.), *The ethnography of reading* (pp. 238–269). Berkeley: University of California Press.

Sasaki, R. A. (1989). The Loom. In Asian Women United of California (Eds.), *Making waves: An anthology of writings by and about Asian*

American women (pp. 199–214). Boston: Beacon Press.

Saville-Troike, M. (1984). What really matters in second language learning for academic achievement? *TESOL Quarterly,* 18(2), 199–219.

Saville-Troike, M., & Kleifgen, J. (1986). Scripts for school: Cross-cultural communication in the elementary classroom. *Text,* 6(2), 207–221.

Sawchuk, M. T. (Ed.). (1992). *The role of faculty development in multicultural education.* Mount St. Mary's College, Los Angeles: Prism Publishing.

Sawchuk, M. T. (Ed.). (1993). *Infusing multicultural perspectives across the curriculum.* Mount St. Mary's College, Los Angeles: Prism Publishing.

Saxton M., & Howe, F. (1987). *With wings: An anthology of literature by and about women with disabilities.* New York: The Feminist Press.

Schmitz, B. (1991). *The core curriculum and cultural pluralism: A guide for campus planners.* Washington, DC: Association of American Colleges.

Schmitz, B. (1992). *Core curriculum and cultural pluralism: A guide for campus planners.* Washington, DC: Association of American Colleges.

Schoem, D., Frankel, L., Zúñiga, X., & Lewis, E. A. (1993). The meaning of multicultural teaching: An introduction. In D. Schoem, L. Frankel, X. Zúñiga, & E. A. Lewis (Eds.), *Multicultural teaching in the university* (pp. 1–12). Westport, CT: Praeger.

Schofield, A. (1991, May). *Improving the effectiveness of the management of innovation and change in higher education.* Paris: International Institute for Educational Planning.

Science and engineering degrees, by race/ethnicity of recipients: 1977–1990. (1992). Washington, DC: National Science Foundation.

Science for all Americans. (1989). A Project 2061 Report on Literacy Goals in Science, Mathematics, and Technology. Washington, DC: American Association for the Advancement of Science.

Science for all cultures. (1993). Arlington, VA: National Science Teachers Association.

Scott, H. (1989). Issues in increasing minority participation in graduate education. In W. Ward, & M. Cross (Eds.), *Key Issues in Minority Education: Research Directions and Practical Implications* (pp. 97–120). Norman, OK: Center for Research on Minority Education, The University of Oklahoma.

Scott, J. W. (1986). Gender: A useful category of historical analysis. *Journal of the American Historical Society,* 1053–1075. Also in Scott, 1988. *Gender and the politics of history.* New York: Columbia University Press.

Scott, J. W. (1991, November/December) "The Campaign against Political Correctness: What's Really at Stake." *Change,* 23(6), 30–43.

Scriven, M. (1975). Standards for the evaluation of educational programs and products. In G. Borich (Ed.), *Evaluating Educational Programs and Products* (pp. 5–24). Englewood Cliffs, NJ: Educational Technology Publications.

Scriven, M. (1991). *Evaluation thesaurus.* (4th ed.). Newbury Park, CA: Sage.

Selin, H. (1993a). Science across cultures, Part I. *The Science Teacher,* 60, 38–44.

Selin, H. (1993b). Science across cultures, Part II. *The Science Teacher,* 60, 32–36.

Semrau, P., & Boyer, B. A. (1994). Enhancing learning with interactive video. In Diane F. Halpern (Ed.), *Changing college classrooms: New teaching and learning strategies for an increasingly complex world* (pp. 213–229). San Francisco: Jossey-Bass.

Senge, P. M. (1990). *The fifth discipline: The art and practice of the learning organization.* New York: Doubleday.

Sennet, R. & Cobb, J. (1973). *The hidden injuries of class.* New York: Vintage Books.

Seymour, E. (1992). 'The Problem Iceberg' in science, mathematics, and engineering education: Student explanations for high attrition rates. *Journal of College Science Teaching,* 21, 230–238.

Seymour, G. E. (1993, October). *New approaches to military performance assessment.* Paper presented at Assessment 2000, San Diego State University, San Diego, CA.

Shackleford, J. (1992). Feminist pedagogy: A means for bringing critical thinking and creativity to the economics classroom. *American Economic Review, 82*(2), 570–576.

Shade, B. (1982). Afro-American cognitive style: A variable in school success? *Review of Educational Research, 52*(2), 219–244.

Shade, B. J. R. (Ed.). (1989). *Culture, style and the educative process.* Springfield, IL: Charles C. Thomas.

Shoull, R. (1970). The Forward. In P. Freire (Ed.), *Pedagogy of the Oppressed.* New York: Seabury Press.

Sims, C. (1992). What went wrong: Why programs failed. *Science, 258,* 1185–1187.

Sitaram, K. S., & Cogdell, R. T. (1976). *Foundations of intercultural communication.* Columbus, OH: Charles E. Merrill.

Slaughter, H. (1991). "The participation of cultural informants on bilingual and cross-cultural evaluation teams." *Evaluation Practice, 12,* 149–157.

Slavin, R. (1987). Ability grouping and student achievement in elementary schools: A best evidence synthesis. *Review of Educational Research, 57,* 293–337.

Slavin, R. E. (1987). *Cooperative learning: Student teams.* Washington, DC: Education Association.

Sleeter, C. (1985). A need for research on preservice teacher education for mainstreaming and multicultural education. *Journal of Equity and Leadership, 5,* 205–215.

Sleeter, C. E. (Ed.). (1991). *Empowerment through multicultural education.* Albany: State University of New York.

Sleeter, C. (1992). *Keepers of the American dream: A study of staff development and multicultural education.* London: The Falmer Press.

Sleeter, C. E., & Grant, C. A. (1987). An analysis of multicultural education in the United States. *Harvard Educational Review, 57*(4), 421–441.

Smith, D. G. (1989). *The challenge of diversity: Involvement or alienation in the academy?* (Report No. 5). Washington, DC: School of Education and Human Development, The George Washington University.

Smith, J. P. (1980). *Female labor supply: Theory and estimation.* Princeton, NJ: Princeton University Press.

Smith, J. P., & Ward, M. P. (1984). *Women's wages and work in the twentieth century.* Santa Monica, CA: Rand.

Smith, T. W. (1990). *Ethnic images.* (GSS Topical Report No. 19). Chicago: University of Chicago, National Opinion Research Center.

Smoke, T. (1988). Using feedback from ESL students to enhance their success in college. In S. Benesch (Ed.), *Ending remediation: Linking ESL and content in higher education* (pp. 7–19). Washington, DC: TESOL.

Smoyak, S. A. (1979). Nurse and client ethnicity and its effects upon interaction. *A Strategy for Change.* American Nurses' Association, Paper presented at the conference held June 9–10, 1979. Albuquerque, New Mexico by the American Nurses' Association Commission on Human Rights, pp. 51–61.

Sobralske, M. C. (1985). Perceptions of health: Navajo Indians. *Topics in Clinical Nursing, 7*(3), 32–39.

Solow, R. (1990). Correspondence of April 3, 1990 from Solow to Feiner.

Soska, M. (1995). Educational technology enhances the LEP classroom. *NABE News, 18*(4), 9–10.

Soto, G. (1990). *Baseball in April and other stories.* San Diego: Harcourt Brace Jovanovich.

Sowell, T. (1981). *Market and minorities.* New York: Basic Books.

Sowell, T. (1983). *The economics and politics of race.* New York: William Morrow and Company.

Soyibo, K. (1993, August). *Some sources of students' misconceptions in biology: A review.* Paper presented at the Third International Seminar on Misconceptions and Educational Strategies in Science and Mathematics, Cornell University, Ithaca, NY.

Spelman, E. V. (1988). *Inessential woman: problems of exclusion in feminist thought.* Boston: Beacon Press.

Spindler, G. (Ed.). (1987). *Education and the cultural process Anthropological perspectives.* Prospect Heights, IL: Waveland.

Spindler, G., & Spindler, L. (1993). The process of culture and person: Cultural therapy and culturally diverse schools. In P. Phelan & A. L. Davidson (Eds.), *Renegotiating cultural diversity in American schools* (pp. 27–51).

New York: Teachers College, Columbia University.

Stacey, J. (1994). The future of feminist differences. *Contemporary Sociology*, 23(4), 482–486.

Stacey, R. (1992). *Managing the unknowable*. San Francisco: Jossey-Bass.

Stack, C. B. (1990, revised version 1994). Different voices, different visions: Gender, culture, and moral reasoning. In M. B. Zinn & B. T. Dill (Eds.), *Women of color in U.S. society* (pp. 291–301). Philadelphia: Temple University Press.

Stage, F., & Manning, K. (Eds.). (1992). Enhancing multicultural campus environment: A cultural brokering approach. *New Directions for Student Voices*. San Francisco: Jossey-Bass.

Stahlman, J. I., & Pusch, J. D. (1992). A rose by any other name: Would it smell as sweet? *Journal of the Association for Persons with Severe Handicaps, 17*, 93–94.

Stanley, W. B., & Brickhouse, N. W. (1994). Multiculturalism, universalism, and science education. *Science Education, 78*, 387–398.

Stecher, B., & Davis, W. (1987). *How to focus an evaluation*. Newbury Park, CA: Sage Publications.

Stenmark, J. (1989). *Assessment alternatives in mathematics*. Berkeley, CA: Regents, University of California.

Stepan, N. L. (1993). Race and gender: The role of analogy in science. In S. Harding (Ed.), *The "racial" economy of science* (pp. 359–376). Bloomington and Indiana: Indiana University Press.

Sternberg, R. J. (1984). What should intelligence tests test? Implications of a triarchic theory of intelligence for intelligence testing. *Educational Researcher, 13*(1), 5–15.

Sternberg, R. J., Okagaki, L., & Jackson, A. S. (1990). Practical intelligence for success in school. *Educational Leadership, 48*, 35–39.

Stolovitch, H. D., &. Lane, M. (1989, July). *Multicultural training: Designing for affective results. Performance & Instruction*, pp. 10–15.

Stufflebeam, D., McCormick, C., Brinkerhoff, R., & Nelson, C. (1985). *Conducting educational needs assessment*. Boston: Kluwer Nijhoff Publishing.

Sullivan, A. R. (1974). Cultural competence and confidence: A quest for effective teaching in a pluralistic society. *In* W. A. Hunter (Ed.), *Multicultural education through competency-based teacher education* (pp. 56–77). Washington, DC: American Association of Colleges of Teacher Education.

Sutman, F. X., Allen, V. F., & Shoemaker, F. (1986). *Learning English through science*. Washington, DC: National Science Teachers Association.

Suzuki, B. H. (1984). Curriculum transformation for multicultural education. *Education and Urban Society, 16*(3), 294–322.

Tafoya, T. (1993, April). *Sacred healing and the path of the clown*. Presentation at the meeting of the Pediatric Continuity of Care Coalition, San Diego, CA.

Tajima, R. E. (1989). Lotus blossoms don't bleed: Images of Asian women. In Asian Women United of California (Eds.), *Making waves: An anthology of writings by and about Asian American women* (pp. 308–317). Boston: Beacon Press.

Takaki, R. (1987). Reflections on racial patterns in America. R. Takaki (Ed.), *From different shores: Perspectives on race and ethnicity in America* (pp. 26–37). New York: Oxford University Press.

Takaki, R. (1993). *A different mirror*. Boston: Little, Brown and Company.

Tannen, D. (1990). *You just don't understand: Women and men in conversation*. New York: Morrow.

Tatum, B. D. (1992). Talking about race, learning about racism: The application of racial identity development theory in the classroom. *Harvard Educational Review, 62*(1), 1–24.

Taylor, C. (1992). *Multiculturalism and "the politics of recognition."* Princeton: Princeton University Press.

Taylor, S. (1994). Technology as a medium of culture. Manuscript prepared for Title III Planning Committee. San Diego: San Diego State University.

Terrell, M. C., & Wright, D. J. (Eds.). (1988). *From survival to success: Promoting minority student retention*. Washington, DC: National

Association of Student Personnel Administrators, Inc.

Tetreault, M. K. (1993). Classrooms for diversity: Rethinking curriculum and pedagogy. In J. A. Banks & C. A. M. Banks (Eds.), *Multicultural education: Issues and perspectives* (2nd Ed., pp. 129–148). Boston: Allyn and Bacon.

The Editors of the Chronicle of Higher Education. (1992). *The almanac of higher education 1992.* Chicago: The University of Chicago Press.

The Liberal Art of Science. (1990). The Report of the Project on Liberal Education and the Sciences. Washington, DC: American Association for the Advancement of Science.

Thorne, B., Kramarae, C., & Henley, N. (Eds.). (1983). *Language, gender, and society.* Rowley, MA: Newberry House Publishers.

Tiedt, P. L., & Tiedt, I. M. (1990). *Multicultural teaching: A handbook of activities, information, and resources* (3rd ed.). Boston: Allyn & Bacon.

Tierney, W. G. (1989). Advancing democracy: A critical interpretation of leadership. *Peabody Journal of Education, 66*(3), 157–175.

Tobias, S. (1987). *Succeed with math: Every student's guide to conquering math anxiety.* New York: College Entrance Examination Board.

Tobias, S. (1990). Math anxiety: An update. *National Academic Advising Association Journal, 10,* 47–50.

Tobias, S. (1990). *They're not dumb, they're different.* Tucson, AZ: Research Corporation.

Tobias, S. (1991). Math mental health: Going beyond math anxiety. *College Teaching, 39,* 91–93.

Toh, S. H. (1994, February 12). Keynote address at the National Association of Multicultural Educators Annual Conference. Detroit, Michigan.

Treiman, D. J., & Hartmann, H. I. (1981). *Women, work, and wages: Equal pay for jobs of equal value.* Washington DC: National Academy Press.

Treisman, U. (1992). Studying students studying calculus: A look at the lives of minority mathematics students in college. *The College Mathematics Journal, 23,* 362–372.

Trend, D. (1992). *Cultural pedagogy: Art, education, politics.* New York: Bergin & Garvey.

Tripp-Reimer, T. (1984). Cultural assessment. In J. P. Bellack & P. A. Bamford (Eds.), *Nursing assessment: A multidimensional approach* (pp. 226–246). Monterey, California: Wadsworth.

Tripp-Reimer, T., Brink, P. J., & Saunders, J. M. (1984, March/April). Cultural assessment: Content and process. *Nursing Outlook, 32*(2), p. 80.

Tucker-Ladd, P., Merchant, B., & Thurston, P. W. (1992). School leadership: Encouraging leaders for change. *Educational Administration Quarterly, 28*(3), 397–409.

U.S. Commission on Civil Rights. (1988, 1990). *The economic status of Black women: An exploratory investigation.* Washington, DC: Staff Report, U.S. Civil Rights Commission.

U.S. Department of Commerce, Bureau of the Census. (1983). We, the first Americans. Washington, DC: U.S. Government Printing Office.

U.S. Department of Education (1993). *Fall enrollment survey.* National Center for Education Statistics.

U.S. Department of Education (1993). *The condition of education.* Washington, DC: National Center for Educational Statistics, Office of Educational Research and Information.

U.S. Department of Health and Human Services. (1988). Indian Health Service: Chart series book (0–218–547:QL3). Washington, DC: U.S. Government Printing Office.

Undergraduate Science Education: The Impact of Different College Environments on the Educational Pipeline in the Sciences. (1992). Los Angeles, CA: Higher Education Research Institute.

Union for Radical Political Economics. (1978). Political economy of women. *Review of Radical Political Economics,*12(2).

Union for Radical Political Economics. (1984). The political economy of women. *Review of Radical Political Economics ,*16 (1).

Union for Radical Political Economics. (1985). The Political economy of race and class. *Review of Radical Political Economics,* 17(3).

Ventimiglia, L. M. (1994). Cooperative learning at the college level. *Thought and action: The NEA Higher Education Journal, IX:2,* 5–30.

Waggoner, D. (1994). Language-minority school-age population now totals 9.9 million. *NABE News,* 18(1), 1, 24–26.

Walberg, H. (1985). Syntheses of research on teaching. In Wittrock, M. (Ed.), *Handbook of*

Research on Teaching (pp. 214–229). New York: Macmillan.

Walker, A. (1981). Advancing Luna—and Ida B. Wells. *You can't keep a good woman down.* New York: Harcourt Brace Jovanovich.

Walker, A. (1983). *In search of our mothers' gardens.* San Diego: Harcourt Brace Jovanovich.

Walker, J. L. (1988). Young American Indian children. *Teaching Exceptional Children, 20*(4), 50–51.

Warner, L. S., & Hastings, J. D. (1991, April). *American Indian education: Culture and diversity in the 21st century.* Paper presented at Arizona State University-West, 21st Century Project, Phoenix, AZ. (ERIC Document Reproduction Service No. ED 331 664)

Warshaw, C., Olson, J., & Beaudry, J. (1991, April). Implications of Meyer and Scott's theory of institutional environments for the implementation of Cummins' framework for the empowerment of students of bilingual kindergartens, National Clearinghouse for Bilingual Education as abstracted in *Resources in Education* (ERIC No. BE017919).

Washington, V. (1981). Impact of antiracism/multicultural education training on elementary teachers attitudes and classroom behavior. *Elementary School Journal, 81,*186–192.

Watkins, B. (June 14, 1989). Many campuses now challenging minority students to excel in math. *The Chronicle of Higher Education, 35,* A13, 16–17.

Waugh, D., quoting Diane Ravitch, "History textbook feud splits along racial lines," *San Francisco Examiner,* August 30, 1990, p. A-10.

Wayson, W. (1988, April). Multicultural education among seniors in the College of Education at Ohio State University. Paper presented at the meeting of the American Educational Research Association, New Orleans.

Weatherford, J. (1988). *Indian givers: How the Indians of the Americas transformed the world.* New York: Fawcett Columbine.

Weimer, M. (1990). *Improving college teaching: Strategies for developing instructional effectiveness.* San Francisco: Jossey-Bass.

Weimer, M. (1993). *Improving your classroom teaching.* Newbury Park, CA: Sage Publications.

Weinstein, G., & Obear, K. (1992). Bias issues in the classroom: Encounters with the teaching self. In M. Adams (Ed.), *Promoting diversity in college classrooms: Innovative responses for the curriculum, faculty, and institutions* (pp. 39–50). *New Directions for Teaching and Learning,* No. 52. San Francisco: Jossey-Bass.

Weiss, R. (1992). On the track of "killer" TB. *Science, 255,* 148–150.

What works: Building natural science communities— A plan for strengthening undergraduate science and mathematics, Vol. One. (1991). Washington, DC: Project Kaleidoscope.

White, E. F. (1990). Africa on my mind: Gender, counter discourse, and African-American nationalism. *Journal of Women's History,* 2(1), 90–94.

Williams, R. (1994). Being queer, being black: Living out in Afro-American studies. Talk for "Thinking, Writing, Teaching and Creating Social Justice." Unpublished paper. University of Minnesota.

Williams, R. (Forthcoming). Bibliography on "difference" vs. "equality," "nationalism" vs. "assimilation." Institute for Teaching and Research on Women, National Clearinghouse for Curriculum Transformation, Towson State University, Towson, MD.

Williams, W. (1987). *All it takes is guts: A minority view.* Washington, DC: Regency Books.

Willig, A. (1985). A meta-analysis of selected studies on the effectiveness of bilingual education. *Review of Educational Research, 55,* 269–317.

Willis, W. (1992). Families with African American roots. In E. W. Lynch & M. J. Hanson (Eds.), *Developing cross-cultural competence* (pp. 121–150). Baltimore: Paul H. Brookes.

Wilson, D. L. (January 29, 1992). Colleges pressured on computer access for the handicapped. *The Chronicle of Higher Education,* 38(21), A1, A21–A22.

Winn, I. J. (1993, Winter). An ecological approach to multiculturalism. *Thought and Action; The NEA Higher Education Journal,* 8(2), 119–126.

Wolf, K. P. (1991). Teaching portfolios: Focus for new clearinghouse and network. *Portfolio News,* 3(1), 7, 22.

Women's review of books (anonymous interviewer). (1994). The politics of genetics: A conversation with Anne Fausto-Sterling and Diane Paul. With comments by Marsha Saxton and Lydia Villa-Komarov. *Women's review of books* ll (10–11), 17–20.

Woolbright, C. (Ed.). (1989). *Valuing diversity on campus: A multicultural approach,* Monograph 11. Bloomington: Association of College Unions-International.

Woolf, V. (1929, 1957). *A Room of One's Own.* New York: Harcourt Brace Jovanovich.

Worthen, B. R. (1993). Critical issues that will determine the future of alternative assessment. *Phi Delta Kappan, 74,* 444–454.

Worthen, B. R., & Sanders, J. R. (1987). *Educational evaluation: Alternative approaches and practical guidelines.* White Plains, NY: Longman.

Yen, S. (1992). Cultural competence for evaluators working with Asian/Pacific Island-American communities: Some common themes and important implications. In M. Orlandi (Ed.), *Cultural Competence for Evaluators: A Guide for Alcohol and Other Drug Abuse Prevention Practitioners Working with Ethnic/Racial Communities* (pp. 261–292). Rockville, MD: U.S. Dept. of Health and Human Services.

Yezierska, A. (1925, 1952). *The bread givers.* New York: Persea Books.

Zalk, S. R. & Gordon-Kelter, J. (1992). *Revolutions in knowledge: Feminism in the social sciences.* Boulder: Westview Press.

Zandy, J. (1990). *Calling home: Working-class women's writings.* New Brunswick: Rutgers University Press.

Zimmerman, B. (1991). Seeing, reading, knowing: The lesbian appropriation of literature. In J. Hartman & E. Messer-Davidow (Eds.), *(En)gendering knowledge: Feminists in academe* (pp. 85–99). Knoxville: The University of Tennessee Press.

Zimpher, N. L., & Ashburn, E. A. (1992). Countering parochialism in teacher candidates. In M. E. Dilworth (Ed.), *Diversity in teacher education: New expectations* (pp. 40–62). San Francisco: Jossey-Bass.

Zuniga, M. E. (1992). Families with Latino roots. In E. W. Lynch & M. J. Hanson (Eds.), *Developing cross-cultural competence* (pp. 151–179). Baltimore: Paul H. Brookes.

Index